INTERNATIONAL LAW AND THE USE OF FORCE

INTERNATIONAL LAW AND THE USE OF FORCE

A Documentary and Reference Guide

Shirley V. Scott, Anthony John Billingsley, and Christopher Michaelsen

PRAEGER SECURITY INTERNATIONAL
An Imprint of ABC-CLIO, LLC

A B C CLIO

Santa Barbara, California • Denver, Colorado • Oxford, England

Library of Congress Cataloging-in-Publication Data is available at *www.loc.gov*.

14 13 12 11 10 1 2 3 4 5

This book is also available on the World Wide Web as an eBook.
Visit www.abc-clio.com for details.

ABC-CLIO, LLC
130 Cremona Drive, P.O. Box 1911
Santa Barbara, California 93116-1911

This book is printed on acid-free paper ∞
Manufactured in the United States of America

CONTENTS

PREFACE

The invasion of Iraq by the United States, United Kingdom, and Australia in 2003 prompted an enormous volume of debate around the world as to whether it was the right thing to do and whether or not it was legal in terms of the Charter of the United Nations. Many who had previously had little interest in international law were now able to conduct a discussion as to whether the invasion had or had not been authorized by the United Nations Security Council. Public outcry in the United Kingdom and Australia prompted those governments to make public the legal opinion on which they had based their decision to join in the invasion of Iraq, and groups of international lawyers spoke out to express their opposition to those opinions.

Iraq thereby brought starkly into focus the body of international law that seeks to govern whether and when countries may resort to the use of force. In the contemporary world, this body of law has as its centerpiece the Charter of the United Nations of 1945. In the scheme of world history it is therefore a relatively recent development. The attempt to place strict limits on the occasions when a country can use force was one of the great governance innovations of the twentieth century. Although political philosophers and lawyers had long called for this development, there was no proof that it would work. It was a bold experiment, and one that the world could not afford to see fail.

This book responds to this heightened interest in international law addressing the use of force and traces the story of this great experiment in world politics. International law on the use of force traditionally comprises two components: first, the law on the use of force and prevention of war *(jus ad bellum)*, which seeks to regulate the resort to force by States, and, second, the law of armed conflict *(jus in bello)*, which concerns whether military operations are conducted justly and in accordance with international customs and treaties (regardless of whether the initiation of hostilities had been lawful). This book mainly addresses the first component, *jus ad bellum*.

The focus of the early chapters is on the historical process by which incremental steps were taken to outlaw the use of force in relations among countries. The first great step was taken in the Covenant of the League of Nations. The Covenant was unable to prevent World War II, but the lessons that governments and international lawyers took from this and other landmark developments, such as the 1928 Kellogg-Briand Pact, were put to good effect in the UN Charter.

Achieving the prohibition on the use of force in the Charter was by no means the end of the path. Just as a constitution is a living document that must keep up with the changing demands of a national political system, so the interpretation of the UN Charter, which can be considered as a constitution of international society, has had to evolve in an international society that is constantly changing. International lawyers have had a vital role to play in helping to refine the framework outlined in the Charter and in applying it to real world situations.

The bulk of this book addresses some of the key issues that have been raised over the decades since 1945. One of the most vital of these is the content and scope of the right of self-defense. If self-defense is the only permissible exception to the prohibition on the use of force, the exact parameters of that right are deserving of close scrutiny and refinement. Moreover, if the UN Security Council is to have a role in maintaining international peace and security to replace the historical right of a country to wage war in pursuit of its perceived national interests, just when and how the Council is to play that role is crucial.

As will be seen, the United States has had a special role in the creation and refinement of the international law on the use of force. The role of President Woodrow Wilson in establishing the League of Nations is well known, but the contribution of the United States peace movement in bringing about the Kellogg-Briand Pact is less well known. Much of the drafting of the UN Charter took place in the U.S. State Department. This intimate relationship between the United States and the evolution of the international law on the use of force means both that the United States tends to regard its interpretation and application of that law somewhat possessively and that the rest of the international community judges the United States particularly harshly when it does not seem to live up to the standards that it played such an important role in establishing.

While the United States played a pivotal role in establishing this body of international law and, indeed, has continued to shape that law through the conduct and justification of its foreign policy, this book is not about the United States per se. It aims to speak to all peoples who seek clarity on the subject. While the United States has been the subject of extensive criticism, this book does not aim to add to the litany of books condemning U.S. foreign policies. Rather, it aims to provide as objective as possible an account of the engagement of the United States—and of other countries—with the international law on the use of force.

This book examines the international law on the use of force through a selection of documents of fundamental importance to this body of law. Each is of significance for one or more of three reasons. Either it sheds light on the political story through which this body of law evolved; or it is a legal document, a "source" of international law; or, third, it helps us to assess the real-world impact of that law. For, not only does this book examine some of the legal nuances of the framework of the UN Charter, but it considers whether this great experiment in world politics has been successful. Has there in fact been a decline in the incidence of wars, and, if so, is this trend attributable to international law? Special care was taken to select a variety of documents that include extracts of international treaties and UN Security Council and General Assembly resolutions as well as transcripts of important speeches and press conferences.

This book is intended to be user-friendly. Its goal is to explore the international law on the use of force as a political endeavor and to draw some preliminary conclusions regarding the contribution of this evolving body of law to international security. The documents are divided according to their subject matter into ten chapters. Chapters 1 and 2 explain the dream of ending war through an international rule of law and provide historical background to the current legal regime, which outlaws use of force in inter-State relations. Chapter 3 outlines the post–1945 Charter framework regarding the use of force. Chapters 4 through 8 address questions that have arisen or come to the fore during the life of this legal framework, either because something was left unclear in the original plan or because of changing circumstances. Chapter 9 considers the legality of the 2003 invasion of Iraq, and Chapter 10 concludes by seeking to assess whether this great experiment in world history has made the world a more secure place.

Each chapter begins with a very brief introduction to the topic of that chapter and its place within the subject as a whole. This is followed by a selection of documents. Each document is prefaced by a series of bulleted points, which enable the reader to see at a glance (1) the details of the document, (2) the date of the document, (3) where the document was created or the text finalized, and (4) a succinct summary of the significance of the document. Then follows the document itself. Where those documents are long, it was necessary to extract the key section or portions of the document so as not to obscure the key points through unnecessary additional text.

Each document is followed by an analysis that explains in much greater detail its significance and contents. The analysis is accompanied by sidebars containing interesting associated facts or, in some cases, portions of related documents. The reader is invited to explore further any aspects of the topic through following up on the documents and analyses via the further readings listed at the conclusion of each analysis. A much more comprehensive bibliography of additional readings is provided at the end of the volume, listing books and academic journal readings on the subject as well as a range of relevant Web sites.

The book thereby aims to cater to interested members of the general public as well as to students requiring an accessible but accurate and nuanced coverage of the content. The authors have also had in mind as a potential audience those who work in related fields or the world of diplomacy who wish to learn more on the subject in a manner more accessible and "less dry" than the standard international law text. We hope that it will inspire readers to learn more about this and other aspects of international law.

As far as the preparation of the book's substantive chapters is concerned, Shirley Scott covered Chapters 1 through 3; Anthony Billingsley concentrated on Chapters 4, 7, and 9; and Christopher Michaelsen focused on Chapters 5, 6, and 8. The book benefited greatly from the most efficient and thorough research assistance of Orli Zahava, to whom we express our sincere gratitude and appreciation. Her strong organizational skills and dedication to the project have done much to ensure its successful completion. Sascha Knoepfel located graphics and provided technical and research support to the authors during his time as a research practicum student in the School of Social Sciences and International Studies at the University of New South Wales. Needless to say (but we shall say it anyway) we are solely responsible for any errors.

Shirley Scott—Anthony Billingsley—Christopher Michaelsen

INTRODUCTION

The "Dove of Peace." In 1979 Pope John Paul II presented the United Nations with this reproduction of a twelfth-century mosaic. Courtesy of Lois Conner, UN Photo

Warfare and violence have been features of relations between organized communities throughout history. Even before the modern age of weapons of mass destruction, the results of this behavior have often been ruinous. Recognizing the widespread impact of warfare, States have attempted to provide rules or principles to govern armed conflict. Most civilizations have also developed justifications on which to base a decision to go to war. In the West, the most prominent philosophical tradition addressing the initiation and conduct of hostilities has been that of the "just war." This introductory chapter will briefly trace the evolution of just war thinking as an important antecedent of the prohibition on the threat and use of force in the Charter of the United Nations. The Introduction will conclude by outlining the approach this book takes to placing the international law of the use of force in a legal, political, and historical context.

THE ORIGINS OF THE JUST WAR TRADITION

The modern concept of the just war has its origins in a fusion of early Roman and Christian teachings.[1] In the ancient world, the Romans followed the principle that the Republic would initiate hostilities against another State only if there were a just cause.[2] Early Christians did not hold political power and did not attempt to seize it by force; some were pacifists, not accepting war under any circumstances. Once Christianity became the official religion of the Roman Empire, however, the Church had to address the question of the duties of rulers.[3] In his book *De Civitate Dei* (The City of God), St Augustine (A.D. 354–430) set out the view that, although every war was a lamentable phenomenon, the wrong suffered at the hands of the adversary necessitated waging "just wars."[4]

Perhaps the most significant of all philosophers of just war was Thomas Aquinas (1225–1274), who has been described as "the greatest theologian of the medieval, and perhaps of any, era."[5] Aquinas built upon the principles set out by Augustine to develop three criteria of a just war:

1. It must be waged under the authority of a ruler rather than by a private individual.
2. It must have a just cause: "those who are attacked, should be attacked because they deserve it on account of some fault."
3. The belligerents must have a "rightful intention": to advance the good or to avoid evil.[6]

Other writers, such as Francisco de Vitoria (c. 1492–1546), sought to elaborate and refine what constituted a "just cause." Vitoria wrote on the Spanish conquest of Central and South America and concluded that the Spanish invasion *was* justified, on the grounds that, contrary to natural law rules, the Native Americans had unlawfully attempted to exclude Spanish traders from their kingdoms. Vitoria also confessed, however, that his "blood froze in his veins" at the thought of the terrible atrocities committed by the Spanish in the process.[7] His writings on war focused on limiting the horrors of conflict. In principle, he said war could not be justified except as defense against aggression or to right a very great wrong. Moreover, a declaration of war should be preceded by efforts at conciliation and arbitration. A ruler should consider whether the war might not do more harm than good. Innocent people might be killed only if it were impossible to distinguish them from participants. Finally, Vitoria maintained that if a subject's conscience told him a war was wrong, he must not take part in it.[8] At the end of the sixteenth century, Alberico Gentili, an Italian writer and professor at the University of Oxford, brought classical just war theory to bear on a broad range of concrete questions arising from the actual practice of military hostilities.[9]

CLASSICAL WRITING ON THE "JUST WAR" AND THE BIRTH OF MODERN INTERNATIONAL LAW

Hugo Grotius (1583–1645), a Dutch scholar and jurist often considered the father of modern international law, further refined the concept of just war. Grotius was influenced in his thinking by the horrors of the Eighty Years' War between Spain and the Netherlands and the Thirty Years' War between Catholic and Protestant European nations. His contribution to the development of Western thinking on what constitutes a "just war" was to develop a secular form of theorizing.[10] Grotius transformed aspects of natural law theory into what he termed the "law of nations." The distinctive feature of the "law of nations" lay in the fact that it was seen as a body of law distinct from the law of nature and, as a consequence, not as part of law governing human social affairs in general. Instead, it was a set of rules applying specifically to one particular category of human beings: rulers of States.

In his important work *De Jure Belli ac Pacis (On the Law of War and Peace)* Grotius attempted to provide a general ethical basis on which conflicts might be restrained. According to Grotius:

> Fully convinced . . . that there is a common law among nations, which is valid alike for war and in war, I have had many and weighty reasons for undertaking to write upon the subject. Throughout the Christian world I observed a lack of restraint in relation to war, such as even barbarous races should be ashamed of; I observed that men rush to arms for slight causes, or no cause at all, and that when arms have once been taken up there is no longer any respect for law, divine or human; it is as if, in accordance with a general decree, frenzy had openly been let loose for the committing of all crimes.[11]

De Jure Belli ac Pacis contains a set of principles that Grotius believed to be binding on all people and nations regardless of local custom. The book identifies three circumstances in which war can be justifiable (*jus ad bellum*, justice in the resort to war): self-defense, reparation of injury, and punishment. Grotius also took up the issue of the rules that regulate the conduct of war once it has begun (*jus in bello*, justice in the conduct of war). He maintained that all parties to war are bound by such rules, whether or not their cause is just.

The emergent system of international law incorporated elements of natural law thinking, by which the content of the law is said to be set by a divine source or by

Hugo Grotius. Portrait by Jan van Ravesteyn, 1599. Courtesy of Dutch Portraits.

nature and hence to have validity everywhere. Increasingly, however, international law became positivist in orientation, meaning that the content of the law did not derive its validity from divine or moral sources but from criteria internal to the legal system itself. In the late seventeenth and mid-eighteenth century, the German philosophers Samuel Pufendorf (1632–1694) and Christian Wolff (1679–1754) distinguished between natural law, reflecting the influence of God, and voluntary law, resulting from the positive actions of States.[12] Wolff, who had been trained as a mathematician, was criticized for relying too much on a logical structure and failing to take account of the actual behavior of States. Emerich de Vattel (1714–1767) addressed the practical behavior of States in his book *Le Droit des Gens (The Law of Nations)* of 1758. Vattel defined the law of nations as "the science of those rights which exist between nations and States, and of the obligations corresponding to those rights."[13] Vattel argued that each State was sovereign, independent, and equal and that the law of nations could be derived from an examination of writings about State practice, from treaties agreed to by States, and from custom drawn from the implicit acceptance of States. Whereas Wolff had been disdainful of the voluntary law, Vattel fully embraced it.

This had important implications for thinking regarding the legality of war. The natural law theory of just wars allowed a State to resort to force in self-help to vindicate a legal right that had been violated, which meant that in any given conflict, only one side may be fighting justly. The voluntary law, however, was not concerned as to which party to a conflict had a stronger legal claim to use force but treated each side as if it had lawfully resorted to war; it largely contended itself with regulating the conduct of wars.

By the nineteenth century, legal positivism had taken hold. The belief that law is an entirely human institution led eventually to the view that rules agreed upon by States were the *only* true source of international law. As the Permanent Court of Justice would later express it in the *Lotus* case, "the rules of law binding upon States . . . emanate from their own free will."[14] Advocates of legal positivism rejected the distinction between just and unjust wars. From the positivist perspective, a State using armed force was creating a factual situation in which the set of international rules relating to the conduct of hostilities replaced that which applied during peacetime, but international law did not attempt to delve into either the origins or the merit of that act.[15] W. E. Hall asserted that:

> International law has no alternative but to accept war, independently of the justice of its origin, as a relation which the parties to it may set up if they choose, and to busy itself only in regulating the effects of the relations.[16]

From roughly the eighteenth to the twentieth century States were presumed to have a right to wage war in the pursuit of their national interests.[17]

While the decision to resort to war was seen as a legal right intrinsic in the sovereignty of the nation-State, the positivist era of the nineteenth century was the period in which the international community first began "legislating" by way of multilateral treaties—agreements legally binding on those States that have given their consent to be so bound. The Western philosophical tradition of just war theorizing can be seen underpinning some of the early examples of multilateral treaties that attempted to regulate the conduct of hostilities *(jus in bello)*. The first major example of this was the 1856 Declaration of Paris, which, *inter alia*, restricted the capture of private property at sea and abolished privateering. The 1868 Declaration of St. Petersburg introduced a ban on exploding bullets and denounced total-war practices by stating that the only permissible objective of war is the defeat of the enemy's armed forces.

THE INTRODUCTION INTO INTERNATIONAL LAW OF A PROHIBITION ON THE THREAT AND USE OF FORCE

This book is not concerned with the body of positivist international law that has developed in an attempt to regulate the conduct of hostilities once they have commenced, so much as with an arguably more radical legal innovation of the twentieth century. This was the introduction into international law of a prohibition on the first use of force and even of the threat to use force. As will be seen in later chapters, the Treaty of Versailles and the 1928 General Treaty for the Renunciation of War constituted preliminary steps that culminated in Article 2(4) of the Charter of the United Nations. Article 2(4) states:

> All Members shall refrain in their international relations from the threat or use of force against the territorial integrity or political independence of any state, or in any other manner inconsistent with the Purposes of the United Nations.

Article 2(4) can be understood as a general prohibition on the use of force in inter-State relations. The Charter intends the United Nations to enjoy a monopoly over the use of force, permitting States to resort to force only in self-defense or if authorized by the United Nations Security Council (UNSC).

International law in the post-1945 world has, as its two principal sources, treaty law and customary international law. Customary international law is defined as "evidence of a general practice accepted as law."[18] Custom is made up of two elements: State practice and *opinio juris*. State practice refers to a pattern of State behavior, and *opinio juris* is "a belief that this practice is rendered obligatory by the existence of a rule of law requiring it."[19] Both State practice and *opinio juris* must be present in order to find that a rule of customary international law has developed. The International Court of Justice has confirmed that the principles regarding the use of force found in the UN Charter are not only part of treaty law but correspond, in their essentials, to what is found in customary international law.[20] This confirms that the prohibition extends to all States, whether or not they are members of the United Nations. Indeed the prohibition on the first use of force by States in Article 2(4) is widely held to constitute *jus cogens:* a peremptory or absolute rule of international law recognized by the whole community of States, from which no derogation (exemption) may be permitted.

Scholars are divided as to the degree to which the Charter's prohibition on the first use of force is a modern manifestation of the just war tradition. As Lynn Miller observed, "some writers, concerned with the broad concept of the attempt to limit war, have placed the Covenant and the Charter in the tradition of just war theory, whereas others have argued on a somewhat more specific basis that the content of the peacekeeping provisions of these twentieth-century organizations differs from that of the traditional just war doctrine."[21] There is little doubt that the intellectual heritage from which the Charter derived was predominantly Western and that the just war tradition is central to the philosophical heritage of the West as regards questions of war and peace. Not all scholars accept that there is any closer connection between the just war tradition and the prohibition on the use of force in the UN Charter. According to Yoram Dinstein:

> It is wrong to believe that the UN Charter, in forbidding the use of force in international relations, has followed in the footsteps of the 'just war' doctrine. The proscription of inter-State force amounts to a veritable revolution compared to earlier international law. The UN Charter has wiped out the pre-existing permissive legal norms concerning recourse to inter-State force and has introduced a whole new set of legal norms based on a *jus contra bellum*. It is totally irrelevant today whether or not a war is just. The sole question is: is war legal, in accordance with the Charter?[22]

In asserting that it is irrelevant today as to whether a war is just, Dinstein is referring to the content of the contemporary, predominantly positivist, system of international law in which considerations of morality or theology are explicitly excluded from the logic of legal analysis; the content of the law derives its authority from the rules to which States have given their consent. If, however, we recall that the just war tradition began as a Christian practice of theorizing about conditions under which war could be acceptable, we can usefully view the Charter from the perspective of just war:

> Even though just war thinking in the strict sense, in the present world is clearly outdated and it is unequivocally contrary to modern international law, as found in the General Treaty for Renunciation of War in 1928, in Article 2(3) and (4) of the Charter, and Chapter VII of the UN Charter, some provisions of the Charter are similar to jurisprudence upon the *jus ad bellum* and are readily reconcilable with some of the major strands of Christian and secular thinking upon war and armed conflict. . . . The UN Charter's position on the just war question is that it is permissible for States, regardless of their domestic power structures, to go to war, if and only if they are victims of the threat or use of force against their territorial integrity or political independence and only until such time as the UNSC acts to restrain the aggressor.[23]

Neff, in his general history of war and international law, refers to the UN Charter as having reinstated a "full just war system".[24]

In recent conflicts initiated by the West, the public in the United States, in the United Kingdom, and elsewhere have demanded that their leaders explain their rationale for the launch of hostilities. The NATO governments that used force during the Kosovo crisis of 1999 made much of the need to respond to a humanitarian crisis, and the governments involved in the 2003 invasion of Iraq emphasized breaches of international law on the part of Iraq. Both of these lines of justification have echoes of just war theorizing, and, on occasion, national leaders have explicitly invoked the language of a "just war." Tony Blair, Prime Minister of the United Kingdom at the time of the Kosovo crisis, claimed that NATO's war was a just war because it was based not on any territorial ambitions but on values.[25]

The attacks of September 11, 2001, gave rise to a flurry of writing on just war. Faced with new security challenges, the West has arguably felt the need to review its attitude toward war, drawing on this long tradition of philosophical theorizing as to when resort to war might be morally acceptable. A cynic might say that we have seen this revival of just war thinking because the tradition can offer the State more malleable guidelines for the use of force than can modern positivist international law, and it is for this very reason that many international lawyers are strongly opposed to references to the just war that aim to legitimate breaches of the Charter or to weaken its normative pull. The just war tradition is, on the other hand, welcomed by those—including lawyers—who seek to promote the ethical conduct of international affairs. This is so precisely because the tradition offers a framework within which moral considerations on which the Charter is silent can be taken into account. Exploration of the question of whether wars of national liberation could be waged to end colonialism often took place within a just war framework, arguably because the issue had been left unaddressed by the Charter. The Rwandan genocide in 1994 and ongoing atrocities in Darfur (Sudan) have prompted heated debate on the concepts of humanitarian intervention and the "responsibility to protect," which draw heavily on principles developed by the just war doctrine.[26]

THE RATIONALE FOR THE SELECTION OF DOCUMENTS

In considering how to approach this book, we were aware that the use of force is one of the most hotly debated issues in the study of international relations and international law. Attempts to enclose the resort to force by States within a legal framework have run up against traditional patterns of State behavior and the basic instinct of States that their core interests and national honor can be preserved only by their ability to threaten or to use force against other States. We approached our writing from the perspective that international law plays a vital role in assisting States to pursue their interests through nonviolent and rule-governed means. Indeed, we are of the view that international law has contributed greatly to changes in State policy and practice over the past hundred or so years. We are, however, aware that not everyone shares this view. A tradition of thinking associated with realism in international relations dismisses international law as little better than an ideological disguise for the policies of great powers and considers any attempt to constrain the powerful via international law as doomed to failure. We have chosen for analysis documents that highlight the various perspectives involved.

The documents selected include some of the most famous and important in the corpus of international law. They include other documents that are important and illustrative but have been overlooked or forgotten with the passage of time. In addition to treaties, UN resolutions, and judgments of international tribunals, we were careful to include a variety of other sources, including public speeches and press conferences. These sources tend to be excluded in more traditional collections and works on international law. What all selected documents have in common is that they illustrate the relevance of international law to national decision making and to relations among States.

CHAPTER 1: INTERNATIONAL LAW AND THE STRUGGLE FOR WORLD PEACE

The development of an international legal regime addressing the use of force and binding on all States was a twentieth-century development. But, as has already been suggested, the twentieth-century developments cannot be fully understood except within a longer historical context. The tradition of writing on just war is one historical trajectory leading to the present. Chapter 1 introduces others, including that of treaties of alliance that may commit States either to use, or to refrain from using, force in particular situations. The Treaty of Kadesh between the Egyptian and Hittite empires, which is generally dated to 1258 B.C., for example, contained provisions on the nonuse of force between the two parties, guarantees of recognized mutual borders, and the return of refugees. In the nineteenth century, European States created a web of alliances that placed obligations on States either to come to the defense of an ally or to stay neutral in the event of war breaking out. The law of neutrality was intended to enable States not parties to a conflict to continue with trade and commerce without becoming entangled in the war.

An important complement to the introduction of a legal prohibition on the use of force in inter-State relations has been the evolution of a body of international law that aims to help States to settle disputes through peaceful means. This chapter considers the historical antecedents to the web of international courts and tribunals that exist today, and the political impediments that scuttled the first attempts to develop a world court.

CHAPTER 2: THE TREATY OF VERSAILLES AS A TENTATIVE TRIAL RUN

The horrific loss of life and catastrophic economic consequences of World War I prompted attempts to curtail the still-accepted right of a State to use war to achieve its national objectives. The Covenant of the League of Nations prohibited in general terms the resort to force and developed several mechanisms, such as arbitration, a judicial framework in the Permanent Court of International Justice, and elaborate disarmament processes as confidence-building measures. The focus on disarmament was augmented by an attempt to place "collective security" at the heart of the League's powers. As explained in Chapter 2, the League's practical approach was reinforced by the Kellogg-Briand Pact, which sought to provide a broader philosophical imperative whereby States made the abnegation of war a fundamental policy doctrine.

The Peace Palace in The Hague. This was the home of the Permanent Court of International Justice and now houses the International Court of Justice. Courtesy of the International Court of Justice.

The League's failure to prevent a second world war naturally led to widespread questioning of the wisdom of the idea that war could be avoided through reliance on law and international norms. Some people insisted that this was a dangerous approach given the natural tendency of States to rely on force as the basis of their self-defense. Others argued that the disaster was the result of the League being inadequately equipped and supported. It was this perspective that inspired U.S. President Roosevelt when planning began for the post–World War II international order.

CHAPTER 3: THE UN CHARTER REGIME ON THE USE OF FORCE

The text of the United Nations Charter reflects fundamental continuities from the League of Nations and the Kellogg-Briand Pact. The Charter was also a product of World War II, its drafters having endeavored to learn from the experiences of that conflict. Importantly, the Charter gives the Security Council a virtual monopoly on the use of force. Even cases of self-defense are to be referred to the Council for resolution. The new organization incorporates the dispute resolution measures pioneered by the League of Nations. The International Court of Justice serves as the successor to the Permanent Court of International Justice and has addressed questions concerning the law of the use of force in several of its judgments.

The League of Nations had been greatly weakened by the absence of the United States. In planning for a replacement organization, it was perceived as crucial that all the major powers of the day be fully committed to its success. Chapter 3 includes an excerpt from the debate in the United States Senate that preceded America's endorsement of the United Nations. U.S. Senators deemed the United Nations equipped to deal with threats to international peace and security and were reassured that the inclusion of the veto of the permanent members in the Security Council meant that the UN Charter could not unduly curtail U.S. policy choices. Within weeks of the signing of the Charter, the United States dropped the first atomic bomb over Hiroshima. That event, and the reaction of the Soviet Union, created a particular challenge for the Charter regime, which had not been designed for the atomic age.

CHAPTER 4: KEY CHALLENGES TO THE GENERAL PROHIBITION ON THE USE OF FORCE

Chapter 4 examines a range of cases in which the scope and significance of Article 2(4) have been subject to challenge. In some instances States have used force in ways that ostensibly do not comply with the prohibition on the use of force found in Article 2(4), and in such instances the States resorting to force have sometimes attempted to bolster their arguments with the introduction of supposedly new principles of international law. Among the most contentious and tenacious are the concept of humanitarian intervention and the related idea of the responsibility to protect. These ideas emerged out of the tension in the Charter between the principle of the sovereign integrity of States and the responsibility of the international community to protect fundamental human rights and to prevent genocide. Chapter 4 discusses some of the key challenges to the prohibition of the use of force and the response of the international community to those challenges.

Peace stamp of the German Democratic Republic (East-Germany), 1950. Courtesy of the Federal Republic of Germany.

CHAPTER 5: THE RIGHT OF SELF-DEFENSE

Chapter 5 examines the scope and content of the concept of self-defense. As an inherent right of States, self-defense has a long history. The concept was given a significant degree of recognition in the context of the 1837 *Caroline* incident. The modern formulation of the right of self-defense is contained in Article 51 of the UN Charter as an exception to the general prohibition on the threat or use of force. Scholars and policymakers nevertheless continue to disagree on the correct interpretation of Article 51. A particular point of contention is whether, and to what extent, Article 51 is compatible with the concepts of anticipatory and preemptive self-defense. Similarly, there is disagreement on whether the protection or rescue of nationals abroad can be justified by self-defense. The law of self-defense has also been challenged by developments since 1945, including the introduction of nuclear weapons. The international community is split over the legality of these weapons, with supporters highlighting their role in the ultimate security of States and opponents drawing on international humanitarian law to reinforce their case.

CHAPTER 6: THE CRIME OF AGGRESSION?

Chapter 6 considers the crime of aggression in international law. It traces the origin and development of this international crime by looking at the Nuremberg and Tokyo tribunals, which were established in the aftermath of World War II to prosecute Nazi and Japanese war criminals. As with terrorism, the definition of aggression remains controversial. A major step towards a legal definition of aggression came with the adoption by the General Assembly in 1974 of a Declaration on the Definition of Aggression. The Declaration generally reaffirmed the principle that acts of aggression are contrary to the UN Charter and international law. A number of countries were keen to see aggression included in the list of crimes over which the International Criminal Court, established in 1998, could exercise jurisdiction and were successful in achieving its inclusion in the Statute of the Court, but agreement on a definition of aggression was not forthcoming during negotiations. The Court will exercise jurisdiction over the crime of aggression once the definition has been finalized. Recent efforts in this regard appear to have been promising, but agreement remains elusive.

CHAPTER 7: CAN COLLECTIVE SECURITY WORK?

The idea of collective security is central to the United Nations structure for the maintenance of international peace and security but has been difficult to put into practice. After the failure of the League's model of collective security, the drafters of the United Nations Charter sought to base a new approach on more realistic foundations. Chapter 7 demonstrates that the record of success has been mixed. There have been only two occasions on which the United Nations has formally invoked collective security action. Chapter 7 considers these two instances of collective security as well as situations in which an apparent violation of the Charter has not been met by a collective response.

CHAPTER 8: TERRORISM, INTERNATIONAL LAW, AND THE USE OF FORCE

This chapter looks at how the threat of terrorism is addressed by States within the framework of international law. The world has witnessed a range of spectacular acts of terrorism since the early 1960s. The international response has been complicated by an inability to agree on a definition of the term "terrorism" in international law. Despite such problems, the international community has pressed ahead with measures designed to address specific aspects of terrorism. Both the UN General Assembly and the Security Council have confirmed that terrorism qualifies as a threat to international peace and security. The international community has also adopted several multilateral conventions and protocols that address specific criminal acts considered terrorist in nature. The chapter draws attention to the legal basis for military action against Al-Qai'da and the Taliban in Afghanistan and the Bush administration's highly controversial practice of detaining alleged illegal enemy combatants in Guantanamo Bay and elsewhere.

CHAPTER 9: WAS THE U.S. INVASION OF IRAQ LEGAL?

During the 1990s the Security Council devoted much time to the problem of how to deal with Iraq after its expulsion from Kuwait in 1991. Toward the end of the decade, the possibility of military action against Iraq was discussed on several occasions, and Council members made clear their view that any action must first be specifically approved by the Security Council. The 2003 invasion of Iraq by the United States and a small coalition took place without such approval and provoked concern among States and widespread popular opposition. In the public debate in the months immediately before the invasion most States took the view that the invasion represented defiance of the United Nations Security Council and threatened to undermine the rule of law. The United States Administration devoted considerable effort to providing justifications for the invasion under international law. Chapter 9 examines the legal justifications provided by the main protagonists in the context of the crisis and its origins.

CHAPTER 10: CONCLUSIONS: HAS THE INTERNATIONAL LAW RELATING TO THE USE OF FORCE CREATED A MORE PEACEFUL WORLD?

Early attempts by the international community to limit the resort to force by States and to outlaw war failed to prevent the outbreak of World War II. The ideas contained in the Covenant of the League of Nations and in the Kellogg-Briand Pact nevertheless survived and were embodied in the Charter of the United Nations with its broad prohibition of the threat and first use of force. The UN Charter is often likened to an international constitution, and its prohibition on the use of force is widely agreed to represent not only customary international law, but *jus cogens*.

We argue that the establishment in international law of a prohibition on the threat and use of force in interstate relations has had a significant influence on State behavior. This can be seen in the expectation that a breach of the norm will trigger an international response. Given the tumultuous nature of the post–World War II years, including the Cold War and decolonization, it is reasonable to believe that, without Article 2(4), the incidence of international violence would have been much greater than it has been.

While there are always those who doubt that international law can have any independent impact on powerful States, the leaders of even the most powerful States usually perceive a need to offer a legal justification when they do decide to use force in the international arena. International law provides not only an expected standard of behavior but a common means of legitimating—and de-legitimating—the actions of States. It serves to render more predictable the behavior of States and to offer alternatives to settling disputes through armed conflict.

Notes

1. Mohammad Taghi Karoubi, *Just or Unjust War? International Law and Unilateral Use of Armed Force by States at the Turn of the 20th Century* (Hants: Aldershot, 2004), 7.
2. David J. Bederman, *International Law in Antiquity* (Cambridge, UK: Cambridge University Press, 2001), 222.
3. Yoram Dinstein, *War, Aggression and Self-Defence*, 4th ed. (Cambridge, UK: Cambridge University Press, 2005), 64.
4. Dinstein, *War, Aggression and Self-Defence*, 64.
5. Chris Brown, Terry Nardin, and Nicholas Rengger, eds., *International Relations in Political Thought. Texts from the Ancient Greeks to the First World War* (Cambridge, UK: Cambridge University Press, 2002), 213.
6. Brown, Nardin, and Rengger, eds., *International Relations in Political Thought*, 214.
7. Francisco di Vitoria. "On the American Indians," in Anthony Pagden and Jeremy Lawrence, eds., *Political Writings* (Cambridge, UK: Cambridge University Press, 1991), 231–292.
8. Franciscus de Victoria (ed. Ernest Nys, trans. John Pawley Bate), *De Indis et de Ivre Belli. Relectiones: of Relectiones Theologicae XII* [The Second Relectiones of the Reverend Father, Brother Franciscus de Victoria, on the Indians, or on the Law of War made by the Spaniards on the Barbarians], Questions 22 and 23. (New York: Oceana, 1964). http://www.constitution.org/victoria/victoria.txt.
9. Gesina van der Molen, *Alberico Gentili and the Development of International Law* (Leiden: Sijhoff, 1968).
10. Michael Walzer, *Just and Unjust Wars: A Moral Argument with Historical Illustrations* (New York: Basic Books, 1977), xiv.
11. Hugo Grotius, trans. Francis Kelsey, *The Law of War and Peace* (Carnegie edition, 1925), Prol. sect. 28.
12. Joachim von Elbe, "The Evolution of the Concept of the Just War in International Law," *American Journal of International Law* 33 (1939): 682.
13. Emerich de Vattel, *The Law of Nations*, Book One, Introduction, no. 3. 1999 digital edition: http://www.constitution.org/vattel/vattel.txt.
14. Permanent Court of Justice, Lotus, Judgment No. 9 (1927), Ser A, No. 10.
15. Von Elbe, "The Evolution of the Concept of the Just War": 684.

16. W. E. Hall, *International Law*, 8th ed. (Oxford: Clarendon, 1924), 82.
17. Nicholas Rengger, "On the Just War Tradition in the Twenty-first Century," *International Affairs* 78, no.2 (2002): 359.
18. Statute of the International Court of Justice, article 38(1)(b).
19. *North Sea Continental Shelf* cases, [1969] *ICJ Reports*, 44.
20. *Case Concerning Military and Paramilitary Activities in and Against Nicaragua* (Merits), [1986] *ICJ Reports*: 99–101.
21. Lynn H. Miller, "The Contemporary Significance of the Doctrine of Just War," *World Politics* 16, no. 2 (1964): 260.
22. Yoram Dinstein, "Comments on War," *Harvard Journal of International Law and Public Policy* 27 (2003–2004): 879-880.
23. Karoubi, *Just or Unjust War?* 150.
24. Stephen C. Neff, *War and the Law of Nations. A General History* (Cambridge, UK: Cambridge University Press, 2005), 5.
25. Tony Blair, "Doctrine of the International Community," Speech in the Economic Club of Chicago, April 24, 1999. http://www.number10.gov.uk/Page1297.
26. *The Responsibility to Protect: Report of the International Commission on Intervention and State Sovereignty* (2001). http://www.iciss.ca/report2-en.asp.

1

INTERNATIONAL LAW AND THE STRUGGLE FOR WORLD PEACE

Peace Palace Competition. Winning design by J. F. L. Frowein, March 23, 1907. Courtesy of Delft University of Technology Library, The Netherlands.

OVERVIEW

The international legal regime addressing the use of force by States was a twentieth-century development. The ideal of a world governed by law rather than by military might is, however, far older. And, even before there was an attempt to establish a legal prohibition against war, there were treaties of alliance that placed obligations on States, for example, either to come to the defense of an ally or to stay neutral in the event of war breaking out. This chapter looks at what existed before the momentous legal developments of the twentieth century as regards obligations in international law either to use or not use force and to settle disputes by peaceful means. It provides useful historical background for the chapters to follow.

The Peace Movement in the Nineteenth Century

- ***Document:*** Extract from William Ladd, *An Essay on a Congress of Nations for the Adjustment of International Disputes Without Resort to Arms*
- ***Date:*** Originally published by Harvard University, 1840
- ***Where:*** Maine, United States
- ***Significance:*** This is an outline of a very influential nineteenth-century scheme for how to achieve world peace through international law.

DOCUMENT

The chief end and purpose of government is, to prevent one person from injuring another; so that every one may sit under his own vine and fig-tree, with none to molest or make him afraid. This is the object of all our laws, and all the expensive machinery of government, which has taken care that no individual should molest his neighbor; and when disputes arise, so far from leaving each individual to take his cause into his own hands, governments have provided courts of law to decide the controversy. In many governments, the legislative has been entirely separated from the judicial power, and the executive from both. In all of them, the impartiality of the judicial power has been in a ratio equal to the knowledge and virtue of the people. In some of these governments, laws have been made, not only for securing the rights of private individuals, but also of bodies corporate, and even of component parts of the empire which are for many purposes independent. No such thing has yet been done with respect to nations, though courts have been instituted, to decide controversies which have arisen between two or more members of the same confederacy of nations. Our object is to go one step further, and appoint a court, by which contests between nations shall be settled, without resort to arms, when any such controversy shall be brought, by mutual consent, before it.

By consent of all writers on international law, nations are considered as individual, moral persons, perfectly equal and independent of one another. Therefore, the same moral laws which ought to govern individuals, ought to govern nations. What is wrong for an individual, is wrong for a nation. In the intercourse of these moral persons, disputes will arise, injuries will be done, retaliation and revenge will follow, and, unless some means of terminating their disputes by amicable and rational methods are devised, war will be the consequence. There are three ways already in use, whereby war may be avoided. The first is, by cultivating a spirit of peace, which is the spirit of the gospel, and is as much the duty of nations as it is of individuals; by this means, injuries, especially if not very grievous, will be overlooked, or be passed by with a bare remonstrance, and an appeal to the moral sense of the nation that has inflicted the injury. The second is, by negotiation, where the subject in dispute is formally discussed and settled by reparation or compromise. If this cannot be done, the next step is mediation of a friendly power, accompanied with arbitration and the acceptance of the award. The last resort is war, which commonly increases, instead of remedying the evil. We propose a plan more likely to procure justice than either of these.

As government is an ordinance of God, necessary for the safety, happiness and improvement of the human race, and as it is absolutely necessary for the peace of society, that when the selfish passions of man come in conflict, the judgment of the case should not be left with the individuals concerned, but with some impartial tribunal; so it is equally necessary, for the peace and happiness of mankind, that when the selfish passions of *nations* come in conflict, the decision of the case should not be left with an individual nation concerned, but should be referred to some great tribunal, that should give a verdict on the affairs of nations, in the same manner that a civil court decides the disputes of individuals. If it was desirable for individuals, bodies politic, and small independent tribes, to unite in some general system of jurisprudence, why is it not equally desirable for large tribes and nations to do the same?

There are two difficulties in the way, which require our attention; but it will be found that they may as easily be removed as were the difficulties attending the commencement and advancement of institutions for the adjudication of difficulties arising between individuals. The first of these is the want of a body of men to enact and promulgate laws for the government of nations; the other is the want of a physical force to carry the decisions of a court of nations into execution.

As to the first difficulty, the formation of what we call a CONGRESS OF NATIONS is no greater than the assembling of any conversation for the enactment of laws, by mutual consent, for the government of the parties represented. It is not expected, that such a combination of powers would be of a very great geographical extent, as it could only embrace the most civilized, enlightened, and Christian nations that could be represented at one great diet, by their ambassadors; and there form a league and covenant, each with every one, and every one with each, that they would, in their future intercourse, be governed by the laws enacted by the diet or congress and ratified by the governments of all the powers so represented. The world has now a kind of code of *voluntary* international law, laid down by eminent civilians, which is, for the most part, respected, but which is not confirmed, by any compact or agreement, and on which the authors themselves often differ, so that what is now called the law of nations, is but little better than a nose of wax, which may be twisted either way, to suit the purposes of dominant nations.

The magnitude of the second difficulty is apparently greater, but it will be much reduced by reflection. It is true, it would not comport with the peace and happiness of mankind, to invest rulers with the power to compel an acquiescence in the decisions of a COURT OF NATIONS by arms; but if we look into the condition of man in a state of civilization, it will be found, that where one man obeys the laws for fear of the sword of the magistrate, an hundred obey them through fear of public opinion. But I would further observe, 1st, that public opinion has not yet been made to bear on nations, and little or no means have hitherto been used to make it bear on them. The plan we propose is one of the means eminently adapted to make it bear on them, as will be shown in the sequel. 2. We do not know what means the congregated wisdom of Christendom may devise for the enforcement of the decisions of a court of nations, by so regulating the intercourse of nations that a refractory member might be made to feel that its duty is its true interest. 3. As it is not intended that this court of nations shall judge any cases but such as are submitted to it by the mutual consent of both parties concerned, its decisions will have as much to enforce them as the decisions of an individual umpire, which has so often settled disputes between nations. 4. Though at the commencement of this system, its success may not be so great as is desirable, yet, as moral power is every day increasing in a geometrical ratio, it will finally take the place of all wars between civilized and Christian nations, much in the same manner as a civil court has taken the place of the judicial combat.

SOURCE: William Ladd, *An Essay on a Congress of Nations for the Adjustment of International Disputes Without Resort to Arms*. Boston: Whipple and Damrell, 1840.

ANALYSIS

This is an extract from an essay on peace written in 1840. The ideal of peace is probably almost as old as human existence. Ancient philosophers and writers were critical of war, and most religions advocate peace. Political philosophers over the centuries have proposed ways by which peace might become possible. In the early eighteenth century, for example, Charles Irénée Castel, Abbé de Saint-Pierre, drew up a draft treaty, ready for the signature of European Powers, that provided for the creation of a European society. Saint-Pierre had initially decided to devise a plan for a confederation of all kingdoms of the world but had then decided to begin with a scheme to include only Europe so that it would not appear implausible. Saint-Pierre foresaw a general renunciation of war, an obligatory mediation of any dispute, and disarmament such that all States would have the same size armies. His plan even included a prohibition on secret treaties— another twentieth-century legal development; no treaties were to be allowed other than those acceptable to all members of the union.[1] Other thinkers, including Rousseau and Kant, drew inspiration from

St. Pierre's work in developing their own schemes for peace. Rousseau wrote in relation to Saint-Pierre's project:

> The advantages which its realization would bring to each prince, to each nation, to the whole of Europe, are immense, manifest, incontestable; and nothing could be more solid or more precise than the arguments which the author employs to prove them. Realize his commonwealth of Europe for a single day, and you may be sure it will last forever; so fully would experience convince men that their own gain is to be found in the good of all. For all that, the very princes who would defend it with all their might, if it once existed, would resist with all their might any proposal for its creation; they will as infallibly throw obstacles in the way of its establishment as they would in the way of its abolition.[2]

In the nineteenth century, a growing number of people came to believe that the progress of civilization might actually lead to a world without war. Peace campaigners sought to turn public opinion against war and to find the best means of preventing war. A number of peace societies were formed in the United States and in England in the years following the end of the Napoleonic Wars in the early nineteenth century, and peace societies were also formed in other countries, including Switzerland and Germany. Members of the peace societies worked for the cause of world peace. Some produced "tracts" to spread information on war and to convince others that war was wrong. Key organizations included the London Peace Society and the American Peace Society, founded in 1828 by William Ladd, the author of this extract.

Ladd's 1840 *Essay on a Congress of Nations*, extracted here, has been referred to as "one of the most celebrated and influential schemes for peace ever propounded."[3] In the plan devised by Ladd, there would be a congress of ambassadors from all Christian and civilized nations, which would agree on the principles of international law for the preservation of peace. In addition to this diplomatic body there would be a court of nations, but it would be merely advisory; it would have no power to enforce its decisions. Cases would be decided according to existing treaties and laws and, where they failed to decide the issue, the case was to be decided according to principles of equity and justice. The scheme devised by Ladd depended heavily on the force of public opinion. Ladd was convinced that the public was coming to want all nations to settle disputes by peaceful means and in the future would not tolerate their leaders taking them to war. He told a meeting of the American Peace Society, that

> a revolution of public opinion has commenced; and revolutions do not go back. The time will come, and that shortly, when nations will settle their disputes by amicable adjustment or arbitration, and will look back on war with as much amazement, as we do on the ordeal by battle and the burning of heretics.[4]

The idea of third-party dispute resolution as a way of avoiding international conflict was not new; the Greeks had sometimes submitted their disputes to arbitration.[5] Hugo Grotius and Jeremy Bentham had both considered arbitration and judicial settlement to be the most effective way of maintaining peace.[6] During the eighteenth

George Washington, 1795. Courtesy of Adolph Ulrike Wertmuller.

century there was considerable use of mediation. States were, however, often reluctant to turn to mediation when issues of national honor were at stake.[7]

The nineteenth century was the era of arbitration. This was considered to be an advance over mediation. A landmark in the development of modern international arbitration was the Jay Treaty of 1794 between the United States and Great Britain. This agreement was initiated by U.S. President George Washington to deal with issues after the American War of Independence. The most famous nineteenth-century arbitration was that between the United States and Great Britain over the *Alabama*, a ship built in Great Britain and used by the Confederacy in the U.S. Civil War. Great Britain had declared its neutrality during the war, and so should not have been assisting either side or allowing its citizens to assist either side. Under British law, however, the building of the *Alabama* had not been illegal, so long as it was not fitted out as a warship or armed in Britain. The *Alabama* had been built in Birkenhead, England, but was fitted out and crewed in the Azores. It sank many Union vessels before itself being sunk by a U.S. warship. In 1872 an arbitral commission in Geneva ordered Great Britain to pay $15,500,000 in gold.

The *Alabama* arbitration was seen as evidence that even as powerful a country as Great Britain was at that time could agree to comply with the decision of third-party arbitration in an issue of national importance. It increased hopes that arbitration might become the standard way by which international disputes were to be settled.

CSS *Alabama* by J. W. Schmidt, 1961. Courtesy of Naval Historical Foundation.

The United States President during the arbitration, General Ulysses S. Grant, predicted "an epoch when a court recognized by all nations will settle international differences instead of keeping large standing armies."[8]

FURTHER READING

Bingham, Tony. "The *Alabama* Claims Arbitration." *International and Comparative Law Quarterly* 54 (2005): 1–25.

Ceadel, Martin. *The Origins of War Prevention: The British Peace Movement and International Relations, 1730–1854*. Oxford: Clarendon, 1996.

Chatfield, Charles. *The American Peace Movement. Ideals and Activism*. New York: Twayne, 1992.

Janis, Mark Weston. *The American Tradition of International Law: Great Expectations, 1789–1914*. Oxford: Clarendon, 2004. Particularly see Chapter 4, "Utopians: International Courts and World Peace."

Ralston, Jackson H. *International Arbitration, from Athens to Locarno*. Stanford, CA: Stanford University Press, 1929.

The Complex Web of Alliances in Nineteenth-Century Europe

- ***Document:*** The text of the provisions of the Treaty of Alliance between Austria-Hungary and Germany, known as the Dual Alliance
- ***Date:*** October 7, 1879
- ***Significance:*** In the years leading up to the outbreak of World War I in 1914, Europe became divided into opposing groups of States by a web of treaty arrangements, many of which were secret. The Dual Alliance was one of the most important of these agreements.

DOCUMENT

Article I

Should, contrary to their hope, and against the loyal desire of the two High Contracting Parties, one of the two Empires be attacked by Russia the High Contracting Parties are bound to come to the assistance one of the other with the whole war strength of their Empires, and accordingly only to conclude peace together and upon mutual agreement.

Article II

Should one of the High Contracting Parties be attacked by another Power, the other High Contracting Party binds itself hereby, not only not to support the aggressor against its high Ally, but to observe at least a benevolent neutral attitude towards its fellow Contracting Party.

Should, however, the attacking party in such a case be supported by Russia, either by an active cooperation or by military measures which constitute a menace to the Party attacked, then the obligation stipulated in Article 1 of this Treaty, for reciprocal assistance with the whole fighting force, becomes equally operative, and the conduct of the war by the two High Contracting Parties shall in this case also be in common until the conclusion of a common peace.

Article III

The duration of this Treaty shall be provisionally fixed at five years from the day of ratification. One year before the expiration of this period the two High Contracting Parties shall consult together concerning the question whether the conditions serving as the basis of the Treaty still prevail, and reach an agreement in regard to the further continuance or possible modification of certain details.

If in the course of the first month of the last year of the Treaty no invitation has been received from either side to open these negotiations, the Treaty shall be considered as renewed for a further period of three years.

Article IV

This Treaty shall, in conformity with its peaceful character, and to avoid any misinterpretation, be kept secret by the two High Contracting Parties, and only communicated to a third Power upon a joint understanding between the two Parties, and according to the terms of a special Agreement.

The two High Contracting Parties venture to hope, after the sentiments expressed by the Emperor Alexander at the meeting at Alexandrovo, that the armaments of Russia will not in reality prove to be menacing to them, and have on that account no reason for making a communication at present; should, however, this hope, contrary to their expectations, prove to be erroneous, the two High Contracting Parties would consider it their loyal obligation to let the Emperor Alexander know, at least confidentially, that they must consider an attack on either of them as directed against both.

Article V

This Treaty shall derive its validity from the approbation of the two Exalted Sovereigns and shall be ratified within fourteen days after this approbation has been granted by Their Most Exalted Majesties. In witness whereof the Plenipotentiaries have signed this Treaty with their own hands and affixed their arms.

Done at Vienna, October 7, 1879
(L.S.) ANDRASSY (L.S.) H. VII v. REUSS

SOURCE: The Dual Alliance Between Austria-Hungary and Germany, October 7, 1879. *Courtesy of the Avalon Project, Yale Law School Library.*
http://avalon.law.yale.edu/19th_century/dualalli.asp.

ANALYSIS

The development of universal international law forbidding a country to launch a way to achieve its political objectives took place in the twentieth century. This does not mean, however, that an individual country previously was completely free to do

"Triple entente." A Russian poster from 1914. The upper inscription reads "agreement." Shown are the female personifications of France, Russia, and Britain, the Triple Entente allies in World War I. In the center, Russia holds aloft an Orthodox Cross. In the background is a battle scene, with men fighting with guns and swords, some on horseback. Above them is an exploding shell, an early airplane, and an airship. Courtesy of the Russian Federation.

what it liked in terms of launching hostilities. One of the earliest types of agreements between States is that of alliances, and alliances still exist today. Even today a country is allowed to defend itself if attacked and, in some circumstances, to come to the assistance of another State if it is attacked. The right to defend oneself if attacked is a natural right that arguably does not need to be embodied in law. An agreement between a pair of States or small group of States to come to the assistance of one another if attacked is a defensive alliance. States have sometimes also formed offensive alliances. Such agreements have often been negotiated in secret and the agreed text—or an additional agreement added to it or specific articles within the agreement—been kept secret.

The years from 1870 to 1914 are well known for the negotiation of a web of European alliance relationships and secret treaties. This document is the text of the Dual Alliance, an agreement between Germany and Austria-Hungary by which they promised to help each other if attacked by Russia or by a fourth power backed by Russia. If either of them were attacked by another country, without Russian backing, the other was, at the very least, to remain neutral. The treaty was secret by Article 4. The Dual Alliance was prolonged by a protocol of March 22, 1883, and renewed on June 1, 1902.[9] On May 18, 1881, Chancellor Bismarck issued a secret Ministerial Declaration that this alliance would remain valid and binding after the upcoming Triple Agreement or League of the Three Emperors (a secret treaty between Austria-Hungary, Germany, and Russia that was primarily concerned with the status of the Balkan Peninsula).[10] The League was extended, with minor alterations, by a treaty of March 27, 1884, and replaced in 1887 by another secret treaty between Germany and Russia. In 1882 Austria-Hungary, Germany, and Italy signed the First Treaty of Triple Alliance by which, *inter alia*, if any one of the parties were attacked by two or more Great Powers not signatories of the treaty, the other two were to go to its assistance.[11] The Triple Alliance was extended by treaties of 1887, 1891, 1902, and 1912.[12] The terms of the Triple Alliance remained so secret that, even when the agreement broke down in 1915, only those diplomats and statesmen directly involved knew what they contained.[13] There were, of course, plenty of rumors, generally wrong.

In 1892 France and Russia negotiated an agreement by which, if either were attacked by Germany or by Austria-Hungary, both would retaliate, forcing Germany to fight on two fronts.[14] This gave France greater security against the threat from Germany but did not seem enough to balance the Triple Alliance. The French Foreign Minister therefore opened negotiations with Britain, and in 1904 France and Britain signed several conventions dealing with colonial

DID YOU KNOW?

Bismarck and His Foreign Policy

Otto Eduard Leopold von Bismarck (1815–1898) was an important figure in nineteenth-century German politics and in European history. What is now Germany had, since the days of the Holy Roman Empire, existed as a set of principalities. Bismarck can take considerable credit for the unification of these separate areas into the German State in 1871. Germany became a federation and a particularly powerful State in the center of Europe. As the first chancellor of this State, Bismarck came to be known as the Iron Chancellor. Bismarck sought to keep the peace in Europe and further German interests through keeping on good terms with other European States, particularly Austria and Russia, while diplomatically isolating France.

issues, so removing some points of friction in their bilateral relationship.[15] France was also keen to improve relations between Britain and Russia. In 1907 Britain and Russia negotiated a treaty on Persia, Afghanistan, and Tibet.[16] After 1907 this loose alliance of Britain, France, and Russia—an attempt to provide a counterweight to the Triple Alliance—was known as the Triple Entente.

By the early years of the twentieth century, Europe was thus balanced into two opposing groups of States, an inherently unstable situation made worse by the rise of the United States and Japan outside Europe and by the combination of States within each of the two principal groupings. France and Britain had traditionally been enemies, and Russia and Britain had competed with each other in the Middle East throughout

Engraving of Otto von Bismarck, 1873. Courtesy of Evert A. Duykinck.

> **DID YOU KNOW?**
>
> **States and World Politics**
>
> The term "state" is used to refer to a political division within a federation—Alabama in the United States and Queensland in Australia, for example. "State" is also the official term for "country"; when used in that sense in this book, the word is usually capitalized. The world of international politics has changed dramatically since the nineteenth century. Representatives of twenty-six States attended the First International Peace Conference in 1899. The United Nations today includes more than 190 States. The Montevideo Convention on Rights and Duties of States (1933) contains what is generally regarded as the classic definition of a State. According to this Convention, a State must have a permanent population, a defined territory, and a government capable of maintaining effective control over its territory and of conducting international relations with other States.

the nineteenth century. Germany and Austria had been bitter enemies prior to the Austro-Prussian War of 1866, and Austria had traditionally been an enemy of Italy. Although a member of the Triple Entente, Italy negotiated a number of secret treaties with both Great Britain and France. The German Empire had been bolstered by the humiliating defeat of France in the Franco-Prussian War of 1870–1871, and the Triple Alliance made it feel even more secure against a war of revenge by France. Germany nevertheless feared encirclement by members of the Triple Entente. The Triple Entente, on the other hand, feared the growing power and aggressive foreign policy of Germany, which in 1898 began a program of rapid naval expansion.

The complex web of alliances in nineteenth-century Europe cannot be understood except in the context of the dominant understanding of how to maintain peace. This was the doctrine of balance of power. According to this doctrine, no single country should be permitted to dominate over others. Where this was looming as a possibility, the threatened States should combine so as to counterbalance the prevailing power. The balance-of-power principle is thought to date from the ancient world and is still frequently used by both scholars and practitioners to account for aspects of the dynamics of international relations and to inform foreign policy. It also underpinned an ad hoc system of conferences held by the major European powers between 1815 and 1854. At these conferences, the great powers sought to "tutor, guide, and control" the balance of power in Europe.[17] The Concert of Europe was a largely reactionary grouping of States, which sought to suppress revolution and maintain the status quo in Europe. It can be regarded as a forerunner of attempts to prevent war through collective arrangements that were much more formally developed and given a basis in international law in the twentieth century.

FURTHER READING

Berger, Stefan, ed. *A Companion to Nineteenth-Century Europe*. Malden, MA: Blackwell Publishing, 2006.

Grosek, Edward. *The Secret Treaties of History*. Buffalo, NY: William S. Hein & Co., 2007.

Joll, James, and Gordon Martel. *The Origins of the First World War*. 3rd ed. New York: Pearson Longman, 2007. Especially see Chapter 3, "The Alliance System and the Old Diplomacy."

Richardson, Louise. "The Concert of Europe and Security Management in the Nineteenth Century." In Helga Haftendorn, Robert O. Keohane, and Celeste A. Wallander, eds. *Imperfect Unions: Security Institutions over Time and Space*. Oxford: Oxford University Press, 1999, 48–79.

The First Hague Peace Conference

- ***Document:*** Note from Tsar Nicholas II of Russia to the diplomatic representatives based in St. Petersburg
- ***Date:*** August 12, 1898
- ***Where:*** St. Petersburg, Russia
- ***Significance:*** This led to the First Hague Peace Conference the following year, which was a landmark on the path toward developing international law and organizations dedicated to the maintenance of world peace.

DOCUMENT

The maintenance of general peace and a possible reduction of the excessive armaments which weigh upon all nations present themselves, in the existing condition of the whole world, as the ideal towards which the endeavours of all Governments should be directed.

The humanitarian and magnanimous views of His Majesty the Emperor, my august master, are in perfect accord with this sentiment.

In the conviction that this lofty aim is in conformity with the most essential interests and the legitimate aspirations of all Powers, the Imperial Government believes that the present moment would be very favourable for seeking, by means of international discussion, the most effective means of ensuring to all peoples the benefits of a real and lasting peace, and above all of limiting the progressive development of existing armaments.

In the course of the last twenty years the longings for a general state of peace have become especially pronounced in the consciences of civilized nations. The preservation of peace has been put forward as the object of international policy. In its name great States have formed powerful alliances; and for the better guaranty of peace they have developed their military forces to proportions hitherto unknown, and still continue to increase them without hesitating at any sacrifice.

All these efforts nevertheless have not yet led to the beneficent results of the desired pacification.

The ever-increasing financial charges strike and paralyze public prosperity at its source; the intellectual and physical strength of the nations, their labour and capital, are for the most part diverted from their natural application and unproductively consumed; hundreds of millions are spent in acquiring terrible engines of destruction, which though today regarded as the last word of science, are destined to-morrow to lose all value in consequence of some fresh discovery in the same field. National culture, economic progress, and the production of wealth are either paralysed or perverted in their development.

Moreover, in proportion as the armaments of each Power increase, so do they less and less attain the object aimed at by the Governments. Economic crises, due in great part to the system of amassing armaments to the point of exhaustion, and the continual danger which lies in this accumulation of war material, are transforming the armed peace of our days into a crushing burden which the peoples have more and more difficulty in bearing. It appears evident, then, that if this state of affairs be prolonged, it will inevitably lead to the very cataclysm which it is desired to avert, and the impending horrors of which are fearful to every human thought.

In checking these increasing armaments and in seeking the means of averting the calamities which threaten the entire world lies the supreme duty to-day resting upon all States.

Imbued with this idea, His Majesty has been pleased to command me to propose to all the Governments which have accredited representatives at the Imperial Court the holding of a conference to consider this grave problem.

This conference would be, by the help of God, a happy presage for the century about to open. It would converge into a single powerful force the efforts of all the States which sincerely wish the great conception of universal peace to triumph over the elements of disturbance and discord. It would at the same time cement their agreement by a solemn avowal of the principles of equity and law, upon which repose the security of States and the welfare of peoples.

COUNT MOURAVIEFF.
ST PETERSBURG, August 12, 1898.

SOURCE: "Russian Circular Note Proposing the First Peace Conference," August 12, 1898, pp. 1–2 in James Brown Scott, ed. *Reports to the Hague Conferences of 1899 and 1907.* Oxford: Clarendon Press, 1917. *Courtesy of Oxford University Press.*

ANALYSIS

This note was given to diplomats in St. Petersburg, suggesting an international conference to place limits on armaments. The note describes what in International Relations is often referred to as the security dilemma: that a State endeavoring to enhance its own security increases its military capacities, which then makes other countries fearful, so they increase their capacities, and so on in a spiraling process. Recognition of this tendency dates from the time of Thucydides,[18] but is today most commonly associated with the work of John Herz. Writing in 1950, Herz described the security dilemma in this way:

> Groups of individuals living in such a constellation [where a plurality of otherwise interconnected groups constitute ultimate units of political life, that is, where groups live alongside each other without being organized into a higher unity] must be, and usually are, concerned about their security from being attacked,

Andrew Carnegie, American businessman and philanthropist, 1913. Courtesy of Marceau.

subjected, dominated, or annihilated by other groups and individuals. Striving to attain security from such attack, they are driven to acquire more and more power in order to escape the impact of the power of others. This, in turn, renders the others more insecure and compels them to prepare for the worst. Since none can ever feel entirely secure in such a world of competing units, power competition ensues, and the vicious circle of security and power accumulation is on.[19]

A second circular noted that the political horizon had undergone a decided change in the last four months because several powers had been rapidly increasing their armaments and military capacity and queried whether it was therefore an opportune time to discuss the ideas set out in the first circular. Despite these misgivings, the second circular proposed a preliminary exchange of ideas on eight subjects, most of which related to armaments, but the last one of which was "acceptance, in principle, of the use of good offices, mediation, and voluntary arbitration, in cases where they are available, with the purpose of preventing armed conflicts between nations; understanding in relation to their mode of application and establishment of a uniform practice in employing them."[20]

The First International Peace Conference took place from May 23 to July 24, 1899. The success of the *Alabama* arbitration had no doubt contributed to the expectations of the conference. Until then, peace conferences had been held only at the ends of wars, not to find ways of keeping the peace in future. The immediate impact of this conference on the course of world events was not huge, but the participating States did agree to the text of a Convention for the Pacific Settlement of International Disputes, which established the Permanent Court of International Arbitration. The title of the Permanent Court was a little misleading, since the institution to which it gave rise was not really permanent nor a court. Each State would nominate four potential arbitrators, whose names would be given to a bureau established in The Hague. If countries agreed to refer a case to the Court, each country would then select arbitrators from this list according to a particular formula. The Second International Peace Conference, held from June 15 to October 18, 1907, made some revisions to the procedure of the Court and limited the judges to no more than one per country.

DID YOU KNOW?

Andrew Carnegie and the Peace Palace

The Peace Palace in The Hague was built between 1907 and 1913 as the home for the new Permanent Court of International Arbitration. It housed the Permanent Court of International Justice between 1922 and 1946 and has, since 1946, been the home of the International Court of Justice. Andrew Carnegie donated $1.5 million dollars through the Carnegie Foundation for building the Peace Palace. Carnegie was born in Scotland in 1835. He came from a poor family that had immigrated to Pittsburgh in 1848 in search of a better life. Carnegie worked his way up to becoming a captain of industry and the richest man in the world. Toward the end of his life he looked for ways in which his fortune could be used to help create a better world. He funded many public libraries and institutions of higher learning. The Peace Palace was opened with great ceremony in 1913, one year before World War I broke out.

DID YOU KNOW?

The Hague: Legal Capital of the World

A major conference tends to become associated with the country in which it is held, and so it would be easy for a conference dedicated to preserving world peace to become associated with the interests of a Great Power were that country to host the event. The second Russian circular suggested that the proposed conference should not be held in the capital city of a Great Power, because such a choice of venue might detract from progress. The Russian Government subsequently suggested The Hague as a suitable location. The Hague is now sometimes referred to as the "legal capital of the world" because it hosts several of the world's leading legal bodies, including the International Court of Justice, the International Criminal Court, and the Organization for the Prohibition of Chemical Weapons.

It may have been that Russia proposed the idea of limiting armaments because it felt unable to keep up with the increasing militarization in Europe. As one writer described the situation:

> The Tsar of Russia, at the request of his minister of finance, Count Serge Witte, . . . convened at The Hague in 1899 a large international conference which gave attention to disarmament. The Tsar's idealism developed after Witte pointed out that France, Germany and Austria-Hungary were equipping their armies with a new type of field gun, the so-called "French 75," which the Russian treasury would be unable to purchase and at the same time finance some necessary warships. Count Witte, preferring the new warships, hoped that the Tsar could obtain at The Hague a moratorium of 75's in the name of disarmament and world peace. But the other world powers were aware of these Russian motives and nothing came of disarmament.[21]

Another landmark development was the establishment in 1907 of the Central American Court of Justice by Costa Rica, Guatemala, Honduras, Nicaragua, El Salvador, the United States, and Mexico. States agreed to submit all disputes to this Court, including those questions involving "national honor and vital interests." It was in one sense ironic that these momentous developments toward international courts took place at a time of increasing international tensions, culminating in World War I. Viewed from another angle it makes perfect sense that, at a time when tensions were increasing and it was difficult to foresee any endpoint other than war, leaders should make a desperate bid to steer history down another channel. The Central American Court of Justice decided nine cases in the ten years of its existence, though it did not survive World War I. The Permanent Court of International Arbitration heard fourteen cases prior to August 1914. It lost prominence with the establishment of the World Court after World War One.

FURTHER READING

Caron, David D. "War and International Adjudication: Reflections on the 1899 Peace Conference." *American Journal of International Law* 94 (2000): 4–30.

Davis, Calvin DeArmond. *The United States and the First Hague Peace Conference*. Ithaca, NY: Cornell University Press, 1962.

Eyffinger, Arthur. *The 1899 Hague Peace Conference: "The Parliament of Man, the Federation of the World."* The Hague: Kluwer Law International, 1999.

Van Krieken, Peter J., and David McKay, eds. *The Hague—Legal Capital of the World*. Cambridge, UK: Cambridge University Press, 2005.

Nasaw, David. *Andrew Carnegie*. New York: Penguin, 2006.

The International Law of Neutrality

- ***Document:*** Speech by U.S. President Woodrow Wilson to the joint houses of Congress
- ***Date:*** April 2, 1917
- ***Where:*** Washington, DC
- ***Significance:*** This demonstrates the important role that the law of neutrality had in questions of war and peace prior to the development of the international law of collective security in the twentieth century.

DOCUMENT

I have called the Congress into extraordinary session because there are serious, very serious, choices of policy to be made, and made immediately, which it was neither right nor constitutionally permissible that I should assume the responsibility of making.

On the third of February last I officially laid before you the extraordinary announcement of the Imperial German Government that on and after the first day of February it was its purpose to put aside all restraints of law or of humanity and use its submarines to sink every vessel that sought to approach either the ports of Great Britain and Ireland or the western coasts of Europe or any of the ports controlled by the enemies of Germany within the Mediterranean.

That had seemed to be the object of the German submarine warfare earlier in the war, but since April of last year the Imperial Government had somewhat restrained the commanders of its undersea craft in conformity with its promise then given to us that passenger boats should not be sunk and that due warning would be given to all other vessels which its submarines might seek to destroy, when no resistance was offered or escape attempted, and care taken that their crews were given at least a fair chance to save their lives in their open boats.

The precautions taken were meagre and haphazard enough, as was proved in distressing instance after instance in the progress of the cruel and unmanly business, but a certain degree of restraint was observed. The new policy has swept every restriction aside. Vessels of every kind, whatever their flag, their character, their cargo, their destination, their errand, have been ruthlessly sent to the bottom without warning and without thought of help or mercy for those on board, the vessels of friendly neutrals along with those of belligerents.

Even hospital ships and ships carrying relief to the sorely bereaved and stricken people of Belgium, though the latter were provided with safe conduct through the proscribed areas by the German Government itself and were distinguished by unmistakable marks of identity, have been sunk with the same reckless lack of compassion or of principle.

I was for a little while unable to believe that such things would in fact be done by any government that had hitherto subscribed to the humane practices of civilized nations. International law had its origin in the attempt to set up some law which would be respected and observed upon the seas, where no nation had right of dominion and where lay the free highways of the world.

This minimum of right the German Government has swept aside under the plea of retaliation and necessity and because it had no weapons which it could use at sea except these which it is impossible to employ as it is employing them without throwing to the winds all scruples of humanity or of respect for the understandings that were supposed to underlie the intercourse of the world.

I am not now thinking of the loss of property involved, immense and serious as that is, but only of the wanton and wholesale destruction of the lives of non-combatants, men, women, and children, engaged in pursuits which have always, even in the darkest periods of modern history, been deemed innocent and legitimate. Property can be paid for; the lives of peaceful and innocent people cannot be. The present German submarine warfare against commerce is a warfare against mankind.

It is a war against all nations. American ships have been sunk, American lives taken, in ways which it has stirred us very deeply to learn of, but the ships and people of other neutral and friendly nations have been sunk and overwhelmed in the waters in the same way. There has been no discrimination.

The challenge is to all mankind. Each nation must decide for itself how it will meet it. The choice we make for ourselves must be made with a moderation of counsel and a temperateness for judgement befitting our character and our motives as a nation. We must put excited feeling away. Our motive will not be revenge or the victorious assertion of the physical might of the nation, but only the vindication of right, of human right, of which we are only a single champion.

When I addressed the Congress on the twenty-sixth of February last I thought that it would suffice to assert our neutral rights with arms, our right to use the seas against unlawful interference, our right to keep our people safe against unlawful violence.

But armed neutrality, it now appears, is impracticable. Because submarines are in effect outlaws when used as the German submarines have been used against merchant shipping, it is impossible to defend ships against their attacks as the law of nations has assumed that merchantmen would defend themselves against privateers or cruisers, visible craft giving chase upon the open sea. It is common prudence in such circumstances, grim necessity indeed, to endeavour to destroy them before they have shown their own intention.

They must be dealt with upon sight, if dealt with at all. The German Government denies the right of neutrals to use arms at all within the areas of the sea which it has proscribed, even in the defence of rights which no modern publicist has ever before questioned their right to defend.

The intimation is conveyed that the armed guards which we have placed on our merchant ships will be treated as beyond the pale of law and subject to be dealt with as pirates would be. Armed neutrality is ineffectual enough at best; in such circumstances and in the face of such pretensions it is worse than ineffectual: it is likely only to produce what it was meant to prevent; it is practically certain to draw us into the war without either the rights or the effectiveness of belligerents.

There is one choice we cannot make, we are incapable of making: we will not choose the path of submission and suffer the most sacred rights of our Nation and our people to be ignored or violated. The wrongs against which we now array ourselves are no common wrongs; they cut to the very roots of human life.

With a profound sense of the solemn and even tragical character of the step I am taking and of the grave responsibilities which it involves, but in unhesitating obedience to what I deem my constitutional duty, I advise that the Congress declare the recent course of the Imperial German Government to be in fact nothing less than war against the government and people of the United States; that it formally accept the status of belligerent which has thus been thrust upon it; and that it take immediate steps not only to put the country in a more thorough state of defence but also to exert all its power and employ all its resources to bring the Government of the German Empire to terms and end the war.

SOURCE: 55 U.S. Congressional Record, House 118 (1917). *Courtesy of Hein Online.*

ANALYSIS

One body of law that addressed the question of use of force in the era preceding the international prohibition on war was that of the law of neutrality. "Neutrality" refers to the legal status of a State not participating in a war being waged by other States. Neutrality was an option open to a State in the days when war was an accepted instrument of policy. The most fundamental obligation on a neutral State was that it not intervene in a conflict to the advantage of one or other of the belligerents. Neutrality was a way of confining the effects of war by ensuring that third States could continue to trade and engage in daily life without becoming drawn into the war. In the Balkan Wars of 1912–1913, for example, the Great Powers used the law of neutrality to localize the conflicts in the Balkan Peninsula, with the aim of preventing their spread to the European continent.[22]

The United States was a leader in the development of the modern law of neutrality, using this legal option as a way of keeping out of European conflicts. The United States passed domestic legislation to prevent U.S. citizens acting in a way contrary to that required of a neutral. The first U.S. Neutrality Act, passed on June 5, 1794, included a prohibition on American citizens enlisting in foreign military forces and on the fitting out or arming of ships for belligerents. Permanent legislation, focusing on maritime neutrality, was enacted on April 20, 1818.[23] The British Foreign Enlistment Act of 1819 was modeled on the U.S. Act.[24] It prohibited foreign enlistment, the equipping of armed ships for belligerent use and the reinforcement of belligerent warships in British waters. It was replaced in 1870 by the Foreign Enlistment Act, which contained prohibitions against foreign enlistment, the equipping of armed ships, and the reinforcement of warships in British waters.[25]

We have already seen that neutrality was an issue during the American Civil War. The Union accused Great Britain on more than one occasion of breaching its declared neutrality. Although the international law had been partially codified in the 1856 Declaration of Paris, the details of the law remained unclear. The most serious issue that arose between the Union and Great Britain during the Civil War was that of Britain permitting Confederate warships to be built in and depart from British ports. The Foreign Enlistment Act of 1819 did not expressly prohibit the construction of ships, and the international law of neutrality, while prohibiting a neutral State from supplying war materiel to a belligerent, did not extend this obligation to a private party. British courts required only that, when the ships departed British waters, they remained "incapable of attack and defense." This meant that a ship could be fitted with armaments and manning, even from the same British port, so long as the fitting happened elsewhere.[26] Britain and the United States nearly went to war at several stages during the Civil War.[27] After the war, the *Alabama* arbitration settled issues related to British neutrality during the war.

World War I broke out in August 1914, and the United States adopted a policy of neutrality. What was to become a major issue for the United States was, however, the attitude it would take toward British actions in relation to the laws of neutrality. Britain imposed a blockade on Germany, asserting the right to stop and search neutral ships carrying contraband—materials with which to wage war—to the Central Powers. Germany responded to the blockade with submarine attacks on Allied and neutral shipping. On May 7, 1915, a German submarine sank the *Lusitania*, a British passenger ship with many Americans on board as well as munitions for Great

> **DID YOU KNOW?**
>
> **Lawyers and U.S. Foreign Policy**
>
> The international law of neutrality played a central role in the international diplomacy leading up to U.S. entry into World War I. International law has been central to the conduct of U.S. foreign policy. It is often recognized that the United States has a particularly legalistic culture. This has also been reflected in the professional background of those who play significant roles in the nation's foreign relations. The vast majority of Secretaries of State have been lawyers by background. Woodrow Wilson was a lawyer who had been a professor of political science before entering politics. Of the previous twenty-seven presidents, eighteen had been lawyers. Of the thirty-four men who had chaired the influential Senate Foreign Relations Committee between 1816 and 1918, all but three had been lawyers.

> **DID YOU KNOW?**
>
> **Woodrow Wilson and International Law**
>
> President Woodrow Wilson is famous for his promotion of international law and institutions; indeed "Wilsonian" is use as an adjective to refer to a belief in employing international law to advance the interests of justice and world peace. But, according to Mark Janis, there was nothing particularly "Wilsonian" about Wilson's own analysis of the potential of international law during his days as a professor of international law; his conversion probably took place during World War I.[29] Not all historians believe that, even during and after the War, Wilson was as idealistic or as "Wilsonian" as he is usually portrayed.

Britain. Germany had warned that it regarded attack on that vessel as justified. This is seen as a turning point in U.S. foreign policy, because of the strong U.S. protest to Germany, without a corresponding protest to Britain in relation to its blockade. President Wilson found it increasingly difficult to pursue a policy of neutrality, and the United States gradually became drawn toward the Allied side of the war.

Although President Wilson wanted to remain neutral and to use that position to mediate an end to the war, his suggestions to the European powers were not well received, and the United States was drawn closer to involvement in the war when Wilson demanded that German submarines not attack merchant ships. Wilson

President Woodrow Wilson, December 2, 1912. Courtesy of the Pach Brothers.

explained his ideas for postwar Europe to Congress on January 22, 1917, declaring that a balance of power should be replaced with a community of power. As referred to near the beginning of this document, on February 1, 1917, Germany began a policy of total submarine warfare, by which all ships in war zones were fair game, including U.S. merchant ships. On February 26, 1917, Wilson asked Congress to finance "armed neutrality," by which merchant ships would be armed. When the Senate did not comply with Wilson's request, he went ahead anyway, acting on the basis of an "almost forgotten" law of the eighteenth century.[28]

The speech extracted in this document made the case for why the United States should declare war on Germany. A prime reason given was Germany's lack of respect for the law of neutrality, which "thrust" the status of belligerent on the United States. This speech was followed by a formal declaration of war on April 6, 1917.

Notes

1. Sylvester John Hemleben, *Plans for World Peace Through Six Centuries* (Chicago: University of Chicago Press, 1943), 56–73.
2. Chris Brown, Terry Nardin, and Nicholas Rengger, eds., *International Relations in Political Thought. Texts from the Ancient Greeks to the First World War* (Cambridge, UK: Cambridge University Press, 2002), 426–427.
3. Hemleben, *Plans for World Peace Through Six Centuries*, 105.
4. William Ladd, "Address Delivered at the Tenth Anniversary of the Massachusetts Peace Society," December 25, 1825, cited in Hemleben, *Plans for World Peace through Six Centuries*, 111.
5. David J. Bederman, *International Law in Antiquity* (Cambridge, UK: Cambridge University Press, 2001), 82–84.
6. Hans-Jürgen Schlochauer, "Arbitration," in Rudolf Bernhardt, ed., *Encyclopedia of Public International Law,* Instalment 1 (1981): 16.
7. Hemleben, *Plans for World Peace Through Six Centuries*, 191.
8. C. D. Davis, *The United States and the First Hague Peace Conference* (Ithaca, NY: Cornell University Press, 1962), 13–14.
9. Michael Hurst, ed., *Key Treaties for the Great Powers, 1814–1914,* Vol. 2 (Newton Abbot: David & Charles, 1972), 629–30; 732.
10. Edward Grosek, *The Secret Treaties of History* (Philadelphia: Xlibris, 2004), 126.
11. The text is in Hurst, ed., *Key Treaties for the Great Powers*, vol. 2., 611–613.
12. For the texts of these see Hurst, ed., *Key Treaties for the Great Powers*, vol. 2, 639, 658, 738, 833.
13. Denys P. Myers and J. G. D'Arcy Paul, eds., *The Secret Treaties of Austria-Hungary Vol. I. Texts of the Treaties and Agreements* (Cambridge, MA: Harvard University Press, 1920), 4.
14. "Draft of Military Convention Between France and Russia, 1892," in Hurst, ed., *Key Treaties for the Great Powers*, vol. 2, 668–670.
15. The texts are in Hurst, ed., *Key Treaties for the Great Powers*, vol. 2, 756–765.
16. "Convention between Great Britain and Russia relating to Persia, Afghanistan and Thibet," August 31, 1907, in Hurst, ed., *Key Treaties for the Great Powers*, vol. 2, 805–809.

17. Graham Evans and Jeffrey Newnham, *The Penguin Dictionary of International Relations* (London: Penguin, 1998), 91.
18. Robert Jervis, "Was the Cold War a Security Dilemma?" *Journal of Cold War Studies* 3:1 (2001): 36, fn. 1.
19. John H. Herz, "Idealist Internationalism and the Security Dilemma," *World Politics* 2 (1950): 157.
20. "Russian Circular Note Proposing the Programme of the First Conference," December 30, 1898, reproduced in James Brown Scott, ed., *The Reports to the Hague Conferences of 1899 and 1907* (Oxford: Clarendon, 1917), 2–4.
21. Robert H. Ferrell, "The Peace Movement." in Alexander DeConde, ed., *Isolation and Security* (Durham, NC: Duke University Press, 1957), 91.
22. Elizabeth Chadwick, *Traditional Neutrality Revisited: Law, Theory and Case Studies* (The Hague: Kluwer, 2002), 14.
23. Erich Kussbach, "Neutrality Laws," in Rudolf Bernhardt, ed., *Encyclopedia of Public International Law* vol. 4 (1982): 28.
24. *British and Foreign States Papers* 6 (1818–1819): 130.
25. J. H. W. Verzijl, *International Law in Historical Perspective. Part IX-B The Law of Neutrality* (Akogeb aab den Rijn: Sijthoff & Noordhoff, 1979), 108.
26. Chadwick, *Traditional Neutrality Revisited*, 38–39.
27. Chadwick, *Traditional Neutrality Revisited*, 40.
28. Walter LaFeber, *The American Age. U.S. Foreign Policy at Home and Abroad, 1750 to the Present*, 2nd ed. (New York: W. W. Norton, 1989), 295.
29. Mark Weston Janis, *The American Tradition of International Law: Great Expectations, 1789–1914* (Oxford: Clarendon, 2004), 128.

FURTHER READING

Clements, Kendrick A. *Woodrow Wilson, World Statesman*. rev. ed. Chicago: I.R. Dee, 1999.

Coogan, John W. *The End of Neutrality: The United States, Britain, and Maritime Rights, 1899–1915*. Ithaca, NY: Cornell University Press, 1981.

Hall, William Edward. *The Rights and Duties of Neutrals*. London: Longmans, 1874.

LaFeber, Walter. *The American Age. U.S. Foreign Policy at Home and Abroad. 1750 to the Present*. 2nd ed. New York: W.W. Norton, 1989.

"Proclamation of April 6, 1917, of the Existence of a State of War between the United States and Germany by the President of the United States of America." Reprinted in United States Department of State, *Papers Relating to the Foreign Relations of the United States, 1917. Supplement 1, The World War (1917)*. 207–208. http://digicoll.library.wisc.edu/FRUS/.

2

THE TREATY OF VERSAILLES AS A TENTATIVE TRIAL RUN

Palais des Nations, former headquarters of the League of Nations. Courtesy of CORBIS.

OVERVIEW

The first significant step toward an international legal regime outlawing the use of force came with the Covenant of the League of Nations, followed relatively closely by what is colloquially known as the Kellogg-Briand Pact of 1928. This chapter looks at these developments between the World Wars as precursors to the establishment of the United Nations.

The League of Nations

- ***Document:*** The Covenant of the League of Nations (including amendments adopted to December 1924)
- ***Date:*** June 28, 1919; entered into force January 10, 1920
- ***Where:*** The Treaty was signed at the Versailles Palace, near Paris.
- ***Significance:*** This treaty represented a midway point between the era in which States regarded it as their sovereign right to wage war and the contemporary era, in which there is a general prohibition on the use of force in inter-State relations.

DOCUMENT

THE HIGH CONTRACTING PARTIES, In order to promote international co-operation and to achieve international peace and security by the acceptance of obligations not to resort to war, by the prescription of open, just and honourable relations between nations, by the firm establishment of the understandings of international law as the actual rule of conduct among Governments, and by the maintenance of justice and a scrupulous respect for all treaty obligations in the dealings of organised peoples with one another,

Agree to this Covenant of the League of Nations.

Article 1

The original Members of the League of Nations shall be those of the Signatories which are named in the Annex to this Covenant and also such of those other States named in the Annex as shall accede without reservation to this Covenant.

Such accession shall be effected by a Declaration deposited with the Secretariat within two months of the coming into force of the Covenant. Notice thereof shall be sent to all other Members of the League.

Any fully self-governing State, Dominion or Colony not named in the Annex may become a Member of the League if its admission is agreed to by two-thirds of the Assembly, provided that it shall give effective guarantees of its sincere intention to observe its international obligations, and shall accept such regulations as may be prescribed by the League in regard to its military, naval and air forces and armaments.

Any Member of the League may, after two years' notice of its intention so to do, withdraw from the League, provided that all its international obligations and all its obligations under this Covenant shall have been fulfilled at the time of its withdrawal.

Article 2

The action of the League under this Covenant shall be effected through the instrumentality of an Assembly and of a Council, with a permanent Secretariat.

Article 11

Any war or threat of war, whether immediately affecting any of the Members of the League or not, is hereby declared a matter of concern to the whole League, and the League shall take any action that may be deemed wise and effectual to safeguard the peace of nations.

In case any such emergency should arise the Secretary General shall on the request of any Member of the League forthwith summon a meeting of the Council. It is also declared to be the friendly right of each Member of the League to bring to the attention of the Assembly or of the Council any circumstance whatever affecting international relations which threatens to disturb international peace or the good understanding between nations upon which peace depends.

Article 12

The Members of the League agree that, if there should arise between them any dispute likely to lead to a rupture they will submit the matter either to arbitration or judicial settlement or to enquiry by the Council, and they agree in no case to resort to war until three months after the award by the arbitrators or the judicial decision, or the report by the Council.

In any case under this Article the award of the arbitrators or the judicial decision shall be made within a reasonable time, and the report of the Council shall be made within six months after the submission of the dispute.

Article 13

The Members of the League agree that whenever any dispute shall arise between them which they recognise to be suitable for submission to arbitration or judicial settlement and which cannot be satisfactorily settled by diplomacy, they will submit the whole subject-matter to arbitration or judicial settlement.

Disputes as to the interpretation of a treaty, as to any question of international law, as to the existence of any fact which if established would constitute a breach of any international obligation, or as to the extent and nature of the reparation to be made for any such breach, are declared to be among those which are generally suitable for submission to arbitration or judicial settlement.

For the consideration of any such dispute, the court to which the case is referred shall be the Permanent Court of International Justice, established in accordance with Article 14, or any tribunal agreed on by the parties to the dispute or stipulated in any convention existing between them.

The Members of the League agree that they will carry out in full good faith any award or decision that may be rendered, and that they will not resort to war against a Member of the League which complies therewith. In the event of any failure to carry out such an award or decision, the Council shall propose what steps should be taken to give effect thereto.

Article 14

The Council shall formulate and submit to the Members of the League for adoption plans for the establishment of a Permanent Court of International Justice.

The Court shall be competent to hear and determine any dispute of an international character which the parties thereto submit to it. The Court may also give an advisory opinion upon any dispute or question referred to it by the Council or by the Assembly.

Article 15

If there should arise between Members of the League any dispute likely to lead to a rupture, which is not submitted to arbitration or judicial settlement in accordance with Article 13, the Members of the League agree that they will submit the matter to the Council.

Any party to the dispute may effect such submission by giving notice of the existence of the dispute to the Secretary General, who will make all necessary arrangements for a full investigation and consideration thereof.

For this purpose the parties to the dispute will communicate to the Secretary General, as promptly as possible, statements of their case with all the relevant facts and papers, and the Council may forthwith direct the publication thereof.

The Council shall endeavour to effect a settlement of the dispute, and if such efforts are successful, a statement shall be made public giving such facts and explanations regarding the dispute and the terms of settlement thereof as the Council may deem appropriate.

If the dispute is not thus settled, the Council either unanimously or by a majority vote shall make and publish a report containing a statement of the facts of the dispute and the recommendations which are deemed just and proper in regard thereto.

Any Member of the League represented on the Council may make public a statement of the facts of the dispute and of its conclusions regarding the same.

If a report by the Council is unanimously agreed to by the members thereof other than the Representatives of one or more of the parties to the dispute, the Members of the League agree that they will not go to war with any party to the dispute which complies with the recommendations of the report.

If the Council fails to reach a report which is unanimously agreed to by the members thereof, other than the Representatives of one or more of the parties to the dispute, the Members of the League reserve to themselves the right to take such action as they shall consider necessary for the maintenance of right and justice.

If the dispute between the parties is claimed by one of them, and is found by the Council, to arise out of a matter which by international law is solely within the domestic jurisdiction of that party, the Council shall so report, and shall make no recommendation as to its settlement.

The Council may in any case under this Article refer the dispute to the Assembly. The dispute shall be so referred at the request of either party to the dispute, provided that such request be made within fourteen days after the submission of the dispute to the Council.

In any case referred to the Assembly, all the provisions of this Article and of Article 12 relating to the action and powers of the Council shall apply to the action and powers of the Assembly, provided that a report made by the Assembly, if concurred in by the Representatives of those Members of the League represented on the Council and of a majority of the other Members of the League, exclusive in each case of the Representatives of the parties to the dispute, shall have the same force as a report by the Council concurred in by all the members thereof other than the Representatives of one or more of the parties to the dispute.

Article 16

Should any Member of the League resort to war in disregard of its covenants under Articles 12, 13 or 15, it shall ipso facto be deemed to have committed an act of war against all other Members of the League, which hereby undertake immediately to subject it to the severance of all trade or financial relations, the prohibition of all intercourse between their nationals and the nationals of the covenant-breaking State, and the prevention of all financial, commercial or personal intercourse between the nationals of the covenant-breaking State and the nationals of any other State, whether a Member of the League or not.

It shall be the duty of the Council in such case to recommend to the several Governments concerned what effective military, naval or air force the Members of the League shall severally contribute to the armed forces to be used to protect the covenants of the League.

The Members of the League agree, further, that they will mutually support one another in the financial and economic measures which are taken under this Article, in order to minimise the loss and inconvenience resulting from the above measures, and that they will mutually support one another in resisting any special measures aimed at one of their number by the covenant-breaking State, and that they will take the necessary steps to afford passage through their territory to the forces of any of the Members of the League which are co-operating to protect the covenants of the League.

Any Member of the League which has violated any covenant of the League may be declared to be no longer a Member of the League by a vote of the Council concurred in by the Representatives of all the other Members of the League represented thereon.

Article 17

In the event of a dispute between a Member of the League and a State which is not a Member of the League, or between States not Members of the League, the State or States not Members of the League shall be invited to accept the obligations of membership in the League for the purposes of such dispute, upon such conditions as the Council may deem just.

If such invitation is accepted, the provisions of Articles 12 to 16 inclusive shall be applied with such modifications as may be deemed necessary by the Council. Upon such invitation being given the Council shall immediately institute an inquiry into the circumstances of the dispute and recommend such action as may seem best and most effectual in the circumstances.

If a State so invited shall refuse to accept the obligations of membership in the League for the purposes of such dispute, and shall resort to war against a Member of the League, the provisions of Article 16 shall be applicable as against the State taking such action.

If both parties to the dispute when so invited refuse to accept the obligations of membership in the League for the purposes of such dispute, the Council may take such measures and make such recommendations as will prevent hostilities and will result in the settlement of the dispute.

Article 18

Every treaty or international engagement entered into hereafter by any Member of the League shall be forthwith registered with the Secretariat and shall as soon as possible be published by it. No such treaty or international engagement shall be binding until so registered.

Article 19

The Assembly may from time to time advise the reconsideration by Members of the League of treaties which have become inapplicable and the consideration of international conditions whose continuance might endanger the peace of the world.

Article 20

The Members of the League severally agree that this Covenant is accepted as abrogating all obligations or understandings inter se which are inconsistent with the terms thereof, and solemnly undertake that they will not hereafter enter into any engagements inconsistent with the terms thereof.

In case any Member of the League shall, before becoming a Member of the League, have undertaken any obligations inconsistent with the terms of this Covenant, it shall be the duty of such Member to take immediate steps to procure its release from such obligations.

SOURCE: Covenant of the League Nations, *Courtesy of The Avalon Project Yale Law School Library*. http://avalon.law.yale.edu/20th_century/leagcov.asp.

ANALYSIS

Several peace treaties were concluded at the end of World War I. The Treaty of Versailles, the peace treaty between Germany and the Allied Powers, was signed on June 28, 1919. Article 231 assigned Germany full responsibility for the war and imposed harsh economic penalties on Germany. The war-guilt clause and the reparations obligations forced on Germany fostered resentment in Germany and contributed to the rise of Hitler's national socialism, paving the way for a second world war. For the purpose of understanding the evolution of international law toward the prohibition of the use of force, however, it is Part I of the Treaty of Versailles that is of most direct importance. Part I established the League of Nations, the forerunner to the United Nations.

The Covenant of the League was drafted relatively rapidly. U.S. President Woodrow Wilson proclaimed the need for an international organization in the last of his famous Fourteen Points of January 8, 1914.

> A general association of nations must be formed under specific covenants for the purpose of affording mutual guarantees of political independence and territorial integrity to great and small states alike.

The first formulation of League of Nations suggestions in a definite text under governmental direction was a draft treaty prepared by a committee chaired by Lord Phillimore and submitted to the British Government on March 20, 1918.[1] The French Government also appointed a committee, which on June 8, 1918, produced a report on the potential for such an organization. In the United States, Colonel House and his advisers drew on the Phillimore Plan in preparing a draft covenant; it was presented to Wilson on July 16, 1918.[2]

Following further preparatory work, an international Commission on the League of Nations, chaired by President Wilson, held ten sessions between February 3 and February 13, 1919. The draft was made public on February 14, 1919, and on March 20 and 21 the commission met with representatives of States that had been neutral during the war. After five other meetings, the Covenant was completed, and on April 28 it was accepted by a plenary session of the Conference.[3] The Covenant was incorporated as Part I of the peace treaties with Germany, Austria, Bulgaria, and Hungary.

The League of Nations was based in Geneva, Switzerland. From 1938 its home was the Palais des Nations, a building that still houses the UN Office at Geneva, the biggest United Nations duty station outside of headquarters in New York. The League was made up of an Assembly (the equivalent of today's UN General Assembly), a Council (the equivalent to today's UN Security Council), the Permanent Court of International Justice (the forerunner to the International Court of Justice), and a Secretariat, the administrative organ. There were also a several agencies and other bodies associated with the League, including the Slavery Commission and the International Labor Organization, each addressing a specific issue of the day. The main organs took up issues including reducing armaments and establishing a mandates system to deal with colonies.

At the heart of the Organization was, however, the question of war and peace, and the attempt to further develop international law to prevent war. The Covenant of the League of Nations did not outlaw war as such; that did not come until the Charter of the United Nations after World War II. But the Covenant did take an important step toward the general prohibition on the use of force. Article 12 of the Covenant of the League of Nations provided that, if a member of the League had a dispute with another State, it would submit that matter for resolution by one of three methods. One alternative was arbitration, which would give rise to an arbitral "award" or decision; the second was to take the issue to Court, which would give rise to a formal judicial decision; the third was for the Council of the League of Nations

The League of Nations at its opening session in Geneva on November 15, 1920. Courtesy of UN Photo.

Nations Unitas. This poster, created by the U.S. Office of War Information in 1943, represents the origins of the United Nations in the 1942 Declaration of United Nations. The poster depicts the flags of the countries and of those governments-in-exile that pledged to support the Allied effort, above the ongoing war machine of the United Nations. The Free French flag is missing. Courtesy of Office of War Information, U.S. Federal Government.

to undertake an inquiry, which would result in a report of the Council. Member States agreed that they would not "resort to war" until three months after the arbitral award, judicial decision, or report of the Council, and further that they would carry out the award or decision and not resort to war against a member of the League that complied. The Council was to propose what to do in the event that a State failed to carry out the award or decision.

Underlying key provisions of the Covenant was therefore the assumption that States go to war as a way of resolving disputes. The Covenant sought to build in alternative, peaceful, methods of dispute resolution or, at minimum, a cooling-off period. We can see, therefore, how the international law against the use of force evolved hand in hand with the international law of dispute resolution. Article 14 of the Covenant provided for the establishment of a permanent international court, by which was meant a court established on an ongoing basis rather than on an ad hoc basis to deal with a specific set of issues or disputes. The Covenant assigned responsibility for drawing up plans for an international court to the League Council. In 1920 the Executive Council of the League of Nations commissioned an Advisory Committee of Jurists to prepare a draft statute for what came to be the Permanent Court of International Justice (PCIJ). The Advisory Committee met at The Hague from June 16 to July 24, 1920, by the end of which they had agreed to a draft Statute. The draft was accepted with modifications by the Council on August 5, 1920, and by the Assembly of the League of Nations on December 13, 1920.

Particularly contentious had been the question as to whether the Court would have compulsory jurisdiction. In other words, would it be compulsory for a country to take a dispute to the Court, or would the Court be able to decide a case involving a country only if that country has agreed to its doing so? The draft Statute prepared by the Advisory Committee of Jurists provided for compulsory jurisdiction whenever any party to a dispute took the matter to the court. This was believed to be in the interests of smaller powers, redressing to some extent the balance within the Council. The idea was popular with the Belgian, Portuguese, and several South American governments but opposed by Britain, France, and Japan.[4] As a consequence, the Court was *not* given compulsory jurisdiction, but a compromise was reached by which those States that wished to do so could *accept* the compulsory jurisdiction of the Court in those instances in which the other State involved did so too. The so-called "optional clause" was a bitter disappointment to those committed to establishing an international rule of law. The PCIJ was formally inaugurated in 1922 and was housed in the Peace Palace in The Hague. The Court dealt with sixty-six cases between 1922 and 1939.

The system established by the League not only substituted third-party dispute resolution for "resorting" to war. Another important dimension to the work of the League was disarmament. Disarmament has long been on the agenda of those seeking to develop a system of international law as an avenue to peace. In the eighteenth century Immanuel Kant and Jean-Jacques Rousseau wrote of a completely disarmed world, and their ideas have been influential in the peace movement over subsequent centuries. Disarmament had been one of the topics addressed at the First Hague Peace Conference in 1899, although nothing had been achieved. Article 8 of the Covenant of the League of Nations referred to "the reduction of national armaments to the lowest point consistent with national safety and the enforcement by common action of international obligations." This reflected what seemed to be an obvious lesson of World War I: that the steady increase in armaments of European nations had made hostilities inevitable; the smallest diplomatic crisis had been sufficient to spark an enormous explosion.[5]

In the relatively peaceful world of the 1920s, disarmament did not seem only idealistic but realistic. Naval disarmament conferences were held in 1921–22, 1927, 1930, and 1935–36, and a World Disarmament Conference was held in 1932–34. But by the mid-1930s, disarmament had become a far-from-realistic option for the Allied countries. Adolf Hitler had become Chancellor of Germany in 1933. Intent on rebuilding German military power, he withdrew Germany from the disarmament conference and then from the League of Nations. The stronger Germany became, the more difficult it would be for militarily run-down Allied countries to confront Hitler. It is little wonder that, alongside appeasement, disarmament became largely discredited.

A third, and perhaps the most important aspect of the League of Nations was its attempt to establish a system of "collective security." As we saw in Chapter 1, nineteenth-century European States and their overseas offshoots developed a complicated network of alliances, the underlying assumption of which was that peace could most likely be preserved where there was a balance of power. The theory of collective security was an attempt to substitute protection by other members of one's "team" with protection by the rest of the international community. The theory is that any individual State can be kept in check where all the other States in the international community agree to do so collectively—no aggression is likely to take place if it is certain that all States will act against an aggressor. This is what is meant in Article 16 when it stipulates: "Should any Member of the League resort to war in disregard of its covenants under Articles 12, 13 or 15, it shall *ipso facto*

DID YOU KNOW?

Key Personalities at Versailles

Three of the key figures at the peace negotiations after World War I were David Lloyd George, Prime Minister of Great Britain; Georges Clemenceau, Premier of France; and Woodrow Wilson, President of the United States. Wilson had already set out his "Fourteen Points," one of which was that an international organization should be set up, though interestingly, the list did not include the establishment of a world court. David Lloyd George sought a reasonable settlement, although he was under domestic pressure to "squeeze Germany until the pips squeak." Clemenceau, known as "The Tiger," sought harsh terms. The following reported comments of Clemenceau illustrate his attitude:

> "Mr Wilson," the Tiger said on one occasion, "if I accepted what you propose as ample for the security of France, after the millions who have died and the millions who have suffered, I believe—and indeed, I hope—that my successor in office would take me by the nape of the neck and have me shot before the donjon of Vincennes!"
>
> "You wish to do justice to the Germans," he said to Wilson on another occasion. "Do not believe that they will ever forgive us. They will seek only the chance of revenge. Nothing will suppress the fury of those who hoped to dominate the world and believed success so near."
>
> "Pray, Monsieur Clemenceau," Wilson asked the premier at one point, "have you ever been to Germany?"
>
> "No, sir!" said the Tiger. "But twice in my lifetime the Germans have been to France."[7]

Notably, Clemenceau was subsequently criticized at home for having agreed to a "soft" treaty.

DID YOU KNOW?

Comparison of the League of Nations and the United Nations

	League of Nations	United Nations
Headquarters	Geneva	New York
Term first used by	U.S. President Woodrow Wilson	U.S. President Franklin D. Roosevelt
Founding Document	Covenant of the League of Nations	Charter of the United Nations
Permanent Members of the Council	British Empire, France, Italy, Japan, and the USSR (1934–35)	France, China, USSR, UK, USA
Membership at its highest	59 (1935)	192 (2008)
Official Languages	English, French, Spanish (from 1920)	Arabic, Chinese, English, French, Russian, Spanish

be deemed to have committed an act of war against all other Members of the League." The term "League" refers to a "military, political, or commercial covenant or compact made between parties for their mutual protection and assistance against a common enemy."[6]

The Covenant provided for the Council to impose economic and political sanctions and for force to be used if required, but the language used in Article 16 was recommendatory only. Should any Member of the League "resort to war in disregard of its covenants under Articles 12, 13 or 15" the Council would by Article 16 have the "duty" to "recommend to the several Governments concerned what effective military, naval or air force the Members of the League shall severally contribute to the armed forces to be used to protect the covenants of the League." That the League was meant to constitute a decisive break from the reliance on alliances in the nineteenth century was reflected in its forbidding the existence of secret treaties. By Article 18, all treaties were to be registered with the secretariat and published. This had been one of Wilson's "Fourteen Points" and was designed to increase transparency in relations among States.

The League is generally regarded as having been successful on many social and economic issues, although it clearly failed to achieve and maintain international peace.

FURTHER READING

Allain, Jean. *A Century of International Adjudication. The Rule of Law and Its Limits*. The Hague: T.M.C. Asser Press, 2000.

Cooper, John Milton. *Breaking the Heart of the World: Woodrow Wilson and the Fight for the League of Nations*. Cambridge, UK: Cambridge University Press, 2001.

Fleming, Denna Frank. *The United States and the League of Nations, 1918–1920*. New York: G.P. Putnam's Sons, 1932.

Mee, Charles L., Jr. *The End of Order: Versailles 1919*. London: Secker & Warburg, 1981.

Miller, David Hunter. *The Drafting of the Covenant*, 2 vols. New York: G.P. Putnam's Sons, 1928.

Myers, Denys P. *Handbook of the League of Nations. A Comprehensive Account of Its Structure, Operation and Activities*. Boston: World Peace Foundation, 1935.

Spiermann, Ole. "'Who Attempts Too Much Does Nothing Well': The 1920 Advisory Committee of Jurists and the Statute of the Permanent Court of International Justice." *British Yearbook of International Law* 73 (2002): 187–260.

Zimmern, Alfred. *The League of Nations and the Rule of Law, 1918–1935*. Holmes Beach, FL: Gaunt, 1998.

The Kellogg-Briand Pact

- ***Document:*** Extract of the Treaty Between the United States and Other Powers Providing for the Renunciation of War as an Instrument of National Policy, also known as the Pact of Paris and the Kellogg-Briand Pact
- ***Date:*** August 27, 1928
- ***Where:*** Paris
- ***Significance:*** This treaty was negotiated between the French foreign minister, Aristide Briand, and the U.S. Secretary of State, Frank B. Kellogg. It was a landmark en route to the inclusion in international law of a general prohibition against the use of force.

DOCUMENT

Article I

The High Contracting Parties solemnly declare in the names of their respective peoples that they condemn recourse to war for the solution of international controversies, and renounce it, as an instrument of national policy in their relations with one another.

Article II

The High Contracting Parties agree that the settlement or solution of all disputes or conflicts of whatever nature or of whatever origin they may be, which may arise among them, shall never be sought except by pacific means.

SOURCE: United States Statutes at Large, Vol. 46, Part 2: 2343.
http://avalon.law.yale.edu/20th_century/kbpact.asp
Courtesy of the Avalon Project, Yale Law School Library.

ANALYSIS

This treaty is of great importance because it represented another important step toward a legal prohibition of the use of force. By Article I, Parties "condemn recourse to war for the solution of international controversies, and renounce it, as an instrument of national policy in their relations with one another." Note that, like the Covenant of the League of Nations, this assumes that States initiate wars because of disagreements with other States, so that the way to avoid war is to develop alternatives methods of dispute resolution. By Article II, States agreed to use only peaceful methods of dispute resolution. The treaty incorporates no means of monitoring the behavior of States in practice or of doing anything about breaches of this obligation.

There are two historical trajectories that merged in this treaty. The first was the peace movement. The heyday of the U.S. peace movement came between the World Wars. Disillusionment with World War I gave added impetus to the movement. A whole array of peace societies worked hard for the cause of peace in the 1920s, including the American Committee for the Cause and Cure of War, the National Council for Prevention of War, the Women's International League for Peace and Freedom, the American Committee for the Outlawry of War and Stop Organized Slaughter. The American peace movement had been born in the early years of the

Calvin Coolidge, Herbert Hoover, and Frank B. Kellogg, standing, with representatives of the governments that ratified the Treaty Between the United States and Other Powers Providing for the Renunciation of War as an Instrument of National Policy. Courtesy of Library of Congress, U.S. Federal Government.

James Shotwell, 1874–1965. Courtesy of CORBIS.

nineteenth century but was to reach the height of its influence in the years leading up to the attack on Pearl Harbor.[8] Even though government officials knew that some of the ideas of the movement were impracticable, they were nevertheless unable to simply dismiss the peace agitators because of the breadth of support they received. Women played a strong role in the movement, and since universal female suffrage had been introduced only in 1920, the impact of women's organizations on the American political balance was not yet known.[9]

The timing of such a seemingly idealistic treaty has similarities with the Hague Peace Conferences of the 1890s, which had been held at a time of increasing armaments and tensions. But there is a second context within which the conclusion of the Pact of Paris needs to be understood. This was that of the considerable number of security treaties that were signed in Europe after World War I. The creation of the League of Nations had not put an end to the negotiation of treaties of alliance. France was unsure of how much support it would get from either Britain or the United States in the event of another war with Germany. Although there was no doubt that France would need U.S. economic support in such a situation, American public opinion and investors were increasingly favoring Germany.[10] In a desperate quest for security, France entered into a secret military understanding with Belgium (1920), a political agreement with Poland (1921); a treaty of alliance and friendship with Czechoslovakia (1924); treaties of mutual guarantee with Czechoslovakia and Poland (1925); a treaty of friendship with Romania (1926); and a treaty of "Friendly Understanding" with Yugoslavia (1927).[11]

Here, then, is the context within which Professor Shotwell, a leader in the U.S. peace movement, obtained an interview with French Foreign Minister Briand in 1927. Shotwell suggested that Briand could best meet suspicion of French militarism and improve relations with the United States by proposing renunciation of war as an instrument of national policy and that a treaty be made along that line. They agreed that Briand should address a letter to the American people.[12] This took the form of a letter published in the *New York Times* and the *Herald Tribune* on April 6, 1927, on the tenth anniversary of the entry of the United States into the World War. The latter read in part:

> If there were any need between these two great democracies to testify more convincingly in favor of peace and to present to the peoples a more solemn example, France would be ready publicly to subscribe, with the United States, to any mutual engagement tending, as between those two countries, to 'outlaw war,' to use an American expression.[13]

On June 20, 1927 the Department of State received from Briand the text of a Pact of Perpetual Friendship between France and the United States. Article I condemned recourse to war and renounced war as an instrument of national policy as

DID YOU KNOW?

James Shotwell, 1874–1965

James Thomson Shotwell was a leading advocate of internationalism and collective security in the United States in the period between the two World Wars. Until 1917 Shotwell had been an academic historian, teaching medieval and modern European history at Columbia University. After World War I he turned his attention to the possibility of eliminating war. He believed that the world could be made a better place through rational thought, commitment, and dedication. This optimistic starting point strongly influenced the U.S. peace movement and U.S. foreign policy. Upon his death the *New York Times* credited Shotwell with contributing "mightily to the slow and sometimes painful shift in American public opinion from the isolationism of the nineteen-twenties to the internationalism of today." Although he emphasized the need to be practical, most would refer to him as idealistic. Shotwell appears to have been the first to use the phrase "as an instrument of national policy," which featured in the wording of the 1928 Pact. He apparently adapted the term from a book by Carl von Clausewitz.[18] According to Shotwell, "war which was once a directable instrument of policy has now changed its nature with the nature of modern society and ceases to be controllable and directable in the hands of statements." The industrialization of war meant that war had become a contagion among nations "and one cannot safely use a contagion as an instrument."[19]

between France and the United States, and Article II stated that disputes between the two were to be settled only by peaceful means.[14] This was very similar to French alliances with Rumania and Yugoslavia that had been negotiated in 1926. U.S. Secretary of State Kellogg saw Briand's proposal as a negative military alliance, a non-aggression pact that might, in the event of France being involved in a future war, hamper the United States from defending itself against French violations of American neutrality.[15] The United States responded on December 28, 1927, with a counterproposal: the two countries should promote a multilateral renunciation of war. This was not at all what Briand had wanted.

By the end of April there were two competing texts; the French version included reservations to protect the French alliance system.[16] In late July 1928 Briand finally accepted the U.S. draft. Accompanied by considerable publicity, the Treaty was signed in late August by Kellogg, Briand, and delegations from the major powers. The parties understood it as making exceptions for self-defense, collective action for the enforcement of international obligations, war between a signatory and a non-signatory, and war with a violator of the Pact, although these exceptions were not written into the final version of the text.[17] Whether for the fact that these span most of the obvious reasons for war, or because the treaty, even with its terms interpreted more broadly, is without enforcement provisions, the Kellogg-Briand Pact has sometimes been described as "anodyne."

FURTHER READING

Byrn-Jones, David. *Frank B. Kellogg: A Biography*. New York: Putnam, 1937.

Ferrell, Robert H. *Peace in Their Time: The Origins of the Kellogg-Briand Pact*. Hamden, CT: Archon Books, 1968.

Josephson, Harold. "Outlawing War: Internationalism and the Pact of Paris." *Diplomatic History* 3:4 (1979): 377–390.

Miller, David H. *The Peace Pact of Paris. A Study of the Briand-Kellogg Treaty*. New York: G. P. Putnam's Sons, 1928.

The Twenty Years' Crisis

- ***Document:*** Extracts from *The Twenty Years' Crisis* by E. H. Carr
- ***Date:*** 1940
- ***Where:*** United Kingdom
- ***Significance:*** The book from which these extracts derive is a classic in the discipline of International Relations. Carr's analysis of what had gone wrong since World War II influenced the political realism of the postwar years. But this was not a work of a pure realism, either, and *The Twenty Years Crisis* is valuable for its attempt to assess what difference international law and organizations could make in a world of great powers and national ambition.

DOCUMENT

Politically, the doctrine of the identity of interests has commonly taken the form of an assumption that every nation has an identical interest in peace, and that any nation which desires to disturb the peace is therefore both irrational and immoral. This view bears clear marks of its Anglo-Saxon origin. It has been easy since 1918 to convince that part of mankind which lives in English-speaking countries that war profits nobody. The argument did not seem particularly convincing to Germans, who had profited largely from the wars of 1866 and 1870, and who attributed their more recent sufferings, not to the War of 1914, but to the fact that they had lost it; or to Italians, who blamed not the War, but the treachery of Allies, who defrauded them in the peace settlement; or to Poles or Czecho-Slovaks who, far from deploring the War, owed their national existence to it; or to Frenchmen, who could not unreservedly regret a war which had restored Alsace-Lorraine to France; or to people of other nationalities who remembered profitable wars waged by Great Britain and the United

States in the past. But these people had fortunately little influence over the formation of post-War theories of international relations, which emanated almost exclusively from the English-speaking countries. British and American writers continued to assume that the uselessness of war had been irrefutably demonstrated by the experience of 1914–18, and that an intellectual grasp of this fact was all that was necessary to induce the nations to keep the peace in the future; and they have been sincerely puzzled as well as disappointed at the failure of other countries to share this view. . . . The utopian assumption that there is a world interest in peace which is identifiable with the interests of each individual nation has helped politicians and political writers everywhere to evade the unpalatable fact of a fundamental divergence of interest between nations desirous of maintaining the *status quo* and nations desirous of changing it. . . . The fact of divergent interests is disguised and falsified by the platitude of a general desire to avoid conflict.

E. H. Carr. Courtesy of the Australian National University.

Periods of crisis have been common in history. The characteristic feature of the present crisis, seen in the light of the twenty years between 1919 and 1939, has been the abrupt descent from the visionary hopes of the first post-War decade to the grim despair of the second, from a utopia which took little account of reality to a reality from which every element of utopia seems rigorously excluded. . . .

The first and most obvious tragedy of this utopia was its ignominous collapse, and the despair which this collapse brought with it. . . . It was no longer possible

Council of Four at the Versailles Peace Conference, 1919: Lloyd George, Vittorio Emanuele Orlando, Georges Clemenceau, President Woodrow Wilson. Photograph taken by Captain Jackson of the U.S. Army Signal Corps. Courtesy of National Archives of the United States.

to rationalise international relations by pretending that what was good for Great Britain was also good for Yugoslavia and what was good for Germany was also good for Poland, so that international conflicts were merely the transient products of avoidable misunderstanding or curable ill-will. For more than a hundred years, the reality of conflict had been spirited out of sight by the political thinkers of Western civilization. In the last decade, we have returned shocked and bewildered to the world of nature.

The Rabbit: "My offensive equipment being practically nil, it remains for me to fascinate him with the power of my eye." "Moral Suasion." Cartoon by Bernard Partridge. Published July 28, 1920. Courtesy of Punch Cartoons.

SOURCE: Edward Hallett Carr, *The Twenty Years' Crisis 1919–1939*. London: Macmillan, 1940. *By permission of Macmillan.*

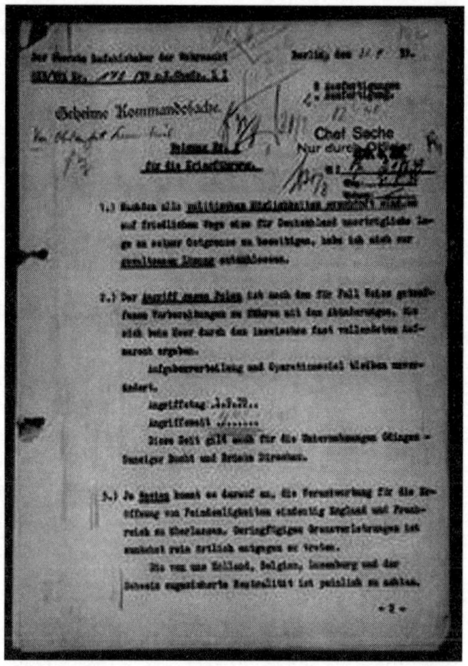

The first page of an official order of Adolf Hitler dated August 31, 1939, for an attack against Poland. Germany invaded the following day. Courtesy of the Government of Germany.

ANALYSIS

Edward Carr worked for the British Foreign Office and was a member of the British delegation to the Peace Conference at Versailles. Like several members of the British delegation, Carr believed that the Versailles Treaty was too harsh on Germany. His antagonism toward the Versailles Treaty meant that he did not recognize Hitler as a serious danger until 1938. By then he had been appointed the Woodrow Wilson Professor of International Politics at the University College of Wales, Aberystwyth. *The Twenty Years' Crisis* was in the process of being published when war broke out. In 1941 Carr became Assistant Editor of *The Times*, an influential British newspaper, in which position he played an influential role in shaping public opinion. He looked back on this book as strongly realist—that is, erring on the side that political outcomes are determined primarily by the distribution of power—although the text criticizes both extreme utopianism and extreme realism.[20]

The outbreak of World War II represented the ultimate failure of the League attempt to prevent war through collective security, but this was the culmination of a number of smaller failures. These included the inability of the League to influence Japan when it invaded Manchuria in 1931, Italy when it invaded Abysinnia (Ethiopia) in 1935, or Japan when it invaded China in 1937. The League did not attempt to address German reoccupation of the Rhineland in 1936, annexation of Austria and the Sudetenland in 1938, or of Czechoslovakia and Poland in 1939. It never used force in response to an act of aggression and had difficulty in summoning up the political will necessary for stringent economic sanctions.

As it became apparent in the late 1930s that world war would likely break out again, those who had believed in, and worked hard for, the ideals of the League of Nations were bitterly disappointed and disillusioned. In these passages, Carr referred to a utopianism that had been embodied in the League of Nations. The doctrine of the harmony of interests had been popularized in political economy, holding that the economic interests of the individual were identical with those of the community.[21] This doctrine had more recently been applied to the postwar situation, largely through the American influence, where it held that all countries want peace. The assumption was evident in the Covenant, which provided for methods

DID YOU KNOW?

The United States and the League of Nations

The United States was listed in the Annex of the Covenant as an "original" Member, but it never assumed membership. It was nevertheless an active participant in several of the activities of the League. Following an "understanding" of January 1934, the United States registered its treaties as per Article 18 of the Covenant. The United States accepted membership in the International Labor Organization on August 20, 1934. The United States participated in almost all of the standing committees of the League, and its representatives even sat on the Council as *ad hoc* members to express views and contribute to the making of appointments.[23]

DID YOU KNOW?

The End of the League of Nations

As the 1930s wore on and the League proved incapable of curbing aggression, its authority declined. The September 1939 meetings of the League Assembly and Council were postponed, and only a minimum of League activities continued. The League was a flurry of activity once more from December 9 to 14, 1939, when it expelled the USSR following the Soviet invasion of Finland. The Secretary-General of the League at the time was Joseph Avenol, a former French diplomat. He welcomed the possibility of a Europe unified under Germany and the demise of the League. When Avenol was eventually forced out, Simon Lester, an Irishman who had been Deputy Secretary-General of the League since 1937, took over as acting Secretary-General in 1940. Lester managed to keep the less political aspects of the work of the League going during the war such that he could, at the end of the War, hand over a working structure to the founders of the United Nations.

of peaceful dispute resolution and a system of collective security, but that in practice was unable to stop acts of aggression. What the League replacement for the right to go to war did not seem to allow for was the possibility that the leaders of a State might want to initiate war to achieve national goals.

Several reasons are commonly given for the failure of the League of Nations. One of the most commonly cited reasons is that it was not sufficiently strong. The United States never joined the League, the USSR joined in 1934 but was expelled in 1939, Germany became a member in 1926 but withdrew in 1935, and Japan also withdrew in 1935. Although the nonparticipation of the United States certainly weakened the authority of the League, not all analysts are confident that the League would necessarily have been more successful had the United States been a member. The United States may have been no more willing than others to impose effective sanctions, and even if the United States had been willing, this on its own would not have meant that other States would have been.[22]

Notes

1. David Hunter Miller, *The Drafting of the Covenant*, Vol. 1 (New York: G. P. Putnam's Sons, 1928), 3.
2. Miller, *The Drafting of the Covenant*, Vol. 1, 2.
3. Denys P. Myers, *Handbook of the League of Nations. A Comprehensive Account of Its Structure, Operation, and Activities* (Boston: World Peace Foundation, 1935), 3.
4. Lorna Lloyd, *Peace Through Law. Britain and the International Court in the 1920s* (Woodbridge, UK: Boydell, 1997), 12.
5. Robert H. Ferrell, "The Peace Movement," in Alexander DeConde, ed., *Isolation and Security* (Durham, NC: Duke University Press, 1957), 89.
6. *Oxford English Dictionary Online*, 2nd ed. 1989.
7. Charles L. Mee, Jr., *The End of Order: Versailles 1919* (London: Secker & Warburg, 1981), 158.
8. John E. Wiltz, *From Isolation to War, 1931–1941* (London: Routledge and Kegan Paul, 1968), 12.
9. Robert H. Ferrell, "The Peace Movement," 104.
10. Edward David Keeton, *Briand's Locarno Policy. French Economics, Politics, and Diplomacy, 1925–1929* (New York: Garland, 1987), 230.
11. Elizabeth Chadwick, *Traditional Neutrality Revisited: Law, Theory and Case Studies* (The Hague: Kluwer, 2002), 134.

12. Robert H. Ferrell, *Peace in Their Time. The Origins of the Kellogg-Briand Pact* (New Haven, CT: Yale University Press, 1952), 68–9.
13. Cited in Ferrell, *Peace in Their Time*, 71.
14. Ferrell, *Peace in Their Time*, 96.
15. Ferrell, *Peace in Their Time*, 73.
16. Edward David Keeton, *Briand's Locarno Policy. French Economics, Politics, and Diplomacy, 1925–1929* (New York: Garland, 1987), 240.
17. Stanimir A. Alexandrov, *Self-Defense Against the Use of Force in International Law* (The Hague: Kluwer, 1996), 58.
18. This sidebar draws on information in Harold Josephson, *James T. Shotwell and the Rise of Internationalism in America* (London: Associated University Presses, 1975), especially 9–10, 160, and 301.
19. James T. Shotwell, *War as an Instrument of National Policy and Its Renunciation in the Pact of Paris* (New York: Harcourt, Brace and Company, 1929), 36.
20. R. W. Davies, "Edward Hallett Carr 1892–1982," *Proceedings of the British Academy* 69 (1983): 473–511.
21. Davies, "Edward Hallett Carr 1892–1982": 473–511.
22. Russell S. Sobel, "The League of Nations Covenant and the United Nations Charter: An Analysis of Two International Constitutions," *Constitutional Political Economy* 5:2 (1994): 173–192.
23. Myers, *Handbook of the League of Nations*, 22.

FURTHER READING

Barros, James. *Betrayal from Within. Joseph Avenol, Secretary-General of the League of Nations, 1933–1940*. New Haven, CT: Yale University Press, 1969.

Gageby, Douglas. *The Last Secretary-General: Sean Lester and the League of Nations*. Dublin, Ireland: Town House, 1999.

Moorehouse, Frank. *Grand Days*. Chippendale, NSW: Pan Macmillan, 1993; and *Dark Palace: The Companion Novel to Grand Days*. Milsons Point: Random House Australia, 2000.

Pedersen, Susan. "Review Essay: Back to the League of Nations." *The American Historical Review* 112 (2007). http://www.historycooperative.org/journals/ahr/112.4/pedersen.html.

3

THE UN CHARTER REGIME ON THE USE OF FORCE

United Nations Building, New York. Courtesy of Steve Cadman.

OVERVIEW

This chapter outlines the Charter regime on the use of force and its provisions on the peaceful resolution of international disputes. In doing so it draws comparisons with the League of Nations that the UN replaced. The Chapter concludes by considering the fact that, although the Charter of the United Nations and the atomic bomb both date from 1945, the conclusion of the negotiations for the Charter preceded the atomic era.

A New Epoch in International Law: The Founding of the United Nations

- ***Document:*** Extracts from the Charter of the United Nations of most importance to the international legal regime pertaining to the use of force
- ***Date:*** June 26, 1945 (entered into force October 24, 1945)
- ***Where:*** San Francisco
- ***Significance:*** The UN Charter provides the framework for the contemporary international law regarding whether and when a State may use force against another State.

DOCUMENT

Chapter I: Purposes and Principles

Article 1

The Purposes of the United Nations are:

To maintain international peace and security, and to that end: to take effective collective measures for the prevention and removal of threats to the peace, and for the suppression of acts of aggression or other breaches of the peace, and to bring about by peaceful means, and in conformity with the principles of justice and international law, adjustment or settlement of international disputes or situations which might lead to a breach of the peace;

To develop friendly relations among nations based on respect for the principle of equal rights and self-determination of peoples, and to take other appropriate measures to strengthen universal peace;

To achieve international co-operation in solving international problems of an economic, social, cultural, or humanitarian character, and in promoting and encouraging respect for human rights and for fundamental freedoms for all without distinction as to race, sex, language, or religion; and

To be a centre for harmonizing the actions of nations in the attainment of these common ends.

Article 2(4)

All Members shall refrain in their international relations from the threat or use of force against the territorial integrity or political independence of any State, or in any other manner inconsistent with the Purposes of the United Nations.

Article 2(5)

All Members shall give the United Nations every assistance in any action it takes in accordance with the present Charter, and shall refrain from giving assistance to any State against which the United Nations is taking preventive or enforcement action.

Article 2(7)

Nothing contained in the present Charter shall authorize the United Nations to intervene in matters which are essentially within the domestic jurisdiction of any State or shall require the Members to submit such matters to settlement under the present Charter; but this principle shall not prejudice the application of enforcement measures under Chapter VII.

Chapter V: The Security Council

Article 25

The Members of the United Nations agree to accept and carry out the decisions of the Security Council in accordance with the present Charter.

Chapter VII: Action with Respect to Threats to the Peace, Breaches of the Peace, and Acts of Aggression

Article 39

The Security Council shall determine the existence of any threat to the peace, breach of the peace, or act of aggression and shall make recommendations, or decide what measures shall be taken in accordance with Articles 41 and 42, to maintain or restore international peace and security.

Article 41

The Security Council may decide what measures not involving the use of armed force are to be employed to give effect to its decisions, and it may call upon the

Members of the United Nations to apply such measures. These may include complete or partial interruption of economic relations and of rail, sea, air, postal, telegraphic, radio, and other means of communication, and the severance of diplomatic relations.

Article 42

Should the Security Council consider that measures provided for in Article 41 would be inadequate or have proved to be inadequate, it may take such action by air, sea, or land forces as may be necessary to maintain or restore international peace and security. Such action may include demonstrations, blockade, and other operations by air, sea, or land forces of Members of the United Nations.

Article 51

Nothing in the present Charter shall impair the inherent right of individual or collective self-defense if an armed attack occurs against a Member of the United Nations, until the Security Council has taken measures necessary to maintain international peace and security. Measures taken by Members in the exercise of this right of self-defense shall be immediately reported to the Security Council and shall not in any way affect the authority and responsibility of the Security Council under the present Charter to take at any time such action as it deems necessary in order to maintain or restore international peace and security.

Chapter XVI: Miscellaneous Provisions

Article 103

In the event of a conflict between the obligations of the Members of the United Nations under the present Charter and their obligations under any other international agreement, their obligations under the present Charter shall prevail.

SOURCE: Charter of the United Nations, http://www.un.org/aboutun/charter/.

ANALYSIS

This document is an extract from the Charter of the United Nations. The Charter was finalized at the United Nations Conference on International Organization, a meeting of fifty governments, held in San Francisco from April 25 to June 26, 1945. Much of the early preparation for the new collective security organization had been carried out in the U.S. Department of State during the War. Some consideration had been given to the possibility of creating a covenant of peace that would build on the Kellogg-Briand Pact, but the general consensus in the United States was that what was needed was peace guaranteed by force. It was decided to start again with a whole new collective security organization. U.S. officials held "conversations" with officials from the United Kingdom (UK), the Union of Soviet Socialist Republics (USSR), and China at the Dumbarton Oaks Estate in Washington, DC, from August 21 to October 7, 1944. Following further discussions by Stalin, Churchill, and Roosevelt, plans were finalized for the San Francisco conference.

The U.S. and UK influence on the new collective security organization was evident even in the title of the Organization. The United Nations had been the name of the wartime alliance against the Axis powers. In 1941, before the United States entered the War, the United States and the United Kingdom had signed the Atlantic Charter, a statement of broad objectives that included renouncing territorial aggrandizement, supporting self-determination, and working for the establishment of a permanent system of security. The United States saw the Atlantic Charter as providing a framework within which plans for a peaceful future world could be developed. The following year twenty-six other States signed the "Declaration by the United Nations," expressing agreement with those principles.

The Charter of the United Nations is made up of nineteen chapters. There was not a chapter dedicated to the question of when a State can use force; the relevant

The Egyptian delegation and the UN Charter at the signing ceremony, San Francisco, June 26, 1945. Courtesy of UN Photo.

provisions are found in several sections of the Charter. Article 2(4) is found within a chapter on the general obligations of UN members. This reinforces the fact that the provisions regarding use of force were part of a total package that incorporated measures for informal dispute resolution, resolution by the International Court of Justice (ICJ), and collective security. Although the extract above contains some of the most important provisions, it would be difficult to overemphasize the value of reading the whole Charter. The text can readily be found on the Internet or in a book of international law documents.

Viewed in one way, Article 2(4) represents no dramatic change from the Covenant of the League, for States had not been supposed to use force for political objectives during the years of the League either. The provisions of the Kellogg-Briand Pact had arguably already become customary international law.[1] It was less a case of radical change to the provisions on use of force than of the language being refined. The reference to "war" in the Covenant and Kellogg-Briand Pact had left a loophole: if war is what happens following a declaration of war, what if a State undertakes an act of aggression without having declared war?

The answer was Article 2(4). International lawyers engage in numerous debates regarding the interpretation of this provision, which will be examined in Chapter 4. For now, it is sufficient to note that Article 2(4) is widely accepted as constituting a general prohibition on the use of armed force in relations among Sates. In order to close the loophole of the Covenant and Kellogg-Briand Pact, the Charter adopts the language of "use of force" rather than "war." Article 2(4) bans not only the use of force but also the threat of using force. Article 2(4) is thus the cornerstone of attempts to prevent another world war via international law. It remains the starting point in any contemporary legal discussion regarding use of force.

The Charter does, however, recognize self-defense as a legitimate exception to the prohibition on the use of force. The right to defend oneself if attacked could be regarded as so fundamental a right as to be logically prior to the development of law. This is why Article 51 does not in itself "give" a State the right to use self-defense but refers to an "inherent right." A close reading of Article 51 reveals that it refers to both individual and collective self-defense. Collective self-defense

DID YOU KNOW?

In History: Text of the Declaration of United Nations, 1942

The title of the United Nations came from the wartime alliance of the same name. Here is its text:

A Joint Declaration by the United States, the United Kingdom, the Union of Soviet Socialist Republics, China, Australia, Belgium, Canada, Costa Rica, Cuba, Czechoslovakia, Dominican Republic, El Salvador, Greece, Guatemala, Haiti, Honduras, India, Luxembourg, Netherlands, New Zealand, Nicaragua, Norway, Panama, Poland, South Africa, Yugoslavia.

The Governments signatory hereto,

Having subscribed to a common program of purposes and principles embodied in the Joint Declaration of the President of the United States of America and the Prime Minister of the United Kingdom of Great Britain and Northern Ireland dated August 14, 1941, known as the Atlantic Charter.

Being convinced that complete victory over their enemies is essential to defend life, liberty, independence and religious freedom, and to preserve human rights and justice in their own lands as well as in other lands, and that they are now engaged in a common struggle against savage and brutal forces seeking to subjugate the world,

DECLARE:

(1) Each Government pledges itself to employ its full resources, military or economic, against those members of the Tripartite Pact: and its adherents with which such government is at war.

(2) Each Government pledges itself to cooperate with the Governments signatory hereto and not to make a separate armistice or peace with the enemies.

The foregoing declaration may be adhered to by other nations which are, or which may be, rendering material assistance and contributions in the struggle for victory over Hitlerism.

Done at Washington
January First, 1942

The cornerstone of the United Nations Permanent Headquarters was laid at a special open-air General Assembly meeting held on the site of the Headquarters building in Manhattan, New York, on the fourth anniversary of the United Nations, October 24, 1949. Courtesy of UN Photo.

involves a situation in which a State comes to the assistance of a State that has been attacked. Acts of self-defense are to be reported to the Security Council, and Article 51 assumes that the Security Council will then take the lead in addressing the situation. Although it would be difficult to deny the right to self-defense, there are many questions marks regarding the exact scope of this legal right. These will be explored in Chapter 5.

The UN Charter is not so idealistic as to anticipate a world in which force is never used. Rather, it gives the Security Council a virtual monopoly on the legitimate use of force. The UN Charter system is a system of collective security, by which a central body essentially takes primary responsibility for maintaining international peace and security. Articles 39, 41, and 42 should be read together to give a sense of how, in legal terms, the system of collective security led by the Security Council is to function. If and when members of the Security Council "determine the existence of any threat to the peace, breach of the peace,

DID YOU KNOW?

Franklin D. Roosevelt was a strong supporter of the new organization to be established after the war, but on April 12, 1945, Roosevelt died and was replaced by Vice-President Harry S. Truman. This was less than two weeks before the scheduled San Francisco conference. The first decision Truman made as President of the United States was that the conference should go ahead as scheduled. Like Roosevelt, Truman believed the new organization to be essential for maintaining peace in the postwar world.[5]

or act of aggression," they can decide either to address it through the use of peaceful measures such as sanctions, or, if the Council deems that peaceful measures "would be inadequate or have proved to be inadequate," it can go so far as to authorize the military action necessary to maintain or restore international peace and security. The details of how this was designed to work and has worked in practice will be examined in Chapter 7. Note that the system was not intended to replace regional collective security organizations but to work in conjunction with them.

With the Security Council wielding such enormous power, the question of Security Council voting became a highly contentious political issue. The Americans, the British, and the Soviets all believed that there could be no peace in the postwar world if the United States and the Soviet Union did not agree.[2] The Soviet Union advocated a simple majority, while the United Kingdom and China proposed a two-thirds majority. At a meeting of President Roosevelt, Prime Minister Churchill and Premier Stalin at Yalta in February 1945, the United States presented a compromise proposal. Known as the Yalta voting formula, this provided for a majority of seven, including all of the permanent members, for important decisions.

Opposing opinions on voting in the Security Council were held so strongly at San Francisco that in mid-May the conference seemed doomed.[3] On June 7 the Great Powers presented a "Statement by the Delegations of the Four Sponsoring Governments on Voting Procedure in the Security Council." The statement set out the rationale for the veto: that the permanent members could not be expected to assume the obligation to take action to maintain peace and security upon a decision in which they had not concurred. When the question of the veto came to a head in plenary,

> Senator Connally, an old-fashioned, flamboyant speaker, told the other delegates, "You may go home from San Francisco, if you wish, and report that you have defeated the veto. . . . But you can also say, 'We tore up the charter'." Whereupon the senator picked up his copy of a draft of the charter, tore it into shreds, and flung the scraps upon the negotiating table. The histrionic threat that the choice lay between a strong veto and no U.N. at all carried the day. By a vote of twenty to ten (with fifteen abstaining and five absent), the conference decided to keep the Yalta veto formula.[4]

DID YOU KNOW?

In History: Timeline of Some Significant Events Relating to the End of World War II and the Establishment of the United Nations

Jan. 1, 1942	Declaration of United Nations
Aug. 21–Oct. 7, 1944	Informal talks at the Dumbarton Oaks Estate
Apr. 12, 1945	Death of Franklin D. Roosevelt Harry S. Truman becomes President
Apr. 25, 1945	San Francisco conference begins
May 7, 1945	Germany signs an Instrument of Surrender
June 26, 1945	Conclusion of negotiations at San Francisco
Aug. 6, 1945	The United States drops an atomic bomb on Hiroshima
Aug. 9, 1945	The United States drops an atomic bomb on Nagasaki
Sep. 2, 1945	Japan signs an instrument of surrender to the Allied Powers
Oct. 24, 1945	UN Charter enters into force
Jan. 10, 1946	First meeting of the UN General Assembly, in London
Jan. 18, 1946	First meeting of the UN Security Council, in London
Apr. 18, 1946	Assembly of the League of Nations passes a resolution to dissolve the League of Nations and transfer its assets and responsibilities to the United Nations

"After You" by David Low. Published in the *Evening Standard* on April 26, 1945. Courtesy of the British Cartoon Archive, University of Kent, www.cartoons.ac.uk.

FURTHER READING

"Charter of the United Nations," at http://www.un.org/aboutun/charter/or in Scott, Shirley V., ed. *International Law and Politics. Key Documents*. Boulder, CO: Lynne Rienner, 2006.

Gray, Christine. *International Law and the Use of Force*. 2nd ed. Oxford: Oxford University Press, 2004, particularly Chapter 2 on "The Prohibition on the Use of Force."

Greenwood, Christopher. "The Concept of War in Modern International Law." *International and Comparative Law Quarterly* 36 (1987): 283–306.

Schlesinger, Stephen C. *Act of Creation. The Founding of the United Nations. A Story of Superpowers, Secret Agents, Wartime Allies and Enemies, and Their Quest for a Peaceful World*. Colorado: Westview Press, 2003.

Simma, Bruno, ed. *The Charter of the United Nations. A Commentary*. 2nd ed. New York: Oxford University Press, 2002.

Ziring, Lawrence, Robert E. Riggs, and Jack C. Plano. *The United Nations. International Organization and World Politics*. 4th ed. Belmont, CA: Thomson Wadsworth, 2005, particularly Chapter 5 on "Security Through Collective Action".

Would the U.S. Senate Reject the UN as It Had the League?

- ***Document:*** Excerpt from a speech by Mr. Connally, Chairman of the Committee on Foreign Relations, to the U.S. Senate
- ***Date:*** July 23, 1945
- ***Where:*** Washington, DC
- ***Significance:*** It was crucial for the new world organization that it receive the support of the U.S. Senate. In this speech Senator Connally (Democrat), explained why he believed that the Senate should support the Charter. Mr Connally drew comparisons between the United Nations and the League of Nations, as did many commentators of the day.

DOCUMENT

Mr President, in conclusion, permit me to say that ever since World War I there has been among the people of the United States and, I think, among the people of the world a feeling, growing over the years, that the statesmen of the world were challenged and that civilization was being challenged by our failure to erect some kind of international machinery for the cooperation of the peoples of the earth who do not want war, to bring about situations which would at least minimize the danger of war and advance the cause of peace.

We all know that the United States did not want to become involved in the First World War or in the present World War. We did not want to send our sons to foreign territory, there to be sacrificed upon the bloody altars of war. We did not want to pour out our treasure in destructive activities. However, we did just that. We were drawn into the First World War. During the Second World War we were ruthlessly and treacherously attacked at Pearl Harbor, and the allies of Japan namely Hitler, Mussolini, and others, declared war upon the United States before we drew the sword.

So, Mr President, in this modern time when the tides of war are running high, it is almost impossible for the United States to keep itself out of involvement. We know the price which we are now paying. That price consists of more than a million casualties, some of them bearing on their bodies the mark of their courage all the way to the tomb. We have suffered more than a million casualties of the finest young manhood of this Republic. Billions upon billions of dollars of treasure have been poured in order to advance the cause of the war. There will be repercussions of a postwar character which will perhaps dislocate our economic life, and disrupt a return to civilian life of the soldiers and sailors who have fought so gallantly. That is a stupendous price to pay for war. We want no more of it. Therefore, the growing sentiment against war has resulted in the United States in the proposal of measures of various kinds. I refer to the resolution of the Foreign Relations Committee, the Fulbright resolution adopted by the House, the Dumbarton Oaks Conference, and recently, the charter which was agreed to at San Francisco, and which is now before the Senate.

Mr President, the longings to which I have referred for an organization for world peace have brought about the Charter which was agreed to at San Francisco. We advance it not as a magical instrument which will guarantee that there shall be no more wars. We realize that any instrumentality will have its imperfections and weaknesses. This charter is not an absolute guaranty that there shall never be another war. However, Mr President, it is an advance over the ground where we now stand. It is an approach. It brings into contact the nations of the world. It brings them into contact in the General Assembly where they may freely discuss international questions, and do so with no restrictions being placed upon them. More than that, in the Security Council the great nations of the earth are brought into contact with each other, such as nations who today possess military and material resources, armies and navies, and air forces which are capable of making war, and are therefore capable of keeping the peace. The Security Council brings together great nations who, by appending their signatures to the Charter, made solemn pledges with each other to settle their disputes by peaceful means, to support the Charter, and to undertake to bring their influences and resources to the execution of the policies and doctrines of the charter. Mr President, if the charter does no more than to assemble in solemn conferences the representatives of the 50 nations who will make up the assembly, and the representatives of those same nations in the Security Council, to discuss and express their views respecting international questions which are fraught with the danger of war, it represents a great advance of the forces of peace out yonder into the territory of darkness and danger in which we have groped in the past.

But it does more than that, Mr President. It establishes agencies for the settlement of disputes. It establishes a World Court to which may be referred justiciable questions. It sets up an assembly where matters may be freely discussed by the humblest, smallest, and weakest nation, as well as by the mightiest nation. It will be one place where the equality of all nations will be recognized.

The Charter also establishes a Security Council. It places upon the Security Council and the great nations which possess powerful military, naval, and material resources, the primary obligation of preserving the peace. It is so written in the bond. It is denominated in the charter that the primary responsibility for preserving the peace of the world rests upon the Security Council. When a dispute is submitted to the Security Council it may be discussed, considered freely, and debated. If the Security Council takes jurisdiction of the matter, there are set forth in the Charter a number of steps which may be taken to bring about a settlement of the dispute. First, in order to preserve peace, and in order to bring about peaceful settlements, the Security Council suggests to the disputants, "Submit your case, Settle it between yourselves if you can do so. If you cannot settle it by diplomatic action, try arbitration or negotiation, and endeavor to adjust your dispute by peaceful means. If you cannot adjust your differences by peaceful means, the Security Council will have to adopt its own program." That program, Mr President may be a suggestion to the parties as to how the dispute should be settled. It would be merely a suggestion, however. There would be no exercise of compulsion. There is no jurisdiction or authority in the Security Council to compel the disputants to accept the formula which may be submitted. If all these measures fail, and as a result thereof violence is threatened, the Security Council may, as a last resort, and as a final effort to preserve peace, employ armed forces to prevent aggression and preserve the peace.

Mr President, I regard this document as a great instrument in the history of the world, a great instrument in the field of international relations. To my mind it is the greatest document of its kind that has ever been formulated. It is far superior to the League of Nations. The League of Nations did much good. The League of Nations, even through its failures and its weaknesses helped light the way to future international negotiations and to the construction of this Charter itself. The League of Nations carried the matter of agreement further than the pending Charter. Under the League there had to be unanimity of agreement as to every member of the Council, and when they agreed, while the League could persuade and could beg, it had no compulsive powers whatever; it could not enforce a peace; it could not prevent armed aggression; it had no authority and no power in those respects.

So, Mr President, we do not advance this instrument as embodying perfection. I dare say that ingenious Senators can take any statute that we pass here and find many things in it they do not like and which, if they were writing it, they would change. So I venture to say that if now the rewriting of this entire Charter were committed to individual Senators, when they got through, instead of having 1 charter, we would have 95 charters, and, if there were not a vacancy in the Senate, we would have 96 charters. Somewhere along the line every Senator would deviate from his colleagues, perhaps not on fundamental principles, but when it came to details there would be disagreement. So we have got to accept this Charter on the over-all picture, on its entirety.

Think about the 50 nations that met at San Francisco, many of which had divergent views. Many of them did not like certain things in the Charter, but they tried to look ahead, they tried to look down the vista of the years, they tried to envision what the future would hold, and finally they came to say, "Regardless of our objections to the voting procedure and to the Security Council, regardless of our views about the Assembly, we think the Charter is the best hope for peace and world security, and we will vote to ratify it."

Mr President, you would have been stirred, I am sure, had you been on the steering committee representing all 50 of the nations, when the roll was called and every nation responded "yea." It was a historic event, it was a stirring event, when the vote was recorded and it was announced that 50 nations had recorded their views that the Charter ought to be ratified.

Mr President, do not misunderstand me. Those who expect an automatic piece of machinery which it is necessary only to set up and then they can go ahead about their business and it will preserve the peace and stop war, will not have their expectations met by this Charter. This Charter is going to require the constant support and assistance of those who love peace, the nations who love peace and the peoples who love peace, if it is to be successful and if it is to achieve the high objectives for which it is designed.

Those who want to join a league that is magic, that requires no care, that requires no fuel, that requires no sacrifice on our part, that requires the sending of no troops by us if it comes to that point, are doomed to disappointment. There is no such league; there never has been such a league, and there never will be such a league. There has got to be constant cooperation of the nations of the earth in support of the spirit as well as the letter of the Charter and the high purposes which it envisions.

Mr President, these are the general principles upon which we base our appeal for the ratification of this charter. Let me say in closing that ratification of the Charter by the Senate may well give a tremendous impulse to its ratification by the other nations of the earth. It will mean that we shall be the first of the great powers to ratify the treaty. Strange as it may seem, in view of the practical unanimity of the people of the United States in support of the Charter, many representatives of foreign nations are still doubtful as to what the vote on the charter will be here in the Senate. They remember 1919. They know how the League of Nations was slaughtered here on the floor. Can you not still see the blood on the floor? Can you not see upon the walls the marks of the conflict that raged here in the Chamber where the League of Nations was done to death? They fear that that same sentiment may keep the United States from ratifying this Charter. Our ratification of it will instill hope into the hearts of the peoples of the earth. We heard it constantly at San Francisco. Not publicly in debate but privately delegates would approach us and inquire what we thought about the prospects of the ratification of the charter. So I trust that the Senate, after such debate as it sees fit to indulge upon the subject, will ratify this Charter by a vote so overwhelming as to carry the conviction over the earth that the United States expects to assume its obligations for the purpose of keeping them, for the purpose of living up to them, for the purpose of supporting a world organization for peace with all our spirit and with all our hearts.

SOURCE: U.S. Congressional Record, *July 23, 1945, 7953–7954. Courtesy of Hein Online.*

ANALYSIS

A potential stumbling block to the creation after World War II of an effective global collective security organization was the possibility of the Charter not being acceptable to the U.S. Senate. The United States had never become a member of the League of Nations, despite its own important role in establishing the organization, and it is generally thought that the absence of the United States was detrimental to the League. This time it was going to be different. U.S. involvement in creating the United Nations had proceeded along bipartisan lines. Recognizing that the Charter gave the United States a veto both on war and on any steps leading to war, Republicans in the Senate supported the Charter. This excerpt comes from the Senate debate that preceded the vote on ratification. On July 28, the Senate passed the Charter by a vote of 89 to 2, with no reservations.

Participants in the Senate debate and in contemporary scholarly debate drew comparisons between the League of Nations and the United Nations. There were strong institutional continuities between the two. Changes to the structure and working of the Council—now to be called the Security Council—would, so it was claimed, make the Council more able and ready to act. The modifications reflected a widely held belief that the League had failed because it had not been sufficiently strong to deal with aggression by Japan, Italy, or Germany, meaning that the new body would need to be stronger. One change was the basis on which the Security Council could act. Article XVI of the Covenant had defined precisely the event upon which the Council could take action: resort to war by a member State in disregard of its covenants. The UN Charter left the exact nature of the event undefined; it was to be in response to a "threat to the peace, breach of the peace, or act of aggression." Secondly, the Covenant of the League had provided that substantive decisions of the Council could be taken only by the unanimous vote of all its Members, whether permanent or not, with the exception of parties to a dispute under Article XV. In practice, most disputes brought before the League had been dealt with, and decisions to undertake investigations made, under Article XI, by which not even parties to a dispute were excluded from voting.[6] A decision of the UN Security Council, on the other hand, was not going to depend on unanimity; the Security Council was to be subject only to the veto of the Great Powers.

In the lead up to establishing the United Nations, the Great Powers presented the abandonment of the unanimity provision as likely to remove an impediment to action, by making the Council less liable to obstruction. Not all commentators agreed with this analysis. Leland M. Goodrich took the view that the fact that the Great Powers retained the veto meant that the United Nations was not necessarily going to be any more effective than the League had been.

> It can, however, be queried whether the Charter system will be more effective than the League system, in view of the requirement of unanimity of the permanent members of the Security Council. If we imagine its application in situations such as the Italian-Ethiopian and Sino-Japanese affairs, it is difficult to see how the United Nations would achieve any better results than did the League. Like the League, but for somewhat different technical reasons, the United Nations, in so far as its enforcement activities are concerned, is an organization for the enforcement of peace among the smaller states. If the permanent members of the Security Council are in agreement, it will be possible to take effective action under the Charter. It is not likely that such agreement will be reached to take measures against one of these great powers or against a protégé of such a great power. Consequently the sphere of effective enforcement action

> by the United Nations is restricted in advance, even more perhaps than was that of the League. Within the area of possible operation, the actual effectiveness of the United Nations system will depend upon political conditions which, if they had existed, would have also assured the success of the League of Nations.[7]

Others went further. James L. Brierly, Chichele Professor of Public International Law at the University of Oxford, told an audience in 1947 that "what we have done is to exchange a scheme which might or might not have worked for one which cannot work, and that instead of limiting the sovereignty of States we have actually extended the sovereignty of the Great Powers, the only States whose sovereignty is still a formidable reality in the modern world."[8] Brierly disagreed that the League had failed because of its own weakness, arguing that the aggressions of the interwar period proved nothing about the merits or defects of the Charter.

Sean Lester, the third and last Secretary-General of the League of Nations, reached a similar verdict. In October 1945 he wrote:

> The peoples of the world, searching for means to avoid the inhumanity and folly of war, constantly becoming more terrible and destructive, made a

"History Doesn't Repeat Itself" by David Low. Published in the *Evening Standard,* June 30, 1950. Courtesy of the British Cartoon Archive, University of Kent, www.cartoons.ac.uk.

United Nations Security Council meets in London, March 29, 1946. Courtesy of Hulton-Deutsch Collection/CORBIS.

> covenant and a league of peace. They did not keep the covenant; they broke the league; and a new war smashed across Europe and leaped the oceans. Aggression and ambition, on one side, timidity of Governments and short-sighted vision of the peoples themselves, on the other, led straight to the catastrophe.
>
> The League of Nations as an organization no doubt had faults, but it is dangerous nonsense to say that war came because of those faults. The League did not fail; it was the nations which failed to use it.[9]

According to Brierly, the problem had been the level of political support accorded the League by the Great Powers of the day.[10]

> The principle of the Covenant is very simple. It was intended that it should create a system of co-operation between States, which were to retain their sovereignty but to agree to do and not to do certain things in the exercise of their sovereign rights. The Covenant did not contain even the beginnings of a system of international government in the proper sense of the word 'government'. I remember in the early days of the League meeting a member of Parliament who had just returned from a first visit to Geneva. He said he had discovered that the League was not 'it' but 'they', and he was perfectly right. As a corporate body there was hardly anything that the League could do; in fact, there is, I think, only one Article in the Covenant which envisages action by the League

Knotted gun sculpture at UN Headquarters Building, New York. Courtesy of Marlith.

as such at all, and I suspect that this provision was a mere slip of drafting. Article XI does say that in the event of war or any threat of war 'the League shall take any action that may be deemed wise and effectual to safeguard the peace of nations', but elsewhere throughout the Covenant it is normally 'the members of the League' who undertake to act in some particular way in a certain event, and so far as I know the departure from the usual terminology in Article XI had no special significance in the practice of the League.[11]

Brierly therefore regarded the crucial innovation of the Charter as member States conferring a power of directing how they should act on an organ of the collective body rather than a Covenant system of States binding themselves individually to act in certain specified ways.[12] From his perspective, the fact that it could take action only against small Powers meant that it did not deserve being called a system of collective security. Gilbert Murray, another writer of the day, commented: "The rest of the world might well ask what good could be expected from an elaborate and

DID YOU KNOW?

The Choice of New York for UN Headquarters

The Covenant of the League of Nations had specified where the permanent headquarters of the organization was to be located. In the case of the United Nations, this was left to the Preparatory Commission. After receiving and considering many submissions, the Preparatory Commission recommended that the headquarters be in the United States. On February 14, 1946, the General Assembly voted that the temporary headquarters be in New York. On December 14 of that year the final decision was taken as to the location of the permanent headquarters. John D. Rockefeller, Jr., offered the sum of $8.5 million to acquire land in Manhattan. Construction was completed in 1950. Visitors to New York can join a guided tour of the buildings.

high-sounding convention which was to be rigidly binding upon all nations except those likely to break it."[13]

FURTHER READING

Ambrosius, Lloyd E. *Woodrow Wilson and the American Diplomatic Tradition: The Treaty Fight in Perspective.* Cambridge, UK: Cambridge University Press, 1987.

Goodrich, Leland M. "From League of Nations to United Nations." *International Organization* 1 (1947): 3–21.

Grigorescu, Alexandru. "Mapping the UN–League of Nations Analogy: Are There Still Lessons to Be Learned from the League?" *Global Governance* 11 (2005): 25–42.

Gross, Leo. "The Charter of the United Nations and the Lodge Reservations." *American Journal of International Law* 41 (1947): 531–554.

Hoopes, Townsend, and Douglas Brinkley. *FDR and the Creation of the UN*. New Haven, CT: Yale University Press, 1997.

Lodge, Henry Cabot. *The Senate and the League of Nations*. New York: Scribner, 1925.

Schild, Georg. "The Roosevelt Administration and the United Nations: Re-creation or Rejection of the League Experience?" *World Affairs* 158 (1995): 26–34.

Sobel, Russell S. "The League of Nations Covenant and the United Nations Charter: An Analysis of Two International Constitutions." *Constitutional Political Economy* 5:2 (1994): 173–192.

DID YOU KNOW?

The U.S. Senate and Treaties

The Charter of the United Nations is a treaty. Becoming party to a treaty is an international act, but every country needs an internal process by which to decide whether or not to take on the legal obligations contained in a treaty. The constitution of the United States requires that a treaty gain the approval of two-thirds of the Senate, a provision intended to ensure that a treaty has received broad political support before the United States becomes party to it. An example of a relatively recent treaty rejected by the U.S. Senate is the 1996 Comprehensive Nuclear Test Ban Treaty. On other occasions, however, a treaty is not even presented to the Senate because defeat is certain. Even before the text of the Kyoto Protocol on climate change was finally agreed, Republicans in the Senate declared that the treaty would be "dead on arrival" in the Senate.

The Peaceful Resolution of International Disputes and the Role of the International Court of Justice

- ***Document:*** Some key provisions in the UN Charter relating to the peaceful resolution of international disputes
- ***Date:*** June 26, 1945 (entered into force October 24, 1945)
- ***Where it is:*** San Francisco
- ***Significance:*** The UN Charter did not simply outlaw the use of force but did so as part of a package of "war prevention measures." One important component of the package was a set of provisions for the peaceful resolution of international disputes. These include options ranging from the least to the most formal and may include recourse to the International Court of Justice or Security Council.

DOCUMENT

Chapter 1: Purposes and Principles

Article 2(3)

All Members shall settle their international disputes by peaceful means in such a manner that international peace and security, and justice, are not endangered.

Chapter VI: Pacific Settlement of Disputes

Article 33(1)

The parties to any dispute, the continuance of which is likely to endanger the maintenance of international peace and security, shall, first of all, seek a solution by negotiation, enquiry, mediation, conciliation, arbitration, judicial settlement, resort to regional agencies or arrangements, or other peaceful means of their own choice.

Article 36(1)

The Security Council may, at any stage of a dispute of the nature referred to in Article 33 or of a situation of like nature, recommend appropriate procedures or methods of adjustment.

Article 37

(1) Should the parties to a dispute of the nature referred to in Article 33 fail to settle it by the means indicated in that Article, they shall refer it to the Security Council.

(2) If the Security Council deems that the continuance of the dispute is in fact likely to endanger the maintenance of international peace and security, it shall decide whether to take action under Article 36 or to recommend such terms of settlement as it may consider appropriate.

Article 38

Without prejudice to the provisions of Articles 33 to 37, the Security Council may, if all the parties to any dispute so request, make recommendations to the parties with a view to a pacific settlement of the dispute.

SOURCE: Charter of the United Nations. http://www.un.org/aboutun/charter/.

ANALYSIS

As we have seen, the prohibition on the use of force in the UN Charter was not introduced in isolation. If States were legally required to refrain from the use of force in international relations, there also needed to be alternative processes in place by which disputes could be peacefully resolved. The first-listed purpose of the United Nations in Article 1 is to maintain international peace and security. Article 2(3) of the UN Charter places a basic obligation on all member States to "settle their international disputes by peaceful means in such a manner that international peace and security, and justice, are not endangered." Article 33(1) offers them a range of ways by which they might go about doing so: negotiation, enquiry, mediation, conciliation, arbitration, judicial settlement, resort to regional agencies or arrangements, or other peaceful means of their own choice. These are often used in combination. It should be noted that the terms found in Article 33(1) are not terms of art with precise definitions in international law; the differences between mediation and conciliation, for example, may depend upon their usage in a particular context. A sense of what each of these terms mean can nevertheless be gleaned from understanding that the list moves from negotiation as the least formal but most commonly used method of resolving disputes between States, to judicial settlement as the most formal but least used.

Enquiry refers to a process in which a third party is asked to provide the answers to certain questions of fact, which can then be used as a basis of negotiation. Mediation involves a neutral, third person approved by both sides attempting to help bring about a compromise. Typically, however, a mediator does not take the initiative in recommending a course of action but facilitates the parties reaching their own resolution of the matter. A similar term to mediation is "good offices." This term is not specifically used in Article 33(1), and some assume that this is because it is synonymous with mediation. In comparison, conciliation involves a third party such as a commission or committee making advisory proposals for settlement. We looked briefly at arbitration in Chapter 1. Arbitration involves a third party making a decision with which the parties agree to comply. The parties to the dispute generally agree to a document that outlines the subject matter of the dispute, the composition of the arbitral tribunal, its procedure, and possibly the law to be applied. A permanent arbitral agreement may be established by treaty to decide any future disputes that may arise. Although the States are to be bound by the decision of a third party, they have thus had considerable say in how that third party is to arrive at the decision.

Public hearings of the International Court of Justice presided over by H.E. Judge Rosalyn Higgins, February/March 2006. Courtesy of the International Court of Justice.

Inaugural session of the International Court of Justice, April 18, 1946, held in the Great Hall of Justice at the Peace Palace in the presence of Their Royal Highnesses Princess Juliana and Prince Bernhard of The Netherlands. Courtesy of the International Court of Justice.

Judicial settlement is the most formal method of dispute resolution in international law. It involves a third party making a decision legally binding on the parties, and doing so on the basis of existing rules of procedure. The International Court of Justice (ICJ) is integral to the package of institutional devices and actions designed to prevent the use of force in world politics. This may not seem obvious if we look at the international landscape today, but is certainly apparent if we view the United Nations system as a progression from the League. There was very considerable continuity from the Permanent Court of International Justice (PCIJ) to the ICJ.

One of the most significant similarities between the two concerned the question of whether it would be compulsory for States to be subject to the jurisdiction of the Court or whether it would be optional for them to take a dispute to the Court. If the rule of law is to be established at an international level equivalent to that which functions within Western democracies, the sovereignty of States would need to be subject to the decisions of an international judicial body. But States had not been prepared to surrender so much of their sovereignty in either 1899 nor in 1920. The compromise when the Permanent Court was established was the "optional clause" system by which States could choose whether or not to opt for obligatory adjudication. This system was transferred across to the International Court of Justice. Article 36(3) of the Charter of the United Nations states that "legal disputes should as a general rule be referred by the parties to the International Court of Justice," while

Article 36(1) of the Statute of the ICJ confers jurisdiction on the Court in "all cases which the parties refer to it."

Another question concerning international courts that is politically contentious is that of how the judges are to be appointed. The ICJ is composed of fifteen judges. The judges are elected by separate absolute majorities of the General Assembly and Security Council and serve nine-year renewable terms. Ad hoc judges may be appointed for particular cases when one, but not another, State party to a dispute has a national on the Court. Judges are not meant to represent their States, but it has been more common for them to find in favor of their country than against.

The caseload of the Court has been much more complex than that of the PCIJ. The Court has heard cases on a wide range of subjects, including the law of the sea and the location of maritime boundaries. Notably, it has also heard cases relating to territorial sovereignty, the location of territorial boundaries and the disposition of large tracts of land with large populations.[14] Examples include the Case concerning the Territorial Dispute [Libyan Arab Jamahiriya/Chad] over the Aouzou Strip, the judgment being handed down in 1994, and the Case concerning the Land and Maritime Boundary between Cameroon and Nigeria, a judgment regarding which was given in 2002. Although the primary function of the ICJ is to facilitate the peaceful settlement of international disputes, a by-product of that process has been its contribution to the evolution of the bodies of international law on which it has needed to make a determination. As will be seen in subsequent chapters, these include that of use of force.

Chapter VI of the Charter, which encompasses Articles 33–38, gives the Security Council a role in the peaceful resolution of disputes. A key idea in this chapter is that the Council should not wait until a dispute erupts into a conflict but should investigate any situation with the potential to cause conflict. It can make suggestions for peaceful resolution and may make use of the range of methods of dispute resolution listed in Article 33(1). The Secretary-General has on a number of occasions offered or performed "good offices," as for example, in relation to Cyprus from 1964; Kampuchea 1989; and Afghanistan 1988. This has produced some successes and some failures. In 1982, for example, Javier Pérez de Cuéllar, UN Secretary General, met separately with Britain and Argentina on a number of occasions after they severed diplomatic relations over the Falkland Islands issue but his efforts met with no success. The United Kingdom went ahead with landings.

UN mediation successes in the 1980s and 1990s are said to include the Iran–Iraq war, El Salvador, Cambodia, Mozambique, Guatemala, and Tajikistan.[15] Perhaps naturally, mediation tends to have been most successful where the parties were already looking for a way out. Similarly, the International Court of Justice has been most successful where the States involved in a dispute wanted to have the Court settle the matter.

DID YOU KNOW?

The Legal Basis on Which the ICJ Operates

There are three legal documents that together constitute the basis for the functioning of the International Court of Justice. First is the Charter of the United Nations. The International Court of Justice is referred to at several points in the Charter. Article 7(1) of the UN Charter establishes the Court as a principal organ of the organization, and Article 92 refers to it as the principal judicial organ of the United Nations. By Article 94, Members of the United Nations agree to comply with the decision of the Court in any case to which it is a party and that, if a State does not comply, the other party to the dispute may have recourse to the Security Council. Annexed to the Charter is the Statute of the ICJ, which provides further details on how the Court is to function, including the basis on which the Court is to decide a case. The third document, the Rules of Court, sets out how the Court is going to comply in practice with the Statute and hence serves as a supplement to the Statute.

Where one of the parties regards its position as not amenable to compromise, it is less likely that a third party can facilitate dispute resolution. It also needs to be borne in mind that winning a legal skirmish does not necessarily equate with settling the political score. The United States may have defeated Iran in the *Case Concerning United States Diplomatic and Consular Staff in Tehran* (1980), but the hostages remained in Tehran. The dispute was finally settled through mediation by Algeria.

DID YOU KNOW?

Some Key International Judicial and Quasi-Judicial Bodies Today

There has been a proliferation of international dispute resolution bodies over recent decades. While the International Court of Justice is the best known and can deal with a wide range of subjects, there are several other dispute resolution bodies to address disputes concerning particular subjects. The International Tribunal for the Law of the Sea addresses issues relating to the law of the sea; the World Trade Organization has its own dispute resolution body, and the International Criminal Court has been established to prosecute international criminal law. The International Criminal Court has jurisdiction over individuals rather than States. Regional human rights judicial bodies include the European Court of Human Rights, the African Court on Human and Peoples' Rights, and the Inter-American Court of Human Rights. Quasi-judicial bodies include the Committees established to monitor the implementation of United Nations treaties on human rights and those to monitor compliance with international environmental agreements.

FURTHER READING

Allain, Jean. *A Century of International Adjudication: The Rule of Law and its Limits*. The Hague: T.M.C. Asser Press, 2000.

The International Court of Justice. *Selected Documents Relating to the Drafting of the Statute*. Washington, DC: Government Printing Office, 1946.

Merrills, J. G. *International Dispute Settlement*. 4th ed. Cambridge, UK: Cambridge University Press, 2005.

Patel, Bimal N. *The World Court Reference Guide. Judgments, Advisory Opinions and Orders of the Permanent Court of International Justice and the International Court of Justice (1922–2000)*. The Hague: Kluwer Law International, 2002.

Peace Negotiations Watch is a weekly publication prepared by the Public International Law & Policy Group (PILPG) detailing current events relating to conflict and peace processes in selected countries. To view the latest edition and/or subscribe, visit the PILPG Web site at http://www.publicinternationallaw.org/.

The Project on International Courts and Tribunals. Synoptic Chart of the International Judiciary in Context and much other useful information. http://www.pict-pcti.org/.

Rosenne, Shabtai, with the assistance of Yaël Ronen. *The Law and Practice of the International Court, 1920–2005*. 4th ed. Leiden: Martinus Nijhoff, 2006.

The Web site of the International Court of Justice provides a wealth of valuable and accessible information http://www.icj-cij.org/.

The UN Charter Enters the Nuclear Age

- ***Document:*** An article featured the memories of a survivor of the atomic bomb dropped on Hiroshima on the sixtieth anniversary of the bombing
- ***Date:*** August 5, 2005
- ***Where:*** Voice of America, New York
- ***Significance:*** Disarmament and the regulation of armaments can be understood to have been part of the overall package of war prevention measures in the Charter era.

DOCUMENT

Hiroshima Survivor Recalls Day Atomic Bomb Was Dropped

By Adam Phillips

Sixty years ago, on August 5, 1945, in Washington and August 6, in Japan, the United States dropped an atomic bomb on Hiroshima. It was the first of 2 U.S. nuclear attacks on Japan that hastened the end of World War II and set the stage for the post-war nuclear arms race.

In 1945, Tomiko Morimoto was a 13-year-old schoolgirl. She recalls feeling no particular fear when she and her classmates heard the lone American B-29 bomber droning through the cloudless skies above Hiroshima. Her city had never been bombed, and she assumed the plane was simply on a reconnaissance mission, like the others she had seen.

Then she saw the flash. "You know how you see the bright sun that's going down on a very hot day? Bright red—orange red. That's what it was like," she recalls. "After we heard a big noise like a 'BOONG!' 'BOONG!' Like that. That was the sound."

After the sound, she recalls, "everything started falling down; all the buildings started flying around all over the place. Then something wet started coming down, like rain. I guess that's what they call black rain. In my child's mind, I thought it was oil. I thought the Americans were going to burn us to death. And we kept running. And fire was coming out right behind us, you know."

Adults at the school led Tomiko and her classmates across the Motoyasu River to a plateau on the outskirts of Hiroshima, and told them to wait for family members to come get them. All night long, they watched their city burning below. The next morning, no parents had come, and the children were released to find their way home on their own. For Ms. Morimoto, that meant trying to find a bridge into the city that had not been destroyed.

She remembers seeing "dead people all over. All over! Particularly, I can remember . . . I saw a Japanese soldier that was still mounted right on his horse—just dead! Also that a streetcar had stopped just at that moment [of the bomb] and the people still standing, dead."

Finally, Ms. Morimoto says she found a bridge she and her classmates could cross safely—a railroad bridge. She recalls looking down through the spaces between the railroad ties. Normally, one would see the river flowing there underneath. But she says, instead she saw "a sea of dead people. There was not one space for the water, just people lying there and dead."

Survivors she encountered begged for water. "Mainly, I just wanted to find my people. Finally—finally!—I reached home and of course my home was gone and I couldn't find anybody."

The only person who recognized Ms. Morimoto was a family hired man, who told her her grandparents had taken refuge with some neighbors in a certain nearby cave.

"And I found my grandmother and grandfather among them. Of course my grandfather was terribly hurt," she says. "He had glass lodged all over his back, bleeding. My grandmother, she wasn't hurt but she couldn't stand up from shock. My mother, I didn't find her for a week or so, and she was burned underneath a building. I hoped she died instantly."

Tomiko Morimoto now lives in rural, upstate New York. She says surviving the bombing of Hiroshima has made her appreciate even the smallest things. "I go out the first thing in the morning and look at the sky and the sun and I am very appreciative of everything I have right now. You don't always have that," she says. "I carry that [sad] emotion, yes, and when I talk about it, it comes back. And I just take my hand and I erase the picture from in my mind. And that's how I cope with it."

But she also lives with fear. "I'm always afraid as more countries have the atomic bomb. I fear the end of the world," she says. "I would say never let there be another bombing like that. We all have to work towards peace. That's the only way I can summarize it."

Ironically, Tomiko Morimoto is not among those who believe that American forces should never have dropped the atomic bomb. She believes that only a total unequivocal victory by the Allies would have convinced the Japanese population that their war effort was hopeless, that they must lay down their arms and try to move on.

Today, 60 years after the bomb fell on Hiroshima, we remember not only those who died in that war, but also those who lived.

SOURCE: Courtesy of Voice of America, www.voanews.com/english/archive/2005-08/2005-08-05-voa38.cfm.

ANALYSIS

Six weeks after the signing of the Charter, the United States dropped one atomic bomb over Hiroshima and, three days later, another over Nagasaki. At that moment the world entered a new era, in which the prospect of a third world war with nuclear weapons was unthinkable. The imperative of "getting it right" in terms of establishing a new world order had been made clear. The Charter, on the other hand, was a "pre-atomic" document—the Trinity test, the first explosion using the new nuclear technology, took place only on July 16, 1945. The Charter provided for the maintenance of peace by collective security, but the fact that it was followed so closely by the Cold War nuclear arms race means that some might say that in practice it was for the next half century the principle of mutually assured destruction, rather than that of collective security, that was more significant in preventing a third world war.

Disarmament does not feature prominently in the UN Charter, although Article 11 states:

> The General Assembly may consider the general principles of cooperation in the maintenance of international peace and security, including the principles governing disarmament and the regulation of armaments, and may make recommendations with regard to such principles to the Members or to the Security Council or to both.

Aftermath of Hiroshima, Japan, 1945. Courtesy of United States Navy Office of Information.

The General Assembly established a series of committees, the first of which focuses on disarmament and security questions and provides draft resolutions to the Assembly. According to Article 26 of the UN Charter:

> In order to promote the establishment and maintenance of international peace and security with the least diversion for armaments of the world's human and economic resources, the Security Council shall be responsible for formulating . . . plans . . . for the establishment of a system for the regulation of armaments.

The text of the UN Charter was finalized too early to incorporate provisions specifically on nuclear weapons. By 1964 five countries had developed and tested nuclear weapons: China, France, the USSR, the UK, and the United States of America. There was a perceived need for a separate treaty with the aim of limiting the spread of nuclear weaponry to more and more countries. The Treaty on the Non-Proliferation of Nuclear Weapons (NPT) was opened for signature on July 1, 1968. The NPT obliged existing nuclear weapon States not to assist others to join the "nuclear club" while requiring nonnuclear weapon States not to receive or control any nuclear weapons or other nuclear explosive devices and not to seek or receive any assistance in manufacturing such weapons or devices. While one assumption underpinning the NPT is that the spread of nuclear weapons increases the dangers of nuclear war, it is important to note that another key principle in the treaty is that the peaceful application of nuclear energy should be made universally available.

During the Cold War the term "arms control" came into use to refer to rules for limiting competition in armaments, of which disarmament—the actual reduction or elimination of armaments—may be one aspect. Article VI of the NPT, on nuclear disarmament, was worded much less tightly than those on nonproliferation. It provided:

> Each of the Parties to the Treaty undertakes to pursue negotiations in good faith on effective measures relating to cessation of the nuclear arms race at an early date and to nuclear disarmament, and on a treaty on general and complete disarmament.

DID YOU KNOW?

A Selection of Important Post 1945 Treaties on Disarmament and Arms Control

1959	The Antarctic Treaty
1967	Treaty for the Prohibition of Nuclear Weapons in Latin America
1968	Treaty on the Non-Proliferation of Nuclear Weapons
1980	Convention on Prohibitions or Restrictions on the Use of Certain Conventional Weapons Which May be Deemed to Be Excessively Injurious or to Have Indiscriminate Effects
1993	Convention on the Prohibition of the Development, Production, Stockpiling, and Use of Chemical Weapons and on Their Destruction
1996	Treaty on the Nuclear Weapon Free Zone in Africa
1996	Comprehensive Nuclear Test Ban Treaty
1997	Convention on the Prohibition of the Use, Stockpiling, Production, and Transfer of Anti-Personnel Mines and on Their Destruction
2008	Convention on Cluster Munitions

DID YOU KNOW?

The Pacifist Legacy of Hiroshima and Nagasaki

After Japan's defeat in World War II and its experience of the atomic bomb, Japan became a strongly pacifist country in which it was taboo to even consider publicly the possibility of Japan becoming a nuclear weapon State. The young people in Japan were far more pacifist than their counterparts in other countries. In recent years there have been signs that this is beginning to change. This is probably primarily a generational change, as memories of Hiroshima and Nagasaki are lost. The shift is significant not only if it leads to concrete changes in Japan's foreign policy and role within the nuclear nonproliferation regime but if it affects Japan's sensitive relations with neighboring countries, including China and the Koreas.

The first session of the United Nations General Assembly opened on January 10, 1946, at Central Hall in London. Clement Attlee, Prime Minister of the United Kingdom, is addressing the General Assembly. Courtesy of UN Photo.

Arms control agreements may respond to the proliferation of weapons of mass destruction—nuclear, biological, and chemical weapons—or of conventional weaponry. A considerable body of international law on arms control has developed under UN auspices. One of the most recent additions is the Convention on Cluster Munitions, which was adopted in May 2008. This treaty prohibits the stockpiling, production, and transfer of cluster munitions and also addresses the destruction of stockpiles.

Notes

1. Albrecht Randelzhoffer, "Article 2(4)," in Bruno Simma, ed. *The Charter of the United Nations. A Commentary* (Oxford: Oxford University Press, 1994), 111.
2. Stanley Meisler, *United Nations: The First Fifty Years* (New York: The Atlantic Monthly Press, 1995), 11.
3. Meisler, *United Nations*, 17.
4. Meisler, *United Nations*, 19.
5. Meisler, *United Nations*, 2.
6. *Yearbook of the United Nations 1946–47* (Lake Success, NY: Department of Public Information, 1947): 24.

7. Leland M. Goodrich, "From League of Nations to United Nations," *International Organization* 1 (1947): 3–21.
8. J. L. Brierly, *The Covenant and the Charter* (Cambridge, UK: Cambridge University Press, 1947), 23.
9. Sean Lester, *The Work of the League During the War*, cited in Douglas Gageby, *The Last Secretary General. Sean Lester and the League of Nations* (Dublin: Town House, 1999), 262.
10. Brierly, *The Covenant and the Charter*, 6.
11. Brierly, *The Covenant and the Charter*, 7.
12. Brierly, *The Covenant and the Charter*, 16.
13. Gilbert Murray, *From the League to UN* (London: Oxford University Press, 1948), 158.
14. Shabtai Rosenne, "International Court of Justice," in Rüdiger Wolfrum, ed. *Max Planck Encyclopedia of Public International Law* (Oxford: Oxford University Press, 2008) online edition, http://www.mpepil.com/, 23.
15. Edward C. Luck, *UN Security Council: Practice and Promise* (London: Routledge, 2006), 35.

FURTHER READING

The Arms Control Association. A U.S. nonpartisan organization dedicated to promoting public understanding of and support for effective arms control policies. It produces a magazine on current issues in arms control, titled *Arms Control Today*. http://www.armscontrol.org/.

Blix, Hans. *Why Nuclear Disarmament Matters*. Cambridge, MA: MIT Press, 2008. The Convention on Cluster Munitions. http://www.clusterconvention.org/.

DiFilippo, Anthony. *Japan's Nuclear Disarmament Policy and the US Security Umbrella*. New York: Palgrave Macmillan, 2006.

Larsen, Jeffrey Arthur, and James M. Smith, *Historical Dictionary of Arms Control and Disarmament*. Lanham, MD: Scarecrow Press, 2005.

The United Nations Office for Disarmament Affairs. http://www.un.org/disarmament/.

4

KEY CHALLENGES TO THE GENERAL PROHIBITION ON THE USE OF FORCE

"And they shall beat their swords into ploughshares" (Isaiah 2:4). Bronze sculpture created by Soviet artist Evgeny Vuchetich and presented to the United Nations in December 1959 by the Government of the USSR. The sculpture is meant to symbolize man's desire to put an end to war and to convert the means of destruction into creative tools for the benefit of mankind. The sculpture is located in the North Garden of the UN Headquarters, New York. Courtesy of Nicolas Kuskin, UN Photo.

OVERVIEW

Article 2(4) of the UN Charter is widely regarded as the contemporary expression of treaty and customary law with regard to the use of force.[1] Some observers consider the article to have resulted in a fundamental change in the attitude of States toward the use of force and argue that it has directly contributed to a significant reduction in the resort to force by States.[2] There is, however, also a view that States have failed to comply with the requirements of Article 2(4) to such an extent as to render the article meaningless.[3] Some of the skeptics have gone so far as to suggest that attempts to limit the resort to force are doomed to failure because they are, in the words of Bernard Meltzer, seeking "order and morality where only anarchy and amorality prevail"—that "[w]ar in Europe had been almost as natural a relation as peace" and that there was a tradition in Europe of "aggression and its moral acceptance in an area bristling with long standing hates, fears and rivalries."[4]

In the light of the extensive differences of opinion this chapter sets out to examine a range of cases in which Article 2(4) has been "put to the test." Each case has raised a particular question as to the scope, interpretation, or application of the Charter provisions on the use of force. The international community has in each instance had to decide whether the use of force in question is best understood as a straightforward violation of the Charter or whether it is perhaps compatible with Article 2(4) despite that particular scenario not having been envisaged by the drafters of the Charter.

Should Article 2(4) Be Interpreted Broadly or Narrowly?

- ***Document:*** Extracts from the Judgment of the International Court of Justice in the Corfu Channel Case between Albania and the United Kingdom
- ***Date:*** April 9, 1949
- ***Where:*** The Peace Palace, The Hague
- ***Significance:*** The Corfu Channel case addressed the related issues of innocent passage through international waterways, the significance to international law of the territorial sovereignty of a State, and the law's tolerance of external intervention.

DOCUMENT

In addition to the passage of the United Kingdom warships on October 22nd, 1946, the second question in the Special Agreement relates to the acts of the Royal Navy in Albanian waters on November 12th and 13th, 1946. This is the minesweeping operation called 'Operation Retail' by the Parties during the proceedings. This name will be used in the present Judgment.

After the explosions of October 22nd, the United Kingdom Government sent a note to the Albanian Government, in which it announced its intention to sweep the Corfu Channel shortly. The Albanian reply, which was received in London on October 31st, stated that the Albanian Government would not give its consent to this unless the operation in question took place outside Albanian territorial waters. Meanwhile, at the United Kingdom Government's request, the International Central Mine Clearance Board decided, in a resolution of November 1st, 1946, that there should be a further sweep of the Channel, subject to Albania's consent. The United Kingdom Government having informed the Albanian Government, in a communication of November 10th, that the proposed sweep would take place on November 12th, the Albanian Government replied on the 11th, protesting against this "unilateral decision of His Majesty's Government." It said it did not consider it inconvenient that the British fleet should undertake the sweeping of the channel of navigation, but added that, before sweeping was carried out, it considered it indispensable to decide what area of the sea should be deemed to constitute this channel, and proposed the establishment of a Mixed Commission for the purpose. It ended by saying that any sweeping undertaken without the consent of the Albanian Government outside the channel thus constituted, i.e., inside Albanian territorial waters where foreign warships have no reason to sail, could only be considered as a deliberate violation of Albanian territory and sovereignty.

After this exchange of notes, "Operation Retail" took place on November 12th and 13th. Commander Mestre, of the French Navy, was asked to attend as observer, and was present at the sweep on November 13th. The operation was carried out under the protection of an important covering force composed of an aircraft carrier, cruisers and other war vessels. This covering force remained throughout the operation at a certain distance to the west of the Channel, except for the frigate *St. Bride's Bay*, which was stationed in the Channel south-east of Cape Kiephali. The sweep began in the morning of November 13th, at about 9 o'clock, and ended in the afternoon near nightfall. The area swept was in Albanian territorial waters, and within the limits of the channel previously swept.

The United Kingdom Government does not dispute that "Operation Retail" was carried out against the clearly expressed wish of the Albanian Government. It recognizes that the operation had not the consent of the international mine clearance organizations, that it could not be justified as the exercise of a right of innocent passage, and lastly that, in principle, international law does not allow a State to assemble a large number of warships in the territorial waters of another State and to carry out minesweeping in those waters. The United Kingdom Government states that the operation was one of extreme urgency, and that it considered itself entitled to carry it out without anybody's consent.

The United Kingdom Government put forward two reasons in justification. First, the Agreement of November 22nd, 1945, signed by the Governments of the United Kingdom, France, the Soviet Union and the United States of America, authorizing regional mine clearance organizations, such as the Mediterranean Zone Board, to divide the sectors in their respective zones amongst the States concerned for sweeping. Relying on the circumstance that the Corfu Channel was in the sector allotted to Greece by the Mediterranean Zone Board on November 5th, i.e., before the signing of the above-mentioned Agreement, the United Kingdom Government put forward a permission given by the Hellenic Government to resweep the navigable channel.

The Court does not consider this argument convincing. It must be noted that, as the United Kingdom Government admits, the need for resweeping the Channel was not under consideration in November, 1945; for previous sweeps in 1944 and 1945 were considered as having effected complete safety. As a consequence, the allocation of the sector in question to Greece, and, therefore, the permission of the Hellenic Government, which is relied on, were both of them merely nominal. It is also to be remarked that Albania was not consulted regarding the allocation to Greece of the sector in question, despite the fact that the Channel passed through Albanian territorial waters.

But, in fact, the explosions of October 22nd, 1946, in a channel declared safe for navigation, and one which the United Kingdom Government, more than any other government, had reason to consider safe, raised quite a different problem from that of a routine sweep carried out under the orders of the mine-clearance organizations. These explosions were suspicious; they raised a question of responsibility.

Accordingly, this was the ground on which the United Kingdom Government chose to establish its main line of defence. According to that Government, the *corpora delicti* must be secured as quickly as possible, for fear they should be taken away, without leaving traces, by the authors of the mine-laying or by the Albanian authorities. This justification took two distinct forms in the United Kingdom Government's arguments. It was presented first as a new and special application of the theory of intervention, by means of which the State intervening would secure possession of evidence in the territory of another State, in order to submit it to an international tribunal and thus facilitate its task.

The Court cannot accept such a line of defence. The Court can only regard the alleged right of intervention as the manifestation of a policy of force, such as has, in the past, given rise to most serious abuses and such as cannot, whatever be the present defects in international organization, find a place in international law. Intervention is perhaps still less admissible in the particular form it would take here; for, from the nature of things, it would be reserved for the most powerful States, and might easily lead to perverting the administration of international justice itself.

The United Kingdom Agent, in his speech in reply, has further classified "Operation Retail" among methods of self-protection or self-help. The Court cannot accept this defence either. Between independent States, respect for territorial sovereignty is an essential foundation of international relations. The Court recognizes that the Albanian Government's complete failure to carry out its duties after the explosions, and the dilatory nature of its diplomatic notes, are extenuating circumstances for the action of the United Kingdom Government. But to ensure respect for international law, of which it is the organ, the Court must declare that the action of the British Navy constituted a violation of Albanian sovereignty. This declaration is in accordance with the request made by Albania through her Counsel, and is in itself appropriate satisfaction.

The method of carrying out "Operation Retail" has also been criticized by the Albanian Government, the main ground of complaint being that the United Kingdom, on that occasion, made use of an unnecessarily large display of force, out of proportion to the requirements of the sweep. The Court thinks that this criticism is not justified. It does not consider that the action of the British Navy was a demonstration of force for the purpose of exercising political pressure on Albania. The responsible naval commander, who kept his ships at a distance from the coast, cannot be reproached for having employed an important covering force in a region where twice within a few months his ships had been the object of serious outrages.

For these reasons, the Court unanimously:

gives judgment that by reason of the acts of the British Navy in Albanian waters in the course of the Operation of November 12th and 13th, 1946, the United Kingdom violated the sovereignty of the People's Republic of Albania, and that this declaration by the Court constitutes in itself appropriate satisfaction.

SOURCE: "Corfu Channel Case," Judgment of April 9, 1949, *ICJ Reports* 1949, pp. 32–36. *Courtesy of the International Court of Justice.*

ANALYSIS

Article 2(4) of the United Nations Charter requires States to "refrain in their international relations from the threat or use of force against the territorial integrity or political independence of any State, or in any other manner inconsistent with the Purposes of the United Nations," and by Article 2(3), States have committed to settling their international disputes by peaceful means. These two obligations are interrelated in that, if a State is to agree not to settle disputes through threat or use of force, there should ideally be an alternative avenue by which to do so. The Corfu Channel case, in which the International Court of Justice (ICJ) handed down its judgment in 1949, was significant as the first post-Charter use of force to be subjected to third-party dispute resolution before the International Court of Justice. As such, it marked a major departure from State practice in the past.[5] In this case, use of force—a traditional approach to the pursuit of State interests—collided with the new emphasis on international law and judicial settlement. The case and its outcome could, therefore, be described as indicative of a significant shift in the attitude of States to the resort to force. As one writer observed:

> Sixty years ago, a Balkan incident like the mining of the destroyers in the Corfu Channel would probably have led to an immediate British ultimatum to Albania, with limitless vistas of punitive war and Great Power intervention on opposite sides. This was in the days before observance of international law had developed into the standard of conduct for civilized states, and it is a mark of the advance made in at least some directions that the damage and loss of life last October were not followed at once by anarchic reprisals, bombardments of the Albanian coast, and demands for indemnities. Instead, Britain subjected the facts to the third party judgement of the Security Council of the United Nations, and, when the Russian veto blocked a decision in her favour, allowed the dispute to go before the International Court, thus transforming a serious political embroilment into a legal issue, and incidentally giving a lesson in the way to stop war.[6]

The Corfu Channel case is well known for having addressed the question of whether warships had the right of innocent passage through the territorial waters of a State where those waters formed part of an international strait. The case resulted from an incident in 1946 in which several British warships were engaged in innocent passage through the Corfu Channel, an international waterway that runs between the Greek island of Corfu and the Albanian mainland and is bordered by Greece and Albania. In the course of the passage, two warships were seriously damaged by mines. In response, the British navy conducted a minesweeping operation in Albanian territorial waters and collected a number of mines without the approval of the Albanian Government. In response to the angry reaction of Albania and its supporters, Britain initially sought the support of the UN Security Council but was frustrated by opposition from the Soviet Union. The British then approached the International Court of Justice for a resolution. Albania expressed its concern about the referral to the Court but also stated its willingness to appear and ultimately took an active part in the proceedings.

In justifying its actions before the Court, the British Government argued that Albania must have planted the mines that damaged the British ships or have known of their placement and that Albania therefore bore responsibility for the incident. Implying that Albania could not be trusted to cooperate with any investigation into the incident, the British argued that their action was designed to assist the legal process by collecting necessary evidence and that this intervention did not violate the prohibition on the use of force as it was not aimed at interfering with Albania's territorial integrity and political independence. As such, the British action raised the question as to just how Article 2(4) should best be interpreted: "should the words 'against the territorial integrity or political independence of any State, or in any other manner inconsistent with the purposes of the United Nations' be construed as a strict prohibition on all use of force against another State, or did they allow the use of force provided that the aim was not to overthrow the government or seize the territory of the State and provided that the action was consistent with the purposes of the UN?"[7]

In its judgment, the Court confirmed the entitlement of the British navy to assert its right of passage through the Corfu Channel. The Court noted the suspicious nature of the incident and the provocative behavior of the Albanian authorities over some time. It also commented on a number of serious failings on the part of the Government of Albania after the British ships were damaged. The Court nevertheless emphasized the need to ensure respect for international law and emphasized that respect for the sovereignty and territorial integrity of States was "an essential foundation of international relations." The decision of the ICJ confirmed that the Charter contains a general prohibition on a State using force against another State, to which the only permissible exception is self-defense. To claim that a use of force is not illegal because it is not directed against the territorial integrity of the other State is not a correct interpretation of the Charter. Although some scholars believe that the Court was not rejecting the narrow interpretation of Article 2(4) but rather the British claim on the particular facts,[8] an examination of the *travaux préparatoires* (documents involved in the preparation) of Article 2(4) confirms that the terms "territorial integrity" and "political independence" were not intended to restrict the scope of the prohibition on the use of force.[9] These variants had not been part of the Dumbarton Oaks proposals and were introduced at the San Francisco conference at the request of several smaller States that wanted particular emphasis to be placed on the protection of territorial integrity and political independence by means of the prohibition on the use of force. Nevertheless, the question as to whether Article 2(4) can be subject to a narrow interpretation has recently resurfaced in the discourse on the legality of intervention for human protection purposes.

UN Security Council vote on a resolution on Situation in Czechoslovakia. Yakov Malik (Soviet Union) vetoing the resolution. In the center is Lord Caradon (United Kingdom). At right is George Ball (United States). August 22, 1968, United Nations, New York. Courtesy of UN Photo.

The British preparedness to submit its use of force to the judgment of the International Court of Justice has regrettably not been followed in all instances. Notably, when the International Court of Justice found in 1984 that it did indeed have jurisdiction to hear a case brought against the United States by Nicaragua for the unlawful use of force against the Government of Nicaragua and for its intervention through support for military and paramilitary activities of the *contra* forces, the United States failed to participate further in the proceedings and rejected the Court's subsequent judgment on the merits.

FURTHER READING

Baxter. R. R. "Passage of Ships Through International Waterways in Time of War." *British Year Book of International Law* 31 (1954): 187–216.

Gazzini, Tarcisio. *The Changing Rules on the Use of Force in International Law*. Manchester: Juris, 2005.

Johnson, D. H. N. "Some Legal Problems of International Waterways, with Particular Reference to the Straits of Tiran and the Suez Canal." *Modern Law Review* 31, no. 2 (1968): 153–164.

Leigh, Monroe. "Military and Paramilitary Activities in and Against Nicaragua (Nicaragua v. United States of America) 1986 ICJ Rep. 14." *American Journal of International Law* 81, no. 1 (1987): 206–211.

Wright, Quincy. "The Corfu Channel Case." *American Journal of International Law* 43, no. 3 (1949): 491–494.

Is It Legal to Intervene with Force If Invited to Do So?

- ***Document A:*** Extract from a letter dated May 22, 1958, from the Representative of Lebanon addressed to the President of the Security Council
- ***Date:*** May 23, 1958
- ***Where:*** United Nations, New York
- ***Significance:*** This short letter from the Government of Lebanon to the Security Council highlights some of the complexities facing attempts to apply international legal considerations to issues of civil war and intervention by invitation.

DOCUMENT A

Upon instructions from my Government, I have the honour to request you, in your capacity as President of the Security Council, to call an urgent meeting of the Council to consider the following question:

> "Complaint by Lebanon in respect of a situation arising from the intervention of the United Arab Republic in the internal affairs of Lebanon, the continuance of which is likely to endanger the maintenance of international peace and security."

The said intervention consists *inter alia* of the following acts: the infiltration of armed bands from Syria into Lebanon, the destruction of Lebanese life and property by such bands, the participation of United Arab Republic nationals in acts of terrorism and rebellion against the established authorities in Lebanon, the supply of arms from Syria to individuals and bands in Lebanon rebelling against the established authorities, and the waging of a violent radio and press campaign in the

United Arab Republic calling for strikes, demonstrations and the overthrow of the established authorities in Lebanon, and through other provocative acts.
Please accept, etc.
(Signed) Karim Azkoul
Permanent Representative of
Lebanon to the United Nations

SOURCE: UN Security Council Records, 13th session, supplement for April–June 1958, UN Doc. S/4007 (1958).

- ***Document B:*** Statement by the Telegraph Agency of the Soviet Union (TASS) justifying the military intervention of Warsaw Pact nations into Czechoslovakia on August 20–21, 1968.
- ***Date:*** August 21, 1968.
- ***Where:*** Moscow.
- ***Significance:*** The TASS statement represented the attempt by the Soviet leadership to explain and justify the invasion by the Soviet Union of Czechoslovakia in August 1968 in the face of widespread international hostility.

DOCUMENT B

TASS is authorised to state that Party and Government leaders of the Czechoslovak Socialist Republic have asked the Soviet Union and other allied states to render the fraternal Czechoslovak people urgent assistance, including assistance with armed forces. This request was brought about by the threat which has arisen to the socialist system in Czechoslovakia and to the statehood established by the Constitution. The threat emanates from the counter-revolutionary forces which have entered into collusion with foreign forces hostile to socialism.

The events in and around Czechoslovakia were repeatedly the subject of exchange of views between leaders of fraternal socialist countries, including the leaders of Czechoslovakia. These countries are unanimous in that the support, consolidation and defence of the people's socialist gains is a common internationalist duty of all the socialist states. This common stand was solemnly proclaimed in the Bratislava Statement.

The further aggravation of the situation in Czechoslovakia affects the vital interests of the Soviet Union and other socialist states, the interests of the security of the states of the socialist community. The threat to the socialist system in Czechoslovakia constitutes at the same time a threat to the mainstays of European peace.

The Soviet Government and the governments of the allied countries—the People's Republic of Bulgaria, the Hungarian People's Republic, the German Democratic Republic, the Polish People's Republic—proceeding from the principles of unseverable friendship and cooperation, and in accordance with the existing contractual commitments, have decided to meet the above-mentioned request for rendering necessary help to the Czechoslovak people.

This decision is fully in accord with the rights of states to individual and collective self-defence envisaged in treaties of alliance concluded between the fraternal socialist countries. This decision is also in line with vital interests of our countries in safeguarding European peace against forces of militarism, aggression and revanche which have more than once plunged the peoples of Europe into wars.

Soviet armed units, together with armed units of the above-mentioned allied countries, entered the territory of Czechoslovakia on 21 August. They will be immediately withdrawn from the Czechoslovak Socialist Republic as soon as the obtaining threat to the gains of socialism in Czechoslovakia, the threat to the security of the socialist community countries is eliminated and the lawful authorities find that the further presence of these armed units there is no longer necessary.

The actions which are being taken are not directed against any state and in no measure infringe upon any state's interests. They serve the purpose of peace and have been prompted by concern for its consolidation.

The fraternal countries firmly and resolutely counterpose their unbreakable solidarity to any threat from outside. Nobody will ever be allowed to wrest a single link from the community of socialist states.

SOURCE: International Legal Materials 7 (1968): 1283–1284. *Courtesy of Hein Online.*

ANALYSIS

The UN Charter is built on respect for sovereignty and nonuse of force by any one State against the territorial integrity of another State. It has, however, been uncontroversial since 1945 that a State may intervene militarily in another State if it does so at the request of the government in power or to maintain domestic order.[10] A State may not intervene in support of anti-government forces. What has challenged Article 2(4) in this instance is not, therefore, the relevant law, but how to apply it to particular incidents in which there may be dispute regarding the facts of the situation. There may be disagreement, for example, as to whether the State is experiencing civil unrest or has moved into civil war, whether those opposing the ruling government are being supported internationally, or even as to who represents the true government of a country.

Document A concerns a decision of the United States to intervene in a domestic conflict within another State. This letter submitted by the Government of Lebanon to the President of the Security Council alleged external interference in its domestic affairs through support, both material and political, of its domestic opponents. The crisis itself resulted from local issues arising out of rumors that the President of Lebanon, Camille Chamoun, intended to have the constitution amended to allow him to serve a second term in office. The rumors provoked clashes between militia groups supporting and opposed to Chamoun. When the Lebanese army refused to be drawn in, neither group was able to establish dominance, and the resulting stalemate led to the Lebanese Government seeking Security Council help in devising "appropriate . . . methods of adjustment under Article 36(1)." In response to the Lebanese

DID YOU KNOW?

The Brezhnev Doctrine (Abridged)

Concerning Czechoslovakia the interdependence of the national interests of the socialist countries and their international duties acquire particular importance. Measures taken by the Soviet Union, with other socialist countries, in defending socialist gains of the Czechoslovak people are significant in strengthening the socialist community, the main achievement of the international working class.

People of socialist and Communist parties have and should have freedom to determine how to advance their countries. However, none of their decisions should damage socialism in their country or the fundamental interests of other socialist countries, and the working class. This means each Communist party is responsible not only to its people, but to all socialist countries, to the entire Communist movement.

Just as, in Lenin's words, a man in a society cannot be free from the society, a socialist state, in a system of other states composing the socialist community, cannot be free from the common interests of that community. Lenin demanded Communists fight against small-nation narrow-mindedness and isolation, subordinate the particular to the general interest.

Socialist states respect democratic norms of international law. They have proved this more than once, by resisting attempts of imperialism to violate the sovereignty and independence of nations. It is from these positions that they reject the leftist, adventurist conception of 'exporting revolution,' of 'bringing happiness' to other peoples. . . From a Marxist view, the norms of law cannot be interpreted narrowly, formally, and in isolation from the context of class struggle in the world.

Each Communist party is free to apply principles of Marxism Leninism and socialism in its country, but it cannot depart from these principles. . . . Lenin said: 'Each man must choose between joining our side or the other side. Any attempt to avoid taking sides in this issue must end in fiasco.'

Source: *Pravda,* September 25, 1968; translated by Novosti, Soviet Press Agency.

appeal, the Council dispatched an observation group to ensure that no infiltration of fighters or arms was taking place across Lebanon's borders.[11] The group reported to the Council that there had been no massive infiltration and that most of the combatants were Lebanese.

The United States decided to intervene in Lebanon in response to a coup in Iraq, which it saw as being promoted by the United Arab Republic (the union of Syria and Egypt from 1958 to 1961). The coup and the events in Lebanon came, in American eyes, to represent parts of a plot to drive Western influence out of the Middle East. In response, the United States advised the Security Council that it was sending troops to Lebanon in response to an invitation by President Chamoun. This led to a Security Council debate during which two draft resolutions were tabled but vetoed by the United States. Debate in the Council focused on the issues of self-defense and intervention by invitation. The Americans supported their decision to intervene by claiming that they had acted to preserve Lebanon's territorial integrity and independence and to protect the many American citizens resident in Lebanon.[12] They also argued that their goal was "to exert a calming psychological influence that would enable the Lebanese . . . to set their own house in order."[13] This was consistent with the actions of U.S. forces once they had landed in Lebanon, where they avoided involvement with rebel militias and, instead, helped to maintain the status quo.[14] The American insistence that its intervention was also to secure the safety of American citizens resident in Lebanon—which would generally be considered a claim to self-defense—clouded what was otherwise a relatively clear-cut example of intervention by invitation during domestic disorder.

The United Arab Republic disputed Lebanon's claim of outside intervention in its affairs. The Soviet Union went further and argued that since the Security Council had become seized of the matter, the United States was acting in violation of Article 51 of the Charter. Article 51 confirms the right of collective self-defense "until the Security Council has taken measures necessary to maintain international peace and security." Other Council members expressed concern that there was no suggestion in the Lebanese submission or any independent evidence that an armed attack had occurred, as would be required for action to be taken under Article 51.

In response, the United States claimed that its actions were justified until the Security Council had taken "sufficient" steps to maintain international peace and security in the crisis and that Resolution 128, setting up the Observer Group, did not go far enough. Ultimately, given the stalemate between the United States and the Soviet Union, the matter was referred to the UN General Assembly, and, by Resolution 1237 (ES-III) of August 7, 1958, the American position was endorsed unanimously.

U.S. Marines patrolling the streets of Beirut, Lebanon, 1958. Courtesy of US Foreign Policy in Perspective.

Widespread acceptance of the legitimacy of the request of the Lebanese Government for assistance added legitimacy to the American claim of intervention by invitation. As such, the United States' intervention in Lebanon provides a useful yardstick against which other interventions, including that in the Dominican Republic in 1965, the 1966–89 civil war in Chad, the 1958 Soviet invasion of Czechoslovakia, and the 1979 Soviet intervention in Afghanistan can be measured.

Document B relates to the invasion of Czechoslovakia in August 1968 by approximately 600,000 troops from the Soviet Union, East Germany, Bulgaria, Hungary, and Poland. This followed the election of Alexander Dubcek as First Secretary of the Czechoslovak Communist Party and the consequent adoption of a variety of reforms, including the abolition of censorship and a relaxation of rules preventing public criticism of the government. These changes suggested a move away from one-party rule and a reorientation of the country toward the West. This provides an interesting contrast to the intervention by invitation with which Document A was concerned, because the invasion provoked widespread opposition around the world, including among governments and people who might otherwise be regarded as sympathetic to the Soviet Union.

This document, a Soviet statement on the invasion, provided a series of arguments to explain and justify the invasion. It was directed to supporters of the Soviet Union in Eastern and Western Europe and in the developing world. The Soviet Union claimed that the invading forces had been invited in to meet a threat from counter-revolutionary forces in collusion with international opponents of socialism and that the developments in Czechoslovakia threatened the vital interests of the Soviet Union and its allies as well as European peace. The invasion was, TASS declared, an example of collective self-defense and self-help, intended to preserve the socialist revolutions that had taken place in Eastern Europe. A similar argument has been used by the United States over the years to justify its own interventions in other States. During the Vietnam War, for example, Secretary of State Dean Rusk claimed that the "United States cannot be secure until the total international environment is ideologically safe."[15]

The Soviet Union was forced to modify its arguments in the light of international criticism and in the face of the persistent refusal of Czechoslovak authorities, including the National Assembly, to support the claim that the invading forces had been invited to intervene. The Czechoslovak Foreign Ministry specifically rejected the Soviet claim in a letter to the UN Security Council. The invasion was submitted to the Security Council. During the debate, the Soviet Union concentrated on the general argument that it was acting in self-defense. It supported this claim with reference to the Brezhnev Doctrine, which asserted the right of socialist States to intervene in other socialist States in order to resist threats to socialism. The Soviet arguments, however, were received with considerable skepticism, and a Security Council resolution was drafted that would have affirmed the sovereign and political independence and territorial integrity of Czechoslovakia, condemned the armed intervention of the Warsaw Pact, and called for the immediate withdrawal of foreign forces.[16] The draft described the invasion as a violation of the UN Charter. Such was the concern felt by Council members that not even the nonaligned members of the Council would support the Soviet Union, and it was only the resort to the veto by the Soviet Union that prevented adoption of the resolution.

FURTHER READING

Epstein, Leon D. "Partisan Foreign Policy: Britain in the Suez Crisis." *World Politics* 12, no. 3 (1960): 201–224.

Fisher, Eugene M., and M. Cherif Bassiouni. *Storm over the Arab World.* Chicago: Follett, 1972: 134–144.

Golan, Galia. *The Czechoslovak Reform Movement: Communism in Crisis, 1962–1968.* Cambridge, UK: Cambridge University Press, 1971.

Golan, Galia. *Reform Rule in Czechoslovakia: The Dubcek Era, 1968–1969.* Cambridge, UK: Cambridge University Press, 1973.

Gray, Christine. *International Law and the Use of Force.* 2nd ed. Chapter 3: "Invitation and Intervention: Civil Wars and the Use of Force." Oxford: Oxford University Press, 2004.

Heykal, Mohammed H. *Cutting the Lion's Tail: Suez Through Egyptian Eyes.* London: Andre Deutsch, 1986.

Kusin, Vladimir. *The Intellectual Origins of the Prague Spring; the Development of Reformist Ideas in Czechoslovakia, 1956–1967.* Cambridge, UK: Cambridge University Press, 1971.

Nutting, Anthony. *Nasser.* London: Constable, 1972.

Paul, David W. "Soviet Foreign Policy and the Invasion of Czechoslovakia." *International Studies Quarterly* 15, no. 2 (1971): 159–202.

Ronzitti, Natalino. *Rescuing Nationals Abroad Through Military Coercion and Intervention on Grounds of Humanity.* Dordrecht: Martinus Nijhoff, 1985.

Starr, Harvey, "A Collective Goods Analysis of the Warsaw Pact after Czechoslovakia." *International Organization* 28, no. 3 (1974): 521–523.

Is Humanitarian Intervention Compatible with Article 2(4)?

- ***Document:*** North Atlantic Treaty Organization (NATO) statement on the situation in Kosovo
- ***Date:*** April 24, 1999
- ***Where:*** NATO headquarters, Brussels
- ***Significance:*** This statement explained and justified NATO military action against the Federal Republic of Yugoslavia, which began on March 24, 1999. The statement made little attempt to align NATO's actions with the position of the United Nations Security Council or to place its actions within the UN framework but instead assigned a limited, supporting role to the United Nations.

DOCUMENT

Statement on Kosovo

Issued by the Heads of State and Government at the meeting of the North Atlantic Council in Washington, DC on 23rd and 24th April, 1999:

1. The crisis in Kosovo represents a fundamental challenge to the values for which NATO has stood since its foundation: democracy, human rights and the rule of law. It is the culmination of a deliberate policy of oppression, ethnic cleansing and violence pursued by the Belgrade regime under the direction of President Milosevic. We will not allow this campaign of terror to succeed. NATO is determined to prevail.
2. NATO's military action against the Federal Republic of Yugoslavia (FRY) supports the political aims of the international community, which were reaffirmed in recent statements by the UN Secretary-General and the European

Union: a peaceful, multi-ethnic and democratic Kosovo where all its people can live in security and enjoy universal human rights and freedoms on an equal basis.

3. Our military actions are directed not at the Serb people but at the policies of the regime in Belgrade, which has repeatedly rejected all efforts to solve the crisis peacefully. President Milosevic must:
   - Ensure a verifiable stop to all military action and the immediate ending of violence and repression in Kosovo;
   - Withdraw from Kosovo his military, police and paramilitary forces;
   - Agree to the stationing in Kosovo of an international military presence;
   - Agree to the unconditional and safe return of all refugees and displaced persons, and unhindered access to them by humanitarian aid organisations; and
   - Provide credible assurance of his willingness to work for the establishment of a political framework agreement based on the Rambouillet accords.
4. There can be no compromise on these conditions. As long as Belgrade fails to meet the legitimate demands of the international community and continues to inflict immense human suffering, Alliance air operations against the Yugoslav war machine will continue. We hold President Milosevic and the Belgrade leadership responsible for the safety of all Kosovar citizens. We will fulfil our promise to the Kosovar people that they can return to their homes and live in peace and security.
5. We are intensifying NATO's military actions to increase the pressure on Belgrade. Allied governments are putting in place additional measures to tighten the constraints on the Belgrade regime. These include intensified implementation of economic sanctions, and an embargo on petroleum products on which we welcome the EU lead. We have directed our Defence Ministers to determine ways that NATO can contribute to halting the delivery of war material including by launching maritime operations, taking into account the possible consequences on Montenegro.
6. NATO is prepared to suspend its air strikes once Belgrade has unequivocally accepted the above mentioned conditions and demonstrably begun to withdraw its forces from Kosovo according to a precise and rapid timetable. This could follow the passage of a United Nations Security Council resolution, which we will seek, requiring the withdrawal of Serb forces and the demilitarisation of Kosovo and encompassing the deployment of an international military force to safeguard the swift return of all refugees and displaced persons as well as the establishment of an international provisional administration of Kosovo under which its people can enjoy substantial autonomy within the FRY. NATO remains ready to form the core of such an international military force. It would be multinational in character with contributions from non-NATO countries.
7. Russia has a particular responsibility in the United Nations and an important role to play in the search for a solution to the conflict in Kosovo. Such a solution must be based on the conditions of the international community as laid out above. President Milosevic's offers to date do not meet this test. We want to work constructively with Russia, in the spirit of the Founding Act.

8. The long-planned, unrestrained and continuing assault by Yugoslav military, police and paramilitary forces on Kosovars and the repression directed against other minorities of the FRY are aggravating the already massive humanitarian catastrophe. This threatens to destabilise the surrounding region.
9. NATO, its members and its Partners have responded to the humanitarian emergency and are intensifying their refugee and humanitarian relief operations in close cooperation with the UNHCR, the lead agency in this field, and with other relevant organisations. We will continue our assistance as long as necessary. NATO forces are making a major contribution to this task.
10. We pay tribute to the servicemen and women of NATO whose courage and dedication are ensuring the success of our military and humanitarian operations.
11. Atrocities against the people of Kosovo by FRY military, police and paramilitary forces represent a flagrant violation of international law. Our governments will co-operate with the International Criminal Tribunal for the former Yugoslavia (ICTY) to support investigation of all those, including at the highest levels, responsible for war crimes and crimes against humanity. NATO will support the ICTY in its efforts to secure relevant information. There can be no lasting peace without justice.
12. We acknowledge and welcome the courageous support that states in the region are providing to our efforts in Kosovo. The former Yugoslav Republic of Macedonia and Albania have played a particularly important role, not least in accepting hundreds of thousands of refugees from Kosovo. The states in the region are bearing substantial economic and social burdens stemming from the current conflict.
13. We will not tolerate threats by the Belgrade regime to the security of its neighbours. We will respond to such challenges by Belgrade to its neighbours resulting from the presence of NATO forces or their activities on their territory during this crisis.
14. We reaffirm our support for the territorial integrity and sovereignty of all countries in the region.
15. We reaffirm our strong support for the democratically elected government of Montenegro. Any move by Belgrade to undermine the government of President Djukanovic will have grave consequences. FRY forces should leave the demilitarised zone of Prevlaka immediately.
16. The objective of a free, prosperous, open and economically integrated Southeast Europe cannot be fully assured until the FRY embarks upon the transition to democracy. Accordingly, we express our support for the objective of a democratic FRY which protects the rights of all minorities, including those in Vojvodina and Sandjak, and promise to work for such change through and beyond the current conflict.
17. It is our aim to make stability in Southeast Europe a priority of our transatlantic agenda. Our governments will co-operate urgently through NATO as well as through the OSCE, and for those of us which are members, the European Union, to support the nations of Southeast Europe in forging a

better future for their region—one based upon democracy, justice, economic integration, and security co-operation.

SOURCE: http://www.nato.int/docu/pr/1999/p99-062e.htm. *Courtesy of NATO.*

ANALYSIS

The North Atlantic Treaty Organization (NATO) bombing of Yugoslavia on March 23, 1999, raised questions about the legality of regional organizations taking military action without specific UN Security Council authorization and about the compatibility of so-called humanitarian intervention with Article 2(4) of the UN Charter. In the above statement, NATO focused on humanitarian aspects of the crisis and claimed that its actions were consistent with the political aims of the international community. This and other statements by NATO and some NATO members have been interpreted by observers as indicating that the Organization's action was based on the principle of humanitarian intervention—that is, the use of force to intervene in a State in response to a humanitarian emergency.

The UN Charter makes no explicit mention of intervention for this purpose, and a strict interpretation of Article 2(4) would therefore suggest that the use of force, even for humanitarian protection purposes, is prohibited. During the Security Council debate on March 26, 1999, the United Kingdom argued that "in the current circumstances, military intervention was justified as an exceptional measure to prevent an overwhelming humanitarian catastrophe."[17] In its submission to a subsequent hearing before the International Court of Justice in a Case on the legality of the attacks, Belgium drew on the narrow interpretation of Article 2(4) to argue that the intervention was

> not an intervention directed against the territorial integrity or the independence of the Republic of Yugoslavia. It is an armed, humanitarian intervention to rescue a population in danger, in deep distress. For this reason the Kingdom of Belgium takes the view that this is an armed humanitarian intervention, compatible with Article 2, paragraph 4, of the Charter, which covers only intervention against the territorial integrity or political independence of a State.[18]

There is widespread agreement that a humanitarian emergency can constitute a threat to international peace and security, thereby paving the way for Security Council involvement in civil wars and other ostensibly domestic issues under Chapter VII of the Charter. This has been made clear in several Security Council resolutions, including Resolution 794 (1992) on the situation in Somalia. In that resolution the Council determined that "the magnitude of the human tragedy caused by the conflict in Somalia, further exacerbated by the obstacles being created to the distribution of humanitarian assistance[,] constitutes a threat to international peace and security." There is also acceptance of the practice of the Security Council of "contracting out" the task of enforcing its resolutions. This could extend to individual countries, coalitions of countries, such as in the Kuwait crisis of 1990–1991, and regional organizations, the latter being specifically allowed for in Article 53 of the Charter.

In this case, however, there had been no explicit authorization by the Security Council. The NATO action was conducted in the context of Security Council resolutions 1199 and 1203, which had defined the Yugoslav Government's assault on Kosovo as a threat to peace under Chapter VII of the Charter. The resolutions had not approved the use of force, instead declaring that the Council would "consider further action and additional measures to maintain or restore peace and stability in the region."[19] In the course of Security Council debate, however, it became clear that Russia and China would resist any additional measures being extended to include military action.[20] This left the Council stalemated, and in response, the United States bypassed the Security Council, working through NATO to take action against Belgrade. In doing so, the members of NATO exposed themselves to accusations of having violated UN Charter Articles 2(4), 2(7), and 53.

The problem for advocates of humanitarian intervention not authorized by the Security Council is that there is no evidence of consistent State practice to support their view that it is compatible with international law. Moreover, if there had been pre-Charter customary law in support of humanitarian intervention, it arguably did not survive the entry into force of the United Nations Charter. Most of the interventions that might have been described as humanitarian intervention—India in East Pakistan (Bangladesh; 1971), Vietnam in Cambodia (Kampuchea; 1978), and Tanzania in Uganda (1979)—were at the time justified in terms of self-defense and, with the exception of Tanzania, condemned by the United Nations. In the Security Council debate on Vietnam's invasion of Kampuchea, the British delegate stated: "Whatever is said about human rights in Kampuchea, it cannot excuse Vietnam, whose own human rights record is deplorable, for violating the territorial integrity of Democratic Kampuchea." Australia's representative declared that it could not accept "that the internal policies of any government, no matter how reprehensible" could "justify a military attack on it by another government."[21]

It is notable that in NATO's case, the United States and France avoided reference to humanitarian intervention, claiming instead that they were implementing

DID YOU KNOW?

Extract from a Debate on Kosovo in the UN Security Council.

Mr Lavrov (Russian Federation): The Russian Federation is profoundly outraged at the use by the North Atlantic Treaty Organization (NATO) of military force against the Federal Republic of Yugoslavia. . . .

Those who are involved in this unilateral use of force against the sovereign Federal Republic of Yugoslavia—carried out in violation of the Charter of the United Nations and without the authorization of the Security Council—must realize the heavy responsibility they bear for subverting the Charter and other norms of international law and for attempting to establish in the world, *de facto,* the primacy of force and unilateral diktat.

The members of NATO are not entitled to decide the fate of other sovereign and independent States. . . .

Attempts to justify the NATO strikes with arguments about preventing a humanitarian catastrophe in Kosovo are completely untenable. Not only are these attempts in no way based on the Charter or other generally recognized rules of international law, but the unilateral use of force will lead precisely to a situation with truly devastating humanitarian consequences. Moreover, by the terms of the definition of aggression adopted by the General Assembly in 1974,

"No consideration of whatever nature, whether political, economic, military or otherwise, may serve as a justification for aggression". *(General Assembly resolution 3314 (XXIX), annex, article 5, para. 1)*

Source: United Nations Security Council 3988th meeting, March 24, 1999, S/PV.3988, pp. 2–3.

Kosovar refugees fleeing their homeland. [Blace area, the former Yugoslav Republic of Macedonia], March 1, 1999. Courtesy of R. LeMoyne, UN Photo.

Security Council resolutions under Chapter VII. Article 53 of the UN Charter allows for regional organizations to enforce Security Council decisions. But the article also specifically states that "no enforcement action shall be taken under regional arrangements or by regional agencies without the authorization of the Security Council." In this instance there was an attempt to claim implied authorization of the Council for military action, but, given the opposition of two permanent members of the Council, there was little support for this assertion. The idea of "implied authorization" by the Security Council had first emerged when the United States and Britain had sought a legal basis for the exclusion zones they had created in the south and north of Iraq in 1991 and for subsequent attacks on Iraq. The notion of implied authorization had met with some resistance at that time, but nothing as intense as the reaction when the United States and United Kingdom attempted to raise it again in 1998 in relation to Kosovo. Council members insisted that authorization for the use of force be granted in advance and expressed specifically in clear and precise terms.

A final line of argument pursued by NATO and its members was that the action might have been illegal in the strict sense of the word but that it was, nevertheless, legitimate and reflected public opinion. While this may have been correct with regard to opinion in the West, the attitude in other parts of the world was less sympathetic, and it is of note that the NATO members did not seek UN General Assembly endorsement, for example, through a Uniting for Peace resolution, which might have given some substance to such a claim.

FURTHER READING

Bhuta, Nehal. "'Paved with Good Intentions'—Humanitarian War, the New Interventionism and Legal Regulation of the Use of Force." *Melbourne University Law Review* 28 (2001): 843–858.

Falk, Richard A. "Kosovo, World Order and the Future of International Law." *American Journal of International Law* 93, no. 4 (1999): 847–857.

Guicherd, Catherine. "International Law and the War in Kosovo." *Survival* 41, no. 2 (1999): 19–33.

Murphy, Sean D. *Humanitarian Intervention: the United Nations in an Evolving World Order*. Philadelphia: University of Pennsylvania Press, 1996.

Ronzitti, Natalino. "Lessons of International Law from NATO's Armed Intervention Against the Federal Republic of Yugoslavia." *International Spectator* XXXIV, no. 3 (1999): 45–54.

Ronzitti, Natalino. *Rescuing Nationals Abroad Through Military Coercion and Intervention on Grounds of Humanity*. Dordrecht: Martinus Nijhoff, 1985.

What Is the Status in International Law of the Responsibility to Protect?

- ***Document:*** Extracts from *The Responsibility to Protect: Report of the International Commission on Intervention and State Sovereignty*, Synopsis, pp. XI–XIII
- ***Date:*** December 2001
- ***Where:*** Ottawa, Canada
- ***Significance:*** A major attempt to provide a legal and theoretical basis for the idea of humanitarian intervention.

DOCUMENT

The Responsibility to Protect: Core Principles

Synopsis

(1) BASIC PRINCIPLES

A. State sovereignty implies responsibility, and the primary responsibility for the protection of its people lies with the state itself.

B. Where a population is suffering serious harm, as a result of internal war, insurgency, repression or state failure, and the state in question is unwilling or unable to halt or avert it, the principle of non-intervention yields to the international responsibility to protect.

(2) FOUNDATIONS

The foundations of the responsibility to protect, as a guiding principle for the international community of states, lie in:

A. obligations inherent in the concept of sovereignty;
B. the responsibility of the Security Council, under Article 24 of the UN Charter, for the maintenance of international peace and security;
C. specific legal obligations under human rights and human protection declarations, covenants and treaties, international humanitarian law and national law;
D. the developing practice of states, regional organizations and the Security Council itself.

(3) Elements

The responsibility to protect embraces three specific responsibilities:

A. **The responsibility to prevent:** to address both the root causes and direct causes of internal conflict and other man-made crises putting populations at risk.
B. **The responsibility to react:** to respond to situations of compelling human need with appropriate measures, which may include coercive measures like sanctions and international prosecution, and in extreme cases military intervention.
C. **The responsibility to rebuild:** to provide, particularly after a military intervention, full assistance with recovery, reconstruction and reconciliation, addressing the causes of the harm the intervention was designed to halt or avert.

(4) Priorities

A. **Prevention is the single most important dimension of the responsibility to protect:** prevention options should always be exhausted before intervention is contemplated, and more commitment and resources must be devoted to it.
B. The exercise of the responsibility to both prevent and react should always involve less intrusive and coercive measures being considered before more coercive and intrusive ones are applied.

The Responsibility to Protect: Principles for Military Intervention

(1) The Just Cause Threshold

Military intervention for human protection purposes is an exceptional and extraordinary measure. To be warranted, there must be serious and irreparable harm occurring to human beings, or imminently likely to occur, of the following kind:

A. large scale loss of life, actual or apprehended, with genocidal intent or not, which is the product either of deliberate state action, or state neglect or inability to act, or a failed state situation; or
B. large scale 'ethnic cleansing', actual or apprehended, whether carried out by killing, forced expulsion, acts of terror or rape.

(2) THE PRECAUTIONARY PRINCIPLES

A. **Right intention:** The primary purpose of the intervention, whatever other motives intervening states may have, must be to halt or avert human suffering. Right intention is better assured with multilateral operations, clearly supported by regional opinion and the victims concerned.
B. **Last resort:** Military intervention can only be justified when every non-military option for the prevention or peaceful resolution of the crisis has been explored, with reasonable grounds for believing lesser measures would not have succeeded.
C. **Proportional means:** The scale, duration and intensity of the planned military intervention should be the minimum necessary to secure the defined human protection objective.
D. **Reasonable prospects:** There must be a reasonable chance of success in halting or averting the suffering which has justified the intervention, with the consequences of action not likely to be worse than the consequences of inaction.

(3) RIGHT AUTHORITY

A. There is no better or more appropriate body than the United Nations Security Council to authorize military intervention for human protection purposes. The task is not to find alternatives to the Security Council as a source of authority, but to make the Security Council work better than it has.
B. Security Council authorization should in all cases be sought prior to any military intervention action being carried out. Those calling for an intervention should formally request such authorization, or have the Council raise the matter on its own initiative, or have the Secretary-General raise it under Article 99 of the UN Charter.
C. The Security Council should deal promptly with any request for authority to intervene where there are allegations of large scale loss of human life or ethnic cleansing. It should in this context seek adequate verification of facts or conditions on the ground that might support a military intervention.
D. The Permanent Five members of the Security Council should agree not to apply their veto power, in matters where their vital state interests are not involved, to obstruct the passage of resolutions authorizing military intervention for human protection purposes for which there is otherwise majority support.
E. If the Security Council rejects a proposal or fails to deal with it in a reasonable time, alternative options are:
   I. consideration of the matter by the General Assembly in Emergency Special Session under the "Uniting for Peace" procedure; and
   II. action within area of jurisdiction by regional or sub-regional organizations under Chapter VIII of the Charter, subject to their seeking subsequent authorization from the Security Council.

F. The Security Council should take into account in all its deliberations that, if it fails to discharge its responsibility to protect in conscience-shocking situations crying out for action, concerned states may not rule out other means to meet the gravity and urgency of that situation—and that the stature and credibility of the United Nations may suffer thereby.

(4) OPERATIONAL PRINCIPLES

A. Clear objectives; clear and unambiguous mandate at all times; and resources to match.
B. Common military approach among involved partners; unity of command; clear and unequivocal communications and chain of command.
C. Acceptance of limitations, incrementalism and gradualism in the application of force, the objective being protection of a population, not defeat of a state.
D. Rules of engagement which fit the operational concept; are precise; reflect the principle of proportionality; and involve total adherence to international humanitarian law.
E. Acceptance that force protection cannot become the principal objective.
F. Maximum possible coordination with humanitarian organizations."

SOURCE: *The Responsibility to Protect: Report of the International Commission on Intervention and State Sovereignty*, International Development Research Centre, Ottawa, 2001, pp. XI–XIII. http://www.iciss.ca/report-en.asp.

ANALYSIS

The response of the international community to gross violations of human rights as occurred, for example, in Kampuchea and Rwanda, has proven to be one of the most difficult and divisive issues facing international law. Western publics, in particular, have been shocked into demanding that governments not allow such practices to continue. In other parts of the world, however, people are often suspicious of the motives of the powerful Western States that are most inclined to intervene, ostensibly in the name of human rights. Still others, considering the experience of situations such as Kosovo and Haiti, are concerned that with the best will in the world, outside intervention simply does not work in the absence of almost universal support and commitment and results in political failure and stalemate, despite initial military success. Nearly ten years after the NATO intervention in the Balkans, a report to the European Union warned that the region threatened to become a "marginalized black hole".[22]

Nevertheless, there have been serious attempts to provide a legal framework for intervention to remedy a gross violation of human rights when the Security Council is unable or unwilling to take sufficient action, as was the case in relation to Rwanda, Kosovo, and Darfur. General Assembly debates on humanitarian intervention in the wake of the Kosovo intervention served only to highlight the oppositional perspectives of, on the one hand, those countries that could imagine their being the subject of a possible "humanitarian intervention" and, on the other, governments whose publics were demanding that their governments no longer permit large-scale human rights atrocities to occur without response. In an attempt to move beyond that stalemate, the Government of Canada, on the initiative of then Foreign Minister Lloyd Axworthy, with funding from several U.S. foundations and the UK and Swiss Governments, established the International Commission on Intervention and State Sovereignty.

The Commission decided to move away from the by-now well-rehearsed legal and political issues surrounding humanitarian intervention and to advocate the concept of a "responsibility to protect." The concept of "humanitarian intervention" had juxtaposed humanitarian concerns with a term closely associated with coercive military action, whereas the new term was intended to encourage thinking of sovereignty in terms of responsibilities, not simply control. The concept had already been used by scholars Francis Deng and Roberta Cohen and was here being given fuller formulation.[23] While a State has primary responsibility to protect the people within its territory, if that State is unable or unwilling to do so, the international community must step in to meet that responsibility. As summarized in this document, the Commission developed the principle of the responsibility to protect to include three separate responsibilities: the responsibility to prevent, the responsibility to react, and the responsibility to rebuild. The use of coercive military force is only the last resort in meeting the second of these responsibilities.

The Responsibility to Protect accords a central role to the UN Security Council, stressing that the "task is not to find alternatives to the Security Council as a source of authority, but to make the Security Council work better than it has." Should the Security Council fail to deal promptly with any request for authority to intervene where there are allegations of large-scale loss of human life or ethnic cleansing, the document provides recourse to the General Assembly under the Uniting for Peace mechanism and action by regional or subregional organizations under Chapter VIII of the Charter, subject to their seeking subsequent authorization from the Security Council. Significantly, however, the drafters of the document did not rule out other means to meet the gravity and urgency of a situation should all other avenues be blocked. In so doing, *The Responsibility to Protect* is arguably placing a small number of States above the international legal structure designed to reduce the resort to force among States and potentially ignoring the political considerations that might have led to resistance to action by the Security Council or the General Assembly.

The Responsibility to Protect appeared to receive endorsement from heads of state and government at the 2005 World Summit. The Outcome Document stated:

> Each individual State has the responsibility to protect its populations from genocide, war crimes, ethnic cleansing and crimes against humanity. The responsibility entails the prevention of such crimes, including their incitement. . . . The international community, through the United Nations, also has the responsibility to use appropriate diplomatic, humanitarian and other peaceful means . . . to help to protect populations.[24]

The Responsibility to Protect is a political rather than a legal norm, but many of its advocates clearly hope that it may in time evolve into a principle of international law. Louise Arbour, a former UN High Commissioner for Human Rights and President of the International Crisis Group, for example, has downplayed its novelty and emphasized that, as least so far as genocide is concerned, "the heart of the responsibility to protect doctrine already rests upon an undisputed obligation of international law: the prevention and punishment of genocide."[25] Gareth Evans, a former Australian Foreign Minister and cochair of the International Commission on Intervention and State Sovereignty, concluded in 2004:

> While there is not yet a sufficiently strong basis to claim the emergence, in all of this, of something as formal as a new principle of customary international law, growing state and regional organization practice as well as Security Council precedent do suggest an emerging norm, or guiding principle, which can usefully be described, in the Commission's language, as 'the responsibility to protect'.[26]

The well-intentioned efforts of the drafters of *The Responsibility to Protect* highlight one of the great dilemmas of international law. It is perhaps inevitable that there will continue to be instances of large numbers of people experiencing serious harm around the world. These threats to human security will result from government negligence or deliberate policy and will range from human rights abuses as serious as those inflicted by the Pol Pot, Idi Amin, and Robert Mugabe regimes to,

Dennis Byron, President of the International Criminal Tribunal for Rwanda, addresses a Security Council meeting on the work of the Tribunal. United Nations, New York, December 12, 2008. Courtesy of Ryan Brown, UN Photo.

DID YOU KNOW?

"Responsibility to Protect—the Implications of Inaction," pp. 54–55.

6.36 Interventions by ad hoc coalitions (or, even more, individual States) acting without the approval of the Security Council, or the General Assembly, or a regional or sub-regional grouping of which the target State is a member, do not—it would be an understatement to say—find wide favour. Even those countries involved in the Kosovo intervention, and prepared to passionately defend its legitimacy by reference to all the threshold and precautionary criteria we have identified in this report, for the most part acknowledge its highly exceptional character, and express the view that it would have been much preferable to have secured the Security Council's—or failing that the General Assembly's—endorsement. One view that has some currency is that an *ex post facto* authorization, of the kind that has occurred for the African regional instances mentioned above, might conceivably have been obtained in the Kosovo and Rwanda cases, and may offer a way out of the dilemma should any such case occur again in the future.

6.37 As a matter of political reality, it would be impossible to find consensus, in the Commission's view, around any set of proposals for military intervention which acknowledged the validity of any intervention not authorized by the Security Council or General Assembly. But that may still leave circumstances when the Security Council fails to discharge what this Commission would regard as its responsibility to protect, in a conscience-shocking situation crying out for action. It is a real question in these circumstances where lies the most harm: in the damage to international order if the Security Council is bypassed or in the damage to that order if human beings are slaughtered while the Security Council stands by.

increasingly, natural disasters such as that experienced in Burma as a result of Cyclone Nargis. There will be a persistent demand for the international community to develop a coherent and consistent response to such instances, but the possibility of success in this area would appear to be remote. Until now, the response to humanitarian disasters has largely been a function of political considerations. For example, the West ultimately acted firmly to address the problems of the disintegrating Yugoslavia, including Kosovo, but ignored the Rwandan genocide, a human rights tragedy on an even larger scale. There has never been any suggestion that the international community would take strong action against Russia over its suppression of Chechen separatism or its 2008 invasion of Georgia or against China over its treatment of Tibet—all instances that have prompted accusations of serious human rights violations.

It would appear that the approach whereby policy considerations will override legal considerations in cases of humanitarian emergencies is likely to remain dominant. States will consciously ignore the failure of the United Nations to endorse their actions and violate legal provisions designed to limit the use of force to end humanitarian crises in the expectation that the violation will be tolerated by the rest of the international community where the intervention is genuinely justifiable on humanitarian and ethical grounds. They might even seek retrospective endorsement by the United Nations. Some writers regard this as the best possible outcome. In opposing formalization of the practice of humanitarian intervention, Sean D. Murphy, for example, suggested that "developing criteria (to legitimize humanitarian intervention outside the Security Council's mandate) might serve less to constrain unilateral humanitarian intervention and more to provide a pretext for abusive intervention."[27]

FURTHER READING

Arbour, Louise. "The Responsibility to Protect as a Duty of Care in International Law and Practice." *Review of International Studies* 34 (2008): 445–458.

Bellamy, Alex J. "Whither the Responsibility to Protect? Humanitarian Intervention and the 2005 World Summit." *Ethics & International Affairs* 20, no. 2 (2006): 143–169.

Evans, Gareth. "The Responsibility to Protect: An Idea Whose Time Has Come . . . and Gone?" *International Relations* 22, no. 3 (2008): 283–298.

Gazzini, Tarcisio. *The Changing Rules on the Use of Force in International Law*. Manchester: Juris, 2005.

Hilpold, Peter. "Humanitarian Intervention: Is There a Need for a Legal Reappraisal?" *European Journal of International Law* 12, no. 3 (2001): 437–467.

Murphy, Sean D. *Humanitarian Intervention: The United Nations in an Evolving World Order*. Philadelphia: University of Pennsylvania Press, 1996.

Nuclear Weapons: The Ultimate Challenge to the Charter Framework

- ***Document:*** United Nations General Assembly Resolution 1(I), Establishment of a Commission to deal with the problems raised by the discovery of atomic energy—the United Nations Atomic Energy Commission
- ***Date:*** January 24, 1946
- ***Where:*** Central Hall, Westminster, London
- ***Significance:*** The development of weapons of mass destruction, especially nuclear, has been put forward as a reason why the law relating to the use of force needs to be reassessed. This, the first resolution adopted by the General Assembly, represents early recognition by the international community of this challenge.

DOCUMENT

Resolved by the General Assembly of the United Nations to establish a Commission, with the composition and competence set out hereunder, to deal with the problems raised by the discovery of atomic energy and other related matters:

1. Establishment of the Commission

A Commission is hereby established by the General Assembly with the terms of reference set out under section 5 below.

2. Relations of the Commission with the Organs of the United Nations

(a) The Commission shall submit its reports and recommendations to the Security Council, and such reports shall be made public unless the Security Council, in the interest of peace and security, otherwise directs. In the appropriate cases the Security Council should transmit these reports to the General Assembly and the Members of the United Nations, as well as to the Economic and Social Council and other organs within the framework of the United Nations.

(b) In view of the Security Council's primary responsibility under the Charter of the United Nations for the maintenance of international peace and security, the Security Council shall issue instructions to the Commission in matters affecting security. On these matters, the Commission shall be accountable for its work to the Security Council.

3. Composition of the Commission

The Commission shall be composed of one representative from each of those states represented on the Security Council, and Canada, when that state is not a member of the Security Council. Each representative on the Commission may have such assistance as he may desire.

4. Rules of Procedure

The Commission shall have whatever staff it may deem necessary, and shall make recommendations for its rules of procedure to the Security Council, which shall approve them as a procedural matter.

5. Terms of Reference of the Commission

The Commission shall proceed with the utmost dispatch and enquire into all phases of the problem, and make such recommendations from time to time with respect to them as it finds possible. In particular, the Commission shall make specific proposals:

(a) for extending between all nations the exchange of basic scientific information for peaceful ends;
(b) for control of atomic energy to the extent necessary to ensure its use only for peaceful purposes;
(c) for the elimination from national armaments of atomic weapons and of all other major weapons adaptable to mass destruction;
(d) for effective safeguards by way of inspection and other means to protect complying states against the hazards of violations and evasions.

The work of the Commission should proceed by separate stages, the successful completion of each of which will develop the necessary confidence of the world before the next stage is undertaken.

The Commission shall not infringe upon the responsibilities of any organ of the United Nations, but should present recommendations for the consideration of those organs in the performance of their tasks under the terms of the United Nations Charter.

SOURCE: United Nations General Assembly Resolutions, First Session. http://daccessdds.un.org/doc/RESOLUTION/GEN/NR0/032/52/IMG/NR003252.pdf?OpenElement.

ANALYSIS

Albert Einstein once commented, "The unleashed power of the atom has changed everything save our modes of thinking, and we thus drift toward unparalleled catastrophe."[28] Einstein was highlighting the gap between our technical capabilities and our emotional and psychological ability to manage the technology we develop, specifically with regards to weaponry. International law has a long history of attempting to address this gap, going back to the Hague Conventions of 1899 and 1907. At that time it was becoming evident that our ability to kill and destroy was rising to a new level of effectiveness. The international community was in broad agreement about the need to control the use of mass-destructive weapons, in no small part because poison gas was available to most countries. With the advent of nuclear weapons, however, the situation changed significantly. The destructive power of these weapons was clearly greater than that of any other weapon ever devised, but the level of scientific, technological, and economic sophistication necessary to develop, deploy, and use nuclear weapons meant that they were beyond the capacity of all but the most developed States, and so there was less likelihood of a unanimous community decision to eliminate this form of weaponry.

International opinion has tended to support the idea that international law, including the UN Charter, does and should apply to nuclear weapons. The view has strengthened that the destructive power and the potential for proliferation of nuclear weapons means that they cannot be regarded as just another form of weaponry or just another threat to Article 2(4). Because of their likely impact, nuclear weapons potentially undermine any authority international law might possess in the area of the use of force, and they draw into question attempts to impose constraints and accountability on the way in which warfare is conducted. There was early recognition that, if international law is to continue to address the use of force in a meaningful way, it must deal specifically with the challenges posed by these weapons.

As seen in this document, the first resolution adopted by the United Nations General Assembly was addressed to this problem. Among other things, it established the Atomic Energy Commission with broad responsibility to examine issues related to the discovery of atomic energy. The Commission's mandate had a two-pronged focus. One was to prevent the use of atomic weapons—to ban them as an acceptable part of warfare. The second was to create the circumstances whereby atomic power might safely be exploited for peaceful purposes. Establishment of the Commission was a triumph for concerned elements in the United States, which had overcome the Truman administration's initial doubts and sought to build on the Acheson-Lilienthal Plan of March 1946. This proposed an Atomic Development Authority, the banning of atomic weapons, and the elimination of existing (i.e. American) atomic weapons. By mid-1946, however, U.S. policy changed with the presentation to the Commission of the Baruch Plan, which proposed that nuclear weapons be banned and U.S. weapons eliminated at the end of an extensive process of inspection to ensure compliance with the ban. This was seen by the Soviet Union as an attempt by the United States to consolidate its advantage in this area and resulted in a Cold War stalemate and the effective end of the Commission's work.

The demise of this initiative did not bring an end to international efforts to eliminate nuclear weapons. The two main foci of the Atomic Energy Commission—the elimination of atomic weapons and the development of peaceful atomic power—became the focus of subsequent international efforts. Central to the international law and politics of nuclear weapons since 1968 has been the Nuclear Non-Proliferation Treaty (NPT). On paper, the NPT is a significant attempt at reversing the reliance of the major powers on nuclear weapons and at reducing the attractiveness of the weapons to nonnuclear weapons States. It requires the five States in possession of nuclear weapons in 1968 to refrain from assisting other countries to develop nuclear weapons capabilities and to work among themselves toward complete nuclear disarmament. The treaty required non-nuclear-armed States to commit themselves not to attempt to develop a nuclear weapons capacity and to submit to inspections by the International Atomic Energy Agency. The treaty was nevertheless supportive of the peaceful use of nuclear energy by any State.

Since the NPT came into force there have been a few failures of the system, and there have been claims that the Treaty is no longer relevant. Israel, India, and Pakistan have nuclear weapons, and North Korea is suspected of having a rudimentary capability. Iran has been accused of planning to develop nuclear weapons, although the Iranian Government insists that it is only interested in peaceful nuclear energy, as is its entitlement under the NPT. The matter can, however, be viewed from the perspective of the concern expressed by U.S. President John F. Kennedy in 1960 that by 1964 there could be as many as twenty nuclear-armed States. Given that until now there have been only eight nuclear-armed States and that several countries, notably South Africa, have abandoned their nuclear arsenal, the Treaty could be said to have been a success, albeit qualified.

The NPT regime has come under increasing pressure. The fact that the NPT is unable to accommodate the latecomers to the nuclear weapons "club" (India, Israel, and Pakistan) and that countries including Iran and North Korea have sought to test the limits of the Treaty's support of nuclear energy for peaceful uses is of concern. Of equal concern has been the growing inclination of the nuclear powers recognized by the NPT (China, France, Russia, the United Kingdom, and the United States) to interpret somewhat liberally the spirit and the letter of the Treaty. None of the recognized nuclear powers has made any serious and sustained attempt to meet the requirement of article VI of the NPT to work toward complete nuclear disarmament. Indeed, in some cases, the nuclear powers could be accused of defying that provision. The development of smaller, tactical nuclear weapons may mean that nuclear weapons will become easier to use.

Doomsday Clock. Courtesy of Bulletin of the Atomic Scientists.

Article X (1) of the NPT states:

> **DID YOU KNOW?**
>
> **Key Extracts from the U.S. Nuclear Posture Review, January 2001**
>
> "Nuclear weapons play a critical role in the defence capabilities of the United States, its allies and friends. They provide credible military options to deter a wide range of threats, including WMD and large-scale conventional military force. These nuclear capabilities possess unique properties that give the United States options to hold at risk classes of targets [that are] important to achieve strategic and political objectives." (p. 7)
>
> "Greater flexibility is needed with respect to nuclear forces and planning than was the case during the Cold War. The assets most valued by the spectrum of potential adversaries in the new security environment may be diverse and, in some cases, US understanding of what an adversary values may evolve. Consequently, although the number of weapons needed to hold those assets at risk has declined, US nuclear forces still require the capability to hold at risk a wide range of target types. This capability is key to the role of nuclear forces in supporting an effective deterrence strategy relative to a broad spectrum of potential opponents under a variety of contingencies. Nuclear attack options that vary in scale, scope, and purpose will complement other military capabilities." (p. 7)
>
> "Missile defences are beginning to emerge as systems that can have an effect on the strategic and operational calculations of potential adversaries. They are now capable of providing active defence against short- to medium-range threats." (p. 11)
>
> US military forces themselves, including nuclear forces will now be used to "dissuade adversaries from undertaking military programs or operations that could threaten US interests or those of allies and friends." (p. 9)
>
> "A modern, responsive nuclear weapons sector of the infrastructure is indispensable, especially as the size of the operationally deployed nuclear arsenal is reduced." (pp. 10–11)

> Each Party shall in exercising its national sovereignty have the right to withdraw from the Treaty if it decides that extraordinary events, related to the subject matter of this Treaty, have jeopardized the supreme interests of its country. It shall give notice of such withdrawal to all other Parties to the Treaty and to the United Nations Security Council three months in advance. Such notice shall include a statement of the extraordinary events it regards as having jeopardized its supreme interests.[29]

This provision enables any member State intending to use such weapons to do so without violating the Treaty. North Korea relied on this clause when it announced its intention to withdraw from the NPT in 2003.

Some writers have maintained that the issues surrounding nuclear weapons—issues dealing with the ultimate survival of States—are too important to be subjected to international law and the implied involvement of third parties in matters of national security. Such writers argue that no State is going to subject its ultimate survival to the judgments of others. W. Michael Reisman and Myers S. McDougal, for example, have suggested that measures put forward as law relating to nuclear weapons are simply wishful thinking. Reisman asks whether it would be "more appropriate to infer certain shared expectations from the fact that these elites [in the major nuclear powers] are frenetically building, stocking and developing contingency plans for the use of these weapons?"[30] He suggests that such behavior indicates that there is no law that would make the use of nuclear weapons unlawful. In support of Reisman's argument, one can refer to the field manuals of the U.S. Army and Navy and to the U.S. Nuclear Posture Review.

Other writers assert that the use of nuclear weapons is addressed by international law and is already prohibited. There is more than one basis on which this argument can be built. Among the more frequently cited are the Nuremberg Principles, widely regarded as an authoritative statement of customary law as it relates to individual responsibility for war crimes. Article 6(b) of the Nuremberg Charter, which is based on those principles, defines a war crime as "wanton destruction of cities, towns or villages, or devastation not justified by military necessity." Another important basis for those arguing for the applicability of

DID YOU KNOW?

In History: Timeline of Nuclear Treaties

Date	The Treaty	Brief Name
1959	Antarctic Treaty.	
1963	Treaty Banning Nuclear Weapon Tests in the Atmosphere, in Outer Space and Under Water	Limited Test-Ban Treaty
1967	Treaty for the Prohibition of Nuclear Weapons in Latin America	Treaty of Tlatelolco
	Treaty on Principles Governing the Activities of States in the exploration and Use of Outer Space, Including the Moon and other Celestial Bodies	Outer Space Treaty
1968	Treaty on the Non-Proliferation of Nuclear Weapons	NPT
1972	End of first round of the Strategic Arms Limitation Talks	SALT I
	Treaty Between the United States of America and the Union of Soviet Socialist Republics on the Limitation of Anti-Ballistic Missile Systems	ABM Treaty
	Interim Agreement on Strategic Offensive ArmsTreaty.	SALT I
1974	Treaty Between the United States of America and the Union of Soviet Socialist Republics on the Limitation of Underground Nuclear Weapon Tests	TTBT
1976	Treaty Between the United States of America and the Union of Soviet Socialist Republics on Underground Nuclear Explosions for Peaceful Purposes.	PNET
1979	Treaty Between the United States of America and the Union of Soviet Socialist Republics on the Limitation of Strategic Offensive Arms, Together with Agreed Statements and Common Understandings Regarding the Treaty	SALT II
1985	South Pacific Nuclear-Free Zone Treaty	Treaty of Rarotonga
1987	Treaty Between the United States of America and the Union of Soviet Socialist Republics on the Elimination of Their Intermediate-Range and Shorter-Range Missiles.	INF Treaty
1991	Treaty Between the United States of America and the Union of Soviet Socialist Republics on the Reduction and Limitation of Strategic Offensive Arms	START I
1993	Treaty Between the United States of America and the Union of Soviet Socialist Republics on Further Reduction and Limitation of Strategic Offensive Arms	START II
1994	African Nuclear Weapon Free Zone Treaty	Pelinbada Treaty
2002	The Moscow Treaty on Strategic Offensive Reductions	SORT

Source: http://www.globalsecurity.org/wmd/library/policy/dod/npr.htm

Courtesy of the Office of the Deputy Assistant to the Secretary of Defense for Nuclear Matters

international humanitarian law to nuclear weapons is the "Martens Clause," which first appeared in the Hague Convention of 1899. The clause states:

> Until a more complete code of the laws of war is issued, the High Contracting Parties think it right to declare that in cases not included in the Regulations adopted by them, populations and belligerents remain under the protection and empire of the principles of international law, as they result from the usages established between civilized nations, from the laws of humanity and the requirements of the public conscience.[31]

Principles contained in The Hague and Geneva Conventions could therefore be said to apply to nuclear weapons.

On December 15, 1994, the UN General Assembly requested the International Court of Justice to deliver an advisory opinion on the question: "Is the threat or use of nuclear weapons in any circumstances permitted under international law?"[32] The majority Opinion found:

> The threat or use of nuclear weapons would generally be contrary to the rules of international law applicable in armed conflict, and in particular the principles and rules of humanitarian law.[33]

The Court stated that it could not "definitively [conclude] whether the threat or use of nuclear weapons would be lawful or unlawful in an extreme circumstance of self-defense, in which the very survival of a State would be at stake." The Martens Clause had formed an important part of submissions made to the Court, but, beyond the Court noting that the Clause was a rule of customary international law, it is not clear as to the extent to which it influenced the thinking of the judges. Despite the Court finding that there was no basis in customary or treaty law either to authorize or to prohibit specifically the threat or use of nuclear weapons, the Court stressed fundamental principles of international humanitarian law, including the prohibition of the use of weapons that are incapable of differentiating between civilian and military targets, describing such principles as "intransgressible principles of international customary law."[34] The Court stressed the legal obligation of the nuclear powers to pursue in good faith the objective of complete nuclear disarmament contained in the NPT.

This Advisory Opinion demonstrates the Court at its political best. The Court did not simply pander to the interests of the nuclear–weapon States, but neither did it try to force the hand of those States in

DID YOU KNOW?

In History: Excerpt from Farewell Address by U.S. President Harry Truman, January 15, 1953

Now, once in a while, I get a letter from some impatient person asking, why don't we get it over with? Why don't we issue an ultimatum, make all-out war, drop the atomic bomb?

For most Americans, the answer is quite simple: We are not made that way. We are a moral people. Peace is our goal, with justice and freedom. We cannot, of our own free will, violate the very principles that we are striving to defend. The whole purpose of what we are doing is to prevent World War III. Starting a war is no way to make peace.

But if anyone still thinks that just this once, bad means can bring good ends, then let me remind you of this: We are living in the eighth year of the atomic age. We are not the only nation that is learning to unleash the power of the atom. A third world war might dig the grave not only of our Communist opponents but also of our own society, our world as well as theirs.

Starting an atomic war is totally unthinkable for rational men.

Source: http://www.trumanlibrary.org/calendar/viewpapers.php?pid=2059

View from the top of the Red Cross Hospital in Hiroshima looking northwest. Frame buildings recently erected. 1945. Courtesy of U.S. Department of Defense.

terms of eliminating their nuclear weapons. In steering a middle line between the two positions, the Court could be interpreted as having responded to the political reality that nuclear weapon States would have been unlikely to eliminate their weapons even if the Court were to find them illegal, with concomitant damage to the Court's standing.

Notes

1. Tarcisio Gazzini, *The Changing Rules on the Use of Force in International Law* (Manchester, Juris, 2005), 122–123.
2. See for example, Louis Henkin, "The Reports of the Death of Article 2(4) Are Greatly Exaggerated," *American Journal of International Law* 65, no. 3 (1971): 544–548.
3. See for example, Thomas M. Franck, "Who Killed Article 2(4)? Or: Changing Norms Governing the Use of Force by States," *American Journal of International Law* 64, no. 4 (1970): 809–837, and Oscar Schachter, "In Defence of International Rules on the Use of Force," *University of Chicago Law Review* 53, no. 1 (1986): 113–146.

4. Bernard D. Meltzer, "A Note on Some Aspects of the Nuremberg Debate," *University of Chicago Law Review* 14, no. 3 (1947): 459.
5. "Corfu Channel Case," Summaries of Judgements, Judgement of April 9, 1949, International Court of Justice: 7. http://www.icj-cij.org/docket/files/1/1647.pdf.
6. Hector A. Munro, "The Case of the Corfu Minefield," *Modern Law Review* 10, no. 4 (1947): 363.
7. Christine Gray, *International Law and the Use of Force*, 2nd ed. (Oxford: Oxford University Press, 2004), 29.
8. Gray, *International Law and the Use of Force*, 30.
9. Ian Brownlie, *International Law and the Use of Force by States* (Oxford: Clarendon Press, 1963), 265–267.
10. Gray, *International Law and the Use of Force*, 72.
11. The UN Observation Group in Lebanon (UNOGIL)—Security Council Resolution 128, 13th session, 825th meeting, UN Doc. S/4023 (1958).
12. Franck, "Who Killed Article 2(4)?" 815.
13. Quoted in Christopher J. LeMon, "Unilateral Intervention by Invitation in Civil Wars: the Effective Control Test Tested," *NYU International Law and Politics* 35 (2003): 757.
14. Anthony Nutting, *Nasser* (London: Constable, 1972), 240.
15. Christopher Layne, "Kant or Cant: The Myth of Democratic Peace," in Andrew Linklater, ed., *International Relations: Critical Concepts in Political Science* (London and New York, Taylor and Francis, 2000), 988.
16. United Nations Security Council meeting, August 23, 1968. Doc. S/8761 and Add. 1.
17. United Nations Security Council Resolution 794 (1992), December 3, 1992, Somalia.
18. Submission by Belgium to the International Court of Justice, May 10, 1999. http://www.icj-cij.org/docket/files/105/4515.pdf.
19. United Nations Security Council Resolution 1199 (1998), September 23, 1988, Kosovo.
20. United Nations Security Council, 3989th meeting, March 26, 1999, p. 7. http://www.securitycouncilreport.org/atf/cf/%7B65BFCF9B-6D27-4E9C-8CD3-CF6E4FF96FF9%7D/kos%20SPV3989.pdf
21. Both statements are in Natalino Ronzitti, *Rescuing Nationals Abroad Through Military Coercion and Intervention on Grounds of Humanity* (Dordrecht: Martinus Nijhoff, 1985), 100–101.
22. Ian Traynor, "'Black hole' in the Balkans," *The Guardian*, April 14, 2005, http://www.guardian.co.uk/world/2005/apr/14/balkans.
23. Louise Arbour, "The Responsibility to Protect as a Duty of Care in International Law and Practice," *Review of International Studies* 34 (2008): 447.
24. United Nations General Assembly 60th session, Resolution adopted by the General Assembly 60/1. 2005, World Summit Outcome, October 24, 2005, paras. 138 and 139.
25. Arbour, "The Responsibility to Protect," 450.

26. Gareth Evans, "The Responsibility to Protect: Rethinking Humanitarian Intervention," Address by Gareth Evans, President of the International Crisis Group and Co-Chair of the International Commission on Intervention and State Sovereignty, to The American Society of International Law, 98th Annual Meeting, Panel on "Rethinking Collective Action," Washington DC, April 1, 2004. http://www.crisisgroup.org/home/index.cfm?l=1.
27. Sean D. Murphy, *Humanitarian Intervention: The United Nations in an Evolving World Order* (Philadelphia: University of Pennsylvania Press, 1996), 384.
28. Alice Calaprice, ed. *The Expanded Quotable Einstein* (Princeton, NJ: Princeton University Press, 2000), 184.
29. Treaty on the Non-Proliferation of Nuclear Weapons, 1968. http://www.iaea.org/Publications/Documents/Infcircs/Others/infcirc140.pdf.
30. W. Michael Reisman, "Nuclear Weapons in International Law," *New York Law School Journal of International and Comparative Law* 4 (1982–1983): 340.
31. Convention with Respect to the Laws of War on Land (Hague II), July 29, 1899.
32. Request for an Advisory Opinion from the ICJ on the Legality of the Threat or Use of Nuclear Weapons. Resolution 49/75 K, December 15, 1994. http://daccessdds.un.org/doc/UNDOC/GEN/N95/760/03/PDF/N9576003.pdf?OpenElement.
33. International Court of Justice, "Legality of the Threat or Use of Nuclear Weapons." Advisory Opinion of July 8, 1996, *ICJ Reports* (1996): 257, para. 105(2)(E).
34. International Court of Justice, "Legality of the Threat or Use of Nuclear Weapons," para. 79.

FURTHER READING

Boyle, Francis A. "The Relevance of International Law to the 'Paradox' of Nuclear Deterrence." *Northwestern University Law Review* 80, no. 6 (1986): 1407–1448.

Bugnion, Francois. "The International Committee of the Red Cross and Nuclear Weapons: from Hiroshima to the Dawn of the 21st Century." *International Review of the Red Cross* 87, no. 859 (2005): 511–524.

Granoff, Jonathan. "Nuclear Weapons, Ethics, Morals and Law." *Brigham Young University Law Review* (2000): 1413–1442.

Kaysen, Carl, Robert S. McNamara, and George W. Rathjens. "Nuclear Weapons after the Cold War." *Foreign Affairs* 70, no. 4 (1991): 95–110.

Lifton, Robert J., and Richard Falk. *Indefensible Weapons*. Toronto: Canadian Broadcasting Commission, 1982.

Los Alamos Study Group. http://www.lasg.org/legal.htm.

Mearsheimer, John J. "Nuclear Weapons and Deterrence in Europe." *International Security* 9, no. 3 (1984-1985): 19–46.

Miller, Arthur S., and Martin Feinrider. *Nuclear Weapons and Law*. Westport, CT, and London: Greenwood, 1984.

Reisman, W. Michael. "Nuclear Weapons in International Law." *New York Law School Journal of International and Comparative Law* 4 (1982–1983): 339–343.

Ticehurst, Rupert. "The Martens Clause and the Laws of Armed Conflict." *International Review of the Red Cross* 317 (April 30, 1997): 125–134.

Treaty on the Non-Proliferation of Nuclear Weapons (NPT Treaty). http://www.iaea.org/Publications/Documents/Treaties/npt.html.

Waltz, Kenneth. "The Spread of Nuclear Weapons: More May Be Better." *Adelphi Papers*. No. 171. London: International Institute for Strategic Studies (1981).

Weston, Burns H. "Nuclear Weapons versus International Law: Contextual Reassessment." *McGill Law Journal* 28 (1982–1983): 542–590.

5

THE RIGHT OF SELF-DEFENSE

Egyptian, Syrian, Omani, and Kuwaiti troops stand ready for review by King Fahd of Saudi Arabia as they take part in an assembly of international coalition forces during Operation Desert Storm in 1991. Courtesy of D. W. Holmes, U.S. Department of Defense.

OVERVIEW

In contemporary international law, self-defense constitutes one of the two exceptions to the general prohibition of the use of force in international relations. In contrast to the "collective security" exception—i.e., the authorization of force by the United Nations Security Council—self-defense is often referred to as a permissible "unilateral" use of force. The notion of self-defense has long been employed as a political and legal justification for the use of force. Indeed, even in cases where it was patently obvious that the use of force was illegal, States have invoked self-defense in attempts to justify military action. This chapter looks at the scope and content of the right of self-defense in detail. It traces the historical origins of the right of self-defense and examines its codification in the UN Charter. Covering the controversial notions of anticipatory and pre-emptive self-defense, the chapter also looks at collective self-defense, self-defense to protect nationals abroad, and the question as to whether nuclear weapons can be used in self-defense.

The *Caroline* Incident and the Customary Right of Self-Defense

- ***Document:*** Letter by the U.S. Secretary of State Daniel Webster addressed to the British Minister in Washington, Henry Fox
- ***Date:*** April 24, 1841
- ***Where:*** Washington, DC
- ***Significance:*** Webster's letter to Mr. Fox is regarded as the classical formulation of the requirements of the customary right of self-defense.

DOCUMENT

Mr Webster to Mr Fox:

The Undersigned has now to signify to Mr Fox that the Government of the United States has not changed the opinion which it has heretofore expressed to Her Majesty's Government, of the character of the act of destroying the *Caroline*. It does not think that that transaction can be justified by any reasonable application or construction of the right of self-defense under the laws of nations. It is admitted that a just right of self-defense attaches always to nations, as well as to individuals, and is equally necessary for the preservation of both. But the extent of this right is a question to be judged of by the circumstances of each particular case; and when its alleged exercise has led to the commission of hostile acts, within the territory of a power at peace, nothing less than a clear and absolute necessity can afford ground of justification. . . .

Under these circumstances, and under those immediately connected with the transaction itself, it will be for Her Majesty's Government to show, upon what state of facts, and what rules of national law, the destruction of the *Caroline* is to be defended. It will be for that Government to show a necessity of self-defense, instant, overwhelming, leaving no choice of means, and no moment for deliberation. It will be for it to show, also, that the local authorities of Canada, even supposing the necessity of the moment authorized them to enter the territories of the United States at all, did nothing unreasonable or excessive; since the act justified by the necessity of self-defense, must be limited by that necessity, and kept clearly within it.

It must be shown that admonition or remonstrance to the persons on board the *Caroline* was impracticable, or would have been unavailing; it must be shewn that daylight could not be waited for; that there could be no attempt at discrimination, between the innocent and the guilty; that it would not have been enough to seize and detain the vessel; but that there was a necessity, present and inevitable, for attacking her, in the darkness of the night, while moored to the shore, and while unarmed men were asleep on board, killing some, and wounding others, and then drawing her into the current, above the cataract, setting her on fire, and, careless to know whether there might not be in her the innocent with the guilty, or the living with the dead, committing her to a fate, which fills the imagination with horror. A necessity for all this, the Government of the United States cannot believe to have existed. . . .

SOURCE: Courtesy of the Avalon Project, Yale Law School Library. http://avalon.law.yale.edu/19th_century/br-1842d.asp.

ANALYSIS

Self-defense constitutes one of the two exceptions to the general prohibition of the use of force in contemporary international relations. It has a long history as political and legal justification for the resort to force by States and is incorporated in article 51 of the UN Charter. The notion of self-defense as a customary right, however, predates the adoption of UN Charter and finds its origins in a series of letters that were exchanged by the American and British governments in the aftermath of the *Caroline* incident. Of particular significance is U.S. Secretary of State Webster's formulation that it is for the "Government to show a necessity of self-defense, instant, overwhelming, leaving no choice of means, and no moment for deliberation." Webster's formulation is generally regarded to contain the classical requirements of the customary right of self-defense. Nonetheless, it needs to be viewed against the background of the general development of public international law. In the nineteenth century, international law permitted States to wage war without legal justification. As a consequence, the notion of self-defense was of only modest significance, and States invoked it mainly for political reasons. The content of the right to self-defense was unclear and its scope relatively broad. It is noteworthy, however, that Webster's formulation

DID YOU KNOW?

In History

The *Caroline* incident arose out of the Upper Canada Rebellion of 1837. Canadian rebels took refuge on Navy Island on the Canadian side of the Niagara River, from which they raided the Canadian shore as well as passing British ships. The rebels were supplied by American sympathizers with money, provisions, and arms via the steamboat SS *Caroline*. On December 29, 1837, the *Caroline* was moored in the American port of Fort Schlosser, close to the Canadian border. British forces attacked the vessel, set it on fire, and sent it over the Niagara Falls. Two American citizens were killed during the attack and several others wounded. The legality of the British acts was raised when Britain sought the release of Alexander McLeod, a British citizen, who had been arrested in the United States on criminal charges for his involvement in the incident.

already contained references to the principles of necessity and proportionality ("nothing unreasonable or excessive") as essential requirements for lawful self-defense.

At the beginning of the twentieth century—in particular, in response to the catastrophic destruction and suffering caused by World War I—the freedom of States to resort to war became more restricted, and public international law moved gradually toward the general prohibition of the use of force in international relations. In this context the notion of self-defense, as an exception to the prohibition of force, gained in significance. The Kellogg-Briand Pact of 1928 (also known as the Paris Pact), for example, contained a general prohibition of war. Although not explicitly stipulated by the treaty itself, it was generally accepted that the prohibition of war was subject to the reservation of self-defense. The development of international law toward the general prohibition of the use of force culminated in the adoption of the UN Charter, which recognizes the right of individual or collective self-defense in Article 51. In contrast to the wide customary notion of self-defense, the right of self-defense as embodied in Article 51 of the UN Charter is generally considered to be more restrictive in scope.

Daniel Webster, U.S. Secretary of State 1841–43 and 1850–52. Photographer unknown.

FURTHER READING

Bowett, Derek W. *Self Defence in International Law*. Manchester: Manchester University Press, 1958.

Dinstein, Yoram. *War, Aggression and Self-Defence*. 4th ed. Cambridge, UK: Cambridge University Press, 2005.

Jennings, Robert Y. "The *Caroline* and McLeod Cases." *American Journal of International Law* 32, no. 1 (1938): 82–99.

Schachter, Oscar. "Self-Defense and the Rule of Law." *American Journal of International Law* 83, no. 2 (1989): 259–277.

Article 51 of the UN Charter

- ***Document:*** The Charter of the United Nations
- ***Date:*** Signed on June 26, 1945 (effective October 24, 1945)
- ***Where:*** San Francisco
- ***Significance:*** Article 51 is the legal basis for lawful self-defense in contemporary international law.

DOCUMENT

Article 51

Nothing in the present Charter shall impair the inherent right of individual or collective self-defense if an armed attack occurs against a Member of the United Nations, until the Security Council has taken measures necessary to maintain international peace and security. Measures taken by Members in the exercise of this right of self-defense shall be immediately reported to the Security Council and shall not in any way affect the authority and responsibility of the Security Council under the present Charter to take at any time such action as it deems necessary in order to maintain or restore international peace and security.

SOURCE: Charter of the United Nations. http://www.un.org/aboutun/charter/chapter7.htm.

ANALYSIS

Article 51 of the UN Charter contains the right of self-defense as an exception to the general prohibition of force in contemporary international relations. However, both the content and scope of the right of self-defense remain contentious and subject to the most fundamental disagreement between States as well as between scholars. The divisions over the scope of the right of self-defense date back to the creation of the United Nations and continue to exist today, not least in the context of the "War on Terror." A central aspect of the controversy concerns the term "inherent" and the question as to whether a customary right of self-defense existed before the adoption of the Charter, and if so, whether Article 51 needs to be interpreted accordingly.

Some scholars argue that the reference to "inherent" preserved an existing customary right of self-defense, as the UN Charter did not take away pre-existing rights.[1] As a consequence, these scholars maintain that Article 51 needs to be read "widely" in order to include actions taken by States in self-defense in cases where there has not been any previous armed attack (e.g., anticipatory self-defense; see below). Particularly in cases where an armed attack is manifestly imminent, States may take action in self-defense in compliance with Article 51 as long as these measures fulfill strict necessity requirements as stipulated by the *Caroline* doctrine.

Other scholars reject this line of reasoning and argue that Article 51 superseded and replaced any customary right of self-defense, in particular for Member States of the United Nations.[2] They maintain that Article 51 is to be read "narrowly" or "restrictively," as limits imposed on self-defense in the UN Charter would be meaningless if a wide customary right of self-defense survived unfettered by these restrictions. Moreover, these scholars point out that the principles of treaty interpretation require Article 51 to be interpreted in accordance with the ordinary meaning to be given to the terms of the treaty in their context and in the light of its object and purpose. The authorization to use force in self-defense in Article 51 is limited by an "if" clause ("if an armed attack occurs"), which constitutes a condition of fact that is clear, objective, and difficult to misinterpret.

There is similar disagreement as to what constitutes an "armed attack" within the meaning of Article 51. Nevertheless, State practice and case law of the International Court of Justice (ICJ) provide some indications as to how to interpret the term. The ICJ, for instance, has referred to provisions of the UN General Assembly's Resolution 3314 (1974) on the Definition of Aggression. Although this resolution does not define the notion of armed attack, it lists examples of "acts of aggression" that can, subject to certain qualifications, be taken to characterize "armed attacks" within the meaning of Article 51 of the UN Charter. These include, in particular, attacks or invasions by the armed forces of a State on the territory of another, the cross-border use of weapons or bombardment of foreign territory, or an effectively maintained blockade of a State's ports or coasts by land, air, or naval forces. Some scholars have argued that developments in weapon technology require Article 51 to be interpreted so as to include situations considered as equivalent to an armed attack.[3] They cite an activation of launch mechanisms of nuclear missiles as a typical example in this regard.

Article 51 restricts the right of self-defense by stipulating that measures taken in self-defense must be reported to the UN Security Council immediately. In the *Nicaragua* Case, the ICJ found this reporting requirement to be largely procedural; noncompliance does not itself invalidate a claim to self-defense. Nonetheless, the ICJ has held that the absence of a report may be one of the factors indicating whether the State in question was itself convinced that it was acting in self-defense. Article 51 further specifies that the right of self-defense is a temporary right, insofar as it terminates as soon as the Security Council has stepped in to take measures to restore international peace and security.

While Article 51 does not mention either principle explicitly, the right of self-defense is also limited by the principles of necessity and proportionality. Both requirements are often traced back to the *Caroline* incident (see above), and their applicability to Article 51 has been reaffirmed by the ICJ. In the context of self-defense necessity and proportionality mean that any measures taken in response to an armed attack must neither be retaliatory nor punitive in nature but rather aimed at halting and repelling an attack. This does not imply, however, that a defending State is restricted to the same weapons or the same number of armed forces as the aggressor; nor are measures of self-defense necessarily limited to action on its own territory.

FURTHER READING

Alexandrov, Stanimir A. *Self-Defence against the Use of Force in International Law*. The Hague: Kluwer, 1996.

Dinstein, Yoram. *War, Aggression and Self-Defence*. 4th ed. Cambridge, UK: Cambridge University Press, 2005.

Glennon, Michael J. "The Fog of Law: Self-Defense, Inherence and Incoherence in Article 51 of the United Nations Charter." *Harvard Journal of Law and Public Policy* 25, no. 2 (2002): 539–558.

Greig, Don W. "Self-Defence and the Security Council: What Does Article 51 Require?" *International Comparative Law Quarterly* 40 (1991): 366–402.

Randelzhoffer, Albrecht. "Article 51," in Bruno Simma, ed. *The Charter of the United Nations. A Commentary*, 2nd ed. Oxford: Oxford University Press, 2002, 788–806.

Anticipatory Self-Defense

- ***Documents:*** Transcript of a debate in the UN Security Council, UN Security Council Resolution 487 (1981)
- ***Date:*** June 1981
- ***Where:*** United Nations, New York City
- ***Significance:*** The UN Security Council debate and subsequent resolution on Israel's airstrike against Iraq's Osirak nuclear reactor illustrate the contentious scope of anticipatory self-defense.

DOCUMENTS

Mr. Blum (Israel):

On Sunday, 7 June 1981, the Israeli Air Force carried out an operation against the Iraqi atomic reactor called "Osirak". That reactor was in its final stages of construction near Baghdad. The pilots' mission was to destroy it. They executed their mission successfully.

In destroying Osirak, Israel performed an elementary act of self-preservation, both morally and legally. In doing so, Israel was exercising its inherent right of self-defense as understood in general international law and as preserved in Article 51 of the Charter of the United Nations.

A threat of nuclear obliteration was being developed against Israel by Iraq, one of Israel's most implacable enemies. Israel tried to have the threat halted by diplomatic means. Our efforts bore no fruit. Ultimately we were left with no choice. We were obliged to remove that mortal danger. We did it cleanly and effectively. The Middle East has become a safer place. We trust that the international community has also been given pause to make the world a safer place.

Those facts and the potential for a safer world are widely recognized. Several States in the Middle East and beyond are sleeping more easily today in the knowledge that Saddam Hussein's nuclear-arms potential has been smashed. . . .

The Government of Israel, like any other Government, has the elementary duty to protect the lives of its citizens. In destroying Osirak last Sunday, Israel was exercising its inherent right to self-defense, as understood in general international law and well within the meaning of Article 51 of the Charter of the United Nations.

Commenting on the meaning of Article 51 of the Charter, Sir Humphrey Waldock, now President of the International Court of Justice, stated in a lecture delivered at The Hague Academy of International Law in 1952 that

> "it would be a travesty of the purposes of the Charter to compel a defending State to allow its assailant to deliver the first and perhaps fatal blow. . . . To read Article 51 otherwise is to protect the aggressor's right to the first strike."

In a similar vein, Professor Morton Kaplan and Nicholas de B. Katzenbach wrote in their book, *The Political Foundations of International Law:*

> "Must a state wait until it is too late before it may defend itself? Must it permit another the advantages of military build-up, surprise attack, and total offense, against which there may be no defense? It would be unreasonable to expect any State to permit this—particularly when given the possibility that a surprise nuclear blow might bring about total destruction, or at least total subjugation, unless the attack were forestalled."

Professor Derek Bowett of Cambridge University, in his authoritative work on *Self-Defense in International Law,* observed:

> "No state can be expected to await an initial attack, which in the present state of armaments, may well destroy the state's capacity for further resistance and so jeopardize its very existence."

So much for the legalities of the case. Still we have been accused of acting unlawfully. Presumably it is lawful for a sovereign State to create an instrument capable of destroying several hundred thousand Israelis; it is unlawful to halt that fatal process before it reaches completion.

The decision taken by my Government in the exercise of its right to self-defense, after the unusual international procedures and avenues had proven futile, was one of the most agonizing we have ever had to take. We sought to act in a manner which would minimize the danger to all concerned, including a large segment of Iraq's population. We waited until the eleventh hour after the diplomatic clock had run out hoping against hope that Iraq's nuclear arms project would be brought to a halt. Our Air Force was only called in when, as I have said, we learned on the basis of completely reliable information that there was less than a month to go before Osirak might have become critical. Our Air Force's operation was consciously launched on a Sunday, and timed for late in the day, the assumption that the workers on the site, including foreign experts employed at the reactor, would have left. That assumption proved correct, and the loss of human life, which we sincerely regret, was minimal.

I should add that those same considerations worked in the opposite direction as regards Iraq's other nuclear facilities and constrained Israel from taking actions against the smaller Western-supplied research reactor, as well as a small Soviet research reactor. Both of these facilities are operational and if attacked, could release substantial amounts of radiation.

In this connection, I wish to deny in the most categorical terms the false allegation made here by the Minister for Foreign Affairs of Iraq—who had the courtesy to leave the Chamber when I started my statement—that Iraq's nuclear installations were attacked by Israel on a date prior to 7 June.

With regard to the statement of the Foreign Minister of Baghdad as a whole, let me just observe that he added yet another tale to the *Tales of 1,001 Nights*, which, if I am not mistaken, were all written, like his statement, in Baghdad.

Mr. Parsons (United Kingdom):

> "The Government have already made plain their view that armed attack in such circumstances cannot be justified. It represents a grave breach of international law."

Mrs. Thatcher was asked about the fact that, whereas Iraq has signed the nuclear Non-Proliferation Treaty and accepted IAEA safeguards, Israel has not. She replied:

> "The Government firmly support the Non-Proliferation Treaty and wish that more countries would become signatories."

She went on to say:

> "A tragedy of this case was that Iraq was a signatory to the Agreement and had been inspected, but neither of these facts protected her. It was an unprovoked attack, which we must condemn. Just because a country is trying to manufacture energy from nuclear sources, it must not be believed that she is doing something totally wrong."

It has been argued that the Israeli attack was an act of self-defense. But it was not a response to an armed attack on Israel by Iraq. There was no instant or overwhelming necessity for self-defense. Nor can it be justified as a forcible measure of self-protection. The Israeli intervention amounted to a use of force which cannot find a place in international law or in the Charter and which violated the sovereignty of Iraq.

It has also been argued that, whatever the legal rights and wrongs of the matter, the international community privately breathed a sigh of relief after the Israeli raid, the suggestion being that the Iraqi Government will not now have a nuclear-weapon potential for some further time to come. That is certainly not the case so far as my Government is concerned. We do not believe that Iraq had the capacity to manufacture fissile material for nuclear weapons. Answering an assertion of this kind in the House of Commons, my Prime Minister replied:

> "Had there been such an attack on Israel of the kind that there has just been on Iraq, I should totally and utterly have condemned it. I therefore totally and utterly condemn the attack on Iraq."

Resolution 487 (1981) of 19 June 1981
Adopted Unanimously at the 2288th Meeting

The Security Council,

Having considered the agenda contained in document S/Agenda/2280,

Having noted the contents of the telegram dated 8 June 1981 from the Foreign Minister of Iraq (S/14509),

Having heard the statements made to the Council on the subject at its 2280th through 2288th meetings,

Taking note of the statement made by the Director-General of the International Atomic Energy Agency (IAEA) to the Agency's Board of Governors on the subject on 9 June 1981 and his statement to the Council at its 2288th meeting on 19 June 1981,

Further taking note of the resolution adopted by the Board of Governors of the IAEA on 12 June 1981 on the "military attack on the Iraq nuclear research centre and its implications for the Agency" (S/14532),

Fully aware of the fact that Iraq has been a party to the Treaty on the Non-Proliferation of Nuclear Weapons since it came into force in 1970, that in accordance with that Treaty Iraq has accepted IAEA safeguards on all its nuclear activities, and that the Agency has testified that these safeguards have been satisfactorily applied to date,

Noting furthermore that Israel has not adhered to the non-proliferation Treaty,

Deeply concerned about the danger to international peace and security created by the premeditated Israeli air attack on Iraqi nuclear installations on 7 June 1981, which could at any time explode the situation in the area, with grave consequences for the vital interests of all States,

Considering that, under the terms of Article 2, paragraph 4, of the Charter of the United Nations: "All Members shall refrain in their international relations from the threat or use of force against the territorial integrity or political independence of any State, or in any other manner inconsistent with the Purposes of the United Nations",

1. *Strongly condemns* the military attack by Israel in clear violation of the Charter of the United Nations and the norms of international conduct;
2. *Calls upon* Israel to refrain in the future from any such acts or threats thereof;
3. *Further considers* that the said attack constitutes a serious threat to the entire IAEA safeguards regime which is the foundation of the non-proliferation Treaty;
4. *Fully recognises* the inalienable sovereign right of Iraq, and all other States, especially the developing countries, to establish programmes of technological and nuclear development to develop their economy and industry for peaceful purposes in accordance with their present and future needs and consistent with the internationally accepted objectives of preventing nuclear-weapons proliferation;
5. *Calls upon* Israel urgently to place its nuclear facilities under IAEA safeguards;
6. *Considers* that Iraq is entitled to appropriate redress for the destruction it has suffered, responsibility for which has been acknowledged by Israel;
7. *Requests* the Secretary-General to keep the Security Council regularly informed of the implementation of this resolution.

Mrs. Kirkpatrick (United States of America):

Like other members of the Council, the United States does not regard the resolution just adopted as a perfect one.

With respect to this resolution, I must point out that my country voted against the resolution of IAEA which is referred to in the present resolution. We continue to oppose it. In addition, our judgement that Israeli actions violated the Charter of the United Nations is based solely on the conviction that Israel failed to exhaust peaceful means for the resolution of this dispute. Finally, we also believe that the question of appropriate redress must be understood in the full legal context of the relationships that exist in the region.

Nothing in this resolution will affect my Government's commitment to Israel's security and nothing in these reservations affects my Government's determination to work with all Governments of the region willing to use appropriate means to enhance the peace and security of the area.

Mr. Al-Qaysi (Iraq):

I apologize to you, Mr. President, and the members of the Council for having asked to be allowed to speak for a few minutes in this late hour.

My purpose in doing so is to recall that the representative of Israel at the end of his statement called this a moment of truth for all of us. Let us see how he has abided by that motto of his statement.

The representative of Israel saw fit in his statement of 12 June [2280th meeting] before the Council and his statement today to quote from an article by Sir Humphrey Waldock, the President of the International Court of Justice. He has also quoted from other sources in a vain attempt to substantiate his allegations. Let us see what the truth of that quotation was.

Sir Humphrey Waldock said exactly the following:

> "The Charter prohibits the use of force except in self-defense. The Charter obliges Members to submit to the Council or Assembly any dispute dangerous to peace which they cannot settle. Members have therefore an imperative duty to invoke the jurisdiction of the United Nations whenever a grave menace to their security develops carrying the probability of armed attack. But, if the action of the United Nations is obstructed, delayed or inadequate and the armed attack becomes manifestly imminent, then it would be a travesty of the purposes of the Charter to compel a defending State to allow its assailant to deliver the first and perhaps fatal blow. If an armed attack is imminent within the strict doctrine of the *Caroline*, then it would seem to bring the case within Article 51. To read Article 51 otherwise is to protect the aggressor's right to the first strike."

That is what was said by Sir Humphrey Waldock in the article referred to by the representative of Israel. Yet, the representative of Israel on two occasions deemed it fit to quote Sir Humphrey Waldock as having said:

> "it would be a travesty of the purposes of the Charter to compel a defending State to allow its assailant to deliver the first and perhaps fatal blow. . . . To read Article 51 otherwise is to protect the aggressor's right to the first strike"

SOURCES: For the transcripts of the UN Security Council debate, see 36 UN SCOR, 2280-2288 mtgs (1981). For Resolution 487 (1981) see: http://domino.un.org/UNISPAl.NSF/2ee9468747556b2d85256cf60060d2a6/6c57312cc8bd93ca852560df00653995!OpenDocument.

ANALYSIS

The debate in the UN Security Council following the Israeli attack on the Iraqi nuclear reactor Osirak illustrates the contentious nature of anticipatory self-defense. Anticipatory self-defense is generally considered to be action taken in the absence of an armed attack, i.e. in "anticipation" of an armed attack. Israel sought to justify its airstrike on Osirak as an act of self-defense. The Security Council did not, however, accept Israel's position and unanimously condemned the attack as a clear violation of the UN Charter and norms of international conduct. While commentators have referred to the Osirak incident as an example of anticipatory self-defense, the Council did not address the question of the legal validity of the concept of anticipatory self-defense as such; nor did the permanent members of the Security Council offer matching explanations for their vote in support of Resolution 487 (1981).

The notion of anticipatory self-defense would at first glance appear to be clearly contrary to the wording of Article 51, which recognizes the right to self-defense "if an armed attack occurs." Scholars have argued that anticipatory self-defense is contrary to the object and purpose of Article 51, namely to restrict, to the greatest extent possible, the unilateral use of force in international relations.[4] Given that the imminence of an attack is usually impossible to determine by way of objective assessment, any decision on this point would necessarily have to be left to the discretion of the State concerned. Such discretion would hold an obvious and legally unacceptable risk of abuse. In contrast to the view that anticipatory self-defense is contrary to the Charter, some scholars argue that practical considerations and developments in weapons technology since the Charter require Article 51 to be interpreted to include anticipatory measures of self-defense. They maintain that the scope of Article 51 extends to include anticipatory self-defense as long as a State can demonstrate a necessity of self-defense that is instant, overwhelming, leaving no choice of means, and no moment for deliberation (*Caroline* standard).[5]

State practice does not provide any clear evidence to suggest that the international community accepts anticipatory self-defense as lawful. Israel's airstrike on Iraq's Osirak reactor attracted widespread condemnation by governments, including the United Kingdom and the United States. Interestingly, Israel did not rely on any examples of State practice to support its position during the Security Council debate and instead attempted to justify its actions solely by referring to academic opinions on the content and scope of Article 51. The absence of relevant State practice and the reluctance of States to expressly invoke anticipatory self-defense indicate the doubtful status of the legality of anticipatory self-defense.[6]

FURTHER READING

Beres, Louis R. "Israel and Anticipatory Self Defense." *Arizona Journal of International and Comparative Law* 8, no. 1 (1991): 89–99.

D'Amato, Anthony. "Israel's Air Strike upon the Iraqi Nuclear Reactor." *American Journal of International Law* 77, no. 3 (1983): 584–588.

Dinstein, Yoram. *War, Aggression and Self-Defence.* 4th ed. Cambridge, UK: Cambridge University Press, 2005.

Kaplan, Neil J. "The Attack on Osirak: Delimitation of Self-Defense under International Law." *New York Law School Journal of International and Comparative Law* 4 (1982–83): 131–156.

McCormack, Timothy L. H. "Anticipatory Self-Defence in the Legislative History of the United Nations Charter." *Israel Law Review* 25, no. 1 (1991): 1–42.

Pre-Emptive Self-Defense

- ***Document:*** Extract from the National Security Strategy of the United States of America
- ***Date:*** September 2002
- ***Where:*** The White House, Washington, DC
- ***Significance:*** The National Security Strategy proposes to extend the notion of self-defense to include the pre-emptive use of military force.

DOCUMENT

Traditional concepts of deterrence will not work against a terrorist enemy whose avowed tactics are wanton destruction and the targeting of innocents; whose so-called soldiers seek martyrdom in death and whose most potent protection is statelessness. The overlap between states that sponsor terror and those that pursue WMD compels us to action.

For centuries, international law recognized that nations need not suffer an attack before they can lawfully take action to defend themselves against forces that present an imminent danger of attack. Legal scholars and international jurists often conditioned the legitimacy of preemption on the existence of an imminent threat—most often a visible mobilization of armies, navies, and air forces preparing to attack.

We must adapt the concept of imminent threat to the capabilities and objectives of today's adversaries. Rogue states and terrorists do not seek to attack us using conventional means. They know such attacks would fail. Instead, they rely on acts of terror and, potentially, the use of weapons of mass destruction—weapons that can be easily concealed, delivered covertly, and used without warning.

The targets of these attacks are our military forces and our civilian population, in direct violation of one of the principal norms of the law of warfare. As was demonstrated by the losses on September 11, 2001, mass civilian casualties is the specific objective of terrorists and these losses would be exponentially more severe if terrorists acquired and used weapons of mass destruction.

The United States has long maintained the option of preemptive actions to counter a sufficient threat to our national security. The greater the threat, the greater is the risk of inaction—and the more compelling the case for taking anticipatory action to defend ourselves, even if uncertainty remains as to the time and place of the enemy's attack. To forestall or prevent such hostile acts by our adversaries, the United States will, if necessary, act preemptively.

The United States will not use force in all cases to preempt emerging threats, nor should nations use preemption as a pretext for aggression. Yet in an age where the enemies of civilization openly and actively seek the world's most destructive technologies, the United States cannot remain idle while dangers gather.

SOURCE: U.S. Government. http://www.whitehouse.gov/nsc/nss.pdf, p. 15.

ANALYSIS

The doctrine of pre-emptive self-defense as formulated by the 2002 National Security Strategy of the United States is highly controversial. It proposes to adapt the concept of self-defense to apply to perceived threats to national security in a way that constitutes a significant expansion of the traditional scope and content of self-defense. In contrast to the already contentious notion of anticipatory self-defense, the concept of pre-emptive self-defense goes one step further by stipulating that an armed attack need not even be imminent. Instead, measures involving the use of force may be taken in self-defense if it can be established that there is a *sufficient* threat to national security.

It is evident that this broad interpretation of self-defense is at odds with the existing right of self-defense as embodied in Article 51 of the UN Charter. The majority of scholars therefore regard pre-emptive self-defense as illegal under international law and argue that both the concept's vagueness and the possibility of abuse require maintaining the traditional strict approach.[7] Irrespective of the legal controversies, the concept of pre-emptive self-defense is also problematic for practical reasons. It necessarily relies on high-quality intelligence, which is often unavailable. Nevertheless, as the Iraq invasion of 2003 and the subsequent absence of any Iraqi WMD have shown, intelligence alone may be a shaky foundation on which to build a justification for the use of force.[8]

It remains to be seen whether the United States is indeed intending to establish a new legal doctrine of self-defense or whether the National Security Strategy of 2002 had a primarily political purpose. It appears plausible at least, that the rhetoric of pre-emption was employed to put pressure on hostile regimes such as Iran and North Korea and/or to build the case for military action against Iraq. The question of the legality of the military operations against Iraq in 2003 will be dealt with in more detail in Chapter 9. Suffice it to note here that two other countries contributing ground forces to the invasion, the United Kingdom and Australia, expressly denied that they were acting in pre-emptive self-defense but rather as a consequence of Iraq's

President George W. Bush meets with, from left, CIA Director George Tenet, Secretary Andy Card (not pictured), Vice President Dick Cheney, and National Security Advisor Condoleezza Rice in the Oval Office, October 7, 2001. Courtesy of the White House, Photo by Eric Draper.

failure to comply with UN Security Council resolutions. This may itself be an indication that the overwhelming majority of UN Member States, including close allies of the United States, do not consider the concept of pre-emptive self-defense lawful.

In March 2006, the White House issued a new National Security Strategy.[9] The 2006 document built on the 2002 Strategy by reaffirming that the "United States can no longer simply rely on deterrence to keep the terrorists at bay or defensive measures to thwart them at the last moment" and that "the fight must be taken to the enemy, to keep them on the run."[10] This could be seen as an indication that the Bush administration continued to espouse the doctrine of pre-emptive self-defense. At the same time, the 2006 Strategy recognized the need for "support and concerted action of friends and allies" and stated that it "is the policy of the United States to seek and support democratic movements and institutions in every nation and culture, with the ultimate goal of ending tyranny in our world."[11] This demonstrates a return to the more multilateral approach of previous administrations which is likely to be pursued further by the White House of President Barack Obama.

FURTHER READING

Arend, Anthony C. "International Law and the Preemptive Use of Military Force." *The Washington Quarterly* 26, no. 2 (2003): 89–103.

Bothe, Michael. "Terrorism and the Legality of Pre-emptive Force." *European Journal of International Law* 14, no. 2 (2003): 227–240.

Byers, Michael. "Preemptive Self-defense: Hegemony, Equality and Strategies of Legal Change." *Journal of Political Philosophy* 11, no. 2 (2003): 171–190.

Gray, Christine. "The US National Security Strategy and the New 'Bush Doctrine' on Preemptive Self-Defense." *Chinese Journal of International Law* 1, no. 2 (2002): 437–448.

Gupta, Sanjay. "The Doctrine of Pre-emptive Strike: Application and Implications during the Administration of President George W. Bush." *International Political Science Review* 29, no. 2 (2008): 181–196.

Sapiro, Miriam. "Iraq: The Shifting Sands of Preemptive Self-Defense." *American Journal of International Law* 97, no. 3 (2003): 599–607.

Collective Self-Defense

- ***Document:*** Extract of the Judgment (Merits) by the International Court of Justice in the case of Military and Paramilitary Activities in and Against Nicaragua *(Nicaragua v. United States of America)*
- ***Date:*** June 27, 1986
- ***Where:*** The Hague, The Netherlands
- ***Significance:*** In the *Nicaragua* judgment, the International Court of Justice confirmed that collective self-defense under Article 51 of the UN Charter is subject to the same requirements and limits as individual self-defense. The Court also held that the lawful exercise of collective self-defense is subject to a further requirement, namely that a request for assistance has to be made to the third State that is claiming to exercise collective self-defense in support of the State that is under attack.

DOCUMENT

196. The question remains whether the lawfulness of the use of collective self-defense by the third State for the benefit of the attacked State also depends on a request addressed by that State to the third State. . . .

199. At all events, the Court finds that in customary international law, whether of a general kind or that particular to the inter-American legal system, there is no rule permitting the exercise of collective self-defense in the absence of a request by the State which regards itself as the victim of an armed attack. The Court concludes that the requirement of a request by the State which is the victim of the alleged attack is additional to the requirement that such a State should have declared itself to have been attacked.

232. The exercise of the right of collective self-defense presupposes that an armed attack has occurred; and it is evident that it is the victim State, being the most directly aware of that fact, which is likely to draw general attention to its plight. It is also evident that if the victim State wishes another State to come to its help in the exercise of the right of collective self-defense, it will normally make an express request to that effect. Thus in the present instance, the Court is entitled to take account, in judging the asserted justification of the exercise of collective self-defense by the United States, of the actual conduct of El Salvador, Honduras and Costa Rica at the relevant time, as indicative of a belief by the State in question that it was the victim of an armed attack by Nicaragua, and of the making of a request by the victim State to the United States for help in the exercise of collective self-defense.

233. The Court has seen no evidence that the conduct of those States was consistent with such a situation, either at the time when the United States first embarked on the activities which were allegedly justified by self-defense, or indeed for a long period subsequently. So far as El Salvador is concerned, it appears to the Court that while El Salvador did in fact officially declare itself the victim of an armed attack, and did ask for the United States to exercise its right of collective self-defense, this occurred only on a date much later than the commencement of the United States activities which were allegedly justified by this request. The Court notes that on 3 April 1984, the representative of El Salvador before the United Nations Security Council, while complaining of the "open foreign intervention practised by Nicaragua in our internal affairs" (9PV.2528, p. 58), refrained from stating that El Salvador had been subjected to armed attack, and made no mention of the right of collective self-defense which it had supposedly asked the United States to exercise. Nor was this mentioned when El Salvador addressed a letter to the Court in April 1984, in connection with Nicaragua's complaint against the United States. It was only in its Declaration of Intervention filed on 15 August 1984, that El Salvador referred to requests addressed at various dates to the United States for the latter to exercise its right of collective self-defense (para. XII), asserting on this occasion that it had been the victim of aggression from Nicaragua "since at least 1980". In that Declaration, El Salvador affirmed that initially it had "not wanted to present any accusation or allegation [against Nicaragua] to any of the jurisdictions to which we have a right to apply", since it sought "a solution of understanding and mutual respect" (para. III).

234. As to Honduras and Costa Rica, they also were prompted by the institution of proceedings in this case to address communications to the Court; in neither of these is there mention of armed attack or collective self-defense. As has already been noted (paragraph 231 above), Honduras in the Security Council in 1984 asserted that Nicaragua had engaged in aggression against it, but did not mention that a request had consequently been made to the United States for assistance by way of collective self-defense. On the contrary, the representative of Honduras emphasized that the matter before the Security Council "is a Central American problem, without exception, and it must be solved regionally" (9PV.2529, p. 38), i.e., through the Contadora process. The representative of Costa Rica also made no reference to collective self-defense. Nor, it may be noted, did the representative of the United States assert during that debate that it had acted in response to requests for assistance in that context.

235. There is also an aspect of the conduct of the United States which the Court is entitled to take into account as indicative of the view of that State on the question of the existence of an armed attack. At no time, up to the present, has the United States Government addressed to the Security Council, in connection with the matters the subject of the present case, the report which is required by Article 51 of the United Nations Charter in respect of measures which a State believes itself bound to take when it exercises the right of individual or collective self-defense. The Court, whose decision has to be made on the basis of customary international law, has already observed that in the context of that law, the reporting obligation enshrined in Article 51 of the Charter of the United Nations does not exist. It does not therefore treat the absence of a report on the part of the United States as the breach of an undertaking forming part of the customary international law applicable to the present dispute. But the Court is justified in observing that this conduct of the United States hardly conforms with the latter's avowed conviction that it was acting in the context of collective self-defense as consecrated by Article 51 of the Charter. This fact is all the more noteworthy because, in the Security Council, the United States has itself taken the view that failure to observe the requirement to make a report contradicted a State's claim to be acting on the basis of collective self-defense (SPV.2187).

236. Similarly, while no strict legal conclusion may be drawn from the date of El Salvador's announcement that it was the victim of an armed attack, and the date of its official request addressed to the United States concerning the exercise of collective self-defense, those dates have a significance as evidence of El Salvador's view of the situation. The declaration and the request of El Salvador, made publicly for the first time in August 1984, do not support the contention that in 1981 there was an armed attack capable of serving as a legal foundation for United States activities which began in the second half of that year. The States concerned did not behave as though there were an armed attack at the time when the activities attributed by the United States to Nicaragua, without actually constituting such an attack, were nevertheless the most accentuated; they did so behave only at a time when these facts fell furthest short of what would be required for the Court to take the view that an armed attack existed on the part of Nicaragua against El Salvador.

238. Accordingly, the Court concludes that the plea of collective self-defense against an alleged armed attack on El Salvador, Honduras or Costa Rica, advanced by the United States to justify its conduct toward Nicaragua, cannot be upheld; and accordingly that the United States has violated the principle

DID YOU KNOW?

In History

The *Nicaragua* case is a famous case decided by the International Court of Justice in 1986. The Court found that the United States had violated international law by supporting Contra guerrillas in their operations against the Nicaraguan government and by mining Nicaragua's harbors. The judgment addressed several issues relating to the prohibition of the use of force and the right of self-defense. However, the Court relied mostly on customary international law for jurisdictional reasons. It held that arming and training the Contras and mining Nicaraguan territorial waters constituted a violation of the principle of nonintervention and the prohibition of use of force. The Court also held that Nicaragua's dealings with the armed opposition in El Salvador, although possibly constituting a violation of the principle of nonintervention and the prohibition of the use of force, did not amount to an armed attack within the meaning of Article 51 of the UN Charter. In addition, the Court did not accept the United States' claim to be acting in collective self-defense of El Salvador, Honduras, or Costa Rica, as those States had never requested the assistance of the United States on the grounds of self-defense.

prohibiting recourse to the threat or use of force by the acts listed in paragraph 227 above, and by its assistance to the contras to the extent that this assistance "involve[s] a threat or use of force" (paragraph 228 above).

SOURCE: Courtesy of the International Court of Justice, http://www.icj-cij.org/docket/index.php?p1=3&p2=3&code=nus&case=70&k=66.

ANALYSIS

Despite the long-standing existence of treaty-based alliances before World War II, the notion of collective self-defense was unknown to traditional international law until 1945, when it first entered negotiations on the UN Charter at the San Francisco conference. Because of its long-term deterrent effect on potential aggressors, collective self-defense is based not only on self-interest but also on a general interest in peace and security. It thus represents an addition to the global system of collective security. Following the adoption of the UN Charter, States concluded a significant number of treaties on collective self-defense, both bilateral and multilateral. Examples include the North Atlantic Treaty (1949) establishing the North Atlantic Treaty Organization (NATO), the Manila Treaty (1954) establishing the Southeast Asia Treaty Organization (SEATO), and the Australia, New Zealand, United States Security Treaty or ANZUS Pact (1951).

U.S. Air Force aircraft of the 4th Fighter Wing fly over Kuwaiti oil fires set by the retreating Iraqi army during Operation Desert Storm in 1991. Courtesy of the U.S. Air Force.

Collective self-defense under Article 51 of the UN Charter is subject to the same requirements and limits as individual self-defense: that is, there must be an armed attack, and the response must conform to the general limits of necessity and proportionality. In its *Nicaragua* judgment, the International Court of Justice held that the lawful exercise of collective self-defense is subject to a further requirement. As in the case of individual self-defense, a State that is the victim of an armed attack must declare that it has been attacked. In addition, a request for assistance has to be made to the third State that is claiming to exercise collective self-defense in support of the State that is under attack. Scholars have since debated whether collective self-defense is the joint exercise of individual rights, or whether it is the exercise of a right by one or more States on behalf of the attacked State.[12] This doctrinal division, however, is of little consequence in practice.

FURTHER READING

Bowett, Derek, W. "Collective Self-Defence Under the Charter of the United Nations." *British Yearbook of International Law* 32 (1955–56): 130–161.

Egan, Patrick T. "The Kosovo Intervention and Collective Self-Defence." *International Peacekeeping* 8, no. 3 (2001): 39–58.

Gill, Terry D. "The Second Gulf Crisis and the Relation Between Collective Security and Collective Self-Defense." *Grotiana* 10, no. 1 (1989): 47–76.

Hargrove, John L. "The *Nicaragua* Judgment and the Future of the Law of Force and Self-defense." *American Journal of International Law* 81, no. 2 (1987): 135–152.

Kelsen, Hans. "Collective Security and Collective Self-Defense under the Charter of the United Nations." *American Journal of International Law* 42, no. 2 (1948): 783–796.

Ruggie, John. "The UN and the Collective Use of Force: Whither or Whether?" *International Peacekeeping* 3, no. 4 (1996): 1–20. http://www.informaworld.com/smpp/title~content=t713635493~db=all~tab=issueslist~branches=3-v3.

The Protection of Nationals

- ***Document:*** Transcript of President George Bush's Address on the Decision to Use Force in Panama
- ***Date:*** December 20, 1989
- ***Where:*** Washington, DC
- ***Significance:*** This statement of President Bush is an example for a government invoking the controversial right to protect or rescue nationals abroad.

DOCUMENT

Fellow citizens, last night I ordered U.S. military forces to Panama. No President takes such action lightly. This morning, I want to tell you what I did and why I did it.

For nearly two years, the United States, nations of Latin America and the Caribbean have worked together to resolve the crisis in Panama. The goals of the United States have been to safeguard the lives of Americans, to defend democracy in Panama, to combat drug trafficking and to protect the integrity of the Panama Canal Treaty. Many attempts have been made to resolve this crisis through diplomacy and negotiations. All were rejected by the dictator of Panama, Gen. Manuel Noriega, an indicted drug trafficker.

Last Friday, Noriega declared his military dictatorship to be in a state of war with the United States and publicly threatened the lives of Americans in Panama. The very next day forces under his command shot and killed an unarmed American serviceman, wounded another, arrested and brutally beat a third American serviceman and then brutally interrogated his wife, threatening her with sexual abuse. That was enough.

General Noriega's reckless threats and attacks upon Americans in Panama created an eminent *(sic)* danger to the 35,000 American citizens in Panama. As President, I have no higher obligation than to safeguard the lives of American citizens. And that is why I directed our armed force to protect the lives of American citizens in Panama, and to bring General Noriega to justice in the United States. I contacted the bipartisan leadership of Congress last night and informed them of this decision, and after taking this action, I also talked with leaders in Latin America, the Caribbean, and those of other U.S. allies.

Lifting of U.S. Sanctions

At this moment, U.S. forces, including forces deployed from the United States last night, are engaged in action in Panama. The United States intends to withdraw the forces newly deployed to Panama as quickly as possible. All forces have conducted themselves courageously and selflessly, and as Commander in Chief, I salute everyone of them and thank them on behalf of our country.

Tragically, some Americans have lost their lives in defense of their fellow citizens, in defense of democracy, and my heart goes out to their families. We also regret and mourn the loss of innocent Panamanians.

The brave Panamanians elected by the people of Panama in the elections last May, President Guillermo Endara and Vice Presidents Calderon and Ford, have assumed the rightful leadership of their country. You remember those horrible pictures of newly elected Vice President Ford covered head to toe with blood, beaten mercilessly by so-called dignity battalions. Well, the United States today recognizes the democratically elected Government of President Endara. I will send our Ambassador back to Panama immediately. Key military objectives have been achieved. Most organized resistance has been eliminated. But the operation is not over yet. General Noriega is in hiding. And nevertheless, yesterday, a dictator ruled Panama, and today, constitutionally elected govern—elected leaders govern.

I have today directed the Secretary of the Treasury and the Secretary of State to lift the economic sanctions with respect to the democratically elected Government of Panama, and in cooperation with that Government, to take steps to effect an orderly unblocking of Panamanian Government assets in the United States.

Reasons for Military Action

I am fully committed to implement the Panama Canal Treaties and turn over the Canal to Panama in the year 2000. The actions we have taken and the cooperation of a new democratic Government in Panama will permit us to honor these commitments. As soon as the new Government recommends a qualified candidate, Panamanian, to be administrator of the canal, as called for in the treaties, I will submit this nominee to the Senate for expedited consideration.

I am committed to strengthening our relationship with the democratic nations in this hemisphere. I will continue to seek solutions to the problems of this region through dialogue and multilateral diplomacy. I took this action only after reaching the conclusion that every other avenue was closed and the lives of American citizens were in grave danger. I hope that the people of Panama will put this dark chapter of dictatorship behind them and move forward together as citizens of a democratic Panama with this Government that they themselves have elected.

The United States is eager to work with the Panamanian people in partnership and friendship to rebuild their economy. The Panamanian people want democracy, peace, and the chance for a better life in dignity and freedom. The people of the United States seek only to support them in pursuit of these noble goals.

Thank you very much.

SOURCE: George Bush Presidential Library and Museum, http://bushlibrary.tamu.edu/research/public_papers.php?id=1356&year=1989&month=12.

ANALYSIS

States have invoked an alleged right to protect or rescue nationals abroad as the basis for the use of force on a number of occasions. Such claims have been made, for instance, in the context of the British intervention in the Suez (1956), the Belgian intervention in the Congo (1960), the Israel raid in Entebbe, Uganda (1976), and the United States military operations in the Dominican Republic (1965), Iran (1980), Grenada (1983), and Panama (1989). In all these cases, States have cited self-defense as at least a partial justification for their action. With regard to the interventions in Iran, Grenada, and Panama, for example, the United States expressly informed the UN Security Council that it was invoking Article 51 as giving an inherent right of self-defense to protect American lives.

The practice of invoking Article 51 of the UN Charter as the basis for protecting or rescuing nationals abroad is controversial. Some scholars support the idea and argue that an armed attack on nationals abroad equates to an attack on the national State. They maintain that rescue operations are justified in cases where there is an imminent threat of injury to nationals, where there is a failure or inability of a foreign State to protect the nationals in question, and where the measures are strictly confined to the object of protection.[13] Other scholars reject this approach and argue that nationals cannot be identified with the national State for all purposes; for instance, a State possesses sovereign immunity in foreign courts, but its nationals do not.[14] These scholars also argue that military operations to protect or rescue nationals abroad cannot be justified by reference to the right of self-defense because Article 51 of the UN Charter requires a narrow interpretation that includes only armed attacks against States. Any other interpretation would hold an unacceptable risk that the protection of nationals is used as a pretext for intervention for other purposes.

Irrespective of these doctrinal divisions, most of the abovementioned interventions (with the exception of the Entebbe raid) could not be justified as protection of

President George H. Bush monitoring events in Panama from the White House with John H. Sununu (right), White House chief of staff, and Brent Scowcroft, national security adviser, December 1989. Courtesy of White House Photo Office.

nationals, as the military operations in question were evidently disproportionate. Grenada, for instance, remained occupied for months—long after the evacuation of American citizens was completed. In the case of Panama, United States forces also remained in the country for a considerable amount of time and, as President Bush expressly stated, the U.S. intervention was aimed not only at the protection of American citizens but also at defending democracy in Panama, combating drug trafficking, and protecting the integrity of the Panama Canal Treaty.

In the recent past, however, there have been examples of rescue operations that were neither raised within the United Nations nor attracted widespread condemnation by the international community. These cases concern the rescue of nationals in countries that had plunged into civil war or were experiencing considerable domestic unrest. Examples include the French-Belgian rescue operations in Rwanda (1994) and the French evacuation operations in Côte d'Ivoire and Liberia in 2002–3. In none of these instances did governments invoke Article 51 of the UN Charter, nor did the State where the intervention took place raise the matter. This can be seen as consent by the government to the rescue operation or simply explained by the fact that the operations took place in countries that did not have an effective government at the time. It may thus be concluded that the international community appears to be willing to acquiesce in the forcible evacuation of nationals in conflict zones in cases where such rescue operations are not conducted as a pretext for an intervention with wider political objectives.

Three members of the 7th Infantry Division walk past a restaurant during Operation Just Cause in Panama. Courtesy of Ken Hammond/U.S. Department of Defense.

FURTHER READING

Akehurst, Michael. "The Use of Force to Protect Nationals Abroad." *International Relations* 5 (1977): 3–29.

D'Angelo, John R. "Resort to Force by States to Protect Nationals: The US Rescue Mission to Iran and Its Legality under International Law." *Virginia Journal of International Law* 21 (1981): 485–519.

Henkin, Louis. "The Invasion of Panama under International Law: A Gross Violation." *Columbia Journal of Transnational Law* 29 (1991): 293–317.

Joyner, Christopher C. "United States Action in Grenada: Reflections on the Lawfulness of Invasion." *American Journal of International Law* 78, no. 1 (1984): 121–144.

Terry, James P. "The Panama Intervention: Law in Support of Policy." *Naval Law Review* 39, no. 4 (1990): 110–118.

Nuclear Weapons and Self-Defense

- ***Document:*** Extract of the Advisory Opinion by the International Court of Justice on the Legality of the Threat or Use of Nuclear Weapons
- ***Date:*** July 8, 1996
- ***Where:*** The Hague, The Netherlands
- ***Significance:*** The Court held that the threat or use of nuclear weapons would generally be contrary to the rules of international law. However, the judges were unable to conclude definitively whether the threat or use of nuclear weapons would be lawful or unlawful in an extreme circumstance of self-defense, in which the very survival of a State would be at stake.

DOCUMENT

37. The Court will now address the question of the legality or illegality of recourse to nuclear weapons in the light of the provisions of the Charter relating to the threat or use of force.

38. The Charter contains several provisions relating to the threat and use of force. In Article 2, paragraph 4, the threat or use of force against the territorial integrity or political independence of another State or in any other manner inconsistent with the purposes of the United Nations is prohibited. That paragraph provides: "All Members shall refrain in their international relations from the threat or use of force against the territorial integrity or political independence of any State, or in any other manner inconsistent with the Purposes of the United Nations." This prohibition of the use of force is to be considered in the light of other relevant provisions of the Charter. In Article 51, the Charter recognizes the inherent right of individual

or collective self-defense if an armed attack occurs. A further lawful use of force is envisaged in Article 42, whereby the Security Council may take military enforcement measures in conformity with Chapter VII of the Charter.

39. These provisions do not refer to specific weapons. They apply to any use of force, regardless of the weapons employed. The Charter neither expressly prohibits, nor permits, the use of any specific weapon, including nuclear weapons. A weapon that is already unlawful per se, whether by treaty or custom, does not become lawful by reason of its being used for a legitimate purpose under the Charter.

40. The entitlement to resort to self-defense under Article 51 is subject to certain constraints. Some of these constraints are inherent in the very concept of self defense. Other requirements are specified in Article 51.

41. The submission of the exercise of the right of self-defense to the conditions of necessity and proportionality is a rule of customary international law. As the Court stated in the case concerning Military and Paramilitary Activities in and against Nicaragua *(Nicaragua v. United States of America)* (I.C.J. Reports 1986, p. 94, para. 176): "there is a specific rule whereby self-defense would warrant only measures which are proportional to the armed attack and necessary to respond to it, a rule well established in customary international law". This dual condition applies equally to Article 51 of the Charter, whatever the means of force employed.

42. The proportionality principle may thus not in itself exclude the use of nuclear weapons in self-defense in all circumstances. But at the same time, a use of force that is proportionate under the law of self-defense, must, in order to be lawful, also meet the requirements of the law applicable in armed conflict which comprise in particular the principles and rules of humanitarian law.

43. Certain States have in their written and oral pleadings suggested that in the case of nuclear weapons, the condition of proportionality must be evaluated in the light of still further factors. They contend that the very nature of nuclear weapons, and the high probability of an escalation of nuclear exchanges, mean that there is an extremely strong risk of devastation. The risk factor is said to negate the possibility of the condition of proportionality being complied with. The Court does not find it necessary to embark upon the quantification of such risks; nor does it need to enquire into the question whether tactical nuclear weapons exist which are sufficiently precise to limit those risks: it suffices for the Court to note that the very nature of all nuclear weapons and the profound risks associated therewith are further considerations to be borne in mind by States believing they can exercise a nuclear response in self-defense in accordance with the requirements of proportionality.

105. (. . .) 2 E By *seven votes to seven, by the President's casting vote,* It follows from the above-mentioned requirements that the threat or use of nuclear weapons would generally be contrary to the rules of international law applicable in armed conflict, and in particular the principles and rules of humanitarian law; However, in view of the current state of international law, and of the elements of fact at its disposal, the Court cannot conclude definitively whether the threat or use of nuclear weapons would be lawful or unlawful in an extreme circumstance of self-defense, in which the very survival of a State would be at stake;

Dissenting Opinion of Judge Weeramantry, pp. 513–517 (Footnotes Omitted)

Self-defense raises probably the most serious problems in this case. The second sentence in paragraph 2 E of the *dispositif* states that, in the current state of international law and of the elements of fact at its disposal, the Court cannot conclude definitively whether the threat or use of nuclear weapons would be lawful or unlawful in an extreme circumstance of self-defense, in which the very survival of a State would be at stake. I have voted against this clause as I am of the view that the threat or use of nuclear weapons would not be lawful in any circumstances whatsoever, as it offends the fundamental principles of the *jus in bello*. This conclusion is clear and follows inexorably from well-established principles of international law.

If a nation is attacked, it is clearly entitled under the United Nations Charter to the right of self-defense. Once a nation thus enters into the domain of the *jus in bello*, the principles of humanitarian law apply to the conduct of self-defense, just as they apply to the conduct of any other aspect of military operations. We must hence examine what principles of the *jus in bello* apply to the use of nuclear weapons in self-defense.

The first point to be noted is that the use of *force* in self-defense (which is an undoubted right) is one thing and the use of *nuclear weapons* in self-defense is another. The permission granted by international law for the first does not embrace the second, which is subject to other governing principles as well. All of the seven principles of humanitarian law discussed in this opinion apply to the use of nuclear weapons in self-defense, just as they apply to their use in any aspect of war. Principles relating to unnecessary suffering, proportionality, discrimination, non-belligerent States, genocide, environmental damage and human rights would all be violated, no less in self-defense than in an open act of aggression. The *jus in bello* covers all use of force, whatever the reasons for resort to force. There can be no exceptions, without violating the essence of its principles.

The State subjected to the first attack could be expected to respond in kind. After the devastation caused by a first attack, especially if it be a nuclear attack, there will be a tendency to respond with any nuclear firepower that is available. Robert McNamara, in dealing with the response to initial strikes, states:

> "But under such circumstances, leaders on both sides would be under unimaginable pressure to avenge their losses and secure the interests being challenged. And each would fear that the opponent might launch a larger attack at any moment. Moreover, they would both be operating with only partial information because of the disruption to communications caused by the chaos on the battlefield (to say nothing of possible strikes against communication facilities). Under such conditions, it is highly likely that rather than surrender, each side would launch a larger attack, hoping that this step would bring the action to a halt by causing the opponent to capitulate."

With such a response, the clock would accelerate towards global catastrophe, for a counter-response would be invited and, indeed, could be automatically triggered off. It is necessary to reiterate here the undoubted right of the State that is attacked to use all the weaponry available to it for the purpose of repulsing the aggressor. Yet this principle holds only *so long as such weapons do not violate the fundamental rules of warfare embodied in those rules*. Within these constraints, and for the purpose of repulsing the enemy, the full military power of the State that is attacked can be unleashed upon the aggressor. While this is incontrovertible, one has yet to hear an argument in any forum, or a contention in any academic literature, that a nation attacked, for example, with chemical or biological weapons is entitled to use chemical or biological weapons in self-defense, or to annihilate the aggressor's population. It is strange that the most devastating of all the weapons of mass destruction can be conceived of as offering a singular exception to this most obvious conclusion following from the bedrock principles of humanitarian law. That said, a short examination follows of the various principles of humanitarian law which could be violated by self-defense.

1. *Unnecessary Suffering*

The harrowing suffering caused by nuclear weapons, as outlined earlier in this opinion, is not confined to the aggressive use of such weapons. The lingering sufferings caused by radiation do not lose their intensity merely because the weapon is used in self-defense.

2. *Proportionality/Error*

The principle of proportionality may on first impressions appear to be satisfied by a nuclear response to a nuclear attack. Yet, viewed more carefully, this principle is violated in many ways. As France observed:

> "The assessment of the necessity and proportionality of a response to attack depends on the nature of the attack, its scope, the danger it poses and the adjustment of the measures of response to the desired defensive purpose." (CR 95/23, pp. 82–83.)

For these very reasons, precise assessment of the nature of the appropriate and proportionate response by a nation stricken by a nuclear attack becomes impossible. If one speaks in terms of a nuclear response to a nuclear attack, that nuclear response will tend, as already noted, to be an all-out nuclear response which opens up all the scenarios of global armageddon which are so vividly depicted in the literature relating to an all-out nuclear exchange.

Moreover, one is here speaking in terms of measurement—measurement of the intensity of the attack and the proportionality of the response. But one can measure only the measurable. With nuclear war, the quality of measurability ceases. Total devastation admits of no scales of measurement. We are in territory where the principle of proportionality becomes devoid of meaning.

It is relevant also, in the context of nuclear weapons, not to lose sight of the possibility of human error. However carefully planned, a nuclear response to a nuclear attack cannot, in the confusion of the moment, be finely graded so as to assess the strength of the weapons of attack, and to respond in like measure. Even in the comparatively tranquil and leisured atmosphere of peace, error is possible, even to the extent of unleashing an unintentional nuclear attack. This has emerged from studies of unintentional nuclear war. The response, under the stress of nuclear attack, would be far more prone to accident.

According to the *Bulletin of the Atomic Scientists:*

> "Top decision-makers as well as their subordinate information suppliers rely on computers and other equipment which have become even more complex and therefore more vulnerable to malfunction. Machine failures or human failures or a combination of the two could, had they not been discovered within minutes, have caused unintended nuclear war in a number of reported cases."

The result would be all-out nuclear war. Here again there is confirmation from statesmen, who have had much experience in matters of foreign and military policy, that all-out nuclear war is likely to ensue. Robert McNamara observes:

> "It is inconceivable to me, as it has been to others who have studied the matter, that 'limited' nuclear wars would remain limited—any decision to use nuclear weapons would imply a high probability of the same cataclysmic consequences as a total nuclear exchange."

Former Secretary of State, Dr. Kissinger, has also written to the same effect:

> "Limited war is not simply a matter of appropriate military forces and doctrines. It also places heavy demands on the discipline and subtlety of the political leadership and on the confidence of the society in it. For limited war is psychologically a much more complex problem than all-out war. . . . An all-out war will in all likelihood be decided so rapidly—if it is possible to speak of decision in such a war—and the suffering it entails will be so vast as to obscure disputes over the nuances of policy."

He proceeds to observe:

> "Limited nuclear war is not only impossible, according to this line of reasoning, but also undesirable. For one thing, it would cause devastation in the combat zone approaching that of thermonuclear war in severity. We would, therefore, be destroying the very people we were seeking to protect."

It is thus no fanciful speculation that the use of nuclear weapons in self-defense would result in a cataclysmic nuclear exchange. That is a risk which humanitarian law would consider to be totally unacceptable. It is a risk which no legal system can sanction.

3. *Discrimination*

As already observed earlier in this opinion, nuclear weapons violate the principle of discrimination between armed forces and civilians. True, other weapons also do, but the intensity of heat and blast, not to speak of radiation, are factors which place the nuclear weapon in a class apart from the others. When one speaks of weapons that count their victims by hundreds of thousands, if not millions, principles of discrimination cease to have any legal relevance.

4. *Non-belligerent States*

One of the principal objections to the use of nuclear weapons in self-defense occurs under this head. Self-defense is a matter of purely internal jurisdiction only if such defense can be undertaken without clearly causing damage to the rights of non-belligerent States. The moment a strategy of self-defense implies damage to a non-belligerent third party, such a matter ceases to be one of purely internal jurisdiction. It may be that the act of self-defense inadvertently and unintentionally causes damage to a third State. Such a situation is understandable and sometimes does occur, but that is not the case here.

DID YOU KNOW?

Advisory Opinions are pronouncements by the International Court of Justice that reflect authoritative views on important issues of international law. The Court may deliver an Advisory Opinion under Chapter IV of its Statute when requested to do so by certain organs or agencies of the United Nations. These Opinions are legally non-binding, but their nonbinding character does not mean that they are without legal effect. In arriving at them, the Court follows the same rules and procedures that govern its binding judgments.

5. *Genocide*

The topic of genocide has already been covered. Self-defense, which will, as shown in the discussion on proportionality, result in all probability in all-out nuclear war, is even more likely to cause genocide than the act of launching an initial strike. If the killing of human beings, in numbers ranging from a million to a billion, does not fall within the definition of genocide, one may well ask what will. No nation can be seen as entitled to risk the destruction of civilization for its own national benefit.

6. *Environmental Damage*

Similar considerations exist here, as in regard to genocide. The widespread contamination of the environment may even lead to a nuclear winter and to the destruction of the ecosystem. These results will ensue equally, whether the nuclear weapons causing them are used in aggression or in self-defense. International law relating to the environment, in so far as it concerns nuclear weapons, is dealt with at greater length in my dissenting opinion on the World Health Organization request (I. C. J. *Reports 1996*, pp. 139–143), and the discussion in that opinion should be considered as supplementary to the above discussion.

The West Australian

BRITAIN TESTS HER FIRST ATOMIC BOMB OFF W.A. COAST

Cloud Billows High Over The Indian Ocean

No Ground Shock Felt

A Faint Wisp Of Cloud

Task For The R.A.A.F.

"A POOR MAN'S BOMB" TO HARWELL MEN

News Travelled Faster Than Shock Wave

Front page of *The West Australian* newspaper, October 4, 1952. Courtesy of *The West Australian.*

7. *Human Rights*

All the items of danger to human rights as recounted earlier in this opinion would be equally operative whether the weapons are used in aggression or in self-defense. The humanitarian principles discussed above have long passed the stage of being merely philosophical aspirations. They are the living law and represent the highwatermark of legal achievement in the difficult task of imposing some restraints on the brutalities of unbridled war. They provide the ground-rules for military action today and have been forged by the community of nations under the impact of the sufferings of untold millions in two global cataclysms and many smaller wars. As with all legal principles, they govern without distinction all nations great and small.

It seems difficult, with any due regard to the consistency that must underlie any credible legal system, to contemplate that all these hard-won principles should bend aside in their course and pass the nuclear weapon by, leaving that unparalleled agency of destruction free to achieve on a magnified scale the very evils which these principles were designed to prevent.

SOURCE: Courtesy of the International Court of Justice, http://www.icj-cij.org/docket/index.php?p1=3&p2=4&k=e1&p3=4&case=95.

Official copy of a judgment of the International Court of Justice, signed and sealed. Courtesy of Jeroen Bouman.

ANALYSIS

In response to a request from the UN General Assembly, the ICJ on July 8, 1996, handed down an advisory opinion on the legality of the threat or use of nuclear weapons. The Opinion provides an authoritative view concerning the legality under international law of the use, or the threat of use, of nuclear weapons. The Court held that neither customary nor conventional international law contained any comprehensive and universal prohibition of the threat or use of nuclear weapons as such. On the other hand it found that the threat or use of nuclear weapons was generally contrary to the rules of international law applicable in armed conflict (so-called international humanitarian law).

The Court then specifically addressed the question of whether nuclear weapons may be used in self-defense. The judges decided that they were unable to conclude definitively whether the threat or use of nuclear weapons would be lawful or unlawful in an extreme circumstance of self-defense in which the very survival of a State would be at stake. This finding, however, was highly controversial, and the Court was split with seven judges voting in favor (including the casting vote of the President), and seven voting against it. The controversies particularly centered on the question of whether the use of nuclear weapons complied with the self-defense requirement of proportionality. Some of the dissenting judges argued that the use of nuclear weapons would always constitute a violation of the principle of proportionality, given that these weapons were incompatible with the law of armed conflict. This argument also found significant support among civil society organizations and in the academic literature on the subject.

Notes

1. Derek W. Bowett, *Self Defence in International Law* (Manchester: Manchester University Press, 1958), 185–186.
2. Ian Brownlie, *International Law and the Use of Force by States* (Oxford: Clarendon Press, 1963), 107–127.

3. John Yoo, "Using Force," *University of Chicago Law Review* 71 (Summer 2004): 742.
4. Albrecht Randelzhoffer, "Article 51," in *The Charter of the United Nations. A Commentary*, 2nd ed., ed. Bruno Simma (Oxford: Oxford University Press, 2002), 803.
5. Bowett, *Self Defence in International Law*, 188–189.
6. Christine Gray, *International Law and the Use of Force*, 2nd ed. (Oxford: Oxford University Press), 130.
7. Michael Bothe, "Terrorism and the Legality of Pre-emptive Force," *European Journal of International Law* 14, no. 2 (2003): 227–240.
8. Christian Enemark and Christopher Michaelsen, "Just War Doctrine and the Invasion of Iraq," *Australian Journal of Politics and History* 51, no. 4 (2005): 548.
9. The National Security Strategy of the United States of America, March 2006, available at http://georgewbush-whitehouse.archives.gov/nsc/nss/2006/.
10. Ibid, p. 8.
11. Ibid, p. 1.
12. Martin Dixon and Robert McCorquodale, *Cases and Materials on International Law*, 3rd ed. (London: Blackstone Press, 2000), 575.
13. Yoram Dinstein, *War, Aggression and Self-Defence*, 4th ed. (Cambridge, UK: Cambridge University Press, 2005), 231.
14. Michael Akehurst, "The Use of Force to Protect Nationals Abroad," *International Relations* 5 (1977): 3–29.

FURTHER READING

Falk, Richard A. "Nuclear Weapons, International Law and the World Court: A Historic Encounter." *American Journal of International Law* 91, no. 1 (1997): 64–74.

Matheson, Michael J. "Opinions of the International Court of Justice on the Threat or Use of Nuclear Weapons." *American Journal of International Law* 91, no. 3 (1997): 417–435.

Pogany, Istvan. "Nuclear Weapons and Self-defense in International Law." *Connecticut Journal of International Law* 2 (1986-87): 97–119.

Singh, Nagendra, and Edward McWhinney. *Nuclear Weapons and Contemporary International Law*. The Hague: Martinus Nijhoff, 1989.

Singh, Nagendra. "The Right to Self-Defense in Relation to the Use of Nuclear Weapons." *Indian Yearbook of International Affairs* 5 (1956): 3–37.

6

THE CRIME OF AGGRESSION

The defendants listen as the prosecution begins introducing documents at the International Military Tribunal trial of war criminals at Nuremberg, November 22, 1945. National Archives. Courtesy of USHMM Photo Archives.

OVERVIEW

This chapter looks at the notion of aggression and its international criminality. Attention is drawn to the charters and judgments of the Nuremberg and Tokyo tribunals of the immediate post–World War II period. These tribunals were the first multinational institutions established for the purpose of prosecuting and punishing international crimes including the planning, preparation, and waging of a war of aggression. The chapter then examines developments in the UN era and discusses key provisions of the UN General Assembly Resolution 3314 (XXIX) on the Definition of Aggression, which generally reaffirmed the principle that acts of aggression are contrary to the UN Charter and international law. Finally, the chapter looks at the 1998 Rome Statute, which explicitly recognizes the criminality of aggressive war under international law and stipulates that this crime is to be prosecuted by the International Criminal Court.

The Nuremberg and Tokyo Trials and the Criminality of Aggressive War

- ***Documents:*** Extracts from the Charter of the International Military Tribunal (Nuremberg), Charter of the International Military Tribunal for the Far East (Tokyo) Control Council Law No. 10 and from the Judgment of the International Military Tribunal
- ***Date:*** 1945–1949
- ***Significance:*** The Nuremberg and Tokyo tribunals were the first multinational institutions established for the purpose of prosecuting and punishing crimes having an international dimension and scope. These crimes included the planning, preparation, and waging of a war of aggression. Today, the Tribunals' charter and judgments form the basis for the criminalization of aggressive war.

DOCUMENTS

Charter of the International Military Tribunal (Nuremberg)

Article 6

The Tribunal established by the Agreement referred to in Article 1 hereof for the trial and punishment of the major war criminals of the European Axis countries shall have the power to try and punish persons who, acting in the interests of the European Axis countries, whether as individuals or as members of organizations, committed any of the following crimes.

The following acts, or any of them, are crimes coming within the jurisdiction of the Tribunal for which there shall be individual responsibility:

(a) *Crimes against Peace*: namely, planning, preparation, initiation or waging of a war of aggression, or a war in violation of international treaties, agreements or assurances, or participation in a common plan or conspiracy for the accomplishment of any of the foregoing;

(b) *War Crimes*: namely, violations of the laws or customs of war. Such violations shall include, but not be limited to, murder, ill-treatment or deportation to slave labor or for any other purpose of civilian population of or in occupied territory, murder or ill-treatment of prisoners of war or persons on the seas, killing of hostages, plunder of public or private property, wanton destruction of cities, towns or villages, or devastation not justified by military necessity;

(c) *Crimes against Humanity*: namely, murder, extermination, enslavement, deportation, and other inhumane acts committed against any civilian population, before or during the war; or persecutions on political, racial or religious grounds in execution of or in connection with any crime within the jurisdiction of the Tribunal, whether or not in violation of the domestic law of the country where perpetrated.

Leaders, organizers, instigators and accomplices participating in the formulation or execution of a common plan or conspiracy to commit any of the foregoing crimes are responsible for all acts performed by any persons in execution of such plan.

Article 7

The official position of defendants, whether as Heads of State or responsible officials in Government Departments, shall not be considered as freeing them from responsibility or mitigating punishment.

Article 8

The fact that the Defendant acted pursuant to order of his Government or of a superior shall not free him from responsibility, but may be considered in mitigation of punishment if the Tribunal determines that justice so requires.

Charter of the International Military Tribunal for the Far East (Tokyo)

Article 5

Jurisdiction over Persons and Offences. The Tribunal shall have the power to try and punish Far Eastern war criminals who as individuals or as members of organizations are charged with offences which include Crimes against Peace.

The following acts, or any of them, are crimes coming within the jurisdiction of the Tribunal for which there shall be individual responsibility:

(a) *Crimes against Peace*: Namely, the planning, preparation, initiation or waging of a declared or undeclared war of aggression, or a war in violation of international law, treaties, agreements or assurances, or participation in a common plan or conspiracy for the accomplishment of any of the foregoing;

(b) *Conventional War Crimes*: Namely, violations of the laws or customs of war;

(c) *Crimes against Humanity*: Namely, murder, extermination, enslavement, deportation, and other inhumane acts committed against any civilian population, before or during the war, or persecutions on political or racial grounds in execution of or in connection with any crime within the jurisdiction of the Tribunal, whether or not in violation of the domestic law of the country where perpetrated. Leaders, organizers, instigators and accomplices participating in the formulation or execution of a common plan or conspiracy to commit any of the foregoing crimes are responsible for all acts performed by any person in execution of such plan.

Control Council Law No. 10

Punishment of Persons Guilty of War Crimes, Crimes against Peace and against Humanity

In order to give effect to the terms of the *Moscow Declaration* of 30 October 1943 and the *London Agreement* of 8 August 1945 and the Charter issued pursuant thereto and in order to establish a uniform legal basis in Germany for the prosecution of war criminals and other similar offenders, other than those dealt with by the International Military Tribunal, the Control Council enacts as follows:

Article I

The *Moscow Declaration* of 30 October 1943 "Concerning Responsibility of Hitlerites for Committed Atrocities" and the *London Agreement* of 8 August 1945 "Concerning Prosecution and Punishment of Major War Criminals of European Axis" are made integral parts of this Law. Adherence to the provisions of the London Agreement by any of the United Nations, as provided for in Article V of that Agreement, shall not entitle such Nation to participate or interfere in the operation of this Law within the Control Council area of authority in Germany.

Article II

1. Each of the following acts is recognized as a crime:
   (a) Crimes against Peace. Initiation of invasions of other countries and wars of aggression in violation of international laws and treaties, including but not limited to planning, preparation, initiation or waging a war of aggression, or a war of violation of international treaties, agreements or assurances, or participation in a common plan or conspiracy for the accomplishment of any of the foregoing.
   (b) War Crimes. Atrocities or offenses against persons or property constituting violations of the laws or customs of war, including but not limited to, murder, ill treatment or deportation to slave labour or for any other purpose, of civilian population from occupied territory, murder or ill treatment of prisoners of war or persons on the seas, killing of hostages, plunder of pub-

lic or private property, wanton destruction of cities, towns or villages, or devastation not justified by military necessity.

(c) Crimes against Humanity. Atrocities and offenses, including but not limited to murder, extermination, enslavement, deportation, imprisonment, torture, rape, or other inhumane acts committed against any civilian population, or persecutions on political, racial or religious grounds whether or not in violation of the domestic laws of the country where perpetrated.

(d) Membership in categories of a criminal group or organization declared criminal by the International Military Tribunal.

2. Any person without regard to nationality or the capacity in which he acted, is deemed to have committed a crime as defined in paragraph 1 of this Article, if he was (a) a principal or (b) was an accessory to the commission of any such crime or ordered or abetted the same or (c) took a consenting part therein or (d) was connected with plans or enterprises involving its commission or (e) was a member of any organization or group connected with the commission of any such crime or (f) with reference to paragraph 1 (a) if he held a high political, civil or military (including General Staff) position in Germany or in one of its Allies, co-belligerents or satellites or held high position in the financial, industrial or economic life of any such country.

3. Any persons found guilty of any of the crimes above mentioned may upon conviction be punished as shall be determined by the tribunal to be just. Such punishment may consist of one or more of the following:

(a) Death.

(b) Imprisonment for life or a term of years, with or without hard labor.

(c) Fine, and imprisonment with or without hard labour, in lieu thereof.

(d) Forfeiture of property.

(e) Restitution of property wrongfully acquired.

(f) Deprivation of some or all civil rights.

Any property declared to be forfeited or the restitution of which is ordered by the Tribunal shall be delivered to the Control Council for Germany, which shall decide on its disposal.

4. (a) The official position of any person, whether as Head of State or as a responsible official in a Government Department, does not free him from responsibility for a crime or entitle him to mitigation of punishment.

(b) The fact that any person acted pursuant to the order of his Government or of a superior does not free him from responsibility for a crime, but may be considered in mitigation.

5. In any trial or prosecution for a crime herein referred to, the accused shall not be entitled to the benefits of any statute of limitation in respect to the period from 30 January 1933 to 1 July 1945, nor shall any immunity, pardon or amnesty granted under the Nazi regime be admitted as a bar to trial or punishment.

Hideki Tojo, Former Japanese General Premier and War Minister from December 2, 1941, to July 1944, takes the stand for the first time during the International Tribunal trials, Tokyo, Japan. Courtesy of the U.S. Government.

International Military Tribunal (Nuremberg), Judgment 1 October 1946

The Tribunal now turns to the consideration of the crimes against peace charged in the Indictment. Count One of the Indictment charges the defendants with conspiring or having a common plan to commit crimes against peace.

Count Two of the Indictment charges the defendants with committing specific crimes against peace by planning, preparing, initiating, and waging wars of aggression against a number of other States. It will be convenient to consider the question of the existence of a common plan and the question of aggressive war together, and to deal later in this Judgment with the question of the individual responsibility of the defendants.

The charges in the Indictment that the defendants planned and waged aggressive wars are charges of the utmost gravity. War is essentially an evil thing. Its consequences are not confined to the belligerent states alone, but affect the whole world.

To initiate a war of aggression, therefore, is not only an international crime; it is the supreme international crime differing only from other war crimes in that it contains within itself the accumulated evil of the whole.

The first acts of aggression referred to in the Indictment are the seizure of Austria and Czechoslovakia and the first war of aggression charged in the Indictment is the war against Poland begun on the 1st September, 1939.

Before examining that charge it is necessary to look more closely at some of the events which preceded these acts of aggression. The war against Poland did not come suddenly out of an otherwise clear sky; the evidence has made it plain that this war of aggression, as well as the seizure of Austria and Czechoslovakia, was pre-meditated and carefully prepared, and was not undertaken until the moment was thought opportune for it to be carried through as a definite part of the pre-ordained scheme and plan.

For the aggressive designs of the Nazi Government were not accidents arising out of the immediate political situation in Europe and the world; they were a deliberate and essential part of Nazi foreign policy.

From the beginning, the National Socialist movement claimed that its object was to unite the German people in the consciousness of their mission and destiny, based on inherent qualities of race, and under the guidance of the Fuehrer.

For its achievement, two things were deemed to be essential: the disruption of the European order as it had existed since the Treaty of Versailles, and the creation of a Greater Germany beyond the frontiers of 1914. This necessarily involved the seizure of foreign territories.

DID YOU KNOW?

The United States–led invasion of Iraq in 2003 was generally considered to be in violation of international law. Nevertheless, it is difficult to argue that the invasion qualifies as a criminal war of aggression. Publicly available evidence does not suggest that the "Coalition of the Willing" was interested in annexing or subjugating Iraq, for instance. The invasion thus appears to have lacked the specific aggressive element necessary under customary international law for a war to be one of aggression.

War was seen to be inevitable, or at the very least, highly probable, if these purposes were to be accomplished. The German people, therefore, with all their resources were to be organised as a great political-military army, schooled to obey without question any policy decreed by the State.

SOURCE: Courtesy of the Lillian Goldman Law Library, Yale Law School, http://avalon.law.yale.edu/imt/judnazi.asp#prep, http://avalon.law.yale.edu/imt/imtconst.asp.

> **DID YOU KNOW?**
>
> **In History: Why Nuremberg?**
>
> The Bavarian city of Nuremberg in southern Germany was chosen as the site for the trials for specific reasons. Its Palace of Justice was spacious and one of the few that had remained largely intact through extensive Allied bombing of Germany. In addition, Nuremberg was considered the ceremonial birthplace of the Nazi Party. It was thus a fitting place to mark the Party's symbolic demise. The prosecution entered indictments against 24 major war criminals and six criminal organizations: the leadership of the Nazi party, the Schutzstaffel (SS) and Sicherheitsdienst (SD), the Gestapo, the Sturmabteilung (SA), and the High Command of the German armed forces (Oberkommando Wehrmacht). Twelve defendants were sentenced to death by hanging, seven defendants were given lengthy prison sentences, and three were acquitted. Of the twelve defendants sentenced to death, two were not hanged: Hermann Göring committed suicide the night before the execution, and Martin Bormann was convicted in absentia. The remaining ten defendants sentenced to death were hanged on October 16, 1946.

ANALYSIS

The Nuremberg and Tokyo Trials were a series of trials most notable for the prosecution of members of the political, military, and economic leadership of Nazi Germany and Imperial Japan after their defeat in World War II. The tribunals were a response to the overwhelming horrors of the Nazi genocide in Europe and the Japanese crimes perpetrated during the wartime occupation of large parts of Southeast and East Asia. As early as 1942, the three major Allied wartime powers—the United States, the Soviet Union, and the United Kingdom—had entered into consultations on the prosecution and punishment of war crimes committed by Nazi Germany and Imperial Japan. The issue was discussed further at the conferences in Tehran (1943), Yalta (1945), and Potsdam (1945). British Prime Minister Winston Churchill initially advocated a policy of summary execution of those primarily responsible for determining and applying Nazi policy.[1] However, this approach was rejected by U.S. President Franklin D. Roosevelt, who insisted on the punishment of Nazi criminals in accordance with principles of the rule of law and due process. It was subsequently agreed to establish the International Military Tribunal in Nuremberg to try the "great Nazi criminals," while lesser Allied tribunals in the four occupied zones of Germany were to deal with minor criminals.

The legal basis for the Nuremberg Trials was established at the London Conference held between June and August 1945. The conference concluded on August 8, 1945, with the adoption of the London Agreement, to which was annexed the Charter of the International Military Tribunal. The Charter provided for the prosecution and punishment of "crimes against peace," "war crimes," and "crimes against humanity." On July 26, 1945, two weeks before the conclusion of the London Conference, the Allied powers announced their intention to try leading Japanese officials for these same crimes. The provisions of the Nuremberg Charter were thus subsequently incorporated into the Charter of the International Military Tribunal for the Far East in Tokyo. They also featured in the Control Council Law No. 10, which the Allied Control Council issued on December 20, 1945, to empower any of the occupying authorities in Germany to prosecute suspected war criminals in their respective occupation zones. Based on this law, the U.S. authorities proceeded after the end of the initial Nuremberg Trial against the major war criminals to hold another twelve trials in Nuremberg.

The subject matter jurisdiction of the tribunals included "crimes against peace," "war crimes," and "crimes against humanity." The notion of "crimes against peace" was generally defined as planning, preparing, initiating, or waging of a war of aggression in violation of international treaties, agreements, or assurances. However, the illegality of war under international law was not itself considered sufficient to make it a war of aggression. Rather, an additional element of aggression was deemed necessary to distinguish a war of aggression from other wars that contravene international law. For instance, the wars initiated by Nazi Germany and Imperial Japan were found to be "aggressive" on the basis that they aimed to annex, totally or partially, the territory of the countries involved, or to subjugate these countries. The proposal to include the provision of "crimes against peace" in the Nuremberg and Tokyo Charters was initially made by the United Sates and formally presented to the London Conference on June 26, 1945. As Benjamin Ferencz, a U.S. prosecutor at the Nuremberg Trials, has pointed out, it was the same day as the San Francisco conference outlawed the use of force in the Charter of the United Nations.[2]

Prosecution and punishment of the leadership of Nazi Germany and Imperial Japan for crimes against peace encountered considerable criticism.[3] The Chief Justice of the U.S. Supreme Court, Harlan Fiske Stone, for instance, called the Nuremberg trials a fraud.[4] In particular, it was argued that crimes against peace were applied *ex post facto* and thus violated fundamental principles of justice such as the notion of *nullum crimen sine lege* ("one cannot be punished for doing something that is not prohibited by law"). As the Dutch judge at the Tokyo Trial, Bert V. A. Röling, pointed out, aggressive war was not a crime under international law at the beginning of the war.[5] Other criticisms included the assertion that justice was applied selectively. One of the charges brought against the German defendants at Nuremberg, for instance, was conspiracy to commit aggression against Poland in 1939. The military aggression against Poland followed the Secret Protocols of the 1939 German-Soviet Non-Aggression Pact, which proposed the partition of Poland between the Germans and the Soviets. Soviet leaders, however, were not tried for being part of the same conspiracy.

Today, the Charters of the Nuremberg and Tokyo Tribunals, as well as the judgments that clarified the offense of crimes against peace, form the basis for the criminalization of aggressive war. They are the starting points for the established *opinio juris* ("an opinion of law") of the international community that waging aggressive war is criminal. The criminality of aggressive war was subsequently reaffirmed by various resolutions of the UN General Assembly including the 1970 UN Friendly Relations Declaration and the 1974 UN Declaration of the Definition of Aggression (see Section 6.2). It was also incorporated into the 1998 Statute of the International Criminal Court (see Section 6.3) as an expression of the criminality of aggression under customary international law.

FURTHER READING

Brackman, Arnold C. *The Other Nuremberg: The Untold Story of the Tokyo War Crimes Trials*. New York: Morrow, 1987.

Buscher Frank M. *The US War Crimes Trial Program in Germany, 1946–1955*. New York: Greenwood Press, 1989.

Mettraux, Guénaël, ed. *Perspectives on the Nuremberg Trial*. Oxford: Oxford University Press, 2008.

Smith, Bradley F., ed. *The American Road to Nuremberg: The Documentary Record, 1944–1945*. Stanford, CA: Hoover Institution Press, 1982.

Wanhong, Zhang. "From Nuremberg to Tokyo: Some Reflections on the Tokyo Trial (On the Sixtieth Anniversary of the Nuremberg Trials)." *Cardozo Law Review* 27, no. 4 (2005–2006): 1673–1682.

The Prohibition of Aggression in the UN Era

- ***Document:*** UN General Assembly Resolution 3314 (XXIX) on the Definition of Aggression
- ***Date:*** December 14, 1974
- ***Where:*** New York City
- ***Significance:*** This General Assembly resolution adopted a definition of aggression and reaffirmed the criminality of aggressive war under international law.

DOCUMENT

UN GA Res. 3314 (XXIX), UN GAOR 29th Sess., Supp. No. 31 (1974)

The General Assembly,

Having considered the report of the Special Committee on the Question of Defining Aggression, established pursuant to its resolution 2330 (XXII) of 18 December 1967, covering the work of its seventh session held from 11 March to 12 April 1974, including the draft Definition of Aggression adopted by the Special Committee by consensus and recommended for adoption by the General Assembly,

Deeply convinced that the adoption of the Definition of Aggression would contribute to the strengthening of international peace and security,

1. *Approves* the Definition of Aggression, the text of which it annexed to the present resolution;
2. *Expresses its appreciation to* the Special Committee on the Question of Defining Aggression for its work which resulted in the elaboration of the Definition of Aggression;

3. *Calls upon* all States to refrain from all acts of aggression and other uses of force contrary to the Charter of the United Nations and the Declaration on Principles of International Law concerning Friendly Relations and Co-operation among States in accordance with the Charter of the United Nations;
4. *Calls the attention* of the Security Council to the Definition of Aggression, as set out below, and recommends that it should, as appropriate, take account of that Definition as guidance in determining, in accordance with the Charter, the existence of an act of aggression.

ANNEX
DEFINITION OF AGGRESSION

The General Assembly,

Basing itself on the fact that one of the fundamental purposes of the United Nations is to maintain international peace and security and to take effective collective measures for the prevention and removal of threats to the peace, and for the suppression of acts of aggression or other breaches of the peace,

Recalling that the Security Council, in accordance with Article 39 of the Charter of the United Nations, shall determine the existence of any threat to the peace, breach of the peace or act of aggression and shall make recommendations, or decide what measures shall be taken in accordance with Articles 41 and 42, to maintain or restore international peace and security,

Recalling also the duty of States under the Charter to settle their international disputes by peaceful means in order not to endanger international peace, security and justice,

Bearing in mind that nothing in this Definition shall be interpreted as in any way affecting the scope of the provisions of the Charter with respect to the functions and powers of the organs of the United Nations,

Considering also that, since aggression is the most serious and dangerous form of the illegal use of force, being fraught, in the conditions created by the existence of all types of weapons of mass destruction, with the possible threat of a world conflict and all its catastrophic consequences, aggression should be defined at the present stage,

Reaffirming the duty of States not to use armed force to deprive peoples of their right to self-determination, freedom and independence, or to disrupt territorial integrity,

Reaffirming also that the territory of a State shall not be violated by being the object, even temporarily, of military occupation or of other measures of force taken by another State in contravention of the Charter, and that it shall not be the object of acquisition by another State resulting from such measures or the threat thereof,

Reaffirming also the provisions of the Declaration on Principles of International Law concerning Friendly Relations and Co-operation among States in accordance with the Charter of the United Nations,

Convinced that the adoption of a definition of aggression ought to have the effect of deterring a potential aggressor, would simplify the determination of acts of aggression and the implementation of measures to suppress them and would also facilitate the protection of the rights and lawful interests of, and the rendering of assistance to, the victim,

Believing that, although the question whether an act of aggression has been committed must be considered in the light of all the circumstances of each particular case, it is nevertheless desirable to formulate basic principles as guidance for such determination,

Adopts the following Definition of Aggression:

Article 1

Aggression is the use of armed force by a State against the sovereignty, territorial integrity or political independence of another State, or in any other manner inconsistent with the Charter of the United Nations, as set out in this Definition.

Explanatory note: In this Definition the term "State":

(a) Is used without prejudice to questions of recognition or to whether a State is a Member of the United Nations;
(b) Includes the concept of a "group of States" where appropriate.

Article 2

The first use of armed force by a State in contravention of the Charter shall constitute *prima facie* evidence of an act of aggression although the Security Council may, in conformity with the Charter, conclude that a determination that an act of aggression has been committed would not be justified in the light of other relevant circumstances, including the fact that the acts concerned or their consequences are not of sufficient gravity.

Article 3

Any of the following acts, regardless of a declaration of war, shall, subject to and in accordance with the provisions of article 2, qualify as an act of aggression:

(a) The invasion or attack by the armed forces of a State of the territory of another State, of any military occupation, however temporary, resulting from such invasion or attack, or any annexation by the use of force of the territory of another State or part thereof;
(b) Bombardment by the armed forces of a State against the territory of another State or the use of any weapons by a State against the territory of another State;
(c) The blockade of the ports or coasts of a State by the armed forces of another State;
(e) The use of armed forces of one State which are within the territory of another State with the agreement of the receiving State, in contravention of the conditions provided for in the agreement or any extension of their presence in such territory beyond the termination of the agreement;

(f) The action of a State in allowing its territory, which it has placed at the disposal of another State, to be used by that other State for perpetrating an act of aggression against a third State;
(g) The sending by or on behalf of a State of armed hands, groups, irregulars or mercenaries, which carry out acts of armed force against another State of such gravity as to amount to the acts listed above, or its substantial involvement therein.

Article 4

The acts enumerated above are not exhaustive and the Security Council may determine that other acts constitute aggression under the provisions of the Charter.

Article 5

1. No consideration of whatever nature, whether political, economic, military or otherwise, may serve as a justification for aggression.
2. A war of aggression is a crime against international peace. Aggression gives rise to international responsibility.
3. No territorial acquisition or special advantage resulting from aggression is or shall be recognized as lawful.

Article 6

Nothing in this Definition shall be construed as in any way enlarging or diminishing the scope of the Charter, including its provisions concerning cases in which the use of force is lawful.

Schedule 7

Nothing in this Definition, and in particular article 3, could in any way prejudice the right to self-determination, freedom and independence, as derived from the Charter, of peoples forcibly deprived of that right and referred to in the Declaration on Principles of International Law concerning Friendly Relations and Co-operation among States in accordance with the Charter of the United Nations, particularly peoples under colonial and racist regimes or other forms of alien domination; nor the right of these peoples to struggle to that end and to seek and receive support, in accordance with the principles of the Charter and in conformity with the above-mentioned Declaration.

Article 8

In their interpretation and application the above provisions are interrelated and each provision should be construed in the context of the other provisions.

Explanatory Notes from the Report of the Special Committee on the Question of Defining Aggression, UN GAOR 29th Sess., Supp. No. 19:

1. With reference to article 3, paragraph (b), the Special Committee agreed that the expression "any weapons" is used without making a distinction between conventional weapons, weapons of mass destruction and any other kind of weapon.
2. With reference to article 5, paragraph 1, the Committee had in mind, in particular, the principle contained in the Declaration on Principles of International Law concerning Friendly Relations and Co-operation among States in accordance with the Charter of the United Nations according to which "No State or group of States has the right to intervene, directly or indirectly for any reason whatever, in the internal affairs of any other State".
3. With reference to article 5, paragraph 2, the words "international responsibility" are used without prejudice to the scope of this term.
4. With reference to article 5, paragraph 3, the Committee states that this paragraph should not be construed so as to prejudice the established principles of international law relating to the inadmissibility of territorial acquisition resulting from the threat or use of force.

SOURCE: UN GA Res. 3314 (XXIX), UN GAOR 29th Sess., Supp. No. 31 (1974).

ANALYSIS

The UN Declaration on the Definition of Aggression was adopted by the UN General Assembly without a vote on December 14, 1974. The Declaration was based on several draft proposals developed by the Special Committee on the Question of Defining Aggression, which had been set up by the General Assembly in 1967. As stated in the Resolution's preamble, the main purpose of adopting a definition of aggression was to contribute to the strengthening of international peace and security. It was thought that international agreement on the definition of aggression would further prevent States from resorting to measures involving the use of force to address international disputes.

One of the key provisions of the Declaration is to be found in Article 5(2), which distinguishes between "aggression" (giving rise to international responsibility) and a "war of aggression" as a crime against international peace. Acts of aggression are defined as armed invasions or attacks, bombardments, blockades, armed violations of territory, permitting other states to use one's own territory to perpetrate acts of aggression, and the employment of armed irregulars or mercenaries to carry out acts of aggression. A war of aggression is a series of acts committed with a sustained intent. Drawing on the Nuremberg Charter and judgments, the definition's distinction between an act of aggression and a war of aggression makes it clear that not every act of aggression would constitute a crime against international peace. This means that criminal liability of individual political leaders arises only in cases where it can be established that they were responsible for launching a war of aggression.

The wording of the definition remains controversial and has been subject to intense debate. Commentators have criticized, for instance, that the definition is highly state-centric in that it deems States to be the only actors liable for acts of aggression.[6] Nonstate actors and insurgent groups do not fall within the scope of the definition. Scholars have further criticized that the Definition of Aggression also did not cover acts by international alliances. The two key military alliances at the time of the definition's adoption, NATO and the Warsaw Pact, were nonstate parties and thus were outside the scope of the definition. Moreover, the formulation in Article 5(2) that aggression "gives rise to international responsibility" is considerably vague. The Explanatory Notes from the Report of the Special Committee on the Question of Defining Aggression stipulate that the term "international responsibility" is used without prejudice to its scope, but they fail to provide any guidance on its interpretation.

A further point of contention is the relevance of the definition of aggression for the interpretation of other key provisions of the Charter. In particular, it is somewhat controversial whether the provisions of the Declaration intend to define more precisely "the use of force" prohibited by Article 2(4) of the UN Charter or concern a closer determination of the notion of "armed attack" as contained in Article 51 of the Charter.[7] It is equally contentious whether the definition of aggression implicitly refers to Article 39 of the UN Charter, which allows the Security Council to resort to collective action in case of "any threat to the peace, breach of the peace or act of aggression."[8] This would mean that the definition could also be applied by the General Assembly, which in the Uniting for Peace Resolution (377 V) declared itself to be empowered to recommend collective action in the event of paralysis of the Security Council when a "breach of the peace or act of aggression" occurs.

These uncertainties notwithstanding, the Declaration on the Definition of Aggression is significant for a number of reasons. It generally reaffirmed the principle that acts of aggression are contrary to the UN Charter. In addition, as confirmed by the International Court of Justice in the *Nicaragua* judgment, some sections of the Declaration represent an expression of customary international law, which is legally binding on all States. The Declaration also confirmed the criminality of aggressive war, which was first recognized in the charters and judgments of the Nuremberg and Tokyo trials. As such it contributed to the legal development of international criminal law and represented an important step toward the establishment of a system of international criminal justice.

DID YOU KNOW?

General Assembly resolutions are generally considered to be legally nonbinding. Articles 10 and 14 of the UN Charter stipulate that the General Assembly may issue mere "recommendations" on questions or matters within the scope of the Charter. The recommendatory nature of General Assembly resolutions has also been repeatedly stressed by the International Court of Justice. Although the decisions of the General Assembly have no legally binding force for governments, they carry the weight of world opinion on major international issues, as well as the moral authority of the world community. Moreover, some resolutions—in particular, General Assembly declarations—reflect customary international law, which is legally binding on all States.

FURTHER READING

Brown-John, Lloyd. "The 1974 Definition of Aggression: A Query." *Canadian Yearbook of International Law* 15 (1977): 301–317.

Ferencz, Benjamin B. "The United Nations Consensus Definition of Aggression: Sieve or Substance?" *Journal of International Law and Economics* 10, no. 2 (1975): 701–724.

Garvey, Jack I. "The UN Definition of 'Aggression': Law and Illusion in the Context of Collective Security." *Virginia Journal of International Law* 17, no. 2 (1977): 177–199.

Röling, Bert V. A. "The 1974 UN Definition of Aggression." In *The Current Legal Regulation of the Use of Force*, edited by Antonio Cassese, 413–422. Dordrecht: Martinus Nijhoff, 1986.

Stone, Julius. "Hopes and Loopholes in the 1974 Definition of Aggression." *American Journal of International Law* 71, no. 2 (1977): 224–246.

Stone, Julius. *Aggression and World Order: A Critique of United Nations Theories of Aggression.* London: Stevens, 1958.

The Crime of Aggression in the Statute of the International Criminal Court

- ***Document:*** Extracts from the Statute of the International Criminal Court
- ***Date:*** July 17, 1998 (entry into force on July 1, 2002)
- ***Where:*** The Statute was adopted in Rome, Italy
- ***Significance:*** The Rome Statute explicitly recognized the criminality of aggressive war under international law and stipulates that this crime is to be prosecuted by the International Criminal Court.

DOCUMENT

Article 5—Crimes within the jurisdiction of the Court

1. The jurisdiction of the Court shall be limited to the most serious crimes of concern to the international community as a whole. The Court has jurisdiction in accordance with this Statute with respect to the following crimes:
   (a) The crime of genocide;
   (b) Crimes against humanity;
   (c) War crimes;
   (d) The crime of aggression.
2. The Court shall exercise jurisdiction over the crime of aggression once a provision is adopted in accordance with articles 121 and 123 defining the crime and setting out the conditions under which the Court shall exercise jurisdiction with respect to this crime. Such a provision shall be consistent with the relevant provisions of the Charter of the United Nations.

Article 121—Amendments

1. After the expiry of seven years from the entry into force of this Statute, any State Party may propose amendments thereto. The text of any proposed amendment shall be submitted to the Secretary-General of the United Nations, who shall promptly circulate it to all States Parties.
2. No sooner than three months from the date of notification, the Assembly of States Parties, at its next meeting, shall, by a majority of those present and voting, decide whether to take up the proposal. The Assembly may deal with the proposal directly or convene a Review Conference if the issue involved so warrants.
3. The adoption of an amendment at a meeting of the Assembly of States Parties or at a Review Conference on which consensus cannot be reached shall require a two-thirds majority of States Parties.
4. Except as provided in paragraph 5, an amendment shall enter into force for all States Parties one year after instruments of ratification or acceptance have been deposited with the Secretary-General of the United Nations by seven-eighths of them.
5. Any amendment to articles 5, 6, 7 and 8 of this Statute shall enter into force for those States Parties which have accepted the amendment one year after the deposit of their instruments of ratification or acceptance. In respect of a State Party which has not accepted the amendment, the Court shall not exercise its jurisdiction regarding a crime covered by the amendment when committed by that State Party's nationals or on its territory.
6. If an amendment has been accepted by seven-eighths of States Parties in accordance with paragraph 4, any State Party which has not accepted the amendment may withdraw from this Statute with immediate effect, notwithstanding article 127, paragraph 1, but subject to article 127, paragraph 2, by giving notice no later than one year after the entry into force of such amendment.
7. The Secretary-General of the United Nations shall circulate to all States Parties any amendment adopted at a meeting of the Assembly of States Parties or at a Review Conference.

Article 123—Review of the Statute

1. Seven years after the entry into force of this Statute the Secretary-General of the United Nations shall convene a Review Conference to consider any amendments to this Statute. Such review may include, but is not limited to, the list of crimes contained in article 5. The Conference shall be open to those participating in the Assembly of States Parties and on the same conditions.
2. At any time thereafter, at the request of a State Party and for the purposes set out in paragraph 1, the Secretary-General of the United Nations shall, upon

approval by a majority of States Parties, convene a Review Conference.

SOURCE: UN Treaty Collection. http://untreaty.un.org/cod/icc/index.html.

ANALYSIS

The crime of aggression was incorporated into Article 5 of the Rome Statute of the International Criminal Court (ICC). Nevertheless, in contrast to the other crimes listed in Article 5—the crime of genocide, crimes against humanity, and war crimes—the Rome Statute does not provide for any definition of the crime of aggression, as the negotiations at the Rome conference failed to reach agreement on the issue. The failure to reach agreement mainly stems from the general problem that acts of aggression are commonly perpetrated by States, whereas international criminal liability for it rests with individuals. A key challenge for the international community is thus to find a formulation of the crime of aggression that addresses this fundamental tension.

> **DID YOU KNOW?**
>
> The International Criminal Court (ICC) is an independent, permanent court that tries persons accused of the most serious crimes of international concern, namely genocide, crimes against humanity, and war crimes. Unlike the International Court of Justice, the ICC is legally and functionally independent from the United Nations. It is based on a treaty, joined by 108 countries. The ICC is a court of last resort. It will not act if a case is investigated or prosecuted by a national judicial system unless the national proceedings are not genuine; for example, if formal proceedings were undertaken solely to shield a person from criminal responsibility. Proceedings before the ICC may be initiated by a State Party, the Prosecutor, or the UN Security Council. The jurisdiction and functioning of the ICC are governed by the Rome Statute. The Court's working languages are English and French.

In 2002, the Assembly of States Parties to the ICC thus established a Special Working Group to prepare a proposal on the definition of the crime of aggression, including conditions under which the Court may exercise jurisdiction. It is envisaged that the Special Working Group reports to the Review Conference, which is to be held in 2009 (Article 123 of the ICC Statute). The Special Working Group has since made significant progress. In June 2008, the Group's Chairman, Ambassador Christian Wenaweser of Liechtenstein, introduced the latest version of a discussion paper on the crime of aggression.[9] This paper defined the crime of aggression as follows:

The International Criminal Court in The Hague, Netherlands. Courtesy of Gebruiker: Hanhil.

1. For the purpose of this Statute, "crime of aggression" means the planning preparation, initiation or execution, by a person in a position effectively to exercise control over or to direct the political or military action of a State, of an act of aggression which, by its character, gravity and scale, constitutes a manifest violation of the Charter of the United Nations.
2. For the purpose of paragraph 1, "act of aggression" means the use of armed force by a State against the sovereignty, territorial integrity or political independence of another State, or in any other manner inconsistent with the Charter of the United Nations. Any of the

DID YOU KNOW?

In History

In June 1998, the United Nations General Assembly convened a five-week diplomatic conference in Rome to finalize and adopt a convention on the establishment of an international criminal court. A key objective of the Rome conference was to achieve the broadest possible acceptance of such a court by mainly adopting into its Statute provisions recognized under customary international law. On July 17, 1998, the Rome Statute was adopted by a vote of 120 to 7, with 21 countries abstaining. The seven countries that voted against the treaty were Iraq, Israel, Libya, the People's Republic of China, Qatar, the United States, and Yemen. Article 126 of the Statute provided that it would enter into force shortly after the number of States that had ratified it reached sixty. This happened on April 11, 2002, when ten countries ratified the statute at the same time at a special ceremony held at the United Nations headquarters in New York. The treaty entered into force on July 1, 2002; the ICC can prosecute only crimes committed on or after that date.

following acts, regardless of a declaration of war, shall, in accordance with United Nations General Assembly resolution 3314 (XXIX) of 14 December 1974, qualify as an act of aggression:

(a) The invasion or attack by the armed forces of a State of the territory of another State, or any military occupation, however temporary, resulting from such invasion or attack, or any annexation by the use of force of the territory of another State or part thereof;
(b) Bombardment by the armed forces of a State against the territory of another State or the use of any weapons by a State against the territory of another State;
(c) The blockade of the ports or coasts of a State by the armed forces of another State;
(d) An attack by the armed forces of a State on the land, sea or air forces, or marine and air fleets of another State;
(e) The use of armed forces of one State which are within the territory of another State with the agreement of the receiving State, in contravention of the conditions provided for in the agreement or any extension of their presence in such territory beyond the termination of the agreement;
(f) The action of a State in allowing its territory, which it has placed at the disposal of another State, to be used by that other State for perpetrating an act of aggression against a third State;

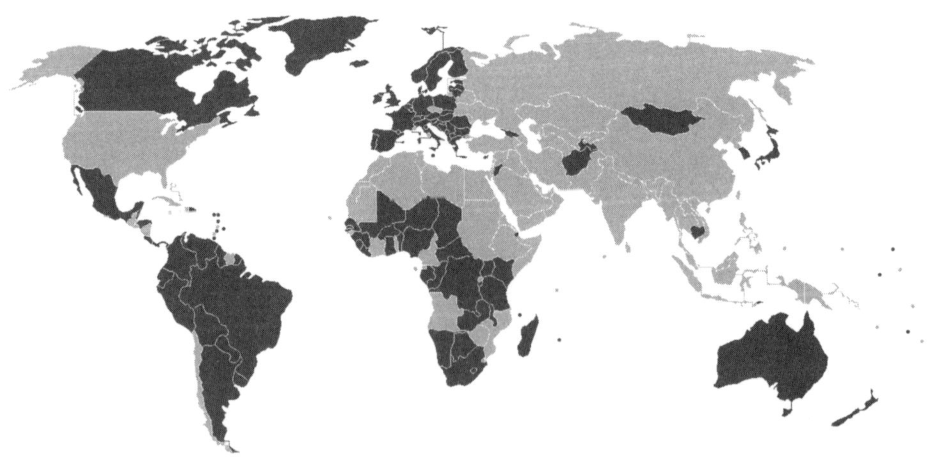

World map indicating States Parties to the Statute of the International Criminal Court. Courtesy of Wiki Commons.

(g) The sending by or on behalf of a State of armed bands, groups, irregulars or mercenaries, which carry out acts of armed force against another State of such gravity as to amount to the acts listed above, or its substantial involvement therein.

The draft paper makes explicit reference to the UN General Assembly resolution 3314 (XXIX) on the Definition of Aggression and proposes to incorporate several of its provisions into the Rome Statute. As such, the proposal goes beyond what is currently criminal under customary international law. It is thus uncertain whether the proposal will receive the support of the Assembly of States Parties to the ICC.

A further point of contention is the role of the UN Security Council in the ICC prosecution of the crime of aggression. According to Article 24 of the UN Charter, the Security Council has primary responsibility for the maintenance of international peace and security. As a consequence, agreement exists that the Security Council should be given priority in determining whether a war of aggression has occurred. The ICC should therefore prosecute aggression only if the Security Council has already dealt with the situation and made a respective determination. Nevertheless, disagreement exists over whether, and to what extent, the ICC may take action in the event that the Security Council, for political or other reasons, does not make any such determination. It has been suggested that in this case the ICC should be able to initiate investigations in the absence of a Security Council decision after a certain period of time. Other proposals include the establishment of a procedure to assign the decision to another organ such as the UN General Assembly or the Court itself. It is unclear at this stage which proposal, if any, will prevail at the end. What is clear, however, is that an adoption of a definition of the crime of aggression under the Rome Statute would represent a milestone in the development of international criminal law, as it would put further pressure on political leaders to carefully assess all consequences before deciding to resort to the use of force.

Notes

1. Antonio Cassese, *International Criminal Law*, 2nd ed. (Oxford: Oxford University Press, 2008), 320.
2. Benjamin B. Ferencz, "Defining Aggression: Where It Stands and Where It's Going," *American Journal of International Law* 66, no. 2 (1972): 492.
3. George A. Finch, "The Nuremburg Trial and International Law," *American Journal of International Law* 41, no. 1 (1947): 24–28.
4. Alpheus T. Mason, *Harlan Fiske Stone: Pillar of the Law* (New York: Viking, 1956).
5. Bert V. A. Röling and Antonio Cassese, *The Tokyo Trial and Beyond* (London: Polity, 1993), 98.
6. Julius Stone, "Hopes and Loopholes in the 1974 Definition of Aggression," *American Journal of International Law* 71, no. 2 (1977): 224–246.
7. Bert V. A. Röling, "The 1974 UN Definition of Aggression," in Antonio Cassese, ed., *The Current Legal Regulation of the Use of Force* (Dordrecht: Martinus Nijhoff, 1986), 413–422.

8. Jochen A. Frowein and Nico Krisch, "Article 39," in Bruno Simma, ed., *The Charter of the United Nations. A Commentary*, 2nd ed. (Oxford: Oxford University Press, 2002), 722.
9. International Criminal Court, Assembly of States Parties, *Discussion Paper on the Crime of Aggression Proposed by the Chairman* (revision June 2008), Doc .ICC-ASP/6/SWGCA/2 (May 14, 2008), http://www.icc-cpi.int/library/asp/ICC-ASP-6-SWGCA-2__English.pdf.

FURTHER READING

Blumenthal, David A., and Timothy L. H. McCormack, eds. *The Legacy of Nuremberg: Civilising Influence or Institutionalised Vengeance?* Leiden: Martinus Nijhoff, 2008.

Cassese, Antonio. *International Criminal Law*. 2nd ed. Oxford: Oxford University Press, 2008.

International Criminal Court, Assembly of States Parties. *Discussion Paper on the Crime of Aggression proposed by the Chairman* (revision June 2008). Doc. ICC-ASP/6/SWGCA/2 (14 May 2008), http://www.icc-cpi.int/library/asp/ICC-ASP-6-SWGCA-2__English.pdf.

Politi, Mauro, and Guiseppe Nesi, eds. *The International Criminal Court and the Crime of Aggression*. Aldershot, UK: Ashgate, 2004.

Politi, Mauro, and Guiseppe Nesi, eds. *The Rome Statute of the International Criminal Court: A Challenge to Impunity*. Aldershot, UK: Ashgate, 2001.

Scharf, Michael P. "Results of the Rome Conference for an International Criminal Court." *American Society of International Law—Insights*, August 1998, http://www.asil.org/insigh23.cfm.

7

CAN COLLECTIVE SECURITY WORK?

Iraqi armored personnel carriers, tanks, and trucks destroyed in a Coalition attack along a road in the Euphrates River Valley during Operation Desert Storm. © U.S. Department of Defense.

OVERVIEW

The idea of collective security is an important feature of the United Nations structure for the maintenance of international peace and security. It has also proven to be one of the difficult features to implement. After the failure of the League of Nations' attempts to promote collective security, the United Nations approach was meant to have been based on more realistic foundations. In the years since the adoption of the UN Charter, however, the experience has been decidedly mixed. There have been only two occasions when the Security Council has formally initiated collective security actions. On other occasions, incidents that might normally have been seen to be in violation of the Charter's prohibition of the use of force have either been ignored or have been explained away behind the justification, usually, of self-defense. This chapter considers examples of when collective security was resorted to, and when the international community decided to ignore an apparent violation of the Charter.

Where Collective Security Has Been Invoked

- ***Document:*** United Nations Security Council Resolutions 82 [S/1501] and 83 [S/1511]
- ***Date:*** Resolution 82 was adopted by the Security Council on June 25, 1950, and Resolution 83 was adopted on June 27, 1950.
- ***Where:*** United Nations, New York
- ***Significance:*** Together, these resolutions provide the basis for the resort to collective security in the Korean peninsula by the United Nations. The Korean action was the only occasion during the Cold War when the Security Council authorized the resort to force following a breach of the peace by a State.

DOCUMENT

Security Council Resolution 82 (1950)

The Security Council,

Recalling the finding of the General Assembly in its resolution 293(IV) of 21 October, 1949, that the Government of the Republic of Korea is a lawfully established government having effective control and jurisdiction over that part of Korea where the United Nations Temporary Commission on Korea was able to observe and consult and in which the great majority of the people of Korea reside; that this government is based on elections which were a valid expression of the free will of the electorate of that part of Korea and which were observed by the Temporary Commission; and that this is the only such Government in Korea,

Mindful of the concern expressed by the General Assembly in its resolutions 195(III) of 12 December, 1948, and 293(IV) of 21 October, 1949, about the consequences which might follow unless member states refrained from acts derogatory to the results sought to be achieved by the United Nations in bringing about the complete independence and unity of Korea; and the concern expressed that the situation described by the United Nations Commission on Korea in its report menaces the safety and well-being of the Republic of Korea and of the people of Korea and might lead to open military conflict there.

Noting with grave concern the armed attack on the Republic of Korea by forces from North Korea,

Determines that this action constitutes a breach of the peace; and

I

Calls for the immediate cessation of hostilities;

Calls upon the authorities in North Korea to withdraw forthwith their armed forces to the 38th parallel;

II

Requests the United Nations Commission on Korea:

(a) To communicate its fully considered recommendations on the situation with the least possible delay;

(b) To observe the withdrawal of North Korean forces to the 38th parallel;

(c) To keep the Security Council informed on the execution of this resolution:

III

Calls upon all member states to render every assistance to the United Nations in the execution of this resolution and to refrain from giving assistance to the North Korean authorities.

Security Council Resolution 83 (1950)

The Security Council,

Having determined that the armed attack upon the Republic of Korea by forces from North Korea constitutes a breach of the peace,

Having called for an immediate cessation of hostilities,

Having called upon the authorities in North Korea to withdraw forthwith their armed forces to the 38th parallel,

Having noted from the report of the United Nations Commission on Korea that the authorities in North Korea have neither ceased hostilities nor withdrawn their armed forces to the 38th parallel, and that urgent military measures are required to restore international peace and security,

Having noted the appeal from the Republic of Korea to the United Nations for immediate and effective steps to secure peace and security,

Recommends that the Members of the United Nations furnish such assistance to the Republic of Korea as may be necessary to repel the armed attack and to restore international peace and security in the area.

SOURCE: *Security Council Resolutions 82 and 83 (1950), Complaint of aggression on the Republic of Korea*. http://daccessdds.un.org/doc/RESOLUTION/GEN/NR0/064/95/IMG/NR006495.pdf?OpenElement.

ANALYSIS

Collective security is a system whereby States belonging to a collective security arrangement are legally and morally bound to go to the assistance of any other member of the arrangement that might be the victim of aggression and to punish the aggressor. Significantly, the use of force, except in cases of self-defense, is to be exercised and legitimized by a quasi-sovereign entity. States thereby effectively surrender an element of their sovereignty—the right to decide where, when, and why they might resort to force.[1] Collective security is a complex and challenging concept in the context of the State-based international system. At its most basic, it is a commitment to maintain the status quo or, at least, to fight against violent change in international relations. In theory, it also involves a commitment of all States to put aside their instincts to rely on self-help and, in the cause of a greater good, to rely on the effectiveness of the system for their own security. Certainly as foreseen under the League of Nations Covenant, a State is expected to make its armed forces available to meet any threat to international peace and security, regardless of how remote the problem might be to that State's interests.

Since the adoption of the UN Charter, the United Nations has fulfilled the role of the entity with ultimate responsibility for collective security. The Charter formalized the concept in several provisions, especially Article 51, which sets out the nature of self-defense in precise terms. These provisions give the United Nations the capacity to adopt a relatively flexible approach to threats to international peace and security that might arise. There are various measures available to the Organization, extending from largely exhortatory or condemnatory Security Council resolutions, through the application of sanctions of varying degrees of intensity and, ultimately, to the resort to force. It is with the last form that we are concerned here.

There is, however, relatively little by way of State practice or United Nations precedent on the resort to collective security in the international system. The first attempt to implement a collective security structure under the League of Nations is widely regarded as having failed. The United Nations has taken over the role of the League and is described as a collective security organization. The Korean action of 1950 to 1953 was the only example of collective security undertaken under the auspices of the United Nations during the Cold War. The next instance was not to occur until the end of the Cold War with the removal of Iraqi forces from Kuwait.

By 1950, the Security Council was largely incapacitated by United States–Soviet Union rivalry, and it could have been expected that the Soviet Union would have ensured that no UN response to the invasion was forthcoming. At the time of the North Korean attack, however, the Soviet Union was boycotting proceedings of the Council in protest at the refusal of the UN to acknowledge the right of the People's Republic of China to a permanent seat on the Security Council. It was only the absence of the

Soviet Union from the debate and vote that avoided a Soviet veto of the two resolutions that authorized the action. This development made the resort to force by the United Nations controversial, at least in Soviet eyes. In addition, Article 27(3) of the UN Charter states that:

> Decisions of the Security Council on all other matters shall be made by an affirmative vote of nine members including the concurring votes of the permanent members; provided that, in decisions under Chapter VI, and under paragraph 3 of Article 52, a party to a dispute shall abstain from voting.

The fact that the Soviet Union, a "permanent member," did not vote could be interpreted as a failure of the Security Council to comply with this provision of the Charter, thereby undermining the legality of the Korean action.[2] In addition, the fact that neither party to the conflict was a member of the United Nations added a further level of complexity to the legal issues involved. Some commentators have argued that the conflict was essentially a domestic issue, at least until the United States, United Nations, and, eventually, China became involved.[3] Finally, the key Security Council resolution (83/1950) recommended but did not make a binding decision that Member States should "furnish such assistance as may be necessary to repel the armed attack." Except indirectly through its reference to a "breach of the peace," the resolution also did not refer to Chapter VII of the Charter, the section

Korean civilians crowd a road seeking safety from the fighting, January 24, 1951. Courtesy of UN Photo.

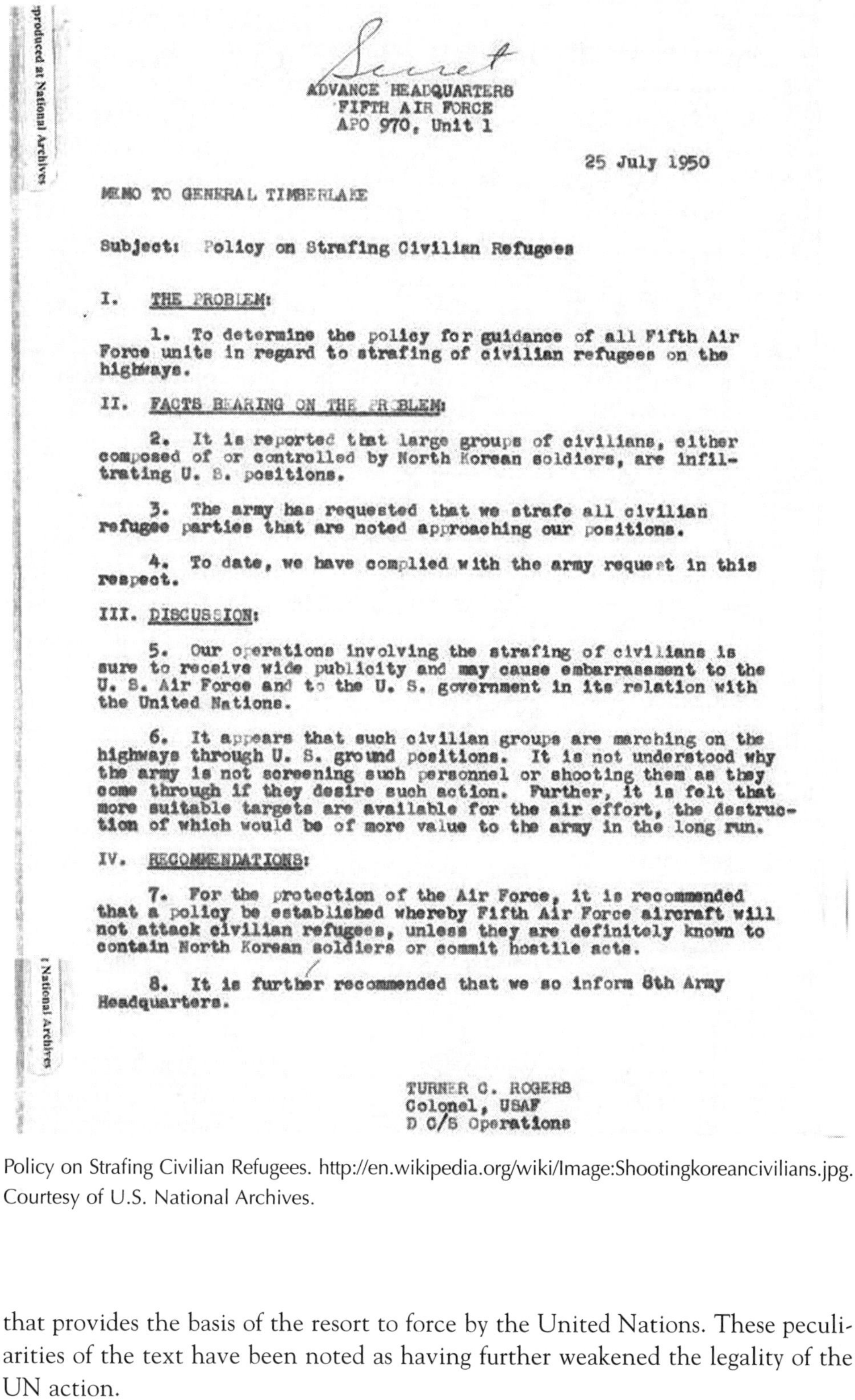

Secret

ADVANCE HEADQUARTERS
FIFTH AIR FORCE
APO 970, Unit 1

25 July 1950

MEMO TO GENERAL TIMBERLAKE

Subject: Policy on Strafing Civilian Refugees

I. THE PROBLEM:

1. To determine the policy for guidance of all Fifth Air Force units in regard to strafing of civilian refugees on the highways.

II. FACTS BEARING ON THE PROBLEM:

2. It is reported that large groups of civilians, either composed of or controlled by North Korean soldiers, are infiltrating U. S. positions.

3. The army has requested that we strafe all civilian refugee parties that are noted approaching our positions.

4. To date, we have complied with the army request in this respect.

III. DISCUSSION:

5. Our operations involving the strafing of civilians is sure to receive wide publicity and may cause embarrassment to the U. S. Air Force and to the U. S. government in its relation with the United Nations.

6. It appears that such civilian groups are marching on the highways through U. S. ground positions. It is not understood why the army is not screening such personnel or shooting them as they come through if they desire such action. Further, it is felt that more suitable targets are available for the air effort, the destruction of which would be of more value to the army in the long run.

IV. RECOMMENDATIONS:

7. For the protection of the Air Force, it is recommended that a policy be established whereby Fifth Air Force aircraft will not attack civilian refugees, unless they are definitely known to contain North Korean soldiers or commit hostile acts.

8. It is further recommended that we so inform 8th Army Headquarters.

TURNER C. ROGERS
Colonel, USAF
D C/S Operations

Policy on Strafing Civilian Refugees. http://en.wikipedia.org/wiki/Image:Shootingkoreancivilians.jpg. Courtesy of U.S. National Archives.

that provides the basis of the resort to force by the United Nations. These peculiarities of the text have been noted as having further weakened the legality of the UN action.

Despite these concerns, the United Nations' action is generally regarded as a legitimate response to North Korean aggression and, as such, provided some indication of the way in which the UN might respond to similar challenges to international peace and security in the future. It also, perhaps, highlighted some of the shortcomings of the idea of collective security as envisaged in the United Nations Charter. In both the Korean and Iraq–Kuwait crises, when the Security Council was provoked by the invasion of one country by another, the UN set as its goal the return to the *status quo ante*. Security Council Resolution 83 called on Members to assist in repelling the North Korean attack and restoring international peace and security. This was to be achieved by forcing North Korea back to the 38th parallel, just as the solution to the problem posed by Iraq's invasion of Kuwait was Iraq's expulsion from Kuwaiti territory (although Security Council resolution 687 of April 3, 1991, subsequently addressed border issues between the two countries).

To determine whether collective security can work, it is necessary to determine what is expected of such an action. If the goal of the collective response to conflict is simply to stop the fighting and return to the physical as opposed to political *status quo ante*, then it could be argued that the task is achievable, albeit, in the Korean case, with great difficulty. If, however, the objective is the achievement of a more lasting solution, then it must be considered that the achievements of collective security initiatives have been less compelling. An armistice agreement was signed by North Korea and the United States in July 1953. Since then, peace and security have been maintained between the two parties, a not inconsiderable achievement given the level of hostility between the two sides. Progress on core issues, however, has been limited. The armistice line and "demilitarized" zone remain a tense and heavily militarized area, contacts between North and South Korea are limited and fraught, and the United States and China are heavily involved in ensuring that frequent increases in tension do not get out of control. Arguably, the threat to international peace and security will remain until a broad framework to govern North–South relations can be developed.

A feature of collective security is its deterrence value. States must believe in the likelihood of a collective response to aggression. They must also believe in the determination of the international system to persist with a collective security action once it has begun. It would seem that North Korea made a serious miscalculation, perhaps misled by a speech in January 1950 by U.S. Secretary of State Dean Acheson, into thinking that the United States did not regard South Korea as a vital strategic interest and would not

DID YOU KNOW?

In History: North Korean atrocities

Evidence by Lt. Colonel J. Todd, JAGC, Chief, War Crimes Division, before the U.S. Senate Subcommittee on Korean War Atrocities, Permanent Subcommittee on Investigations of the Committee on Government Operations, December 3, 1953:

"The field team secures probative evidence of war crimes and charges it against perpetrators. In order that you may appreciate the functions of this organization I should like to outline a typical case, but before doing so I should say there are many deviations from the norm, and they are so numerous I won't comment upon them.

Our team interrogates a prisoner of war who confesses that he participated in the murder of American prisoners of war. He goes into detail, stating that on 30th April, 1951, his unit was engaged in a fight with elements of the 24th US Infantry Division. After a brief encounter the allied troops are pushed off of hill so-and-so and the PW's unit occupies it. After consolidating their positions they organize a search under the command of our PW, a junior lieutenant. This search party rounded up 14 prisoners, several of whom were wounded. He reports this to his battalion commander. The prisoners are herded together and left without medical care or food until the next day. Early next morning, elements of the 24th Division counterattack. When it becomes apparent the Communists must give up the hill, the battalion commander orders our lieutenant to execute the PW because he cannot conveniently evacuate them. Accordingly, the execution is accomplished. When allied troops reoccupy the hill they find the prisoners in a row with a bullet hole in the back of each head, obviously an atrocity. That is the general line of confessions."

Source: *U.S. Government Printing Office, Washington, 1954.*

respond to a military attempt at reunification.[4] The North Koreans and China may also have underestimated the United States' determination to persist with its involvement, despite the difficulty of the campaign.

An interesting element of the UN response to the North Korean attack was the way in which the Organization operated through a proxy, namely the United States. Classic collective security is an enforcement action by all States. This approach is at the heart of the Charter's treatment of the issue (Articles 43–48). The way that the Korean action unfolded, however, created a situation whereby security was restored largely by one State with Security Council approval to act on behalf of all States. Moreover, the UN concept of enforcement action was based on Articles 44 to 47 of the Charter, which deal with agreements covering the availability of national contingents under the strategic direction of the Military Staff Committee. In the case of Korea, however, the UN response was delegated to the United States and the small number of other countries that were in a position to provide meaningful military assistance. This was consistent with Charter Article 48 and was repeated in the next example of collective security, the removal of Iraq from Kuwait.

FURTHER READING

Cumings, Bruce. *The Origins of the Korean War: II, the Roaring of the Cataract, 1947–1950*. Princeton, NJ: Princeton University Press, 1990.

Goulden, Joseph C. *Korea: the Untold Story of the Korean War*. New York: Times Books, 1982.

Halberstam, David. *The Coldest Winter: America and the Korean War*. New York: Hyperion, 2007.

Malkasian, Carter. *The Korean War*. New York: Rosen, 2008.

McWilliams, Wayne C., and Harry Piotrowski. *The World Since 1945*. Boulder, CO: Lynne Rienner, 2005: 60–75.

After Kuwait: A New World Order

- ***Document:*** United Nations Security Council Resolution 678 (1990)
- ***Date:*** Adopted on November 29, 1990
- ***Where:*** United Nations, New York
- ***Significance:*** This resolution provides the authorization for the resort to force in the dispute between Iraq and Kuwait. This was the first time since the end of the Cold War that the Security Council had approved collective security action and was seen as heralding a new approach by the permanent members of the Security Council to their responsibilities.

DOCUMENT

The Security Council,

Recalling, and reaffirming its resolutions 660 (1990) of 2 August (1990), 661 (1990) of 6 August 1990, 662 (1990) of 9 August 1990, 664 (1990) of 18 August 1990, 665 (1990) of 25 August 1990, 666 (1990) of 13 September 1990, 667 (1990) of 16 September 1990, 669 (1990) of 24 September 1990, 670 (1990) of 25 September 1990, 674 (1990) of 29 October 1990 and 677 (1990) of 28 November 1990.

Noting that, despite all efforts by the United Nations, Iraq refuses to comply with its obligation to implement resolution 660 (1990) and the above-mentioned subsequent relevant resolutions, in flagrant contempt of the Security Council,

Mindful of its duties and responsibilities under the Charter of the United Nations for the maintenance and preservation of international peace and security,

Determined to secure full compliance with its decisions,

Acting under Chapter VII of the Charter,

Burning oil wells at Al Magwa with a destroyed Iraqi tank in the foreground. The Iraqi destruction caused tremendous damage to the region's environment. Kuwait, March 25, 1991. Courtesy of John Isaac, UN Photo.

1. *Demands* that Iraq comply fully with resolution 660 (1990) and all subsequent relevant resolutions, and decides, while maintaining all its decisions, to allow Iraq one final opportunity, as a pause of goodwill, to do so;
2. *Authorizes* Member States co-operating with the Government of Kuwait, unless Iraq on or before 15 January 1991 fully implements, as set forth in paragraph 1 above, the above-mentioned resolutions, to use all necessary means to uphold and implement resolution 660 (1990) and all subsequent relevant resolutions and to restore international peace and security in the area;

3. *Requests* all States to provide appropriate support for the actions undertaken in pursuance of paragraph 2 of the present resolution;
4. *Requests* the States concerned to keep the Security Council regularly informed on the progress of actions undertaken pursuant to paragraphs 2 and 3 of the present resolution;
5. *Decides* to remain seized of the matter.

SOURCE: Security Council Resolution 678 (1990), Iraq-Kuwait. http://daccessdds.un.org/doc/RESOLUTION/GEN/NR0/575/28/IMG/NR057528.pdf?OpenElement

---

ANALYSIS

As noted, the military action by the United Nations to drive Iraq from Kuwait in 1991 is only the second instance of collective security instigated by the United Nations Security Council. The action was undertaken in a global atmosphere deeply affected by the fall of the Berlin Wall in 1989 and the dramatic reforms instigated by Soviet President Mikhail Gorbachev, which ultimately led to the collapse of the Soviet Union. There was great hope for a revolution in the way relations between States would be conducted, including in the Security Council. The manner in which the removal of Iraqi troops from Kuwait was authorized and conducted was seen as evidence of this change. U.S. President George H. W. Bush summed up this atmosphere in his address to a joint session of the Congress on September 11, 1990, when he commented:

> A new partnership of nations has begun, and we stand today at a unique and extraordinary moment. The crisis in the Persian Gulf, as grave as it is, also offers a rare opportunity to move toward an historic period of cooperation. Out of these troubled times, our fifth objective—a new world order—can emerge: A new era—freer from the threat of terror, stronger in the pursuit of justice and more secure in the quest for peace. An era in which the nations of the world, east and west, north and south, can prosper and live in harmony.
>
> A hundred generations have searched for this elusive path to peace, while a thousand wars raged across the span of human endeavor, and today that new world is struggling to be born. A world quite different from the one we've known. A world where the rule of law supplants the rule of the jungle. A world in which nations recognize the shared responsibility for freedom and justice. A world where the strong respect the rights of the weak.
>
> This is the vision that I shared with President Gorbachev in Helsinki. He and the other leaders from Europe, the Gulf and around the world understand that how we manage this crisis today could shape the future for generations to come.[5]

In pursuing a collective security response to Iraq's invasion of Kuwait, the Security Council had limited precedent to guide it, the last occasion having been the Korean action. Indeed, aspects of the process were unique. The Council's deliberations were, however, assisted by the approach taken by the Council members. The adoption by the Security Council of the various resolutions, including 678, was remarkable for the unprecedented level of cooperation and goodwill brought to the task, especially by the permanent members of the Council. Nevertheless, the resort to force was not without its controversial aspects. The decision to respond was authorized as an act of collective self-defense. There are established rules governing the exercise of self-defense, one of which is the need for it to be undertaken as an immediate response to an attack. In the case of the Iraqi invasion of Kuwait, however, this requirement was, strictly speaking, not met. The anticipated process of responding to a breach of the peace was reversed, with the Security Council immediately focusing on managing the crisis and attempting to induce Iraq to withdraw by nonmilitary means. The right to resort to force in self-defense was put to the side while this process was being pursued.

On the essential point, that an act of aggression had occurred and that a firm response was called for, there was no significant dispute. It was the first occasion since the Second World War when one country had set out to absorb completely another sovereign State, a point stressed by the UN Secretary-General during Council debate. Iraq's preparations for its invasion of Kuwait and the reasons it gave to justify its action were so patently unacceptable as to leave the international community in no doubt about the illegality of the invasion. The Council would appear to have been reflecting broadly held views when it identified Iraq as the aggressor, a step it has carefully avoided in dealing with other outbreaks of violence between States since the Second World War.

One interesting initiative came from the Soviet Union, when it proposed that military action should be coordinated through the Military Staff Committee, the body established by the UN Charter to "advise and assist the Security Council on all questions relating to the Security Council's military requirements" (Article 47(1)). The Soviets, British, and French seemed to be concerned about American unilateralist tendencies and saw the Committee as a way of imposing limits on American action. In Security Council Resolution 665 of August 25, 1990, the following words were included:

> *Also requests* all States concerned to co-ordinate their actions in pursuit of the above paragraphs of the present resolution using, as appropriate, mechanisms of the Military Staff Committee [6]

In the event, the Americans were able to quarantine the Military Staff Committee to the point where it did little more than approve extensions of national roles in enforcing the initial trade embargo on Iraq. The Americans' concern to avoid a serious role for the Committee influenced their approach to the drafting of Security Council Resolution 678. The text was broadly drafted, with no reference to Article 42 of the Charter, which would have given the Security Council specific control over when force was to be used and might have encouraged the Council to interfere in the conduct of the war. The draft also reflected American hopes that Iraq could be encouraged to evacuate Kuwait peacefully. Finally, the text authorized but did not mandate the use of force (paragraph 2), maintaining a degree of flexibility in the resolution.

The Iraq exercise followed the precedent set by the Korean War experience, insofar as the Security Council authorized States to take action against Iraq in its name, reflecting difficulties the United Nations had regularly encountered when seeking to undertake enforcement or peacekeeping action. This practice was followed throughout the 1990s in Rwanda, Haiti, and East Timor, among other crises. It is different from the approach envisaged under Chapter VII of the Charter but reflects the widespread view[7] that the original structure envisaged by the Charter's framers and spelled out in Chapter VII will not work and that the United Nations should contract out the task of enforcing its decisions. It remains to be seen, however, whether this view will continue to be held in the wake of the American invasion of Iraq in 2003.

FURTHER READING

Bulloch, John, and Harvey Morris. *Saddam's War: Origins of the Kuwait Conflict and the International Response*. London: Faber and Faber, 1991.

Cronin, Bruce, and Ian Hurd, eds. *The UN Security Council and the Politics of International Authority*. London: Routledge, 2008.

Freedman, Lawrence, and Efraim Karsh. *The Gulf Conflict: 1990–1991*. Princeton, NJ: Princeton University Press, 1993.

Gazzani, Tarcisio. *The Changing Rules on the Use of Force in International Law*. Manchester: Juris, 2005.

Gray, Christine. *International Law and the Use of Force*. 2nd ed. Oxford: Oxford University Press, 2004.

Schofield, Richard N. *Kuwait and Iraq: Historical Claims and Territorial Disputes*. London: Royal Institute of International Affairs, 1991.

The General Assembly Takes Over: Uniting for Peace and Suez

- ***Document:*** United Nations General Assembly Resolution 997 (ES-I)
- ***Date:*** Adopted on November 2, 1956
- ***Where:*** United Nations, New York
- ***Significance:*** This resolution addressed the invasion of Egypt by France, Israel, and the United Kingdom. It was adopted under the Uniting for Peace formula (UNGA Resolution 377 (V) of November 3, 1950), by which the General Assembly assumed the power to initiate certain collective security measures in the event of Security Council inaction.

DOCUMENT

The General Assembly,

Noting the disregard on many occasions by parties to the Israel-Arab armistice agreements of 1949 of the terms of such agreements, and that the armed forces of Israel have penetrated deeply into Egyptian territory in violation of the General Armistice Agreement between Egypt and Israel of 24 February, 1949,

Noting that the armed forces of France and the United Kingdom of Great Britain and Northern Ireland are conducting military operations against Egyptian territory,

Noting that traffic through the Suez Canal is now interrupted to the serious prejudice of many nations,

Expressing its grave concern over these developments,

1. *Urges* as a matter of priority that all parties now involved in hostilities in the area now agree to an immediate cease-fire and, as part thereof, halt the movement of military forces and arms into the area;

2. *Urges* the parties to the armistice agreements promptly to withdraw all forces behind the armistice lines, to desist from raids across the armistice lines into neighbouring territory, and to observe scrupulously the provisions of the armistice agreements;
3. *Recommends* that all Member States refrain from introducing military goods in the area of hostilities and in general refrain from any acts which would delay or prevent the implementation of the present resolution;
4. *Urges* that, upon the cease-fire being effective, steps be taken to reopen the Suez Canal and restore secure freedom of navigation;
5. *Requests* the Secretary-General to observe and report promptly on the compliance with the present resolution to the Security Council and to the General Assembly, for such further action as they may deem appropriate in accordance with the Charter;
6. *Decides* to remain in emergency session pending compliance with the present resolution.

SOURCE: *Official records, First Emergency Special Session*, Supplement No. 1, A/3354, 562nd plenary meeting, November 2, 1956. http://www.un.org/ga/search/view_doc.asp?symbol=A/3354&Lang=E.

ANALYSIS

The joint British-French-Israeli invasion of Egypt in October 1956 was generally accepted as being indefensible under the UN Charter and customary international law. There were several reasons for this attitude. International opinion regarded the attack as lacking any substantive justification in fact. Moreover, none of the attacking States attempted to resolve whatever problems they might have had with Egypt through the mechanisms provided by the United Nations, as they were obliged to do under the Charter. Even the legal advisers of the British Government made this point clear in their advice to the Government.[8] The invasion resulted in extensive debate in the Security Council, the General Assembly, and the national parliaments of the parties involved. The debates in the British House of Commons were particularly interesting, as it was in this forum that the government presented its most detailed explanation of its actions and its justifications under international law.

Egypt nationalized the Suez Canal in July 1956. In doing so, Egypt claimed to have honored its obligations under international law, including the payment of appropriate compensation to the former owners.[9] In this, Egypt enjoyed widespread support among governments and analysts around the world. Nevertheless, Britain, France, and Israel rejected the expropriation and determined to use military force against Egypt. The three countries developed a plan whereby Israel would attack Egypt and Britain and France would intervene, ostensibly to separate the two parties and, once in control of the Canal Zone, force the reversal of the nationalization and, if possible, precipitate the downfall of Egypt's President, Gamal Abdel Nasser.

In the event, the day after Israel attacked Egypt, the United States tabled a draft resolution in the Security Council calling for a cease-fire and for Israel to withdraw behind the 1948 armistice lines, the *de facto* borders between Egypt and Israel. The resolution was vetoed by Britain and France, whereupon the United States proposed the above resolution in the UN General Assembly under the Uniting for Peace provision. The resolution was carried overwhelmingly and, in the context of intense American political pressure, provided the legal basis of the three countries' withdrawal from Egypt.

In presenting a legal basis for an attack on Egypt, the British Government developed a number of arguments, including the right of protection of nationals and national interests and anticipatory self-defense. Both of these arguments are controversial. Before the adoption of the UN Charter, it was widely considered that States had a clear right to intervene militarily in another State in order to protect their nationals and the assets of their nationals. With the significant curtailment of the right of States to resort to force in Article 2(4) of the Charter, however, the rights of States to protect their nationals through the use of force has become less clear. State practice in this area is, moreover, not consistent, adding to the difficulty. Controversy has accompanied many interventions on behalf of States' nationals during and after the Cold War, including the Congo in 1960 but especially the U.S. invasions of Grenada (1983) and Panama (1989), which resulted in condemnations by the UN General Assembly. On the other hand, interventions to protect foreign nationals in West Africa in the 1990s seem to have been accepted as valid by the international community. In the case of Suez, the British reliance on the protection-of-nationals argument was described as a "palpably inadequate excuse"[10] and was rejected by most countries. The British case was rejected largely on the grounds that there was no evidence of British nationals and interests being seriously threatened in Egypt.

President Gamal Abdel Nasser meeting Secretary-General U Thant (second from left). At left is Foreign Minister of the United Arab Republic, Mahmoud Riad, and at right are Major General Indar Jit Rikhye, Commander of UNEF, and Dr. Mahmoud Fawzi, Deputy Prime Minister of Foreign Affairs. Cairo, United Arab Republic, May 24, 1967. Courtesy of UN Photo.

Some days after the adoption of Resolution 997, the General Assembly passed a companion resolution (1001 ES-I), which set up the United Nations Emergency Force (UNEF). This was the first UN military force of its kind and was mandated to maintain "quiet" during and after the withdrawal of Israeli, French, and British forces. UNEF provided the General Assembly's intervention with an element of substance, albeit dependent on the goodwill of the parties involved. The force was essentially a peacekeeping operation; however, the UN Secretary-General maintained that the Security Council could widen its mandate to meet Chapter VII criteria.

It is important to note at this point that there is a significant difference between collective security and peacekeeping. While there is no reference to peacekeeping in the UN Charter, there have been many instances of the measure over the years, and peacekeeping has become an important feature in the range of options available to the United Nations. Peacekeeping lacks the coercive nature of collective security and relies largely on the agreement of all parties to a dispute. Secretary-General Kofi Annan commented that "peace-keeping and the use of force (other than self-defense) should be seen as alternative techniques

The trouble with peacekeeping. Courtesy of Jean-Marc Ferré, UN Photo.

and not as adjacent points on a continuum permitting easy transition from one to another'.[11]

The Uniting for Peace measure, which is based on UN General Assembly Resolution 377A of November 1950, became a substitute means of pursuing collective security should the Security Council be unable or unwilling to exercise its primary responsibility for the maintenance of international peace and security. It has been employed ten times,[12] mainly by the United States. One of its strengths is that, by involving all members of the United Nations General Assembly in any decision to use force, a strongly supported resolution can be described as an expression of international opinion. This gives the action an added degree of legitimacy. States are, however, careful about when they seek to resort to this measure. During the Kosovo crisis in 1999, for example, the United States and NATO claimed that international opinion was being frustrated by the threat of a Russian veto of military action in the Security Council. The United States, however, did not expose their intended attack on Yugoslavia to the test of world opinion by seeking authorization through a Uniting for Peace resolution.

FURTHER READING

Fisher, Eugene M., and M. Cherif Bassiouni. *Storm over the Arab World.* Chicago: Follett, 1972, especially pp. 82–93.

Fisk, Robert. *The Great War for Civilisation: the Conquest of the Middle East.* London: Fourth Estate, 2005, esp. pp. 1127–1137.

Hahn, Peter L. "The Suez Crisis: A Crisis That Changed the Balance of Power in the Middle East," *America.gov*, May 8, 2008, http://www.america.gov/st/peacesec-english/2008/May/20080522120851WRybakcuH0.4956781.html.

Lauterpacht, Eli. "The Contemporary Practice of the United Kingdom in the Field of International Law. Survey and Comment III. August 16–December 31, 1956." *International and Comparative Law Quarterly* 6, no. 2 (1957): 301–336.

Marston, Geoffrey. "Armed Intervention in the 1956 Suez Canal Crisis: The Legal Advice Tendered to the British Government." *International and Comparative Law Quarterly* 37, no. 4 (1988): 773–817.

Nutting, A. *Nasser*, London: Constable, 1972.

Where Collective Security Has Not Been Invoked: India's Occupation of Goa

- ***Document:*** Excerpts of statement to the United Nations Security Council by Shri C. S. Jha, Indian Permanent Representative to the United Nations
- ***Date:*** December 18, 1961
- ***Where:*** United Nations, New York
- ***Significance:*** This statement sets out India's argument that, for it, the goal of decolonization took precedence over the prohibition of the use of force contained in the United Nations Charter.

DOCUMENT

My country has never accepted and never will accept any legal, moral or ethical basis for the process by which India became colonised, came under colonial domination. . . .

The greatest thing that has happened in this twentieth century is that no longer can colonialism be tolerated, whether in Asia, in Africa or in Latin America or anywhere else.

That is the situation with which we are faced. It must be realised that this is a colonial question. It is a question of getting rid of the last vestiges of colonialism in India. That is a matter of faith with us. Whatever anyone else may think, Charter or no Charter, Council or no Council, that is our basic faith which we cannot afford to give up at any cost. . . .

The Portuguese not only refused to negotiate, but have invented the myth, the legal fiction, that these are parts of Portugal . . . and for many years they have pursued that fiction in spite of the fact that the general Assembly categorically, in resolution 1542 (XV), has rejected that claim . . . and has laid down that the Portuguese possessions in Africa and Asia . . . are Non-Self-Governing Territories within the meaning of Chapter XI of the Charter.

There is no legal frontier—there can be no legal frontier—between India and Goa. And since the whole occupation is illegal as an issue—it started in an illegal manner, it continues to be illegal today and is even more illegal in the light of resolution 1514—there can be no question of aggression against your own people, whom you want to bring into freedom. . . .

This is the situation. The provocation was theirs; we have been the victims of provocation not only now but for the last fifteen years and, if we go back further in history, for the last 450 years. . . .

With your permission, I should like to read the relevant parts of a proclamation issued by our Government on the morning of 18 December: "To assist resistance movement, protect people from further Portuguese repression and restore law and order following the collapse of the colonial administration, they have instructions to use the minimum force necessary to protect the sanctity of all places of worship. Their primary task is to restore law and order and bring public services back to normal."

This is the objective of the Indian move. Nobody can accuse my Government, through the years, of having any but peaceful intentions; we are a peaceful people. . . . But there are situations when the vindication of justice and freedom becomes of paramount importance. Such is the situation which we now have to face, much against our wishes and very reluctantly. . . .

This is not a question of aggression, this cannot be a question of aggression. If anybody says it is, he is going against the tide of history, he is going against the entire thesis of the United Nations today, he is going against the tide of world history and public opinion because colonialism can no longer be tolerated. . . .

The Prime Minister has said, it is true, "I want a solution of it by peaceful means, but if peaceful means fail then resort to force is not excluded". That is a perfectly straightforward point of view. We are criticised here by various delegations which say, "Why have you used force? The Charter absolutely prohibits force"; but the Charter itself does not completely eschew force, in the sense that force can be used in self-defence, for the protection of the people of a country—and the people of Goa are as much Indians as any other people. We cannot accept any other position. . . .

I have said that we accept international law: we are governed by the tenets of international law, but that we cannot in the twentieth century accept that part of international law which was laid down by European jurists—though great men, great jurists whose contribution to law has been really remarkable—specifying that colonies in Asia and Africa which were acquired by conquest conferred sovereignty on the colonial power. . . .

The step that we have had to take was unavoidable; there was no recourse left to us; there was no choice open to us. Our purpose was not annexation. We have gone into Goa to assist the freedom movement of Goa, to help the resistance movement of Goa. It is our people in Goa whom we have gone to help against Portuguese suppression.

SOURCE: Foreign Affairs Record (India), December 7, 1961: 451–460.

ANALYSIS

India's elimination of Portuguese colonial control of Goa shocked much of the world and appeared to violate the most important principles of the United Nations—namely, not resorting to force to resolve disputes between States and not acquiring territory by force. While claiming that the takeover was consistent with the Charter prohibition of the resort to force and the self-defense exception in Article 51, India also set out to place its actions above the law and suggested that the law it was defying was a Western construct. Indeed, the Indian Security Council representative and other government spokesmen appeared determined to place matters of morality and national pride ("basic faith") above respect for international law.

There is some debate as to why India took the military action it did and why it adopted such a strategy of confrontation with international legal norms. In adopting the arguments and the tone of this document, India opened itself to the criticism that it had not attempted to pursue the possibility of a peaceful solution to the problem. It had not, for example, sought to raise the issue in the UN General Assembly, where it could have been assured of a strong endorsement of its position. The U.S. ambassador to the United Nations, Adlai Stevenson II, commented that "India's armed attack on Goa mocks the good faith of its frequent declarations of lofty principles."[13] One writer suggests that India had been criticised both domestically and by its fellow members of the Non-Aligned Movement for going soft on colonialism.[14] This, of course, was not the argument used in the UN Security Council when the issue came up for debate. It might, however, explain the unusual and dramatic approach adopted by the Indian Government.

India presented several arguments to defend its actions in the Security Council. It suggested that the matter was essentially a domestic issue, that Portugal's excision of Goa from Indian territory had no legitimacy despite the length of time that Portugal had controlled the territory. India also revived the British

DID YOU KNOW?

Challenging the Norm

Had the Security Council intervened, we would not have stopped the action [to take Goa by military force]. We had learned some lessons . . . The nation that behaves well is always in a bad position.

Indian Defence Minister Krishna Menon (1957–1962), quoted in, Nathaniel Berman, "Legitimacy Through Defiance: From Goa to Iraq" [Symposium: Speaking Law to Power: International Law and Foreign Policy], *Wisconsin International Law Journal* 23 (2005) 93–125 at 101.

It is a good precedent . . . If Africa, as such, is unable to take up its responsibilities, it is incumbent on each state to do so. . . . It is a lesson to Amin and people of his kind.

Tanzanian President Julius Nyerere, quoted in Colin Legum, ed., *Africa Contemporary Record* (London: Africana), XI, 1980.

We will work with the UN Security Council for the necessary resolutions. But the purposes of the United States should not be doubted. The Security Council resolutions will be enforced—the just demands of peace and security will be met—or action will be unavoidable. And a regime that has lost its legitimacy will also lose its power.

U.S. President George W. Bush, September 12, 2002. http://www.state.gov/p/nea/rls/rm/13434.htm.

argument from the Suez crisis that it needed to resort to force to defend its citizens. Finally, India sought to claim self-defense, suggesting that Portuguese forces had attacked India.

None of these arguments enjoyed much sympathy in the Security Council, where even India's supporters found it difficult to defend the action on the basis of Charter or customary law. On international legal grounds, India's action in taking over Portuguese colonial territories should have met a collective security response from the international community. This was unlikely on political grounds, given the Soviet Union's support for India. A draft Security Council resolution calling for a cease-fire and for Indian withdrawal from Goa was tabled by Western members of the Council but vetoed by the Soviet Union.

The debate on the draft resolution did, however, highlight some interesting developments in attitudes to international law and the priorities that had, to that point, underpinned it. The debate highlighted diverging interpretations of international law between the West and the rest of the world. The permanent Western members of the Council at the time (the United States, Britain, and France) supported by Nationalist China, Ecuador, Chile, and Turkey, argued that at issue was the problem of the resort to force and the constraints that the UN Charter imposes on the use of force. They argued that the merit of the Indian concern, that Portugal should not still be in colonial possession of part of the Indian homeland, was not at issue—that should be dealt with by other means, bearing in mind the prohibition on the use of force.

India's supporters drew heavily on the UN General Assembly's Declaration on the Granting of Independence to Colonial Countries and Peoples (Resolution 1514 (XV) of December 14, 1960). The Declaration contained the following exhortation in paragraph 5:

> Immediate steps shall be taken, in Trust and Non-Self-Governing Territories or all other territories which have not yet attained independence, to transfer all powers to the peoples of those territories, without any conditions or reservations, in accordance with their freely expressed will and desire, without any distinction as to race, creed or colour, in order to enable them to enjoy complete independence and freedom.

The Soviet delegate suggested during the Security Council debate that, rather than seek to take action against India, the Council should apply sanctions against Portugal for its failure to respond to this part of the Declaration. The basis of their arguments,

DID YOU KNOW?

In History: An Attempt to Censure

Draft Security Council Resolution (S/5033), proposed by France, Turkey, the United Kingdom, and the United States at the 988th meeting of the Security Council on December 18, 1961 (vetoed by the Soviet Union):

The Security Council,

Recalling that in Article 2 of the Charter of the United Nations all Members are obliged to settle their disputes by peaceful means and to refrain from the threat or use of force in a manner inconsistent with the purposes of the United Nations,

Deploring the use of forces by India in Goa, Daman and Diu,

Recalling that Article 1, paragraph 2, of the Charter specifies as one of the purposes of the United Nations to develop friendly relations among nations based on respect for the principle of equal rights and self-determination of peoples,

Calls for an immediate cessation of hostilities;

Calls upon the Government of India to withdraw its forces immediately to positions prevailing before 17 December, 1961;

Urges the parties to work out a permanent solution of their differences by peaceful means in accordance with the principles embodied in the Charter;

Requests the Secretary-General to provide such assistance as may be appropriate.

Ends.

Brigadier Sagat Singh of India's Maroon Beret Parachute Regiment accepts the surrender of Portuguese forces at a military camp in Bambolim. Courtesy of the Government of India.

therefore, appeared to be that the process of decolonization enjoyed a higher priority in international law than the UN Charter's prohibition of the use of force, which underpinned Western approaches to the issue. The end of the colonial period has limited the impact of this apparent precedent on the structure of the law relating to collective self-defense, and it is of note that India adopted a more traditional approach in dealing with other crises concerning the use of force. For example, in commenting on the American invasion of Iraq, the Indian Foreign Ministry insisted that any action against Iraq must be undertaken under the aegis of the Security Council.[15]

An implicit issue underlying the debate and the international community's response to India's actions was that there was widespread acceptance that the result of Portugal's expulsion was beneficial, even if the process by which Portugal was expelled was illegal. The problem of how the international community deals with such contradictions is a constant debate in international legal circles and will be raised in the next document.

FURTHER READING

Berman, Nathaniel. "Legitimacy through Defiance: From Goa to Iraq" (in "Symposium: Speaking Law to Power: International Law and Foreign Policy"), *Wisconsin International Law Journal* 23 (2005): 93–126.

Claude, Inis L. *Swords into Plowshares*. New York: Random House, 1964, especially the section on collective security, pp. 223–238.

Gazzini, Tarcisio. *The Changing Rules on the Use of Force in International Law*. Manchester: Juris, 2005.

Wright, Quincy. "The Goa Incident." *American Journal of International Law* 56 (1962): 617–632.

A Matter of Self-Defense and Self-Help: Tanzania's Overthrow of Idi Amin of Uganda

- *Document:* Statements by the Presidents of Tanzania and Uganda outlining their policies towards their dispute over domestic repression in Uganda and Ugandan incursions into Tanzanian territory
- *Date:* February 5, February 28, and March 26, 1979
- *Where:* Kampala, Uganda, and Dar es Salaam, Tanzania
- *Significance:* Both rulers drew on the principles of noninterference and self-defense in their appeals for international support over their dispute. Despite some criticism of Tanzanian actions, the Tanzania-Uganda conflict and the resultant overthrow of Idi Amin were not raised in the UN Security Council or in the UN General Assembly. It was debated in the Organisation of African Unity (OAU), but Tanzania's actions were not substantively challenged. This silence reflected African and broader international embarrassment with the behavior of Amin.

DOCUMENTS

President Julius Nyerere of Tanzania, report of broadcast on Radio Dar es Salaam

"Toward the end of the third week of last month—and I am saying this purposely—I permitted our young men to cross the border, not to strike with artillery. I allowed them to cross the border to tell Amin that we shall not continue to tolerate his pronouncements, even if they are mere hoaxes. . . . He must not threaten us. . . . We shall no longer ignore him. And this is precisely why I gave our youths the go-ahead." [Nyerere explained that the job of removing Amin was for the Ugandans alone.] "I do not fight for others. . . . The Ugandans do have a reason to remove

Amin, but we don't. It is not our business; we shall not send our troops into Uganda to remove Amin."

President Idi Amin of Uganda, report of message to UN Secretary-General, OAU Secretary-General, and Arab League Secretary-General, February 28, 1979

Uganda has done "everything possible to bring about a peaceful resolution to the conflict." [Amin claimed the war had been started by Tanzania on October 9, 1978, the day Uganda invaded Tanzania.]

President Nyerere, speech calling for the OAU to help by making a statement condemning Amin, February 28, 1979

"If a Boer country had invaded an African country, would the OAU have kept quiet? . . . Invasion is invasion. We cannot argue that this one is alright because it is committed by a person of the same skin colour as me. . . . Despite my dislike for

Idi Amin, President of Uganda, 1971–1979. Courtesy of The New York Times, September 2007.

Amin—and I really do not like him—the Government of Tanzania has no right to enter Uganda in order to topple Amin. . . . No other government in Africa or anywhere else in the world has the right to overthrow Amin's regime. That is a matter of principle. . . . But Amin's regime is a brutal one, and the people of Uganda have that right. All people all over the world have the right to topple regimes they detest. . . . Recently, Iran did likewise . . . and I congratulate them for this."

President Nyerere, Statement Responding to Threats of Intervention by Libya, March 26, 1979

"We will not change our stand on Amin. Amin is a murderer, a liar and a savage. We shall continue to fight those who threaten our security. Since the threats have increased, we shall also intensify our preparations to counter them." [Nyerere pointed out that there were two wars being fought in Uganda:] "First there are the Ugandans fighting to remove the fascist dictator. Then there are the Tanzanians fighting to maintain national security. By threatening to send troops to Uganda, Col. Gaddafy has declared war against Ugandans who have the right to remove any dictatorship."

Cited in Colin Legum, ed., *Africa Contemporary Record* (London: Africana, XI, 1980), 431, 433.

ANALYSIS

As with the Goan crisis discussed above, Tanzania's invasion of Uganda in January 1979 was difficult to reconcile with the basic principles of international law. Tanzania presented its invasion of Uganda and the subsequent overthrow of the Ugandan President, Idi Amin, in terms of self-defense and support for the exercise of self-determination. As with the Indian position on its invasion of Goa, the Tanzanian claims under international law were widely seen as invalid, and their action was regarded, especially in Africa, as inconsistent with international law. Despite this concern, Tanzania's action did not provoke a collective security response by the international community.

The Tanzanian-Ugandan border had been the scene of some low-level conflict including a particularly bloody incursion by Ugandan troops into the northern

DID YOU KNOW?

Idi Amin: President for Life

Idi Amin Dada (c. 1925–2003) was President of Uganda from 1971 to 1979, during which time he earned the reputation as one of the most brutal dictators in modern African history. Amin began his career in the British colonial regiment, the King's African Rifles, where he developed a reputation as a skilled soldier. When independence came to Uganda in 1962, Amin was one of only two African officers in the Ugandan armed forces.

Amin removed President Milton Obote in a coup in January 1971, a step that was initially welcomed because of Obote's reputed corruption. Amin's rule, however, quickly came to be characterized by human rights abuses directed at rival ethnic groups and political opponents. He declared an "economic war" against Uganda's Asian population in 1972 and drove them out of the country. The number of people killed as a result of his misrule is unknown, but estimates from human rights groups range from 100,000 to 500,000.

In office Amin displayed megalomaniac tendencies, eventually titling himself as "His Excellency, President for Life, Field Marshal Al Hadji Doctor Idi Amin Dada, VC, DSO, MC, Lord of All the Beasts of the Earth and Fishes of the Seas and Conqueror of the British Empire in Africa in General and Uganda in Particular." These tendencies ultimately led to his downfall. Dissent within Uganda and Amin's attempt to annex the Kagera Salient of Tanzania in 1978 led to the Uganda-Tanzania War and the fall of his regime. Amin fled to Libya, then to Saudi Arabia in 1981, where he died in 2003.[18]

Julius Nyerere, President of Tanzania, 1964–1985. Courtesy of the Mwalimu Nyerere Foundation.

Kagera salient of Tanzania. Tanzania demanded a condemnation of Ugandan actions by the Organisation of African Unity (OAU). Tanzania maintained throughout the crisis its formal adherence to the inviolability of State borders. Tanzanian statements also highlighted, however, the contradiction between noninterference in the domestic affairs of African nations and the need for the OAU to adopt an approach that would deny African dictators committing human rights abuses the protection of the OAU Charter.

With this in mind, Tanzania developed its argument that the attack on Uganda was part of a two-wars crisis. On one hand, Tanzanian actions in invading Uganda were an exercise in self-defense. Tanzania's President Julius Nyerere insisted that Tanzania had been obliged to intervene because the OAU had failed to take collective security action against Uganda and that Tanzania was fighting "to maintain national security." Nyerere claimed that his country's actions were in response to Ugandan aggression against Tanzania and to prevent a second attack, which he claimed was imminent. On the other hand, the President also promoted an idea that is close to the concept of humanitarian intervention. Nyerere noted the brutality of Idi Amin's regime and claimed that Tanzania was helping the people of Uganda to overthrow a "fascist dictator," which was their right. The implication of this line of argument was that Tanzania was only playing a subsidiary role in the challenge to Amin. This particular Tanzanian argument, however, became increasingly difficult to align with the reality on the ground, as exile forces were unable to make significant gains against Ugandan government troops. Their position became further complicated by the growing involvement of Libyan forces in the defense of the Amin regime. As a result, the Tanzanian military was compelled to play the major role in the invasion.

The international response to Tanzania's removal of Amin was muted. A meeting of OAU heads of State in Monrovia, Liberia, in July 1979 debated the issue, and there was some limited criticism of Tanzania's actions. Nigeria and Kenya described the invasion as being inconsistent with the Charter of the OAU.[16] In addition, the OAU refused to issue a condemnation of the Amin regime. At the same time, however, the meeting did not formally debate the crisis, nor did it make any official comment on developments.

Similarly, in the UN Security Council there was little enthusiasm among members to condemn Tanzania, despite the Council's having condemned Vietnam and imposed various measures against it for its 1978 invasion of Kampuchea (Cambodia) and its overthrow of the Pol Pot regime. Amin wrote on two occasions to the UN Secretary-General asking for a meeting of the Security Council to consider the situation. On the first occasion, the Secretary-General replied that the request was inappropriate. On the second occasion, Amin withdrew his request for a meeting when the African group at the United Nations advised him not to involve the Security Council in the conflict.[17]

The ambivalence of the African nations and the silence of the Security Council on this example of the use of force inconsistent with the UN Charter reflected several factors. First, it would seem clear that most States, including those in Africa, welcomed

DID YOU KNOW?

A Leader of Vision

One of Africa's most respected leaders, Julius Nyerere (1922–1999) was a politician of principle and intelligence. Known as *Mwalimu* (Teacher), he had a vision of education and social action that was designed to lead his country to economic self-sufficiency. Nyerere sought self-sufficiency despite his country's relative lack of natural wealth, and he employed socialist policies, including extensive collectivization, to this end. Nyerere's approach was criticized in the West for having led his country into economic hardship, but over time, Tanzania has achieved a level of political, social, and racial stability and social welfare that is the envy of most of Africa.

A committed pan-African, Nyerere provided a haven for a number of African liberation movements including the African National Congress and the Pan African Congress (PAC) in South Africa, Frelimo in Mozambique, and the Zimbabwe African National Liberation Army (ZANLA, the military wing of Robert Mugabe's Zimbabwe African National Union) in Rhodesia. His decision to overthrow the regime of Idi Amin in Uganda, following a border invasion by Amin in 1978, provoked considerable criticism among other African leaders, who accused him of betraying his commitment to the sovereignty of African states.[19]

the removal of Amin, despite their problems with the manner in which he was overthrown. A second factor, and one that differentiates the Tanzania-Uganda conflict from that between Pol Pot and Vietnam, was that the African problem was isolated from Cold War politics. The Soviet Union, which had been supplying arms to Uganda, was forced by Amin's behavior to back away from supporting him. Western countries simply avoided making any comment on the legitimacy of Nyerere's actions. In both cases, nothing was to be gained by the major powers by making an issue of the invasion.

Notes

1. Dimitris Bourantonis, Kostas Ifantis, and Panayotis Tsakonas, eds., *Multilateralism and Security Institutions in an Era of Globalization* (London: Routledge, 2008), 113
2. Carter Malkasian, *The Korean War: Essential Histories* (London: Osprey, 2001), 16.
3. John W. Young and John Kent. *International Relations Since 1945* (Oxford: Oxford University Press, 2004), 150–152.
4. William R. Keylor, *The Twentieth Century World* (Oxford: Oxford University Press, 2001), 354.
5. Speech by U.S. President George H. W. Bush, to joint session of the United States Congress, Washington, DC, on September 11, 1990. Miller Center of Public Affairs, University of Virginia. http://millercenter.org/scripps/archive/speeches/detail/3425.
6. United Nations Security Council Resolution 665, August 25, 1990.
7. Christine Gray, *International Law and the Use of Force,* 2nd ed. (Oxford: Oxford University Press, 2004), 252.
8. Geoffrey Marston, "Armed Intervention in the 1956 Suez Canal Intervention Crisis: The Legal Advice Tendered to the British Government," *International Comparative Law Quarterly* 37, no. 4 (1988): 773–817.
9. Peter Malanczuk, ed., *Akehurst's Modern Introduction to International Law,* 7th ed. (New York: Routledge: 1997), 235.
10. Rosalyn Higgins, *Problems and Process: International Law and How We Use It* (Oxford: Clarendon, 1994), 220–221.
11. Kofi Annan, *Supplement to an Agenda for Peace,* Report by the United Nations Secretary-General, January 25, 1995, UNSC S/1995/1.
12. Suez, 1956; Hungary, 1956; Middle East, 1958; Congo, 1960; Middle East, 1967; Afghanistan, 1980; Palestine, 1980; Namibia, 1981; Occupied Arab Territories, 1982; Jerusalem and Other Occupied Arab Territories, 2007.
13. Quincy Wright, "The Goa Incident," *American Journal of International Law* 56 (1962): 618.
14. Wright, "The Goa Incident," 629.
15. Indian Ministry of External Affairs statements. http:meaindia.nic.in/.
16. Nicholas J. Wheeler, *Saving Strangers: Humanitarian Intervention in International Society* (Oxford: Oxford University Press, 2002), 127. Also John Darnton, "A Victory for Tanzania: A Worry for Africa," *New York Times* (April 16, 1979): A8.

17. Wheeler, *Saving Strangers*, 123.
18. Kwame A. Appiah and Henry L. Gates, eds., *Africana* (Philadelphia: Running Press, 2003), 24–25.
19. Appiah and Gates, eds., *Africana*, 887–888.

FURTHER READING

Bourantonis, Dimitris, Ifantis Kostas, and Tsakonas Panayotis, eds. *Multilateralism and Security Institutions in an Era of Globalization*. London: Routledge, 2008.

Charter of the Organisation of African Unity, 1963. http://www.africa-union.org/root/au/Documents/Treaties/text/OAU_Charter_1963.pdf.

Chatterjee, S. K. "Some Legal Problems of Support Role in International Law: Tanzania and Uganda." *International and Comparative Law Quarterly* 30, no. 4 (1981): 755–768.

Constitutive Act of the African Union, 2000. http://www.au2002.gov.za/docs/key_oau/au_act.htm.

Gazzini, Tarcisio. *The Changing Rules on the Use of Force in International Law*. Manchester: Juris, 2005.

Murphy, Sean D. *Humanitarian Intervention: The United Nations in an Evolving World Order*. Philadelphia: University of Pennsylvania Press, 1996.

Ronzitti, Natalino. *Rescuing Nationals Abroad Through Military Coercion and Intervention on Grounds of Humanity*. Dordrecht: Martinus Nijhoff, 1985.

"Uganda: Idi Amin Dies Without Facing Justice," *Human Rights Watch*, August 17, 2003. http://www.hrw.org/en/news/2003/08/17/uganda-idi-amin-dies-without-facing-justice.

Wheeler, Nicholas J. *Saving Strangers: Humanitarian Intervention in International Society*. Oxford: Oxford University Press, 2002.

8

TERRORISM, INTERNATIONAL LAW, AND THE USE OF FORCE

The corner of Greenwich and Barclay, facing east, near the destroyed World Trade Center, September 11, 2001. Courtesy of the Prints and Photographs Division, Library of Congress.

OVERVIEW

This chapter looks at how the threat of terrorism is addressed by States within the framework of international law. While international efforts to combat terrorism intensified in the aftermath of the attacks on the United States on September 11, 2001, the issue has been on the agenda of the international community since the early 1960s. Nevertheless, there is still no settled definition of terrorism in international law. This is unfortunate, as a definition would provide legal certainty and prevent governments from using the term for political purposes or to crack down on legitimate political dissent. This chapter discusses key resolutions of the UN General Assembly and the Security Council that confirm that terrorism qualifies as a threat to international peace and security. The chapter also introduces the international legal framework to combat terrorism. This framework consists of several multilateral conventions and protocols adopted between 1963 and 2005 that address specific criminal acts considered terrorist in nature. Attention is then drawn to the legal basis for military action against Al-Qa'ida and the Taliban in Afghanistan and the Bush administration's highly controversial practice of detaining so-called illegal enemy combatants in Guantanamo Bay and elsewhere.

The Definition of Terrorism in International Law

- ***Document:*** UN General Assembly Resolution 49/60 (1994) on Measures to Eliminate International Terrorism
- ***Date:*** December 9, 1994
- ***Where:*** United Nations, New York
- ***Significance:*** The General Assembly Resolution 49/60 (1994) demonstrates that the international community regarded "terrorism" as an issue of serious concern long before 9/11. The resolution also contains an agreement by the international community on core elements of "terrorism." However, there is still no settled definition of "terrorism" in international law.

DOCUMENT

The General Assembly,

Recalling its resolution 46/51 of 9 December 1991 and its decision 48/411 of 9 December 1993,

Taking note of the report of the Secretary-General,

Having considered in depth the question of measures to eliminate international terrorism,

Convinced that the adoption of the declaration on measures to eliminate international terrorism should contribute to the enhancement of the struggle against international terrorism,

1. *Approves* the Declaration on Measures to Eliminate International Terrorism, the text of which is annexed to the present resolution;
2. *Invites* the Secretary-General to inform all States, the Security Council, the International Court of Justice and the relevant specialized agencies, organizations and organisms of the adoption of the Declaration;

3. *Urges* that every effort be made in order that the Declaration becomes generally known and is observed and implemented in full;
4. *Urges* States, in accordance with the provisions of the Declaration, to take all appropriate measures at the national and international levels to eliminate terrorism;
5. *Invites* the Secretary-General to follow up closely the implementation of the present resolution and the Declaration, and to submit to the General Assembly at its fiftieth session a report thereon, relating, in particular, to the modalities of implementation of paragraph 10 of the Declaration;
6. *Decides* to include in the provisional agenda of its fiftieth session the item entitled "Measures to eliminate international terrorism", in order to examine the report of the Secretary-General requested in paragraph 5 above, without prejudice to the annual or biennial consideration of the item.

ANNEX

Declaration on Measures to Eliminate International Terrorism

The General Assembly,

Guided by the purposes and principles of the *Charter of the United Nations*,

Recalling the *Declaration on Principles of International Law concerning Friendly Relations and Cooperation among States in accordance with the Charter of the United Nations*, the *Declaration on the Strengthening of International Security*, the *Definition of Aggression*, the *Declaration on the Enhancement of the Effectiveness of the Principle of Refraining from the Threat or Use of Force in International Relations*, the *Vienna Declaration and Programme of Action*, adopted by the World Conference on Human Rights, the *International Covenant on Economic, Social and Cultural Rights* and the *International Covenant on Civil and Political Rights*,

Deeply disturbed by the world-wide persistence of acts of international terrorism in all its forms and manifestations, including those in which States are directly or indirectly involved, which endanger or take innocent lives, have a deleterious effect on international relations and may jeopardize the security of States,

Deeply concerned by the increase, in many regions of the world, of acts of terrorism based on intolerance or extremism,

Concerned at the growing and dangerous links between terrorist groups and drug traffickers and their paramilitary gangs, which have resorted to all types of violence, thus endangering the constitutional order of States and violating basic human rights,

Convinced of the desirability for closer coordination and cooperation among States in combating crimes closely connected with terrorism, including drug trafficking, unlawful arms trade, money laundering and smuggling of nuclear and other potentially deadly materials, and bearing in mind the role that could be played by both the United Nations and regional organizations in this respect,

Firmly determined to eliminate international terrorism in all its forms and manifestations,

Convinced also that the suppression of acts of international terrorism, including those in which States are directly or indirectly involved, is an essential element for the maintenance of international peace and security,

Convinced further that those responsible for acts of international terrorism must be brought to justice,

Stressing the imperative need to further strengthen international cooperation between States in order to take and adopt practical and effective measures to prevent, combat and eliminate all forms of terrorism that affect the international community as a whole,

Conscious of the important role that might be played by the United Nations, the relevant specialized agencies and States in fostering widespread cooperation in preventing and combating international terrorism, inter alia, by increasing public awareness of the problem,

Recalling the existing international treaties relating to various aspects of the problem of international terrorism, inter alia, the Convention on Offences and Certain Other Acts Committed on Board Aircraft, signed at Tokyo on 14 September 1963, the Convention for the Suppression of Unlawful Seizure of Aircraft, signed at The Hague on 16 December 1970, the Convention for the Suppression of Unlawful Acts against the Safety of Civil Aviation, concluded at Montreal on 23 September 1971, the Convention on the Prevention and Punishment of Crimes against Internationally Protected Persons, including Diplomatic Agents, adopted in New York on 14 December 1973, the International Convention against the Taking of Hostages, adopted in New York on 17 December 1979, the Convention on the Physical Protection of Nuclear Material, adopted at Vienna on 3 March 1980, the Protocol for the Suppression of Unlawful Acts of Violence at Airports Serving International Civil Aviation, supplementary to the Convention for the Suppression of Unlawful Acts against the Safety of Civil Aviation, signed at Montreal on 24 February 1988, the Convention for the Suppression of Unlawful Acts against the Safety of Maritime Navigation, done at Rome on 10 March 1988, the Protocol for the Suppression of Unlawful Acts against the Safety of Fixed Platforms located on the Continental Shelf, done at Rome on 10 March 1988, and the Convention on the Marking of Plastic Explosives for the Purpose of Detection, done at Montreal on 1 March 1991,

Welcoming the conclusion of regional agreements and mutually agreed declarations to combat and eliminate terrorism in all its forms and manifestations,

Convinced of the desirability of keeping under review the scope of existing international legal provisions to combat terrorism in all its forms and manifestations, with the aim of ensuring a comprehensive legal framework for the prevention and elimination of terrorism,

Solemnly declares the following:

I

1. The States Members of the United Nations solemnly reaffirm their unequivocal condemnation of all acts, methods and practices of terrorism, as criminal and unjustifiable, wherever and by whomever committed, including those which jeopardize the friendly relations among States and peoples and threaten the territorial integrity and security of States;
2. Acts, methods and practices of terrorism constitute a grave violation of the purposes and principles of the United Nations, which may pose a threat to

international peace and security, jeopardize friendly relations among States, hinder international cooperation and aim at the destruction of human rights, fundamental freedoms and the democratic bases of society;

3. Criminal acts intended or calculated to provoke a state of terror in the general public, a group of persons or particular persons for political purposes are in any circumstance unjustifiable, whatever the considerations of a political, philosophical, ideological, racial, ethnic, religious or any other nature that may be invoked to justify them;

II

4. States, guided by the purposes and principles of the *Charter of the United Nations* and other relevant rules of international law, must refrain from organizing, instigating, assisting or participating in terrorist acts in territories of other States, or from acquiescing in or encouraging activities within their territories directed towards the commission of such acts;
5. States must also fulfil their obligations under the *Charter of the United Nations* and other provisions of international law with respect to combating international terrorism and are urged to take effective and resolute measures in accordance with the relevant provisions of international law and international standards of human rights for the speedy and final elimination of international terrorism, in particular:

   (a) To refrain from organizing, instigating, facilitating, financing, encouraging or tolerating terrorist activities and to take appropriate practical measures to ensure that their respective territories are not used for terrorist installations or training camps, or for the preparation or organization of terrorist acts intended to be committed against other States or their citizens;

   (b) To ensure the apprehension and prosecution or extradition of perpetrators of terrorist acts, in accordance with the relevant provisions of their national law;

   (c) To endeavour to conclude special agreements to that effect on a bilateral, regional and multilateral basis, and to prepare, to that effect, model agreements on cooperation;

   (d) To cooperate with one another in exchanging relevant information concerning the prevention and combating of terrorism;

   (e) To take promptly all steps necessary to implement the existing international conventions on this subject to which they are parties, including the harmonization of their domestic legislation with those conventions;

   (f) To take appropriate measures, before granting asylum, for the purpose of ensuring that the asylum seeker has not engaged in terrorist activities and, after granting asylum, for the purpose of ensuring that the refugee status is not used in a manner contrary to the provisions set out in subparagraph (a) above;

6. In order to combat effectively the increase in, and the growing international character and effects of, acts of terrorism, States should enhance their cooperation in this area through, in particular, systematizing the exchange of information

concerning the prevention and combating of terrorism, as well as by effective implementation of the relevant international conventions and conclusion of mutual judicial assistance and extradition agreements on a bilateral, regional and multilateral basis;

7. In this context, States are encouraged to review urgently the scope of the existing international legal provisions on the prevention, repression and elimination of terrorism in all its forms and manifestations, with the aim of ensuring that there is a comprehensive legal framework covering all aspects of the matter;
8. Furthermore States that have not yet done so are urged to consider, as a matter of priority, becoming parties to the international conventions and protocols relating to various aspects of international terrorism referred to in the preamble to the present Declaration;

III

9. The United Nations, the relevant specialized agencies and intergovernmental organizations and other relevant bodies must make every effort with a view to promoting measures to combat and eliminate acts of terrorism and to strengthening their role in this field;
10. The Secretary-General should assist in the implementation of the present Declaration by taking, within existing resources, the following practical measures to enhance international cooperation:

    (a) A collection of data on the status and implementation of existing multilateral, regional and bilateral agreements relating to international terrorism, including information on incidents caused by international terrorism and criminal prosecutions and sentencing, based on information received from the depositaries of those agreements and from Member States;
    (b) A compendium of national laws and regulations regarding the prevention and suppression of international terrorism in all its forms and manifestations, based on information received from Member States;
    (c) An analytical review of existing international legal instruments relating to international terrorism, in order to assist States in identifying aspects of this matter that have not been covered by such instruments and could be addressed to develop further a comprehensive legal framework of conventions dealing with international terrorism;
    (d) A review of existing possibilities within the United Nations system for assisting States in organizing workshops and training courses on combating crimes connected with international terrorism;

IV

11. All States are urged to promote and implement in good faith and effectively the provisions of the present Declaration in all its aspects;
12. Emphasis is placed on the need to pursue efforts aiming at eliminating definitively all acts of terrorism by the strengthening of international cooperation and

progressive development of international law and its codification, as well as by enhancement of coordination between, and increase of the efficiency of, the United Nations and the relevant specialized agencies, organizations and bodies.

SOURCE: United Nations. http://www.un.org/documents/ga/res/49/a49r060.htm

---

ANALYSIS

The UN General Assembly has focused on terrorism as an international problem since 1972. In the 1970s and 1980s it addressed the problem through various resolutions. In December 1994, the General Assembly once again redirected attention to the issue of terrorism through a Declaration on Measures to Eliminate International Terrorism. A supplement to this Declaration established an Ad hoc Committee on terrorism in 1996. The 1994 Declaration is significant, as it contains an agreement by the international community on core elements of terrorism. According to the Declaration, terrorist acts are "criminal acts intended or calculated to provoke a state of terror in the general public, a group of persons or particular persons for political purposes," and they "are in any circumstance unjustifiable, whatever the considerations of a political, philosophical, ideological, racial, ethnic, religious or any other nature that may be invoked to justify them." Terrorism is thus primarily regarded as a matter of criminal law.

Despite identifying core elements of terrorism, States have not been able to settle on a definition of the term in international law. As Rosalyn Higgins, a former President of the International Court of Justice, has observed, "terrorism is a term without [international] legal significance. It is merely a convenient way of alluding to activities, whether of States or of individuals, widely disapproved of, and in which either the methods used are unlawful, or the targets protected, or both."[1] The difficulty in defining terrorism is that the use of political violence can be legitimate in particular circumstances. From George Washington to Nelson Mandela, most struggles for independence from colonialism and claims of self-determination have resulted in some form of violence that can be (and have been) described as terrorism. At the same time, an overly broad definition of terrorism can be (and has been) used to shut down nonviolent dissent and undermine democratic society. Nevertheless, ensuring an appropriate definition of terrorism is essential to an effective international approach to combating terrorism. This is not just because of the political and moral connotations that accompany the term, but also because there are significant legal consequences.

In 1996, the Ad Hoc Committee on terrorism commenced negotiations for a Comprehensive Convention on International Terrorism that included a

DID YOU KNOW?

The UN General Assembly is one of the five principal organs of the United Nations and the only one in which all member nations have equal representation. The General Assembly meets in regular yearly sessions, which last from September to December, although it can reconvene for special and emergency special sessions. Its composition, functions, powers, voting, and procedures are set out in Chapter IV of the UN Charter. As a general rule, General Assembly resolutions are not legally binding. However, several resolutions may be constitutive of or proof of international customary law, and therefore binding on Member States.

definition of terrorism.[2] In 2000, India formally circulated in the Committee a revised draft comprehensive treaty originally submitted to the General Assembly's Sixth Committee (Legal) in 1996. Substantial drafting progress was made in 2001 and by 2002 agreement was reached on most of the twenty-seven articles. Negotiations were given further impetus by recommendations to define terrorism by the UN High-Level Panel on Threats, Challenges and Change (2004), the UN Secretary-General's report *In Larger Freedom* (2005) and the UN World Summit (2005). However, several issues remain to be resolved, including the issue of the definition of offenses. The current draft attempts to define terrorist action in article 2 (1), which stipulates that "any person commits an offence within the meaning of this Convention if that person, by any means, unlawfully and intentionally, causes:

(a) death or serious bodily injury to any person; or
(b) serious damage to public or private property, including a place of public use, a State or government facility, a public transportation system, an infrastructure facility or the environment; or
(c) damage to property, places, facilities, or systems referred to in paragraph 1(b) of this article, resulting or likely to result in major economic loss, when the purpose of the conduct, by its nature or context, is to intimidate a population, or to compel a Government or an international organization to do or abstain from doing any act."[3]

> **DID YOU KNOW:**
>
> **The United Nations Global Counter-Terrorism Strategy**
>
> The United Nations Global Counter-Terrorism Strategy was adopted by the UN General Assembly on September 8, 2006, and formally launched on September 19, 2006. It marks the first time that countries around the world agree to a common strategic approach to fight terrorism. The strategy forms a basis for a concrete plan of action: to address the conditions conducive to the spread of terrorism; to prevent and combat terrorism; to take measures to build state capacity to fight terrorism; to strengthen the role of the United Nations in combating terrorism; and to ensure the respect for human rights while countering terrorism. The strategy builds on the unique consensus achieved by world leaders at their 2005 September Summit to condemn terrorism in all its forms and manifestations. The first review of the implementation of the Strategy was held on September 4–5, 2008, and the General Assembly adopted a resolution reaffirming its commitment to the Strategy and its implementation. As one of the inputs to this process, the Secretary-General has compiled a report on activities of the UN system in implementing the Strategy.

This definition has been criticized for its lack of precision.[4] In particular, several Non-Governmental Organizations (NGOs), including Amnesty International and Human Rights Watch, have raised concerns about aspects of the definition and have warned against negative consequences for internationally recognized human rights standards.[5] While there appears to be a basic consensus on the definition of offenses, UN Member States continue to disagree on other aspects of the draft convention.[6] These include the application of the Draft Convention to national liberation forces and the relation between the Draft Convention and sectoral anti-terrorism treaties (see Section 8.2).

FURTHER READING

Friedrichs, Jörg. "Defining the International Public Enemy: The Political Struggle Behind the Legal Debate on International Terrorism." *Leiden Journal of International Law* 19, no. 1 (2006): 69–91.

Glennon, Michael J., and Serge Sur, eds. *Terrorism and International Law.* Leiden: Martinus Nijhoff, 2008.

Guillaume, Gilbert. "Terrorism and International Law." *International and Comparative Law Quarterly* 53, no. 3 (2004): 537–548.

Higgins, Rosalyn, and Maurice Flory, eds. *Terrorism and International Law*. London: Routledge, 1997.

Saul, Ben. *Defining Terrorism in International Law*. Oxford: Oxford University Press, 2006.

Walter, Christian, Silja Vöneky, Volker Röben, and Frank Schorkopf, eds. *Terrorism as a Challenge for National and International Law: Security versus Liberty?* Berlin: Springer, 2004.

The International Legal Framework to Combat Terrorism

- ***Document:*** Overview of the major international conventions and protocols on specific aspects of terrorism
- ***Date:*** 1963–2005
- ***Significance:*** The multilateral conventions and protocols adopted between 1963 and 2005 address specific criminal acts that are considered terrorist in nature. These treaties provide the international legal framework to combat terrorism.

DOCUMENT SUMMARIES

1963 Convention on Offences and Certain Other Acts Committed On Board Aircraft

The Convention on Offences and Certain Other Acts Committed On Board Aircraft was signed in Tokyo on September 14, 1963, and applies to acts affecting in-flight safety. It contains provisions that authorize the aircraft commander to impose reasonable measures, including restraint, on any person he or she has reason to believe has committed or is about to commit an act jeopardizing the safety of the aircraft. The Convention also requires contracting States to take custody of offenders and to return control of the aircraft to the lawful commander.

1970 Convention for the Suppression of Unlawful Seizure of Aircraft (*Hague Convention*)

The Convention for the Suppression of Unlawful Seizure of Aircraft was signed at The Hague on December 16, 1970, and criminalizes acts on board an aircraft that unlawfully, by force or threat thereof, or any other form of intimidation, seize or exercise control of that aircraft. It requires parties to the convention to make hijackings punishable by "severe penalties" and to either extradite offenders or submit respective cases for prosecution. The Convention also requires parties to assist each other in connection with criminal proceedings brought under the Convention.

1971 Convention for the Suppression of Unlawful Acts Against the Safety of Civil Aviation (*Montreal Convention*)

The Convention for the Suppression of Unlawful Acts Against the Safety of Civil Aviation was concluded at Montreal on September 23, 1971. It criminalizes acts of violence against a person on board an aircraft in flight, if that act is likely to endanger the safety of the aircraft. The Montreal Convention further criminalizes placing an explosive device on an aircraft (including attempts at such acts and abetment). It also requires parties to the Convention to make offenses punishable by "severe penalties" and stipulates that either offenders shall be extradited or the case be submitted for prosecution. The 1988 Protocol for the Suppression of Unlawful Acts of Violence at Airports Serving International Aviation extends and supplements the Montreal Convention to encompass terrorist acts at airports serving international civil aviation.

1973 Convention on the Prevention and Punishment of Crimes Against Internationally Protected Persons

The Convention on the Prevention and Punishment of Crimes Against Internationally Protected Persons, Including Diplomatic Agents, was adopted in New York on December 14, 1973. It defines an "internationally protected person" as a Head of State, Minister for Foreign Affairs, or representative or official of a State or international organization who is entitled to special protection in a foreign State, as well as the person's family. The Convention requires parties to criminalize and make punishable "by appropriate penalties which take into account their grave nature" the intentional murder, kidnapping, or other attack upon the person or liberty of an internationally protected person or a violent attack upon the official premises, the private accommodations, or the means of transport of such person. It also criminalizes the threat or attempt to commit such attacks as well as acts "constituting participation as an accomplice."

1979 International Convention Against the Taking of Hostages

The International Convention Against the Taking of Hostages was adopted in New York on December 17, 1979. It stipulates that "any person who seizes or detains and threatens to kill, to injure, or to continue to detain another person in order to compel a third party, namely, a State, an international intergovernmental organization, a natural or juridical person, or a group of persons, to do or abstain from doing any act as an explicit or implicit condition for the release of the hostage commits the offence of taking of hostage within the meaning of this Convention."

1980 Convention on the Physical Protection of Nuclear Material

The Convention on the Physical Protection of Nuclear Material was adopted at Vienna on March 3, 1980. It criminalizes the unlawful possession, use, transfer, or theft of nuclear material and threats to use nuclear material to cause death, serious injury, or substantial property damage.

1988 Convention for the Suppression of Unlawful Acts Against the Safety of Maritime Navigation (*Rome Convention*)

The Convention for the Suppression of Unlawful Acts against the Safety of Maritime Navigation was concluded in Rome on March 10, 1988. It establishes a legal regime applicable to acts against international maritime navigation that is similar to the regimes established for international aviation. The Convention criminalizes the seizure or exercise of control over a ship by force, threat, or intimidation. It also makes it an offense to perform an act of violence against a person on board a ship if that act is likely to endanger the safe navigation of the ship. This includes placing a destructive device or substance aboard a ship.

The 2005 Protocol to the Convention for the Suppression of Unlawful Acts Against the Safety of Maritime Navigation extended the 1988 Convention in that it criminalizes the use of a ship as a device to further an act of terrorism. The Protocol also criminalizes the transport on board a ship of various materials knowing that they are intended to be used to cause, or in a threat to cause, death or serious injury or damage to further an act of terrorism. It makes it an offense to transport persons on board a ship who have committed an act of terrorism. In addition, the Protocol introduces procedures for governing the boarding of a ship believed to have been used in an offense under the Convention.

1988 Protocol for the Suppression of Unlawful Acts Against the Safety of Fixed Platforms Located on the Continental Shelf *(Fixed Platform Protocol)*

The Protocol for the Suppression of Unlawful Acts Against the Safety of Fixed Platforms located on the Continental Shelf was concluded in Rome on March 10, 1988. It establishes a legal regime applicable to acts against fixed platforms on the continental shelf that is similar to the regimes established against international aviation. In 2005, the Protocol to the Protocol for the Suppression of Unlawful Acts Against the Safety of Fixed Platforms Located on the Continental Shelf adapted several changes to the 1988 Convention for the Suppression of Unlawful Acts Against the Safety of Maritime Navigation to the context of fixed platforms located on the continental shelf.

1991 Convention on the Marking of Plastic Explosives for the Purpose of Detection *(Plastic Explosives Convention)*

The Convention on the Marking of Plastic Explosives for the Purpose of Detection was concluded in Montreal on March 1, 1991. It aims to control and limit the used of unmarked and undetectable plastic explosives. Each Party to the Convention is required to take necessary and effective measures to prohibit and prevent the manufacture of unmarked plastic explosives; prevent the movement of unmarked plastic explosives into or out of its territory; exercise strict and effective control over possession and transfer of unmarked explosives made or imported prior to the entry into force of the Convention; ensure that all stocks of unmarked explosives not held by the military or police are destroyed, consumed, marked, or rendered permanently ineffective within three years; take necessary measures to ensure that unmarked plastic explosives held by the military or police are destroyed, consumed, marked, or rendered permanently ineffective within fifteen years; and, ensure the destruction, as soon as possible, of any unmarked explosives manufactured after the date of entry into force of the Convention for that State.

1997 International Convention for the Suppression of Terrorist Bombings (*Terrorist Bombing Convention*)

The International Convention for the Suppression of Terrorist Bombings was concluded in New York on December 15, 1997. It establishes a regime of universal jurisdiction over the unlawful and intentional use of explosives and other lethal devices in, into, or against various defined public places with intent to kill or cause serious bodily injury, or with intent to cause extensive destruction of the public place.

1999 International Convention for the Suppression of the Financing of Terrorism (*Terrorist Financing Convention*)

The International Convention for the Suppression of the Financing of Terrorism was adopted in New York on December 9, 1999. It obligates parties to take steps to prevent and counteract the financing of terrorists, whether direct or indirect, through groups that claim to have charitable, social, or cultural goals or that also engage in illicit activities such as drug trafficking or gun running. The Convention requires parties to hold those who finance terrorism criminally, civilly, or administratively liable for such acts. It also provides for the identification, freezing, and seizure of funds allocated for terrorist activities, as well as for the sharing of the forfeited funds with other States on a case-by-case basis.

2005 International Convention for the Suppression of Act of Nuclear Terrorism (*Nuclear Terrorism Convention*)

The International Convention for the Suppression of Act of Nuclear Terrorism was adopted in New York on April 13, 2005. It covers a broad range of acts and possible targets, including nuclear power plants and nuclear reactors. The Convention also stipulates that offenders shall be either extradited or prosecuted. In addition, it encourages States to cooperate in preventing terrorist attacks by sharing information and assisting each other in connection with criminal investigations and extradition proceedings. The Convention further includes provisions dealing with both crisis situations (assisting States to solve the situation) and post-crisis situations (rendering nuclear material safe through the International Atomic Energy Agency).

SOURCE: United Nations Treaty Collection: Conventions on Terrorism, http://untreaty.un.org/English/Terrorism.asp.

ANALYSIS

Between 1963 and 2005, States concluded several international conventions addressing specific types of terrorism. Most of these multilateral treaties were adopted in response to specific terrorist incidents. A series of attacks on civil aviation in the 1960s and early 1970s, for example, led to the adoption of The Hague and Montreal Conventions; the 1988 Montreal Protocol was a response to terrorist attacks on airports in Rome and Vienna in 1985. Similarly, the 1988 Rome Convention was adopted in the aftermath of the seizure of the Italian cruise ship *Achille Lauro* in 1985.[7] The 1991 Convention on the Marking of Plastic Explosives for the Purpose of Detection was negotiated in the aftermath of the bombing of Pan Am flight 103 on December 21, 1988 (the Lockerbie Air Disaster); the 1997 Convention for the Suppression of Terrorist Bombings was initiated by the United States in response to bombings against U.S. interests in Saudi Arabia and bombings in Sri Lanka, Israel, and the United Kingdom.

Many of the conventions were adopted to fill normative gaps in the regulation of certain activities, such as air and maritime transport, which were spread across

DID YOU KNOW?

The first attempt to define terrorism in an international instrument was made in the 1937 Geneva Convention for the Prevention and Punishment of Genocide, which defined terrorism as "all criminal acts directed against a State and intended or calculated to create a state of terror in the minds of particular persons or a group of persons or the general public." This definition was criticized for its lack of precision, as it encompassed a wide range of criminal acts. The Convention never entered into force, as it did not receive the necessary number of ratifications.

Iran Hostage Crisis, student demonstration, Washington, DC. Courtesy of the Prints and Photographs Division. Library of Congress.

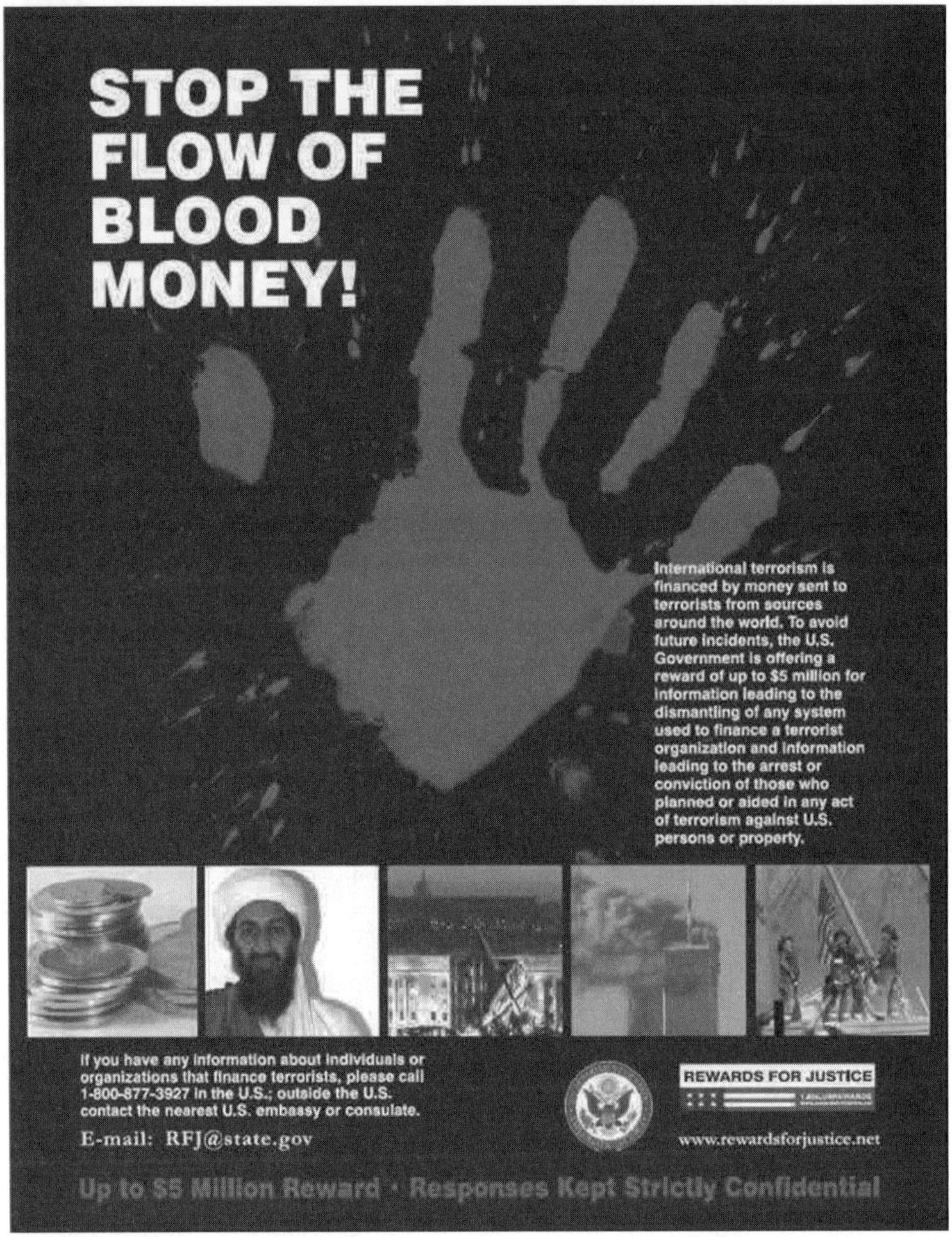

Combating the financing of terrorism is essential for an effective campaign against terrorism. The financing of terrorism is internationally criminalized by the Convention for the Suppression of the Financing of Terrorism, which was adopted in 1999. Courtesy of U.S. Government.

multiple jurisdictions. Some treaties were necessary because norms regulating the subject matter were considered inadequate. The 1988 Rome Convention, for example, was necessary because the crime of piracy was inapplicable to situations like the *Achille Lauro* incident, which lacked the elements of piracy as defined by the 1958 Geneva Convention on the High Seas. The adoption of the conventions and protocols by the majority of States has led to a de facto criminalization of most acts commonly regarded as terrorism. However, some normative gaps in the network of treaties remain.[8] For instance, the existing treaties fail to criminalize internationally the terrorist killings of civilians by any method, as they only criminalize violence by terrorists in specific contexts or by particular methods. This means that the killing of civilians (such as journalists, doctors, or engineers) as well as the killing of hostages is presently not covered by the international legal framework to combat terrorism.

The international legal framework to combat terrorism is complemented by various conventions on the regional level. In Europe, for instance, the Member States of the Council of Europe have adopted the 1977 European Convention on the Suppression of Terrorism with its 2003 Protocol and the 2006 Council of Europe Convention on the Prevention of Terrorism. In the Americas, the Member States of the Organization of American States have adopted the 1971 Convention to Prevent and Punish Acts of Terrorism Taking the Form of Crimes Against Persons and Related Extortion That Are of International Significance and the 2002 Inter-American Convention Against Terrorism. In Africa, Member States of the Organization of African Unity concluded the 1999 Convention on the Prevention and Combating of Terrorism (and 2004 Protocol). Similar conventions have been adopted within the frameworks of the South Asian Association for Regional Cooperation (SAARC), the Association of Southeast Asian Nations (ASEAN), the League of Arab States, and the Organization of the Islamic Conference.

DID YOU KNOW?

In History

On October 7, 1985, four members of the Palestine Liberation Front (PLF) took control of the Italian cruise ship *Achille Lauro* off Egypt as she was sailing from Alexandria to Port Said. Holding the passengers and crew hostage, they directed the vessel to sail to Tartus, Syria, and demanded the release of fifty Palestinians detained in Israeli prisons. After being refused permission to dock at Tartus, the hijackers murdered wheelchair-bound American passenger Leon Klinghoffer and threw his body overboard. The ship headed back toward Port Said, and after two days of negotiations, the hijackers agreed to abandon the cruise ship in exchange for safe conduct. They were subsequently flown towards Tunisia aboard an Egyptian commercial airliner. U.S. President Ronald Reagan ordered that the plane be intercepted by fighter jets from the aircraft carrier USS *Saratoga* and directed to land at a NATO base in Sicily, where the hijackers were arrested by the Italian authorities. The *Achille Lauro* incident led to the adoption of the Convention for the Suppression of Unlawful Acts against the Safety of Maritime Navigation in Rome on March 10, 1988.

FURTHER READING

Elagab, Omer, and Jeehan Elagab, eds. *International Law Documents Relating to Terrorism*. 3rd ed. London: Routledge-Cavendish, 2007.

Lambert, Joseph J. *Terrorism and Hostages in International Law: A Commentary on the Hostages Convention 1979*. Cambridge: Grotius, 1990.

Ramraj, Victor V., Michael Hor, and Kent Roach, eds. *Global Anti-Terrorism Law and Policy*. Cambridge, UK: Cambridge University Press, 2005.

Ronzitti, Natalino, ed. *Maritime Terrorism and International Law*. Dordrecht: Martinus Nijhoff, 1990.

Witten, Samuel M. "The International Convention for the Suppression of Terrorist Bombings." *American Journal of International Law* 92, no. 4 (1998): 774–781.

The UN Security Council and Terrorism as a Threat to Peace and Security

- ***Document:*** UN Security Council Resolutions 1368 (2001) and 1373 (2001)
- ***Date:*** September 12 and 28, 2001
- ***Where:*** United Nations, New York
- ***Significance:*** UN Security Council Resolutions 1368 (2001) and 1373 (2001) stipulate that the 9/11 attacks qualify as a threat to international peace and security.

DOCUMENTS

Resolution 1368 (2001) Adopted by the Security Council at its 4370th meeting, 12 September 2001

The Security Council,

Reaffirming the principles and purposes of the Charter of the United Nations,

Determined to combat by all means threats to international peace and security caused by terrorist acts,

Recognizing the inherent right of individual or collective self-defence in accordance with the Charter,

1. *Unequivocally condemns* in the strongest terms the horrifying terrorist attacks which took place on 11 September 2001 in New York, Washington (D.C.) and Pennsylvania and *regards* such acts, like any act of international terrorism, as a threat to international peace and security;
2. *Expresses* its deepest sympathy and condolences to the victims and their families and to the People and Government of the United States of America;
3. *Calls* on all States to work together urgently to bring to justice the perpetrators, organizers and sponsors of these terrorist attacks and *stresses* that those

responsible for aiding, supporting or harbouring the perpetrators, organizers and sponsors of these acts will be held accountable;

4. *Calls also* on the international community to redouble their efforts to prevent and suppress terrorist acts including by increased cooperation and full implementation of the relevant international anti-terrorist conventions and Security Council resolutions, in particular resolution 1269 of 19 October 1999;
5. *Expresses* its readiness to take all necessary steps to respond to the terrorist attacks of 11 September 2001, and to combat all forms of terrorism, in accordance with its responsibilities under the Charter of the United Nations;
6. *Decides* to remain seized of the matter.

Resolution 1373 (2001) Adopted by the Security Council at its 4385th meeting, on 28 September 2001

The Security Council,

Reaffirming its resolutions 1269 (1999) of 19 October 1999 and 1368 (2001) of 12 September 2001,

Reaffirming also its unequivocal condemnation of the terrorist attacks which took place in New York, Washington, D.C., and Pennsylvania on 11 September 2001, and expressing its determination to prevent all such acts,

Reaffirming further that such acts, like any act of international terrorism, constitute a threat to international peace and security,

Reaffirming the inherent right of individual or collective self-defence as recognized by the Charter of the United Nations as reiterated in resolution 1368 (2001),

Reaffirming the need to combat by all means, in accordance with the Charter of the United Nations, threats to international peace and security caused by terrorist acts,

Deeply concerned by the increase, in various regions of the world, of acts of terrorism motivated by intolerance or extremism,

Calling on States to work together urgently to prevent and suppress terrorist acts, including through increased cooperation and full implementation of the relevant international conventions relating to terrorism,

Recognizing the need for States to complement international cooperation by taking additional measures to prevent and suppress, in their territories through all lawful means, the financing and preparation of any acts of terrorism,

Reaffirming the principle established by the General Assembly in its declaration of October 1970 (resolution 2625 (XXV)) and reiterated by the Security Council in its resolution 1189 (1998) of 13 August 1998, namely that every State has the duty to refrain from organizing, instigating, assisting or participating in terrorist acts in another State or acquiescing in organized activities within its territory directed towards the commission of such acts,

Acting under Chapter VII of the Charter of the United Nations,

1. *Decides* that all States shall:
   (a) Prevent and suppress the financing of terrorist acts;
   (b) Criminalize the wilful provision or collection, by any means, directly or indirectly, of funds by their nationals or in their territories with the intention

that the funds should be used, or in the knowledge that they are to be used, in order to carry out terrorist acts;

(c) Freeze without delay funds and other financial assets or economic resources of persons who commit, or attempt to commit, terrorist acts or participate in or facilitate the commission of terrorist acts; of entities owned or controlled directly or indirectly by such persons; and of persons and entities acting on behalf of, or at the direction of such persons and entities, including funds derived or generated from property owned or controlled directly or indirectly by such persons and associated persons and entities;

(d) Prohibit their nationals or any persons and entities within their territories from making any funds, financial assets or economic resources or financial or other related services available, directly or indirectly, for the benefit of persons who commit or attempt to commit or facilitate or participate in the commission of terrorist acts, of entities owned or controlled, directly or indirectly, by such persons and of persons and entities acting on behalf of or at the direction of such persons;

2. *Decides also* that all States shall:

(a) Refrain from providing any form of support, active or passive, to entities or persons involved in terrorist acts, including by suppressing recruitment of members of terrorist groups and eliminating the supply of weapons to terrorists;

(b) Take the necessary steps to prevent the commission of terrorist acts, including by provision of early warning to other States by exchange of information;

(c) Deny safe haven to those who finance, plan, support, or commit terrorist acts, or provide safe havens;

(d) Prevent those who finance, plan, facilitate or commit terrorist acts from using their respective territories for those purposes against other States or their citizens;

(e) Ensure that any person who participates in the financing, planning, preparation or perpetration of terrorist acts or in supporting terrorist acts is brought to justice and ensure that, in addition to any other measures against them, such terrorist acts are established as serious criminal offences in domestic laws and regulations and that the punishment duly reflects the seriousness of such terrorist acts;

(f) Afford one another the greatest measure of assistance in connection with criminal investigations or criminal proceedings relating to the financing or support of terrorist acts, including assistance in obtaining evidence in their possession necessary for the proceedings;

(g) Prevent the movement of terrorists or terrorist groups by effective border controls and controls on issuance of identity papers and travel documents, and through measures for preventing counterfeiting, forgery or fraudulent use of identity papers and travel documents;

3. *Calls* upon all States to:

(a) Find ways of intensifying and accelerating the exchange of operational information, especially regarding actions or movements of terrorist persons or networks; forged or falsified travel documents; traffic in arms, explosives or sensitive materials; use of communications technologies by terrorist groups; and the threat posed by the possession of weapons of mass destruction by terrorist groups;

(b) Exchange information in accordance with international and domestic law and cooperate on administrative and judicial matters to prevent the commission of terrorist acts;

(c) Cooperate, particularly through bilateral and multilateral arrangements and agreements, to prevent and suppress terrorist attacks and take action against perpetrators of such acts;

(d) Become parties as soon as possible to the relevant international conventions and protocols relating to terrorism, including the International Convention for the Suppression of the Financing of Terrorism of 9 December 1999;

(e) Increase cooperation and fully implement the relevant international conventions and protocols relating to terrorism and Security Council resolutions 1269 (1999) and 1368 (2001);

(f) Take appropriate measures in conformity with the relevant provisions of national and international law, including international standards of human rights, before granting refugee status, for the purpose of ensuring that the asylum seeker has not planned, facilitated or participated in the commission of terrorist acts;

(g) Ensure, in conformity with international law, that refugee status is not abused by the perpetrators, organizers or facilitators of terrorist acts, and that claims of political motivation are not recognized as grounds for refusing requests for the extradition of alleged terrorists;

4. *Notes* with concern the close connection between international terrorism and transnational organized crime, illicit drugs, money-laundering, illegal arms-trafficking, and illegal movement of nuclear, chemical, biological and other potentially deadly materials, and in this regard *emphasizes* the need to enhance coordination of efforts on national, subregional, regional and international levels in order to strengthen a global response to this serious challenge and threat to international security;
5. *Declares* that acts, methods, and practices of terrorism are contrary to the purposes and principles of the United Nations and that knowingly financing, planning and inciting terrorist acts are also contrary to the purposes and principles of the United Nations;
6. *Decides* to establish, in accordance with rule 28 of its provisional rules of procedure, a Committee of the Security Council, consisting of all the members of the Council, to monitor implementation of this resolution, with the assistance of appropriate expertise, and *calls upon* all States to report to the Committee, no later than 90 days from the date of adoption of this resolution and thereafter according to a timetable to be proposed by the Committee, on the steps they have taken to implement this resolution;
7. *Directs* the Committee to delineate its tasks, submit a work programme within 30 days of the adoption of this resolution, and to consider the support it requires, in consultation with the Secretary-General;

8. *Expresses* its determination to take all necessary steps in order to ensure the full implementation of this resolution, in accordance with its responsibilities under the Charter;
9. *Decides* to remain seized of this matter.

SOURCE: United Nations. http://www.un.org/Docs/scres/2001/sc2001.htm,

ANALYSIS

The Security Council has been dealing with terrorism issues since the early 1990s. In the 1990s, its actions took the form of sanctions against States considered to have links to certain acts of terrorism. In 1992, for instance, Libya rejected a request by the United States and the United Kingdom to hand over two Libyans who allegedly acted as agents for Libya and were involved in the 1988 bombing of Pan Am flight 103. The Security Council first supported this request through a nonbinding resolution, and upon Libya's noncompliance adopted resolution 748 (1992) determining "that the failure by the Libyan Government to demonstrate by concrete actions its renunciation of terrorism and in particular its continued failure to respond fully and effectively to the request in Resolution 731 (1992) constitute a threat to peace and security." In 1996, the Security Council adopted a similar approach in resolution 1070 (1996) and subjected Sudan to enforcement measures in response to a failure to comply with earlier requests to extradite terrorist suspects for trial.

In 1999, the Security Council adopted resolution 1267, which requires all States to freeze the assets of, prevent the entry into or transit through their territories by, and prevent the direct or indirect supply, sale, and transfer of arms and military equipment to any individual or entity associated with Al Qa'ida, Osama bin Laden, and/or the Taliban as designated by a subcommittee of the Council, the 1267 Committee. The sanctions regime has since been modified and strengthened by subsequent resolutions, so that the sanctions now cover individuals and entities associated with Al Qa'ida, Osama bin Laden, and/or the Taliban wherever located. In addition to overseeing the implementation of resolution 1267 and subsequent resolutions, the 1267 Committee also maintains a list of individuals and entities with respect to Al Qa'ida, Osama bin Laden, and the Taliban and other individuals, groups, undertakings and entities associated with them. States may request the Committee to add names to this list and the Committee also considers submissions by States to delete names from it. As of September 2009, 509 individuals and/or entities were listed.[9]

The 1267 sanctions regime remains a cornerstone of the UN counter-terrorism efforts. However, it has been criticized for its lack of due process guarantees.[10] For instance, targeted individuals or entities are not informed prior to their being listed and thus do not have any opportunity to prevent the listing by demonstrating that their inclusion in the list is unjustified. Even after an individual or entity is listed, UN Member States do not have an obligation to provide detailed information to the person or entity concerned about reasons for their inclusion. In essence, listed individuals and entities have no means to challenge their inclusion in the list. This has led to a landmark decision of the European Court of Justice in September 2008, which found the implementation of the 1267 regime by the Council of the European Union to be in violation of fundamental rights.[11]

In the immediate aftermath of 9/11 the Security Council further intensified its counter-terrorism efforts. Acting under Chapter VII of the UN Charter, the Council adopted resolutions 1368 and 1373 (2001). Resolution 1373 provides the basis for domestic legal action against terrorism and requires particular domestic action, including legislative measures. The resolution established a subcommittee of the Security Council, the Counter-Terrorism Committee (CTC), to monitor compliance with and implementation of the resolution. States are required to submit reports to the Committee detailing their compliance with resolution 1373 within 90 days of its adoption. Resolution 1373 does not attempt to define terrorism. Instead, each Member State of the UN is required to apply its own laws against terrorism effectively.

Consistent with its practice in certain previous resolutions on terrorism, the Security Council, in resolutions 1368 and 1373 (2001), determined that the 9/11 attacks constituted a threat to international peace and security. In contrast to other resolutions on terrorism, however, the Council also expressly recognized "the inherent right of individual or collective self-defense as recognized by the Charter of the United Nations." This has led to considerable debate among international lawyers. Some scholars have argued that the resolutions confirmed that terrorist attacks amount to an "armed attack" thus triggering the right of self-defense as enshrined in article 51 of the UN Charter.[12] Acknowledging that the right to use force in self-defense against States against terrorism was controversial before 9/11, these scholars cite almost universal support of States for a right of self-defense of the United States in response to the attacks on New York and Washington. Others have expressed doubt about the legal significance of resolutions 1368 and 1373 (2001) and questioned whether these resolutions actually support self-defense against terrorist attacks. They base their reservations on the fact that the reference to self-defense is found in the preamble of the resolutions in question, rather than in their operative part.[13] In addition, these scholars claim that the language is that of "threat to peace and security" rather than "armed attack" under Article 51.

It remains unclear whether 9/11 and the corresponding response of the Security Council brought about a significant change in the law of self-defense. In fact, the practice of the Council suggests that it is not willing to assert a wide right of pre-emptive self-defense. Since the adoption of resolutions 1368 and 1373 the Council has responded to a number of terrorist incidents, including attacks perpetrated by Al Qa'ida. It has adopted resolutions, inter alia, in response to the 2002 Bali bombings (resolution 1438), the 2002 terrorist attacks against a holiday resort and an Israeli airliner in Kenya (resolution 1450), the November 2003 bomb attacks in Istanbul (resolution

DID YOU KNOW?

Chapter VII of the United Nations Charter sets out the UN Security Council's powers to maintain peace. It allows the Council to "determine the existence of any threat to the peace, breach of the peace, or act of aggression" and to take military and nonmilitary action to "restore international peace and security." According to Article 42 of the UN Charter, the Security Council may take such action by air, sea, or land forces as may be necessary to maintain or restore international peace and security in the event that nonmilitary measures provided for in Article 41 are, or have proved to be, inadequate. Enforcement measures involving the use of force may include "demonstrations, blockade, and other operations by air, sea, or land forces of Members of the United Nations."

1516), the 2004 Madrid train bombings (resolution 1530), and the 2005 London Tube bombings (resolution 1611). None of these resolutions made reference to the right of self-defense. Instead the Council repeated that it regards "such acts, like any act of terrorism, as a threat to peace and security," and expressed "its utmost determination to combat terrorism, in accordance with its responsibilities under the Charter of the United Nations." Scholars have argued that this may be taken as an indication that the right to use force in self-defense against terrorist acts may remain exceptional and available only in cases of attacks on territory rather than on nationals abroad.[14]

FURTHER READING

Byers, Michael. "Terrorism, the Use of Force and International Law After 11 September." *International and Comparative Law Quarterly* 51, no. 2 (2002): 401–414.

Cassese, Antonio. "Terrorism Is Also Disrupting Some Crucial Legal Categories of International Law." *European Journal of International Law* 12, no. 5 (2001): 993–1001.

Greenwood, Christopher. "International Law and the 'War against Terrorism'." *International Affairs* 78, no. 2 (2002): 301–317.

McWhinney, Edward. *The September 11 Terrorist Attacks and the Invasion of Iraq in Contemporary International Law*. Leiden: Martinus Nijhoff, 2004.

Murphy, Sean D. "Terrorism and the Concept of Armed Attack in Article 51 of the UN Charter." *Harvard International Law Journal* 43, no. 1 (2002): 41–63.

Rosand, Eric. "Security Council Resolution 1373, the Counter-Terrorism Committee, and the Fight against Terrorism." *American Journal of International Law* 97, no. 2 (2003): 333–341.

Ulfstein, Geir. "Terrorism and the Use of Force." *Security Dialogue*, 34, no. 2 (2003): 153–167.

Afghanistan and Operation Enduring Freedom

- ***Document:*** Presidential Address to the Nation on the Commencement of Military Operations in Afghanistan
- ***Date:*** October 7, 2001
- ***Where:*** The White House, Washington DC
- ***Significance:*** In his Address to the Nation, President Bush outlined the reasons for initiating military operations against the Taliban in Afghanistan.

DOCUMENT

Good afternoon. On my orders, the United States military has begun strikes against al Qaeda terrorist training camps and military installations of the Taliban regime in Afghanistan. These carefully targeted actions are designed to disrupt the use of Afghanistan as a terrorist base of operations, and to attack the military capability of the Taliban regime.

We are joined in this operation by our staunch friend, Great Britain. Other close friends, including Canada, Australia, Germany and France, have pledged forces as the operation unfolds. More than 40 countries in the Middle East, Africa, Europe and across Asia have granted air transit or landing rights. Many more have shared intelligence. We are supported by the collective will of the world.

More than two weeks ago, I gave Taliban leaders a series of clear and specific demands: Close terrorist training camps; hand over leaders of the al Qaeda network; and return all foreign nationals, including American citizens, unjustly detained in your country. None of these demands were met. And now the Taliban will pay a price. By destroying camps and disrupting communications, we will make it more difficult for the terror network to train new recruits and coordinate their evil plans.

Initially, the terrorists may burrow deeper into caves and other entrenched hiding places. Our military action is also designed to clear the way for sustained, comprehensive and relentless operations to drive them out and bring them to justice.

At the same time, the oppressed people of Afghanistan will know the generosity of America and our allies. As we strike military targets, we'll also drop food, medicine and supplies to the starving and suffering men and women and children of Afghanistan.

The United States of America is a friend to the Afghan people, and we are the friends of almost a billion worldwide who practice the Islamic faith. The United States of America is an enemy of those who aid terrorists and of the barbaric criminals who profane a great religion by committing murder in its name.

This military action is a part of our campaign against terrorism, another front in a war that has already been joined through diplomacy, intelligence, the freezing of financial assets and the arrests of known terrorists by law enforcement agents in 38 countries. Given the nature and reach of our enemies, we will win this conflict by the patient accumulation of successes, by meeting a series of challenges with determination and will and purpose.

Today we focus on Afghanistan, but the battle is broader. Every nation has a choice to make. In this conflict, there is no neutral ground. If any government sponsors the outlaws and killers of innocents, they have become outlaws and murderers, themselves. And they will take that lonely path at their own peril.

I'm speaking to you today from the Treaty Room of the White House, a place where American Presidents have worked for peace. We're a peaceful nation. Yet, as we have learned, so suddenly and so tragically, there can be no peace in a world of sudden terror. In the face of today's new threat, the only way to pursue peace is to pursue those who threaten it.

We did not ask for this mission, but we will fulfill it. The name of today's military operation is Enduring Freedom. We defend not only our precious freedoms, but also the freedom of people everywhere to live and raise their children free from fear.

I know many Americans feel fear today. And our government is taking strong precautions. All law enforcement and intelligence agencies are working aggressively around America, around the world and around the clock. At my request, many governors have activated the National Guard to strengthen airport security. We have called up Reserves to reinforce our military capability and strengthen the protection of our homeland.

In the months ahead, our patience will be one of our strengths—patience with the long waits that will result from tighter security; patience and understanding that it will take time to achieve our goals; patience in all the sacrifices that may come.

Today, those sacrifices are being made by members of our Armed Forces who now defend us so far from home, and by their proud and worried families. A Commander-in-Chief sends America's sons and daughters into a battle in a foreign land only after the greatest care and a lot of prayer. We ask a lot of those who wear our uniform. We ask them to leave their loved ones, to travel great distances, to risk injury, even to be prepared to make the ultimate sacrifice of their lives.

They are dedicated, they are honorable; they represent the best of our country. And we are grateful.

To all the men and women in our military—every sailor, every soldier, every airman, every coastguardsman, every Marine—I say this: Your mission is defined; your objectives are clear; your goal is just. You have my full confidence, and you will have every tool you need to carry out your duty.

I recently received a touching letter that says a lot about the state of America in these difficult times—a letter from a 4th-grade girl, with a father in the military: "As much as I don't want my Dad to fight," she wrote, "I'm willing to give him to you."

This is a precious gift, the greatest she could give. This young girl knows what America is all about. Since September 11, an entire generation of young Americans has gained new understanding of the value of freedom, and its cost in duty and in sacrifice.

The battle is now joined on many fronts. We will not waver; we will not tire; we will not falter; and we will not fail. Peace and freedom will prevail.

Thank you. May God continue to bless America.

SOURCE: U.S. Government. http://www.whitehouse.gov/news/releases/2001/10/20011007-8.html

ANALYSIS

On October 7, 2001, the United States commenced military operations against the Taliban in Afghanistan. The United States relied on the right of self-defense as the basis for its use of force. This was made clear by the U.S. ambassador to the United Nations, John Negroponte, who wrote to the President of the Security Council "to report that the United States of America, together with other States, has initiated actions in the exercise of its inherent right of individual and collective self-defense following the armed attacks that were carried out against the United States on September 11th."[15] The letter went on to state that the United States had "clear and compelling information that the Al-Qa'ida organization . . . had a central role in the attacks" of September 11, and stated that the United States might find "that our self-defense requires further actions with respect to other organizations and States."

While the majority of States appear to have supported, or at least tolerated, the United States' decision to use force against the Taliban, international legal scholars have debated at length whether the military operations were justified under Article 51 of the UN Charter. Some scholars have pointed out that the attacks of 9/11 were

DID YOU KNOW?

The International Security Assistance Force (ISAF) is a United Nations–mandated coalition of States, with costs borne by its contributors. As of October 2008, ISAF troops numbered about 50,700 from 26 NATO, 10 partner, and 5 non-NATO/non-partner countries, including contributions from Canada, the United States, the United Kingdom, other European countries, Australia, New Zealand, Azerbaijan, Jordan, Turkey and Singapore. ISAF was initially charged with securing Kabul and surrounding areas from the Taliban, Al Qa'ida, and factional warlords to allow for the establishment of the Afghan Transitional Administration. In October 2003, the UN Security Council authorized the expansion of the ISAF mission throughout Afghanistan, and ISAF subsequently expanded the mission in four main stages over the whole of the country. The command of ISAF initially rotated among different nations on a semiannual basis. In August 2003, however, it was turned over indefinitely to NATO. It is NATO's first deployment outside Europe or North America.

U.S. Marine 1st Lt. Nick Ramseur, platoon leader with Weapons Company, 3rd Battalion, 3rd Marine Regiment, talks to local elders about the damage their houses have sustained from the recent severe weather, during a security operation on March 8, 2005. The Marines are conducting security and stabilization operations in support of Operation Enduring Freedom. Courtesy of Cpl. James L. Yarboro, U.S. Marine Corps.

over long before the United States military response was commenced.[16] As a consequence, the United States could not rely on self-defense as a basis for the use of force. Other scholars rejected this position and maintain that the events of 9/11 could not be considered in isolation.[17] Taken together with other incidents such as the 1998 embassy attacks in Kenya and Tanzania and the attack on the USS *Cole*, for which Al Qa'ida had claimed responsibility, they posed a clear threat of further outrages to come. These scholars argue that the United States was thus justified to launch military operations in self-defense to remove "imminent" future threats.

A further point of contention was the fact that the 9/11 attacks emanated from a terrorist organization rather than from a State. Yet the military action taken by the United States and its allies involved extensive operations on the territory of the State of Afghanistan. This has led some scholars to argue that the U.S. invasion of Afghanistan was disproportionate, and as such not justifiable under Article 51 of the UN Charter.[18] Other scholars disagreed and argued that while the Taliban were not widely recognized as the government of Afghanistan, they controlled most of its territory.[19] In these circumstances, they constituted a *de facto* government, and their actions were to be treated as the actions of the State. By allowing Al Qa'ida to operate from the territory, which it controlled, the Taliban violated the general duty of a State under international law not to allow its territory to be used as a base for attacks on other States. As a consequence, these scholars argue that the United States was entitled to launch attacks against the Taliban in self-defense.

As of September 2009, military operations in Afghanistan continue, both under the auspices of the International Security Assistance Force (ISAF) and as part of Operation Enduring Freedom (OEF). However, ISAF and OEF need to be distinguished for political and legal reasons. ISAF was established as a result of the UN-facilitated talks in Bonn, Germany, in December 2001. The Bonn Agreement laid out a framework and timeline for political recovery and also set the basis for the United Nations Mission in Afghanistan (UNAMA) and ISAF. Its Annex 1 (International Security Force) states that "the participants request the assistance of the international community in helping the new Afghan authorities in the establishment and training of new Afghan security and armed forces."[20] It also included a request for "the early deployment to Afghanistan of a United Nations mandated force."

The Bonn Agreement was endorsed by the UN Security Council in resolution 1386 (2001), which authorized "the establishment for 6 months of an International Security Assistance Force to assist the Afghan Interim Authority in the maintenance of security in Kabul and its surrounding areas, so that the Afghan Interim Authority as well as the personnel of the United Nations can operate in a secure environment." Furthermore, the Security Council called "on Member States participating in ISAF to provide assistance to help the Afghan Interim Authority in the establishment and training of new Afghan security and armed forces." The ISAF mandate was subsequently renewed by several Security Council resolutions, most recently in resolution 1833 (2008), which extended the mandate of ISAF to October 12, 2009.

Marines from Company I, 3rd Battalion, 6th Marine Regiment, patrol on foot through downtown Surobi, Afghanistan, on 23 May 2004. The battalion is conducting security patrols and civil assistance operations throughout the region in support of Operation Enduring Freedom. Courtesy of Lance Cpl. Justin M. Mason, U.S. Department of Defense.

ISAF Logo. The Pashto writing, transliterated Komak wa Hamkari, translates "Help and Cooperation." Courtesy of NATO.

In contrast to the ISAF mission, the legal basis for the U.S. forces in Afghanistan serving as part of Operation Enduring Freedom (OEF) remains somewhat unclear. While some relevant Security Council resolutions on Afghanistan have explicitly acknowledged the existence of OEF forces, the Council has yet to authorize their operation. The United States has also not reached any bilateral "status of forces" agreement with the Afghan government. However, President Bush and the President of Afghanistan, Hamid Karzai, issued a joint declaration of strategic partnership in May 2005.[21] This declaration endorsed the continued stationing of U.S. troops in Afghanistan and entailed regular high-level exchanges in the political, economic, and security fields. It also called for help to organize Afghan security forces, continued antiterrorism activities, strengthening Afghanistan's ties with NATO, and possibly assisting Afghanistan in the case of an external threat. It may thus be argued that U.S. troops operate in Afghanistan with the consent of the local government.

FURTHER READING

Chesterman, Simon. "Humanitarian Intervention and Afghanistan." In *Humanitarian Intervention and International Relations*, edited by Jennifer M. Welsh, 163–175. Oxford: Oxford University Press, 2006.

Drumbl, Mark A. "Self-Defense and the Use of Force: Breaking the Rules, Making the Rules, or Both?" *International Studies Perspectives* 4, no. 4 (2003): 409–431.

Paust, Jordan J. "Use of Force Against Terrorists in Afghanistan, Iraq and Beyond." *Cornell International Law Journal* 35, no. 3 (2002): 533–557.

Rubin, Barnett R. *Afghanistan's Uncertain Transition from Turmoil to Normalcy*. Council on Foreign Relations, CSR No. 12, (2006). http://www.cfr.org/content/publications/attachments/Afghanistan_CSR.pdf.

Schmitt, Michael N. "US Security Strategies: A Legal Assessment." *Harvard Journal of Law & Public Policy* 27, no. 3 (2004):737–764.

Stahn, Carsten. "Terrorist Acts as 'Armed Attack': The Right to Self-Defense, Article 51 (1/2) of the UN Charter, and International Terrorism." *Fletcher Forum of World Affairs* 27, no. 2 (2003): 35–53.

The Practice of Detaining "Illegal Enemy Combatants"

- ***Document*:** Statement by the Press Secretary, Ari Fleischer, on the Geneva Convention
- ***Date*:** May 7, 2003
- ***Where*:** The James S. Brady Briefing Room, The White House, Washington DC
- ***Significance*:** The press statement is an example of the Bush administration's attempts to justify highly questionable practices in the "War on Terror" by presenting an inaccurate and misleading appraisal of fundamental principles of international law.

DOCUMENT

MR. FLEISCHER: I have an announcement to make. Today President Bush affirms our enduring commitment to the important principles of the Geneva Convention. Consistent with American values and the principles of the Geneva Convention, the United States has treated and will continue to treat all Taliban and al Qaeda detainees in Guantanamo Bay humanely and consistent with the principles of the Geneva Convention.

They will continue to receive three appropriate meals a day, excellent medical care, clothing, shelter, showers, and the opportunity to worship. The International Community of the Red Cross can visit each detainee privately.

In addition, President Bush today has decided that the Geneva Convention will apply to the Taliban detainees, but not to the al Qaeda international terrorists.

Afghanistan is a party to the Geneva Convention. Although the United States does not recognize the Taliban as a legitimate Afghani government, the President determined that the Taliban members are covered under the treaty because Afghanistan is a party to the Convention.

Under Article 4 of the Geneva Convention, however, Taliban detainees are not entitled to POW status. To qualify as POWs under Article 4, al Qaeda and Taliban detainees would have to have satisfied four conditions: They would have to be part of a military hierarchy; they would have to have worn uniforms or other distinctive signs visible at a distance; they would have to have carried arms openly; and they would have to have conducted their military operations in accordance with the laws and customs of war.

The Taliban have not effectively distinguished themselves from the civilian population of Afghanistan. Moreover, they have not conducted their operations in accordance with the laws and customs of war. Instead, they have knowingly adopted and provided support to the unlawful terrorist objectives of the al Qaeda.

Al Qaeda is an international terrorist group and cannot be considered a state party to the Geneva Convention. Its members, therefore, are not covered by the Geneva Convention, and are not entitled to POW status under the treaty

The war on terrorism is a war not envisaged when the Geneva Convention was signed in 1949. In this war, global terrorists transcend national boundaries and internationally target the innocent. The President has maintained the United States' commitment to the principles of the Geneva Convention, while recognizing that the Convention simply does not cover every situation in which people may be captured or detained by military forces, as we see in Afghanistan today.

He arrived at a just, principled and practical solution to a difficult issue. The President did so because, as Americans, the way we treat people is a reflection of America's values. The military operates under a code of conduct that upholds these values, based on the dignity of every individual.

The American people can take great pride in the way our military is treating these dangerous detainees. The Convention remains as important today as it was the day it was signed, and the United States is proud of its 50-year history in compliance with the Convention.

Question: Given that the President had long ago determined that none of these folks were prisoners of war, how, if at all, does it change the way the Taliban and, separately, al Qaeda fighters will be treated at Guantanamo Bay? And tell me how this might help protect U.S. forces if they happen to be captured in Afghanistan.

MR. FLEISCHER: What this announcement signifies is the President's dedication to the importance of the Geneva Convention and to the principles that the Geneva Convention holds. In terms of the treatment of the prisoners, even though the President has determined that they will not be treated legally as prisoners of war, they will be afforded every courtesy and every value that this nation applies to treating people well while they're in our custody. So it will not change their material life on a day-to-day basis; they will continue to be treated well because that's what the United States does.

Question: And then why do this? Is it because of the second part of the question?

MR. FLEISCHER: It's because of the first answer I gave, which is because the President believes in the principles and in the law of the Geneva Convention. He believes in its applicability; he believes in its importance; he believes that that plays a role even in today's modern world where the applicability gets somewhat more complicated as a result of an international terrorist organization that doesn't wear uniforms or insignias.

Question: So, Ari, what you're telling us is that the Taliban prisoners, detainees at Guantanamo will not get any more protections than they already are given under the Geneva Convention. What you seem to be telling us is the al Qaeda detainees will get fewer.

MR. FLEISCHER: No. There is no change in the protections they will be provided. They have always been treated consistent with the principles of the Geneva Convention, which means they will be treated well. If you're looking for anything that will not happen as a result of this announcement, it is that they will not receive stipends from the American taxpayers. They will not receive musical instruments courtesy of the United States military. They would have received those had they been declared POWs.

Question: That's true of the Taliban, too, right?

MR. FLEISCHER: Correct.

Question: So what is the difference? How will the al Qaeda and the Taliban detainees be treated differently?

MR. FLEISCHER: What the President is saying here is there's an important legal principle recognizing that Afghanistan is a member state that agreed to the terms of the Geneva Convention. So the President is making distinction between the al Qaeda and the Taliban. But when it comes to the classification as POWs, neither group will be given POW legal designation, although they will continue to be treated humanely, in accordance with America's values, which are reflected in the Convention.

Question: How is there any difference, Ari, in how they are treated? Is there any difference in how they are treated?

MR. FLEISCHER: That's what we've been saying all along. They will continue to be treated well because they're in the custody of America.

Question: They will be treated the same, al Qaeda and Taliban detainees will be treated equally.

MR. FLEISCHER: No distinction will be made in the good treatment given to the al Qaeda or the Taliban.

Question: So this is a distinction without a difference, really?

MR. FLEISCHER: No, it's a distinction based on the legal principle that the President believes in the Geneva Convention and its important principles.

Question: But you have to say, Ari, that day to day nothing is going to change that will be noticeable for these detainees. That's correct, right?

MR. FLEISCHER: They will continue to be treated well. No change in that treatment.

Question: So applying the Convention here is being done solely to protect U.S. citizens, and namely, U.S. soldiers, who may be in a situation overseas held by a foreign government. Is that correct? Is that's the principle that's being upheld?

MR. FLEISCHER: No, the principle is that this country and this President, of course, believe in and adhere to the Geneva Convention. In any case, the United States would always be covered by the Geneva Convention, our military, because as I mentioned, under Article 4, you have to wear a uniform, you have to wear an insignia, carry your weapons outside, be distinguishable from the civilian population, all of which covers our military.

Question: But the concern, the debate here was about if you don't do it here, then U.S. soldiers could be mistreated abroad. Isn't that correct? And so isn't that a big motivation here, to make sure that U.S. soldiers get this same kind of treatment?

MR. FLEISCHER: It's important for all nations, throughout the world, to treat any prisoners well. And that is something the United States always expects, and the United States always does. We have time for one more question, and then there's a pool. David will get one more, and then we'll—

Question: Can you just be responsive to the specific point? Wasn't this an important concern? I understand what the expectations are, but it was important for this administration to be able to say, look, we want to be able to protect our soldiers in similar situations down the line. And if we don't afford privileges under the Geneva Convention, then our soldiers could be in peril?

MR. FLEISCHER: David, I was not in the NSC deliberations where various issues were raised. And so I really—there's no way I can accurately answer that question.

Question: What about the U.S. special forces? They don't—they often do not wear uniforms. They often do not carry their weapons outwardly. If they are captured, they wouldn't be prisoners of war?

MR. FLEISCHER: The terms of the Geneva Convention apply to all, and those terms speak for themselves. Okay, thank you everybody.

SOURCE: U.S. Government. http://www.whitehouse.gov/news/releases/2003/05/20030507-18.html.

ANALYSIS

The practice of detaining "illegal enemy combatants" at the U.S. Naval Base in Guantanamo Bay, Cuba, was a key feature of the Bush administration's "War on Terror." It was part of a series of highly controversial measures that included secret detention, extraordinary rendition, and forced disappearance of terrorism suspects as well as mistreatment of terrorism suspects and prisoners of war in U.S. custody.[22] The latter came to public attention in the context of the abuses of detainees at the Abu Ghraib prison in Iraq, which were reported in an article by Seymour Hersh published in *The New Yorker* magazine as well as by CBS's *60 Minutes* television program.[23] All the above-mentioned practices of the Bush administration raised serious concerns in relation to their compatibility with both international and U.S. law.

As far as the detention of fighters in Afghanistan was concerned, President Bush determined in late 2001 that the Geneva Conventions did not apply to this conflict. This position was revised in early February 2002. However, the Bush administration continued to claim that

DID YOU KNOW?

In History

Guantanamo Bay Naval Base is located at the southeastern end of Cuba and has been used by the United States Navy since the Spanish-American War of 1898. It is the oldest overseas U.S. Navy base, and the only one in a country with which the United States does not have diplomatic relations. Since 2002, the naval base has contained a detention camp for persons alleged to be militant combatants captured in Afghanistan and later in Iraq. Guantanamo became host to Cuba's first and only McDonald's restaurant in 1986. It has been reported that terrorist suspects cooperating with interrogations have been rewarded with Happy Meals from McDonald's.

DID YOU KNOW?

Excerpts from the 1949 Geneva Convention Relative to the Treatment of Prisoners of War

Article 3

In the case of armed conflict not of an international character occurring in the territory of one of the High Contracting Parties, each party to the conflict shall be bound to apply, as a minimum, the following provisions:

1. Persons taking no active part in the hostilities, including members of armed forces who have laid down their arms and those placed hors de combat by sickness, wounds, detention, or any other cause, shall in all circumstances be treated humanely, without any adverse distinction founded on race, colour, religion or faith, sex, birth or wealth, or any other similar criteria. To this end the following acts are and shall remain prohibited at any time and in any place whatsoever with respect to the above-mentioned persons:
   (a) Violence to life and person, in particular murder of all kinds, mutilation, cruel treatment and torture;
   (b) Taking of hostages;
   (c) Outrages upon personal dignity, in particular, humiliating and degrading treatment;
   (d) The passing of sentences and the carrying out of executions without previous judgment pronounced by a regularly constituted court affording all the judicial guarantees which are recognized as indispensable by civilized peoples.
2. The wounded and sick shall be collected and cared for. An impartial humanitarian body, such as the International Committee of the Red Cross, may offer its services to the Parties to the conflict. The Parties to the conflict should further endeavour to bring into force, by means of special agreements, all or part of the other provisions of the present Convention. The application of the preceding provisions shall not affect the legal status of the Parties to the conflict.

Article 4

A. Prisoners of war, in the sense of the present Convention, are persons belonging to one of the following categories, who have fallen into the power of the enemy:
   1. Members of the armed forces of a Party to the conflict as well as members of militias or volunteer corps forming part of such armed forces.
   2. Members of other militias and members of other volunteer corps, including those of organized resistance movements, belonging to a Party to the conflict and operating in or outside their own territory, even if this territory is occupied, provided that such militias or volunteer corps, including such organized resistance movements, fulfil the following conditions:
      (a) That of being commanded by a person responsible for his subordinates;
      (b) That of having a fixed distinctive sign recognizable at a distance;
      (c) That of carrying arms openly;
      (d) That of conducting their operations in accordance with the laws and customs of war.

(Continued)

3. Members of regular armed forces who profess allegiance to a government or an authority not recognized by the Detaining Power.
4. Persons who accompany the armed forces without actually being members thereof, such as civilian members of military aircraft crews, war correspondents, supply contractors, members of labour units or of services responsible for the welfare of the armed forces, provided that they have received authorization from the armed forces which they accompany, who shall provide them for that purpose with an identity card similar to the annexed model.
5. Members of crews, including masters, pilots and apprentices, of the merchant marine and the crews of civil aircraft of the Parties to the conflict, who do not benefit by more favourable treatment under any other provisions of international law.
6. Inhabitants of a non-occupied territory, who on the approach of the enemy spontaneously take up arms to resist the invading forces, without having had time to form themselves into regular armed units, provided they carry arms openly and respect the laws and customs of war.

B. The following shall likewise be treated as prisoners of war under the present Convention:

1. Persons belonging, or having belonged, to the armed forces of the occupied country, if the occupying Power considers it necessary by reason of such allegiance to intern them, even though it has originally liberated them while hostilities were going on outside the territory it occupies, in particular where such persons have made an unsuccessful attempt to rejoin the armed forces to which they belong and which are engaged in combat, or where they fail to comply with a summons made to them with a view to internment.
2. The persons belonging to one of the categories enumerated in the present Article, who have been received by neutral or non-belligerent Powers on their territory and whom these Powers are required to intern under international law, without prejudice to any more favourable treatment which these Powers may choose to give and with the exception of Articles 8, 10, 15, 30, fifth paragraph, 58–67, 92, 126 and, where diplomatic relations exist between the Parties to the conflict and the neutral or non-belligerent Power concerned, those Articles concerning the Protecting Power. Where such diplomatic relations exist, the Parties to a conflict on whom these persons depend shall be allowed to perform towards them the functions of a Protecting Power as provided in the present Convention, without prejudice to the functions which these Parties normally exercise in conformity with diplomatic and consular usage and treaties.

C. This Article shall in no way affect the status of medical personnel and chaplains as provided for in Article 33 of the present Convention.

Article 5

The present Convention shall apply to the persons referred to in Article 4 from the time they fall into the power of the enemy and until their final release and repatriation. Should any doubt arise as to whether persons, having committed a belligerent act and having fallen into the hands of the enemy, belong to any of the categories enumerated in Article 4, such persons shall enjoy the protection of the present Convention until such time as their status has been determined by a competent tribunal.

Source: The Avalon Project, Yale Law School. http://avalon.law.yale.edu/20th_century/geneva03.asp.

U.S. Army Military Police escort a detainee to his cell in Camp X-Ray at Naval Base Guantanamo Bay, Cuba, during inprocessing to the temporary detention facility, January 11, 2002. Courtesy of Petty Officer 1st class Shane T. McCoy, U.S. Navy.

Prison cell in Camp Delta at the U.S. Naval Base at Guantanamo Bay, Cuba. Courtesy of U.S. Department of Defense.

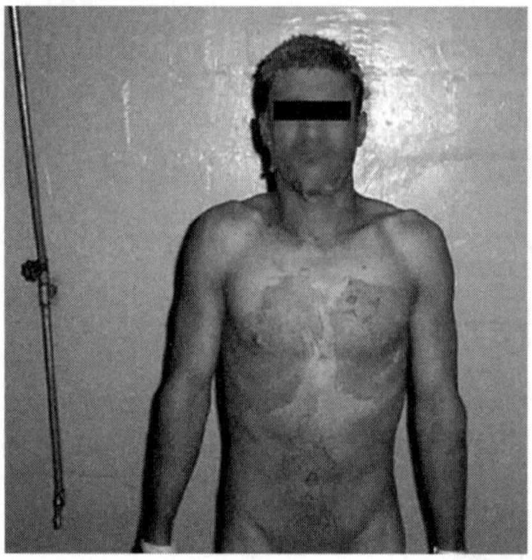

One of the previously unreleased images released in February 2006 by SBS Television in Australia. The picture is showing a man allegedly covered in feces forced to pose for the camera at Abu Ghraib Prison in Iraq. Courtesy of SBS.

key protections of the Geneva Conventions did not apply to Taliban and Al Qa'ida fighters. In particular, the President declared that Taliban and Al Qa'ida fighters were not entitled to prisoner of war status. As evident in the statement by press secretary Ari Fleischer, this assertion was based on two grounds. First, Al Qa'ida was an international terrorist group and could not be considered a State party to the Geneva Convention. Its members, therefore, were not covered by the Geneva Convention and were not entitled to POW status under the treaty. Second, the Taliban did not fulfill the requirements of Article 4A(2) of the 1949 Geneva Convention relative to the Treatment of Prisoners of War (GPW).

These claims demonstrated a remarkable ignorance of the content, nature, and reach of treaties and customary international law.[24] Furthermore, they were based on a highly selective reading of the relevant conventions. Most international lawyers agreed that the protection of Al Qa'ida persons during an armed conflict did not depend on whether Al Qa'ida was a State actor or a party to law of war treaties. Similarly, scholars found it "quite difficult to understand" why the Taliban were not entitled to prisoner of war status.[25] They generally agreed that once it was determined that there was an armed conflict between the United States and enemy military forces in Afghanistan, all persons involved in the conflict were afforded protection by the Geneva Conventions. This was also confirmed by the U.S. Supreme Court in its *Hamdan v. Rumsfeld* decision of June 2006. Challenging the practice of ignoring the Geneva Conventions, the Court ruled that Common Article 3 of the Geneva Conventions applied to all detainees in the "War on Terror" and that the Military Tribunals used to try these suspects were in violation of U.S. and international law.

During his election campaign, Barack Obama pledged to shut down the facility at Guantanamo Bay, and, upon taking office in January 2009, also made this issue one of his first priorities. As of September 2009, however, the detention facility on Guantanamo Bay remains yet to be closed. One of the problems facing the Obama administration is finding countries to take the prisoners. Of those who do not face further charges in the United States, most will be returned to their homes but about 60 detainees cannot be sent back to their own countries for fear of being tortured. Much to the surprise of Obama's supporters and international legal experts, the White House also announced in May 2009 that the administration would continue to prosecute some Guantanamo Bay detainees in a military commission system, a much-criticized centerpiece of the Bush administration's strategy for fighting terrorism.[26]

Notes

1. Rosalyn Higgins, "The General International Law of Terrorism," in Rosalyn Higgins and Maurice Flory, eds. *Terrorism and International Law* (London: Routledge, 1997), 28.
2. Bibi van Ginkel, "The United Nations: Towards a Comprehensive Convention on Combating Terrorism," in Marianne van Leeuwen, ed. *Confronting Terrorism* (The Hague: Kluwer, 2003), 207–221.

3. UN General Assembly, Report of the Ad Hoc Committee established by General Assembly Resolution 51/210 of 17 December 1996, sixth session (January28–February 1, 2002), UN Doc A/57/37.
4. Frederico Andreu-Guzman, ed., *Terrorism and Human Rights No. 2—New Challenges and Old Dangers*, International Commission of Jurists Occasional Papers No. 3 (Geneva: International Commission of Jurists 2003): 34.
5. Amnesty International, "Draft Comprehensive Convention on International Terrorism: A Threat to Human Rights Standards," Statement to the UN General Assembly 56th Session (2002), October 22, 2002.
6. Ben Saul, *Defining Terrorism in International Law* (Oxford: Oxford University Press, 2006), 185–190.
7. Antonio Cassese, *Terrorism, Politics and Law: The Achille Lauro Affair* (London: Polity, 1989).
8. Saul, *Defining Terrorism in International Law*, 135.
9. Figures taken from the official Web site of the 1267 Committee, available at http://www.un.org/sc/committees/1267/consolist.shtml.
10. Bardo Fassbender, *Targeted Sanctions and Due Process* (Berlin: Humboldt-Universität zu Berlin, 2006); http://www.un.org/law/counsel/Fassbender_study.pdf.
11. Judgment of the European Court of Justice in Joined Cases C-402/05 P and C-415/05 P, *Yassin Abdullah Kadi and Al Barakaat International Foundation v Council of the EU and Commission of the EC* (ECJ Judgment), September 3, 2008, http://curia.europa.eu/en/content/juris/index.htm.
12. Christopher Greenwood, "International Law and the 'War against Terrorism'," *International Affairs* 78, no. 2 (2002): 301–317.
13. Antonio Cassese, "Terrorism Is Also Disrupting Some Crucial Legal Categories of International Law," *European Journal of International Law* 12, no. 5 (2001): 993–1001.
14. Christine Gray, *International Law and the Use of Force*, 2nd ed. (Oxford: Oxford University Press), 187.
15. Letter dated October 7, 2001, from the Permanent Representative of the United States of America to the United Nations addressed to the President of the Security Council, UN Doc S/2001/946.
16. Cited in Thomas M. Franck, "Terrorism and the Right of Self-Defense," *American Journal of International Law* 95, no. 4 (2001): 839–842.
17. Greenwood, "International Law and the 'War against Terrorism'": 312.
18. Mark A. Drumbl, "Self-Defense and the Use of Force: Breaking the Rules, Making the Rules, or Both?" *International Studies Perspectives* 4, no. 4 (2003): 409–431.
19. Franck, "Terrorism and the Right of Self-Defense": 340–341.
20. Agreement on Provisional Arrangements in Afghanistan Pending the Re-establishment of Permanent Government Institutions, Bonn, December 5, 2001. http://www.un.org/News/dh/latest/afghan/afghan-agree.htm.
21. White House Press Release, Joint Declaration of the United States–Afghanistan Strategic Partnership, May 23, 2005. http://www.state.gov/p/sca/rls/pr/2005/46628.htm.

22. Stephen Grey, *Ghost Plane: The True Story of the CIA Torture Program* (New York: St. Martin's Press, 2006); Karen J. Greenberg and Joshua L. Dratel, eds., *The Torture Papers: The Road to Abu Ghraib* (New York: Cambridge University Press, 2005).
23. Seymour M. Hersh, "Torture at Abu Ghraib," *The New Yorker* online, May 10, 2004, http://www.newyorker.com/archive/2004/05/10/040510fa_fact.
24. Jordan J. Paust, *Beyond the Law: The Bush Administration's Unlawful Responses in the "War" on Terror* (Cambridge, UK: Cambridge University Press, 2007): 5–12.
25. George H. Aldrich, "Taliban, Al Qaeda, and the Determination of Illegal Combatants," *American Journal of International Law* 96, no. 4 (2002): 893.
26. William Glaberson, "Obama to Keep Tribunals; Stance Angers Some Backers," *New York Times*, May 15, 2009.

FURTHER READING

Aldrich, George H. "Taliban, Al Qaeda, and the Determination of Illegal Combatants." *American Journal of International Law* 96, no. 4 (2002): 891–898.

Berkowitz, Peter, ed. *Terrorism, the Laws of War and the Constitution: Debating the Enemy Combatant Cases*. Stanford, CA: Hoover Institution Press, 2005.

Hamdan v. Rumsfeld, 548 U.S. 557 (2006). http://www.supremecourtus.gov/opinions/05pdf/05-184.pdf.

Harris, George C. "Terrorism, War and Justice: the Concept of the Unlawful Enemy Combatant." *Loyola of Los Angeles International & Comparative Law Review* 26, no. 1 (2003): 31–46.

Hersh, Seymour M. *Chain of Command: The Road from 9/11 to Abu Ghraib*. New York: Harper Collins, 2004.

Paust, Jordan J. "War and Enemy Status after 9/11." *Yale Journal of International Law* 28, no. 2 (2003): 325–335.

Paust, Jordan J. "There is No Need to Revise the Laws of War in Light of September 11th." *The American Society of International Law Task Force Papers on Terrorism*. November 2002. http://www.asil.org/taskforce/paust.pdf.

Paust, Jordan J. *Beyond the Law: The Bush Administration's Unlawful Responses in the "War" on Terror*. Cambridge, UK: Cambridge University Press, 2007.

9

WAS THE U.S. INVASION OF IRAQ LEGAL?

The statue of Saddam Hussein topples in Baghdad's Firdos Square, April 9, 2003. Courtesy of U.S. Department of Defense.

OVERVIEW

The 2003 invasion of Iraq by the United States and a small coalition comprising Britain, Australia, Poland, and Denmark was highly controversial, provoking deep concern among States and widespread popular opposition, including within the countries that participated in the invasion. In debates in the United Nations and in their public statements, most States took the view that the invasion represented outright defiance of the United Nations Security Council and risked undermining the rule of law in international relations. Although, in its campaign to secure public support for the invasion, the United States was openly unconcerned with international opinion, the Administration did devote considerable effort to providing justifications for its actions under international law and to securing United Nations endorsement. Moreover, the crisis developed within an international legal context extending over nearly 13 years, a fact that complicated the debate about the invasion's legality. This chapter examines the legal basis on which the invasion was conducted and the legal justifications provided by the main protagonists as well as some of the factors behind this crisis.

The Basis for Action

- ***Document:*** United Nations Security Council Resolution 1441. This is the key legal document in the lead-up to the invasion of Iraq.
- ***Date:*** The Resolution was adopted unanimously by the Security Council on November 8, 2002.
- ***Where:*** United Nations Headquarters, New York
- ***Significance:*** Resolution 1441 links past Security Council resolutions on Iraq's behavior following the takeover of Kuwait in 1990 to the alleged threat posed by Iraq in 2002. It provides the legal basis for subsequent action by the UN Security Council for Iraq's failure to comply with its demands under Chapter VII of the UN Charter. It was also central to the United States' arguments that its planned invasion was legal.

DOCUMENT

The Security Council,

Recalling all its previous relevant resolutions, in particular its resolutions 661 (1990) of 6 August 1990, 678 (1990) of 29 November 1990, 686 (1991) of 2 March 1991, 687 (1991) of 3 April 1991, 688 (1991) of 5 April 1991, 707 (1991) of 15 August 1991, 715 (1991) of 11 October 1991, 986 (1995) of 14 April 1995, and 1284 (1999) of 17 December 1999, and all the relevant statements of its President,

Recalling also its resolution 1382 (2001) of 29 November 2001 and its intention to implement it fully,

Recognizing the threat Iraq's non-compliance with Council resolutions and proliferation of weapons of mass destruction and long-range missiles poses to international peace and security,

Recalling that its resolution 678 (1990) authorized Member States to use all necessary means to uphold and implement its resolution 660 (1990) of 2 August 1990 and all relevant resolutions subsequent to resolution 660 (1990) and to restore international peace and security in the area,

Further recalling that its resolution 687 (1991) imposed obligations on Iraq as a necessary step for achievement of its stated objective of restoring international peace and security in the area,

Deploring the fact that Iraq has not provided an accurate, full, final, and complete disclosure, as required by resolution 687 (1991), of all aspects of its programmes to develop weapons of mass destruction and ballistic missiles with a range greater than one hundred and fifty kilometres, and of all holdings of such weapons, their components and production facilities and locations, as well as all other nuclear programmes, including any which it claims are for purposes not related to nuclear-weapons-usable material,

Deploring further that Iraq repeatedly obstructed immediate, unconditional, and unrestricted access to sites designated by the United Nations Special Commission (UNSCOM) and the International Atomic Energy Agency (IAEA), failed to cooperate fully and unconditionally with UNSCOM and IAEA weapons inspectors, as required by resolution 687 (1991), and ultimately ceased all cooperation with UNSCOM and the IAEA in 1998,

Deploring the absence, since December 1998, in Iraq of international monitoring, inspection, and verification, as required by relevant resolutions, of weapons of mass destruction and ballistic missiles, in spite of the Council's repeated demands that Iraq provide immediate, unconditional, and unrestricted access to the United Nations Monitoring, Verification and Inspection Commission (UNMOVIC), established in resolution 1284 (1999) as the successor organization to UNSCOM, and the IAEA, and regretting the consequent prolonging of the crisis in the region and the suffering of the Iraqi people,

Deploring also that the Government of Iraq has failed to comply with its commitments pursuant to resolution 687 (1991) with regard to terrorism, pursuant to resolution 688 (1991) to end repression of its civilian population and to provide access by international humanitarian organizations to all those in need of assistance in Iraq, and pursuant to resolutions 686 (1991), 687 (1991), and 1284 (1999) to return or cooperate in accounting for Kuwaiti and third country nationals wrongfully detained by Iraq, or to return Kuwaiti property wrongfully seized by Iraq,

Recalling that in its resolution 687 (1991) the Council declared that a ceasefire would be based on acceptance by Iraq of the provisions of that resolution, including the obligations on Iraq contained therein,

Determined to ensure full and immediate compliance by Iraq without conditions or restrictions with its obligations under resolution 687 (1991) and other relevant resolutions and recalling that the resolutions of the Council constitute the governing standard of Iraqi compliance,

Recalling that the effective operation of UNMOVIC, as the successor organization to the Special Commission, and the IAEA is essential for the implementation of resolution 687 (1991) and other relevant resolutions,

Noting that the letter dated 16 September 2002 from the Minister for Foreign Affairs of Iraq addressed to the Secretary-General is a necessary first step toward rectifying Iraq's continued failure to comply with relevant Council resolutions,

Noting further the letter dated 8 October 2002 from the Executive Chairman of UNMOVIC and the Director-General of the IAEA to General Al-Saadi of the Government of Iraq laying out the practical arrangements, as a follow-up to their meeting in Vienna, that are prerequisites for the resumption of inspections in Iraq by UNMOVIC and the IAEA, and expressing the gravest concern at the continued failure by the Government of Iraq to provide confirmation of the arrangements as laid out in that letter,

Reaffirming the commitment of all Member States to the sovereignty and territorial integrity of Iraq, Kuwait, and the neighbouring States,

Commending the Secretary-General and members of the League of Arab States and its Secretary-General for their efforts in this regard,

Determined to secure full compliance with its decisions,

Acting under Chapter VII of the Charter of the United Nations,

1. *Decides* that Iraq has been and remains in material breach of its obligations under relevant resolutions, including resolution 687 (1991), in particular through Iraq's failure to cooperate with United Nations inspectors and the IAEA, and to complete the actions required under paragraphs 8 to 13 of resolution 687 (1991);
2. *Decides*, while acknowledging paragraph 1 above, to afford Iraq, by this resolution, a final opportunity to comply with its disarmament obligations under relevant resolutions of the Council; and accordingly decides to set up an enhanced inspection regime with the aim of bringing to full and verified completion the disarmament process established by resolution 687 (1991) and subsequent resolutions of the Council;
3. *Decides* that, in order to begin to comply with its disarmament obligations, in addition to submitting the required biannual declarations, the Government of Iraq shall provide to UNMOVIC, the IAEA, and the Council, not later than 30 days from the date of this resolution, a currently accurate, full, and complete declaration of all aspects of its programmes to develop chemical, biological, and nuclear weapons, ballistic missiles, and other delivery systems such as unmanned aerial vehicles and dispersal systems designed for use on aircraft, including any holdings and precise locations of such weapons, components, subcomponents, stocks of agents, and related material and equipment, the locations and work of its research, development and production facilities, as well as all other chemical, biological, and nuclear programmes, including any which it claims are for purposes not related to weapon production or material;

4. *Decides* that false statements or omissions in the declarations submitted by Iraq pursuant to this resolution and failure by Iraq at any time to comply with, and cooperate fully in the implementation of, this resolution shall constitute a further material breach of Iraq's obligations and will be reported to the Council for assessment in accordance with paragraphs 11 and 12 below;
5. *Decides* that Iraq shall provide UNMOVIC and the IAEA immediate, unimpeded, unconditional, and unrestricted access to any and all, including underground, areas, facilities, buildings, equipment, records, and means of transport which they wish to inspect, as well as immediate, unimpeded, unrestricted, and private access to all officials and other persons whom UNMOVIC or the IAEA wish to interview in the mode or location of UNMOVIC's or the IAEA's choice pursuant to any aspect of their mandates; further decides that UNMOVIC and the IAEA may at their discretion conduct interviews inside or outside of Iraq, may facilitate the travel of those interviewed and family members outside of Iraq, and that, at the sole discretion of UNMOVIC and the IAEA, such interviews may occur without the presence of observers from the Iraqi Government; and instructs UNMOVIC and requests the IAEA to resume inspections no later than 45 days following adoption of this resolution and to update the Council 60 days thereafter;
6. *Endorses* the 8 October 2002 letter from the Executive Chairman of UNMOVIC and the Director-General of the IAEA to General Al-Saadi of the Government of Iraq, and decides that the contents of the letter shall be binding upon Iraq;
7. *Decides* further that, in view of the prolonged interruption by Iraq of the presence of UNMOVIC and the IAEA and in order for them to accomplish the tasks set forth in this resolution and all previous relevant resolutions and notwithstanding prior understandings, the Council hereby establishes the following revised or additional authorities, which shall be binding upon Iraq, to facilitate their work in Iraq:

   —UNMOVIC and the IAEA shall determine the composition of their inspection teams and ensure that these teams are composed of the most qualified and experienced experts available;

   —All UNMOVIC and IAEA personnel shall enjoy the privileges and immunities, corresponding to those of experts on mission, provided in the Convention on Privileges and Immunities of the United Nations and the Agreement on the Privileges and Immunities of the IAEA;

   —UNMOVIC and the IAEA shall have unrestricted rights of entry into and out of Iraq, the right to free, unrestricted, and immediate movement to and from inspection sites, and the right to inspect any sites and buildings, including immediate, unimpeded, unconditional, and unrestricted access to Presidential Sites equal to that at other sites, notwithstanding the provisions of resolution 1154 (1998) of 2 March 1998;

   —UNMOVIC and the IAEA shall have the right to be provided by Iraq the names of all personnel currently and formerly associated with Iraq's chemical,

biological, nuclear, and ballistic missile programmes and the associated research, development, and production facilities;
—Security of UNMOVIC and IAEA facilities shall be ensured by sufficient United Nations security guards;
—UNMOVIC and the IAEA shall have the right to declare, for the purposes of freezing a site to be inspected, exclusion zones, including surrounding areas and transit corridors, in which Iraq will suspend ground and aerial movement so that nothing is changed in or taken out of a site being inspected;
—UNMOVIC and the IAEA shall have the free and unrestricted use and landing of fixed- and rotary-winged aircraft, including manned and unmanned reconnaissance vehicles;
—UNMOVIC and the IAEA shall have the right at their sole discretion verifiably to remove, destroy, or render harmless all prohibited weapons, subsystems, components, records, materials, and other related items, and the right to impound or close any facilities or equipment for the production thereof; and
—UNMOVIC and the IAEA shall have the right to free import and use of equipment or materials for inspections and to seize and export any equipment, materials, or documents taken during inspections, without search of UNMOVIC or IAEA personnel or official or personal baggage;

8. *Decides* further that Iraq shall not take or threaten hostile acts directed against any representative or personnel of the United Nations or the IAEA or of any Member State taking action to uphold any Council resolution;
9. *Requests* the Secretary-General immediately to notify Iraq of this resolution, which is binding on Iraq; demands that Iraq confirm within seven days of that notification its intention to comply fully with this resolution; and demands further that Iraq cooperate immediately, unconditionally, and actively with UNMOVIC and the IAEA;
10. *Requests* all Member States to give full support to UNMOVIC and the IAEA in the discharge of their mandates, including by providing any information related to prohibited programmes or other aspects of their mandates, including on Iraqi attempts since 1998 to acquire prohibited items, and by recommending sites to be inspected, persons to be interviewed, conditions of such interviews, and data to be collected, the results of which shall be reported to the Council by UNMOVIC and the IAEA;
11. *Directs* the Executive Chairman of UNMOVIC and the Director-General of the IAEA to report immediately to the Council any interference by Iraq with inspection activities, as well as any failure by Iraq to comply with its disarmament obligations, including its obligations regarding inspections under this resolution;
12. *Decides* to convene immediately upon receipt of a report in accordance with paragraphs 4 or 11 above, in order to consider the situation and the need for full compliance with all of the relevant Council resolutions in order to secure international peace and security;
13. *Recalls*, in that context, that the Council has repeatedly warned Iraq that it will face serious consequences as a result of its continued violations of its obligations;

14. *Decides* to remain seized of the matter.

SOURCE: United Nations Security Council Resolution 1441 (2002), The situation between Iraq and Kuwait. http://www.un.org/Docs/scres/2002/sc2002.htm.

ANALYSIS

The United States, supported by a number of allies, including the United Kingdom, Australia, Denmark, and Poland, invaded Iraq on March 20, 2003. By April 30 the main fighting was over. Baghdad had been taken and Saddam Hussein and his government were in hiding. While the military operation was, predictably, resolved in a short time, the political and legal issues surrounding the invasion continue to generate controversy. It is argued by many that the invasion has led to a marked decline in the United States' global strategic position and to intensified questioning about the United States' commitment to the rule of law. The legality of the invasion has been widely debated, with the majority of opinion assessing that it was a major breach of international law.[1] Support for this conclusion can even be drawn from the actions of the American administration itself, as will be discussed below.

The 2003 invasion should be seen in the context of the expulsion of Iraqi forces from Kuwait in 1991 by American-led United Nations forces, the extensive sanctions imposed by the Security Council in August 1990 and April 1991, and the low-level conflict between Iraqi and American and British forces in the north and the south of the country throughout the 1990s. These developments, the failure of external pressure to provoke regime change in Iraq, and the apparent Iraqi refusal to comply with Security Council resolutions provided the basis on which the U.S. administration built its case for war.

The months leading to the invasion were marked by worldwide debate, with the U.S. and British governments mounting extensive political campaigns to prepare domestic and international opinion for the invasion. This chapter focuses on part of that campaign, the legal debate, which was conducted mainly in the UN Security Council and, to a lesser extent, in the UN General Assembly.

As discussed earlier in this book, the use of force by one country against another has broadly been made illegal by several international treaties, including the Kellogg-Briand Pact and, especially, the UN Charter, which prohibits all resort to force (Article 2(4)). The principle contained in Article 2(4) is generally regarded as *jus cogens* or a peremptory norm of international law, and only two exceptions are allowed: self-defense (Article 51) and action pursuant to Security Council authorization. The United States and Britain sought to present their legal cases within the parameters set by these restrictions.

Security Council Resolution 1441 is the key document that set the scene for the final confrontation between the United States and Iraq. In the wake of the attacks on September 11, 2001, and the invasion of Afghanistan, the U.S. administration began to speak about the need to break the deadlock between the United Nations and Iraq. The Administration demanded that the Security Council be more assertive in enforcing its resolutions and to compel the Iraqi Government to comply with its obligations. Behind this demand was the United States' policy of regime change in Iraq as spelled out in the United States Iraq Liberation Act (1998),[2] although this issue was never raised in the context of Security Council debates.

Secretary of State Colin Powell summed up the United States' legal position during his presentation to the Security Council in February 2003. Powell presented dramatic and, as it turned out, flawed proof of American accusations of Iraqi noncompliance with Security Council resolutions.[3] Central to the Administration's legal argument were the allegations that Iraq had failed to do away with its weapons of mass destruction (chemical, biological, and nuclear weapons) as required under Resolution 687 (1991); that Iraq had long established links with terrorist groups, including Al Qa'ida, and, as a result, that Iraq represented a serious security threat to its neighbors and to the United States. A major element of the American case was the idea of pre-emptive self-defense, in line with the doctrine developed in the 2002 U.S. National Security Strategy. In trying to justify this policy and its apparent inconsistency with the terms of the UN Charter, the United States suggested that there had been a fundamental change in circumstances in the international system in the years since the Charter had been adopted. In particular, there were no nuclear or radiological weapons at that time. Accordingly, the established rules of self-defense drawn from the *Caroline* Case ("It will be for that Government to show a necessity of self-defense, instant, overwhelming, leaving no choice of means, and no moment for deliberation")[4] cannot stand. Instead, the possibility of terrorist groups or rogue States obtaining weapons of mass destruction means that countries must be free to act quickly and flexibly. American academics had provided a basis for this argument. For example, Michael Glennon maintains that the law, as outlined in the Charter and in customary law, no longer constrains State behavior and, therefore, cannot be described as effective. He argues that "justice backed by power" is a higher goal than an international system based on the rule of law.[5]

Although controversial, there is considerable scholarly support for anticipatory self-defense as being consistent with the spirit of the Charter and of international law more generally.[6] It is not regarded as reasonable that a State should be obliged to allow itself to be harmed before resorting to self-defense. The Americans' sweeping interpretation of this concept, however, defined by them as pre-emptive self-defense, went well beyond any established limits on anticipatory self-defense to include potential threats at some unspecified and unknown point in the future. This approach was met by almost total opposition within the Security Council and beyond. In particular, States have rejected the unilateral nature of the decision-making process involved.

Having argued that Iraq represented a threat to international peace and security and was in violation of numerous Security Council resolutions (especially Resolution 687 of April 3, 1991, which established a ceasefire with Iraq, and Resolution 1441), the U.S. Administration maintained that previous Security Council resolutions, specifically Resolution 678 of November 29, 1990, which authorized military action against Iraq, had been revived and, therefore, that an American attack on Iraq already had United Nations Security Council endorsement and would be legal. The Administration then argued that the United States had the right to take unilateral

DID YOU KNOW?

In History

Proclamation of Baghdad

By Sir Stanley Maude, March 19, 1917:

"To the People of Baghdad Vilayet:

Our operations have as their object the defeat of the enemy, and the driving of him from these territories. [O]ur armies do not come as conquerors or enemies, but as liberators. Since the days of Halaka your city and lands have been subject to the tyranny of strangers, and your forefathers and yourselves have groaned in bondage.

But you people of Baghdad are not to understand that it is the wish of the Government to impose upon you alien institutions. It is the hope of the Government that the aspirations of your philosophers and writers shall be realised and that once again the people of Baghdad shall flourish under institutions, which are in consonance with their sacred laws and their racial ideals.

I invite you to participate in the management of your civil affairs in collaboration with the political representatives of Great Britain, so that you may be united with your kinsmen in realising the aspirations of your race."

Source: http://www.harpers.org/archive/2003/05/0079593

action to enforce Security Council decisions. This is an expression of the theory of "implied authorization," which had also arisen in the context of Kosovo. These arguments formed the core of the Americans' dispute with the other members of the Security Council.

Perhaps the high point of U.S. attempts to get the international community, through the UN Security Council, to endorse its planned action against Iraq was the adoption of Security Council Resolution 1441. The Resolution was a compromise between American demands for quick action and the concerns of other members of the Security Council that Iraq should be given more time to comply with the Council's demands.

Resolution 1441 gave Iraq a final opportunity to comply with its obligations and deplored Iraq's failure to allow access to UN weapons inspectors. It demanded that the UN Monitoring, Inspection and Verification Commission (UNMOVIC) and the International Atomic Energy Agency (IAEA) inspectors be allowed full and free access to Iraqi facilities, including to so-called Presidential sites, which had been out of bounds for previous inspections. Under the Resolution, the Council agreed to review the situation after reports from Hans Blix, the UNMOVIC Chief Weapons Inspector, and Mohammed ElBaradei, the Director-General of the IAEA, who had been directed to examine and report on Iraqi compliance. The Resolution also required Iraq to submit a detailed report on all aspects of its chemical, biological, and nuclear facilities, including those claimed not to be related to the development of weapons. It warned of serious consequences if Iraq failed to comply.

The Resolution asserted that Iraq was in "material breach" of previous resolutions (Para. 1), especially Security Council Resolution 678, because of its apparent failure to comply with UNSC demands that it disarm, renounce terrorism, and cooperate with the Council's inspection regime. Security Council Resolution 678 was the resolution that announced, in calling on Iraq to withdraw from Kuwait, its preparedness "to use all necessary means to uphold and implement Resolution 660 (1990) and all subsequent relevant resolutions and to restore international peace and security in the area" (paragraph 2). "All necessary means," a reference to article 42 of the UN Charter, can be read as code for the use of military force.

The Council's reference to "material breach" is a serious step toward a decision to use force. The concept is drawn from the Vienna Convention on the Law of Treaties (Article 60), and, according to the Security Council's interpretation, a material breach of Council resolutions can be regarded as of equal seriousness as the violation of international treaties and, therefore, as a threat to international peace and security. Finding Iraq to be in material breach could provide grounds for the rescinding of the ceasefire put in place at the end of hostilities in 1991.

Initially, American and British representatives accepted the view, widely held among Security Council members and supported publicly by UN Secretary-General Kofi Annan and Chief Weapons Inspector Hans Blix, that the Resolution required the United States to seek Security Council endorsement before initiating military action against Iraq.[7] As the debate developed, however, the American and British representatives began to argue that they did not need to seek specific approval from the Council. They maintained they were already empowered to resort to force in dealing with Iraq by Security Council Resolution 678, which approved "all necessary means . . . to restore international peace and security in the area." The ceasefire suspended but did not cancel that authorization—even though it was ten years old.

The United States pursued this argument as the war approached. It argued that Iraq's failure to comply with the terms of Resolution 1441 was an objective fact that could be determined by an individual mem-

DID YOU KNOW?

President Bush Addresses the Nation

The Cross Hall, March 17, 2003.

"Many Iraqis can hear me tonight in a translated radio broadcast, and I have a message for them. If we must begin a military campaign, it will be directed against the lawless men who rule your country and not against you. As our coalition takes away their power, we will deliver the food and medicine you need. We will tear down the apparatus of terror and we will help you to build a new Iraq that is prosperous and free. The tyrant will soon be gone. The day of your liberation is near."

Source: http://www.whitehouse.gov/news/releases/2003/03/20030317-7.html.

The Oval Office, March 19, 2003.

"We come to Iraq with respect for its citizens, for their great civilization and for the religious faiths they practice. We have no ambition in Iraq, except to remove a threat and restore control of that country to its own people."

Source: http://www.whitehouse.gov/news/releases/2003/03/20030319-17.html.

A general view of the Security Council chamber as Members of the Council vote unanimously to adopt Resolution 1546 (2004) on Iraq. United Nations, New York. June 8, 2004. Courtesy of Mark Garten, UN Photo.

DID YOU KNOW?

Key United Nations Resolutions on Iraq

Resolution No.	Date	What It Did
660	August 2, 1990	Determined that Iraq's invasion of Kuwait constituted a breach of international peace and security and demanded that Iraq withdraw immediately.
661	August 6, 1990	Declared that the Security Council was acting under Chapter VII of the Charter, which meant that the use of force was available to the Council. The Resolution also decided to impose trade and other sanctions on Iraq for its failure to withdraw.
678	November 29, 1990	Gave Iraq until January 15, 1991, to withdraw from Kuwait. Failure to do so would lead to the Council resorting to "all possible means" (code for resort to force) to compel an Iraqi withdrawal.
687	April 3, 1991	Established a formal ceasefire between United Nations and Iraqi forces. Required Iraq to do away with all weapons of mass destruction in its possession and to abandon all programs designed to develop such weapons. Established the United Nations Commission to enforce this process.
986	April 14, 1995	Set up the Oil-for-Food Program.
1284	December 17, 1999	Created the UN Monitoring, Verification and Inspection Commission to replace the Special Commission.
1441	November 8, 2002	The Security Council's final warning to Iraq.

ber of the Security Council. Most other Council members maintained that it was up to the Security Council as a whole to determine the nature of the measures to be taken if Iraq were to have been found in breach of 1441 and other resolutions—not one or two members. This was based on paragraph 4 of the resolution, which is interpreted by most analysts as meaning that a decision on whether a further material breach had occurred was not for a single member of the Council to make but rather one for the Council as a whole to decide.

A problem for the United States' argument lay in the language of Resolution 1441. There are significant differences between the language used in this Resolution and that used in those on which the Americans and British were basing their argument.

President George W. Bush addresses sailors and the nation from the flight deck of the USS *Abraham Lincoln* off the coast of San Diego, California, May 1, 2003. A "Mission Accomplished" banner—which refers to operation Iraqi Freedom—hangs from the control tower in the background. Courtesy of U.S. Government.

U.S. soldiers conducting an exercise near Bahbahani in Iraq. Courtesy U.S. Department of Defense.

DID YOU KNOW?

U.S. Hawk Admits Invasion Was Illegal

Oliver Burkeman and Julian Borger, *The Guardian,* November 20, 2003:

International lawyers and anti-war campaigners reacted with astonishment yesterday after the influential Pentagon hawk, Richard Perle, conceded the invasion of Iraq had been illegal. In a startling break with official White House and Downing Street lines, Perle told an audience in London: "I think in this case international law stood in the way of doing the right thing." Perle said that "international law . . . would have required us to leave Saddam Hussein alone," and this would have been morally unacceptable. French intransigence, he added, meant there had been "no practical mechanism consistent with the rules of the UN for dealing with Saddam Hussein."

President Bush consistently argued the war was legal either because of existing UN Security Council resolutions on Iraq—also the British government's publicly stated view—or as an act of self-defense permitted by international law. On the night bombing began, in March, Bush reiterated America's "sovereign authority to use force" to defeat the threat from Baghdad. UN Secretary General, [Kofi] Annan, questioned that justification, arguing the Security Council would have to rule on whether the US and its allies were under imminent threat.

Source: http://www.guardian.co.uk/uk/2003/nov/20/usa.iraq1

For example, it differed in key areas from Resolution 678, implying that the situation had changed since 1991 and, therefore, that automatic authorization of the use of force could not be assumed. The Resolution talked about "serious consequences" in paragraph 13. This was seen by most Council members as a warning or a reminder, not an authorization. It referred to the need to "secure" international peace and security, implying that the situation was not dire but needed consolidation.

In the face of widespread opposition, the U.S. administration decided to approach the Security Council for a new resolution that, like Resolution 678, would specifically authorize "all necessary means," namely the use of force against Iraq. In so doing, the Administration could be said to have effectively accepted that previous resolutions did not provide the implied authorization they had been claiming. In developing this resolution, the United States and Britain encountered intense resistance from most other members of the Council, including the other Permanent Members. These countries were not necessarily insisting that the military option be abandoned but that the United Nations and the weapons inspectors should be given more time—a position that was reinforced by the encouraging report submitted to the Council by Blix on March 7. In the event, it became apparent that the sponsors of the resolution could not even secure the support of a simple majority of Council members, and they abandoned the effort.

It was clear from the Council debates over some months and from documents submitted that the international community did not accept the basis of the United States' argument. Council members were adamant, moreover, that, despite the "material breach" finding against Iraq in Resolution 1441, they required formal and specific Security Council confirmation that Iraq had failed to comply with the requirements of that Resolution. There was also specific rejection of the Americans' pre-emptive self-defense argument. Even allies such as the United Kingdom and Australia avoided reference to this argument in their legal justifications.

FURTHER READING

Freedman, Lawrence, and Efraim Karsh. *The Gulf Conflict: 1990–1991*. Princeton, NJ: Princeton University Press, 1993.

Gazzini, Tarcisio. *The Changing Rules on the Use of Force in International Law*. Manchester: Juris, 2005.

Glennon, Michael J. "The New Interventionism." *Foreign Affairs* 78, no. 3 (1999): 2–7.

Gray, Christine. *International Law and the Use of Force*. Oxford: Oxford University Press, 2004.

Halabjah Post-Graduate Medical Centre: http://www.nawandihalabja.com/en/index.php?option=com_content&task=view&id=43&Itemid=30.

Rothwell, Donald R. "Anticipatory Self-Defence in the Age of International Terrorism." *University of Queensland Law Journal* 24, no. 2 (2005): 337–354.

Sands, Philippe. *Lawless World*. Camberwell: Allen Lane, 2005. See in particular pages 184–192.

The British Interpretation: The Goldsmith Advice

- ***Document:*** Summary of confidential advice submitted to the British Prime Minister by the UK Attorney General, Lord Goldsmith, on March 7, 2003
- ***Date:*** The advice was publicly released in April 2003.
- ***Where:*** London
- ***Significance:*** The Blair Government had attempted to use the Attorney General's advice to support its position on the legality of an invasion of Iraq through selective release of aspects of the advice. After a series of leaks, however, Blair released the full document. In addition to being an important exposition of the UK Government's case for attacking Iraq, the advice is of interest because of its status as a secret government document that would normally never have seen the light of day.

DOCUMENT

26. To sum up, the language of Resolution 1441 leaves the position unclear and the statements made on adoption of the Resolution suggest that there were differences of view within the Council as to the legal effect of the Resolution. Arguments can be made on both sides. A key question is whether there is in truth a need for an assessment of whether Iraq's conduct constitutes a failure to take the final opportunity or has constituted a failure fully to cooperate within the meaning of OP4 such that the basis of the cease-fire is destroyed. If an assessment is needed of that situation, it would be for the Council to make it. A narrow textual reading of the Resolution suggests that sort of assessment is not needed, because the Council has predetermined the issue. Public statements, on the other hand, say otherwise.

27. In these circumstances, I remain of the opinion that the safest legal course would be to secure the adoption of a further resolution to authorise the use of force. [. . .] The key point is that it should establish that the Council has concluded that Iraq has failed to take the final opportunity offered by Resolution 1441, as in the draft, which has already been tabled.

28. Nevertheless, having regard to the information on the negotiating history, which I have been given and to the arguments of the US Administration, which I heard in Washington, I accept that a reasonable case can be made that Resolution 1441 is capable in principle of reviving the authorisation in 678 without a further resolution.

29. However, the argument that Resolution 1441 alone has revived the authorisation to use force in Resolution 678 will only be sustainable if there are strong factual grounds for concluding that Iraq has failed to take the final opportunity. In other words, we would need to be able to demonstrate hard evidence of non-compliance and non-cooperation. Given the structure of the Resolution as a whole, the views of UNMOVIC and the IAEA will be highly significant in this respect. In the light of the latest reporting by UNMOVIC, you will need to consider very carefully whether the evidence of non-cooperation and non-compliance by Iraq is sufficiently compelling to justify the conclusion that Iraq has failed to take its final opportunity.

30. In reaching my conclusion, I have taken account of the fact that on a number of previous occasions, including in relation to Operation Desert Fox in December, 1998, and Kosovo in 1999, UK forces have participated in military action on the basis of advice from my predecessors that the legality of the action under international law was no more than reasonably arguable. But a "reasonable case" does not mean that if the matter ever came before a court I would be confident that the court would agree with the view. I judge that, having regard to the arguments on both sides, and considering the Resolution as a whole in the light of the statements made on adoption and subsequently, a court might well conclude that OPs 4 and 12 do require a further Council decision in order to revive the authorisation in Resolution 678. But equally I consider that the counter view can be reasonably maintained. However, it must be recognised that on previous occasions when military action was taken on the basis of a reasonably arguable case, the degree of public and Parliamentary scrutiny of the legal issue was nothing as great as it is today.

31. The analysis set out above applies whether a second resolution fails to be adopted because of a lack of votes or because it is vetoed. As I have said before, I do not believe that there is any basis in law for arguing that there is an implied condition of reasonableness which can be read into the power of veto conferred on the permanent members of the Security Council by the UN Charter. So there are no grounds for arguing that an "unreasonable veto" would entitle us to proceed on the basis of a presumed Security Council authorisation. In any event, if the majority of world opinion remains opposed to military action, it is likely to be difficult on the facts to categorise a French veto as "unreasonable." The legal analysis may, however, be affected by the course of events over the next week or so, e.g., the discussions on the draft second resolution. If we fail to achieve the adoption of a second resolution we would need to consider urgently at that stage the strength of our legal case in the light of circumstances at the time.

36. Finally, I must stress that the lawfulness of any military action depends not only on the existence of a legal basis, but also on the question of proportionality. Any force used pursuant to the authorisation in Resolution 678 (whether or not there is a second resolution):

- must have as its objective the enforcement of the terms of the cease-fire contained in Resolution 687 (1990 sic) and subsequent relevant resolutions;
- be limited to what is necessary to achieve that objective; and
- must be a proportionate response to that objective, i.e. securing compliance with Iraq's disarmament obligations.

That is not to say that action may not be taken to remove Saddam Hussein from power if it can be demonstrated that such action is a necessary and proportionate measure to secure the disarmament of Iraq. But regime change cannot be the objective of military action. This should be borne in mind in considering the list of military targets and in making public statements about any campaign.

SOURCE: Confidential advice to British Prime Minister by the Attorney General, March 7, 2003, http://www.number-10.gov.uk/files/pdf/Iraq%20Resolution%201441.pdf. *Reproduced under the terms of the Click-Use License.*

ANALYSIS

Lord Goldsmith's advice was a confidential commentary on legal issues surrounding the American and British plans to invade Iraq. It is important because it was submitted in the context of increasing difficulties being experienced by the promoters of the war in the Security Council and the possibility of their returning to the Council with a recommendation specifically seeking authorization to invade Iraq. It examined in some detail the various legal arguments about the planned invasion and, despite a degree of ambiguity, raised major doubts about the legality of the resort to force. The advice was also significant as a rare example of a confidential Cabinet document dealing with a major issue of national security becoming public property. In the weeks before the invasion, the British Government had quoted selectively from the Opinion to support its claim that the invasion was legal. Subsequently, significant portions were leaked to the public, and eventually the Government felt compelled to release the full document.

The Goldsmith opinion is, not surprisingly, heavily qualified in its conclusions, and it is clearly influenced by aspects of the debate in the Security Council. Goldsmith specifically rejected the pre-emptive self-defense argument on the grounds that it was "not a doctrine which, in [his] opinion, exists or is recognized in international law" (paragraph 3). Goldsmith also rejected humanitarian intervention, a doctrine that had some support in international law, on the grounds that he knew of "no reason why it would be an appropriate basis for action in present circumstances" (paragraph 4). He did, however, suggest that the American-British claim that authorization for the invasion could be drawn from the resolutions adopted in 1990 and 1991 had some merit. He claimed that a narrow textual reading of the Security Council Resolution could be interpreted as the Council having already authorized the use of force (paragraph 26). He noted, however, that public statements by Council members suggested otherwise and commented that, while he regarded this as a "reasonable case," he was not necessarily confident that a court would agree with this view (paragraph 30). Ireland's explanation of its vote during the vote on Resolution 1441 highlights Goldsmith's point:

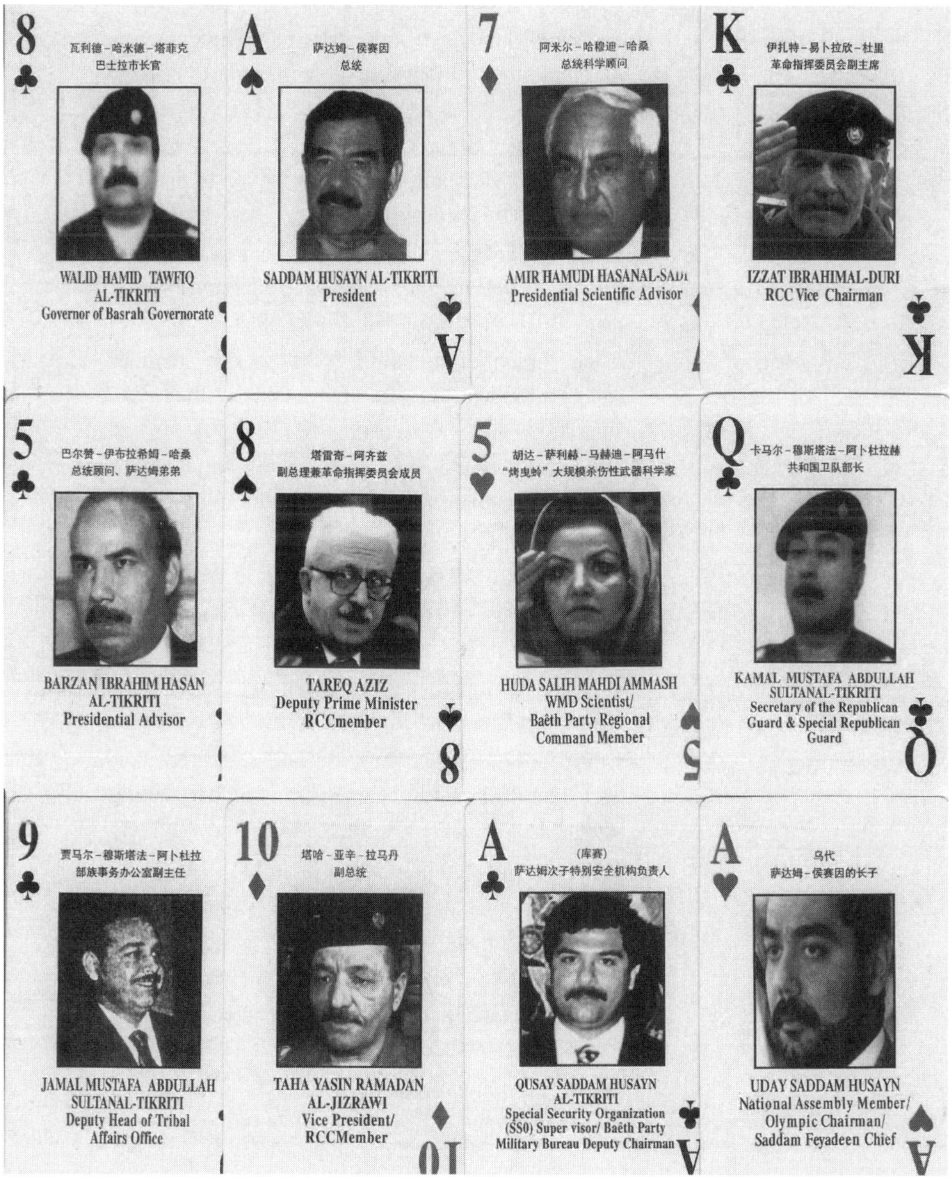

Playing cards issued by the United States featuring wanted members of the regime of Saddam Hussein. Courtesy of U.S. Defense Intelligence Agency.

DID YOU KNOW?

In History: Timeline to Invasion

Year	Month	Event
1990	August	Iraqi invasion of Kuwait
	August	UN sanctions imposed on Iraq
	November	UN Security Council authorizes use of force against Iraq
1991	February	Iraqi forces withdraw from Kuwait
	February	Security Council establishes ceasefire and demands elimination of Iraq's weapons of mass destruction programs
	April	Establishment of the United Nations Special Commission (UNSCOM) to monitor Iraq's destruction of nonnuclear weapons of mass destruction
	April	Establishment by the United States of a zone in the north of Iraq, excluding Iraqi forces (a similar zone was established in the south in August 1992)
1995	April	Establishment of the Oil-for-Food Program, intended to mitigate the worst impact of sanctions on the Iraqi population
1998	October	Adoption by the U.S. Congress of the Iraq Liberation Act, calling, *inter alia*, for the overthrow of the government of Iraq
	December	Withdrawal of UNSCOM from Iraq
	December	Operation Desert Fox, a four-day aerial bombardment of Baghdad by U.S. forces
1999	December	Creation of United Nations Monitoring, Verification and Inspection Commission (UNMOVIC) by the UN Security Council to replace UNSCOM
2002	September	President Bush raises the prospect of military action against Iraq in address to the UN General Assembly
	November	UN Security Council adopts Resolution 1441
2003	February	US Secretary of State Powell gives presentation to the UN Security Council
	March	Report to the Security Council by Chief Weapons Inspector, Hans Blix, on March 7 suggests Iraqi compliance with Council demands
		Beginning of the invasion, March 20

Britain's Prime Minister Tony Blair addresses the 2005 World Summit at UN Headquarters, New York, September 14, 2005. Courtesy of Paulo Filgueiras, UN Photo.

> As far as Ireland is concerned, it is for the Council to decide on any ensuing action. Our debate on 17–18 October made it clear that this is the broadly held view within the United Nations. However, we are confident that should it be necessary, the Council will, in the words of the Secretary-General, face its responsibilities.[8]

Similar comments had been made by the British and American representatives in their explanations of the vote on Resolution 1441. Both denied that there were any "hidden triggers" in the Resolution. As one participant commented, "the Attorney General must have overlooked completely the entire context of the negotiations to reach the conclusion he did in respect of 1441."[9]

Based on these public statements, Goldsmith suggested that a second Security Council resolution authorizing force would be the "safest legal course." Moreover, the Attorney General suggested that the argument that the use of force had already been authorized would only be sustainable if there "strong factual grounds" for determining that Iraq had, indeed, failed to comply with Council demands (paragraph 29). This depended greatly on the reports of the UNMOVIC and IAEA teams, which had been inspecting Iraqi facilities for three months.

The Executive Director of UNMOVIC, Hans Blix, had reported to the Security Council on February 14, 2003, that Iraq was beginning to comply with Resolution 1441's demand that it demonstrate it had disarmed. His report contained examples of Iraqi compliance and questioned some American intelligence that had underpinned Powell's Security Council presentation on February 5. In another report later that month, Blix was more cautious but still identified some significant areas where Iraq was showing signs of compliance. In his last report to the Council on March 7 before the invasion began, the same day that Goldsmith submitted his opinion, Blix was again cautious but reported qualified but significant progress in demonstrating compliance in the destruction of its illegal Samoud 2 missiles. "We are not watching the destruction of toothpicks," he told the Security Council.

The final section of Goldsmith's opinion addressed an issue that had been discussed widely in the United States and Britain before the invasion—regime change. Goldsmith was clear in his advice that the removal of Saddam Hussein could not be a military objective of the invading forces.

FURTHER READING

Bellamy, Alex J. "International Law and the War with Iraq." *Melbourne Journal of International Law* 4, no. 2 (2003): 497–520. http://www.mjil.law.unimelb.edu.au/issues/archive/2003(2)/06Bellamy.pdf.

Blix, Hans. "Oral Introduction of the 12th Quarterly Report of UNMOVIC." Security Council, March 7, 2003. http://www.un.org/Depts/unmovic/SC7asdelivered.htm.

British Government. "JIC Two Document. Version 24 July, 2002." http://foi.fco.gov.uk/content/en/foi-releases/2008a/12.1-iraq-dossier.

Goldsmith, Peter. "Advice to British Government on the legality of military action against Iraq." March 7, 2003. http://www.ico.gov.uk/upload/documents/library/freedomofinformation/notices/annexa-attorney general's advice 070303.pdf.

Smith, Michael. "Blair Planned Iraq War from Start." *Sunday Times*, May 1, 2005. http://www.timesonline.co.uk/article/0,,2087-1592724,00.html.

U.S. Secretary of State Colin Powell holds a model vial of anthrax, arguing that Iraq was likely to possess WMD. United Nations Security Council, February 5, 2003. Courtesy of U.S. Government.

The Trouble with Intelligence: Iraq's Weapons of Mass Destruction

- ***Document:*** British Government assessment of Iraq's Weapons of Mass Destruction, extract from the Executive Summary, pp. 5–7
- ***Date:*** September 2002
- ***Where:*** Downing Street, London
- ***Significance:*** This document was released by UK Prime Minister Blair to reinforce the Government's case for attacking Iraq. It has become known as the "Dodgy Dossier" and includes Blair's claim that "his [Saddam Hussein's] military planning allows for some of the WMD to be ready within 45 minutes of an order to use them."

DOCUMENT

1. Under Saddam Hussein Iraq developed chemical and biological weapons, acquired missiles allowing it to attack neighbouring countries with these weapons and persistently tried to develop a nuclear bomb. Saddam has used chemical weapons, both against Iran and against his own people. Following the Gulf War, Iraq had to admit to all this. And in the ceasefire of 1991 Saddam agreed unconditionally to give up his weapons of mass destruction.
2. Much information about Iraq's weapons of mass destruction is already in the public domain from UN reports and from Iraqi defectors. This points clearly to Iraq's continuing possession, after 1991, of chemical and biological agents and weapons produced before the Gulf War. It shows that Iraq has refurbished sites formerly associated with the production of chemical and biological agents. And it indicates that Iraq remains able to manufacture these agents, and to use bombs, shells, artillery rockets and ballistic missiles to deliver them.
3. An independent and well-researched overview of this public evidence was provided by the International Institute for Strategic Studies (IISS) on September 9.

The IISS report also suggested that Iraq could assemble nuclear weapons within months of obtaining fissile material from foreign sources.

4. As well as the public evidence, however, significant additional information is available to the Government from secret intelligence sources, described in more detail in this paper. This intelligence cannot tell us about everything. However, it provides a fuller picture of Iraqi plans and capabilities. It shows that Saddam Hussein attaches great importance to possessing weapons of mass destruction which he regards as the basis for Iraq's regional power. It shows that he does not regard them only as weapons of last resort. He is ready to use them, including against his own population, and is determined to retain them, in breach of UN Security Council Resolutions (UNSCR).
5. Intelligence also shows that Iraq is preparing plans to conceal evidence of these weapons, including incriminating documents, from renewed inspections. And it confirms that despite sanctions and the policy of containment, Saddam has continued to make progress with his illicit weapons programmes.
6. As a result of the intelligence we judge that Iraq has:
   - continued to produce chemical and biological agents;
   - military plans for the use of chemical and biological weapons, including against its own Shi'a population. Some of these weapons are deployable within 45 minutes of an order to use them;
   - command and control arrangements in place to use chemical and biological weapons. Authority ultimately resides with Saddam Hussein. (There is intelligence that he may have delegated this authority to his son Qusai);
   - developed mobile laboratories for military use, corroborating earlier reports about the mobile production of biological warfare agents;
   - pursued illegal programmes to procure controlled materials of potential use in the production of chemical and biological weapons programmes;
   - tried covertly to acquire technology and materials which could be used in the production of nuclear weapons;
   - sought significant quantities of uranium from Africa, despite having no active civil nuclear power programme that could require it;
   - recalled specialists to work on its nuclear programme;
   - illegally retained up to 20 al-Hussein missiles, with a range of 650km, capable of carrying chemical or biological warheads;
   - started deploying its al-Samoud liquid propellant missile, and has used the absence of weapons inspectors to work on extending its range to at least 200km, which is beyond the limit of 150km imposed by the United Nations;
   - started producing the solid-propellant Ababil-100, and is making efforts to extend its range to at least 200km, which is beyond the limit of 150km imposed by the UN;
   - constructed a new engine test stand for the development of missiles capable of reaching the UK Sovereign Base Areas in Cyprus and NATO members (Greece and Turkey), as well as all Iraq's Gulf neighbours and Israel;
   - pursued illegal programmes to procure materials for use in its illegal development of long range missiles;

- learnt lessons from previous UN weapons inspections and has already begun to conceal sensitive equipment and documentation in advance of the return of inspectors.

7. These judgements reflect the views of the Joint Intelligence Committee (JIC). More details on the judgements and on the development of the JIC's assessments since 1998 are set out in Part 1 of this paper.
8. Iraq's weapons of mass destruction are in breach of international law. Under a series of UNSCR Iraq is obliged to destroy its holdings of these weapons under the supervision of UN inspectors. Part 2 of the paper sets out the key UNSCR. It also summarises the history of the UN inspection regime and Iraq's history of deception, intimidation and concealment in its dealings with the UN inspectors.
9. But the threat from Iraq does not depend solely on the capabilities we have described. It arises also because of the violent and aggressive nature of Saddam Hussein's regime. His record of internal repression and external aggression gives rise to unique concerns about the threat he poses. The paper briefly outlines in Part 3 Saddam's rise to power, the nature of his regime and his history of regional aggression. Saddam's human rights abuses are also catalogued, including his record of torture, mass arrests and summary executions.
10. The paper briefly sets out how Iraq is able to finance its weapons programme. Drawing on illicit earnings generated outside UN control, Iraq generated illegal income of some $3 billion in 2001.

SOURCE: British Government (Joint Intelligence Committee). http://image.guardian.co.uk/sys-files/Politics/documents/2002/09/24/dossier.pdf. *Reproduced under the terms of the Click-Use License.*

ANALYSIS

The months leading to the invasion of Iraq were marked by an intensive campaign by the American and British governments to convince their populations and the rest of the world that Saddam Hussein and his regime represented a major threat to Iraq's own people, its neighbors, to the United States, and to the rest of the world. This involved the governments offering a wide range of reasons as to why Iraq should be attacked. The campaign was largely accepted at face value by the American media and public. Elsewhere, however, American plans for war were met by intense opposition and some of the largest antiwar demonstrations since the Vietnam War.

This document was released by the British Government in the context of increasing American pressure for military action against Iraq. It was debated in the Parliament on September 24, 2002, where there was general acceptance of the Government's claims, if not of its proposed support for invasion. Together with another document released to the media in February 2003, the dossier represented the British Government's most systematic attempt to present a public case for the impending invasion of Iraq. It also served to complement the presentation made to the UN Security Council by U.S. Secretary of State Colin Powell on February 5, 2003. The dossier comprises claims made consistently by the British and American governments until, as the occupying powers, they were unable to deny that the claims were false. These included Iraq's alleged development of weapons of mass destruction, the production of banned ballistic missiles, Saddam Hussein's aggression against his neighbors, and his gross violations of human rights at home.

The focus of the British dossier is Iraq's alleged violation of international law, as defined by the various Security Council resolutions adopted since 1991. This highlights the extent of the powers of the Security Council. The UN Charter gives the Council wide-ranging authority to determine what measures will be necessary to enforce its decisions concerning the maintenance or restoration of international peace and security. This authority is seen by many as empowering the Council to impose obligations that go beyond customary or treaty-based law to the extent that they are almost unlimited.

Iraq was a party to the Nuclear Non-Proliferation Treaty. It was also party to the 1925 Geneva Protocol on Chemical and Biological Warfare and a signatory to the 1972 Biological Weapons Convention. Although it was not a party to the Chemical Weapons Convention, many writers consider that the prohibition of chemical weapons forms part of customary international law. In all these cases, therefore, Iraq could be said to have been broadly bound not to develop weapons of mass destruction. Security Council Resolution 687 (1991), which established the ceasefire between Iraq and the coalition that expelled it from Kuwait, went further, however, and banned Iraq's possession of weapons-usable material (dual use material) that could be used in the manufacture of nuclear, chemical, or biological weapons. The Resolution also banned specific classes of ballistic missile that were not covered by treaty or customary law.

There were several issues that the British Government did not stress in the dossier but that were canvassed in more political contexts. One was Saddam Hussein's alleged links to terrorism. The evidence for this link was so weak that the Government might have decided that to pursue it would have undermined the rest of its case. Another issue, which was discussed at some length by Prime Minister Blair in the Parliamentary debate of the dossier, was the American and British desire to remove Saddam Hussein from power. The idea that one government should attempt to remove another government or its head, known as regime change, has no support in international law, and it would have been an impossible task to sell such an idea to the UN Security Council. It is, nevertheless, a persistent issue in international relations with implications for international law and the use of force.

Chapter 4 discussed one example of regime change: Tanzania's removal of Idi Amin as President of Uganda. Vietnam's overthrow of Pol Pot in Kampuchea has also been mentioned. The international community treated both cases differently. Vietnam was condemned by the UN General Assembly, while Tanzania's action was criticized by some African countries but otherwise ignored by the international system. In both cases, the international reaction was complicated by a general feeling that the world was better off without either regime. Almost alone among nations, the United States has been an active proponent of regime change and has pursued it on numerous occasions in countries such as Panama, Grenada, and even Libya. In the important *Nicaragua* case heard by the International Court of Justice, regime change was addressed by the Court, which expressed the opposition of international law to the practice in direct terms:

> The Court considers that in international law, if one State, with a view to the coercion of another State, supports and assists armed bands in that State whose purpose is to overthrow the government of that State, that amounts to an intervention by the one State in the internal affairs of the other, whether or not the political objective of the State giving such support and assistance is equally far-reaching.[10]

Despite such a rejection, the United States had, as noted in the analysis of the first document of this chapter, adopted regime change in Iraq as official policy in the Iraq Liberation Act of 1998. By contrast, British policy had always been to reject the concept. In the last few months before the invasion, however, the idea began to appear in British political commentary. In response to growing resistance in the UK to an invasion, the Prime Minister began to talk about the human rights violations of Saddam Hussein's regime and the desirability of putting a stop to them by removing him.

In this context, therefore, the task of the British and American governments was to demonstrate to domestic and international opinion that Iraq had been systematically violating international law and the conditions imposed by the Security Council and to convince people that the morality of the invasion was clear. Disappointingly from Blair's perspective, and in contrast to the response in

U.S. Marines from the 1st Battalion, 7th Marines, prepare to enter one of Saddam Hussein's palaces in Baghdad. Courtesy of U.S. Marine Corps.

British forces enter Baghdad. Courtesy of the Gertrude Bell Archive, Newcastle University.

Parliament, the media and public response ranged from skeptical to scornful. One commentator remarked:

> 'I have been increasingly alarmed by the evidence from inside Iraq', says UK Prime Minister Tony Blair in the foreword to the British government's assessment of Iraq's weapons of mass destruction, published today. According to Blair, 'The assessed intelligence has established beyond doubt that Saddam has continued to produce chemical and biological weapons, that he continues in his efforts to develop nuclear weapons, and that he has been able to extend the range of his ballistic missile programme'.
>
> Blair has come a long way since 7 September, 2002. Then, while at Camp David with U.S. President George Bush, he said: "We haven't the faintest idea what has been going on in the last four years . . . other than what we know is an attempt to carry on rebuilding weapons.' From not having the faintest idea to 50-plus pages of 'irrefutable evidence' in just 17 days? That ain't half bad."[11]

Some analysts regarded the invasion as an attempt to dismantle the collective security system or as an opportunity to refashion international law in a way that sidelines the United Nations. The focus of these comments has been largely on American claims to the right of pre-emptive self-defense discussed above. According to Michael Glennon, for example, the United States has abandoned the established UN Charter rules, which attempt to limit external intervention in local conflicts and which have served the international community for sixty years. Glennon argues that the United States has come to favor a less clearly defined approach that is much more tolerant of unilateral military intervention and has few rules by which to judge the action. What rules do exist under this new system seem to be more the result of rationalization after the event than of deliberation and preagreement. The approach seems to assume that the West and the United States, in particular, can be trusted to do the right thing.

> The death of the restrictive old rules on peacekeeping and peacemaking—under which most bloody conflicts were simply ignored as "domestic matters"—should not be mourned. Events since the end of the Cold War starkly show that the anti-interventionist regime has fallen out of sync with modern notions of justice. The crisis in Kosovo illustrates this disjunction and America's

DID YOU KNOW?

Chemical Weapons in Iraq

People in northern Iraq represent the largest civilian populations to be exposed to chemical weapons. Between April 1987 and August 1988, Iraqi forces attacked 250 towns and villages. The population of the area is 4 million, and estimates suggest that up to 250,000 people may have been affected by the chemical weapons. Saddam's regime also used chemical weapons against Iranian soldiers during the Iran-Iraq War and on Shiites and Marsh Arabs in southern Iraq after that conflict.

Perhaps the worst use of weapons of mass destruction was the attack in March 1988, when Halabjah was bombarded with mustard and nerve gases. Up to seven thousand of 80,000 inhabitants died immediately, and 20,000 to 30,000 were injured. Studies indicate over 50 percent of current inhabitants were exposed to the attacks.

While the weapons had terrible direct effects, Iraqi documents indicate they also provoked long-term effects, including cancers, birth defects, neurological problems, and infertility. It is believed Iraq's arsenal included many chemical and biological agents, including those mentioned above and others including anthrax and rotavirus (which causes gastroenteritis and diarrhea in infants and children).

In 1995 the UN Secretary-General documented the weaponization of irradiated zirconium in bombs dropped so as to deliver two curies of radiation over one square kilometer. This radiation can sterilize victims and causes birth defects and cancers. Irradiated zirconium's short half-life enabled the return to targets after two to three months, when no traces of radiation would be found.

> new willingness to do what it thinks right—international law notwithstanding. The horror of ethnic cleansing in the Serbian province was well publicized. As Slobodan Milosevic thumbed his nose at the international community, pressure built to use force against him, whether the UN Charter allowed it or not. Thus when the Western allies launched air strikes, the move was largely popular. It was not, however, technically legal under the old regime. After all, Kosovo is still part of Yugoslavia. No cross-border attack—the one circumstance where the charter allows an international military response—had occurred, and the Security Council had never authorized NATO military measures.[12]

Many observers have focused on the damage that the U.S.-British action had on international relations and on the international legal structure that has guided the international system since the Second World War. International law is an imprecise science, and definite answers to particular issues are often hard to obtain. In the case of the American invasion of Iraq, it is inevitable that there will be some, especially among members of the U.S. foreign policy establishment who supported for various reasons the decision to attack Iraq, who will insist on the legality of the action. And they will have some support among academics and other analysts. Interestingly, some of those supporters who subsequently became critics of the invasion changed their position not so much on the basis of the legality of the action as on the lack of competence shown by the U.S. administration in the post-invasion phase.

The dominant opinion, however, is that the United States and the supporting coalition were in violation of international law in invading Iraq. The anticipatory self-defense argument pursued by the United States was difficult to maintain, being rejected even by the Americans' most important ally, the United Kingdom. And the suggestion that the United States could act unilaterally to enforce Security Council resolutions was widely condemned. This opinion is reinforced by the confidential advice provided to the British Government by the Attorney-General, Lord Goldsmith, on the legality of the intended invasion. The effect of these documents, along with the unsuccessful American attempt to secure passage through the Security Council of a resolution specifically authorizing the resort to force, is to reinforce serious doubts about the legality of the invasion.

DID YOU KNOW?

In History: Iraq's Hostility to External Interference

The invasion of Iraq was portrayed as part of a plan to promote a network of pro-Western democratic Arab states. There was some irony in Bush's choice of Baghdad as the starting point for the new arrangement. Baghdad had given its name to a short-lived British-backed alliance in the 1950s. The Baghdad Pact was formed in 1955 by Britain, Iraq, Turkey, Iran, and Pakistan to promote British power and block Soviet influence in the region. Britain hoped Syria and Jordan would also join. But Britain's plans met with widespread opposition. Syria refused to join, and Jordan's King Hussein bowed to the will of his people, who took to the streets to denounce the Pact. Given the opposition, the Baghdad Pact's prospects were not bright. In the event, Britain's role in the 1956 Suez crisis undermined its standing. Then in 1958, the monarchy installed in Iraq by Britain was overthrown and Iraq withdrew from the Pact, causing it to be renamed the Central Treaty Organization.

Today's world is different. The West's enemy is not communism, but terrorism. But despite the differences, echoes of the Baghdad Pact persist. The players are similar, with America taking over from Britain. Pakistan, after the September 11 attacks, became a crucial American ally. Turkey is an important NATO and regional ally. Iran is the only former Baghdad Pact member outside the framework intended by the United States.

To push the parallel between the modern world and the 1950s too far would be mistaken. Nevertheless, the Bush administration failed to address one factor that has not changed over 50 years: deep Arab hostility to foreign interference in Middle Eastern affairs. That failure has weakened U.S. influence throughout the region.

General Assembly president gets weapons of mass destruction report. Jan Eliasson (right), President of the sixtieth session of the General Assembly, with Hans Blix, Chairman, Commission of Weapons of Mass Destruction, who presented to him the Commission's report "Weapons of Terror: Freeing the World of Nuclear, Biological and Chemical Arms," UN Headquarters in New York. United Nations, New York, June 1, 2006. Courtesy of Evan Schneider, UN Photo.

Notes

1. See "Coalition of the Willing? Make That War Criminals," *Sydney Morning Herald* (February 26, 2003), http://www.smh.com.au/articles/2003/02/25/1046064028608.html and Jim Lobe, "Law Groups Say US Invasion Illegal," *Common Dreams News Centre* (March 21, 2003), http://www.commondreams.org/headlines03/0321-10.htm.
2. "It should be the policy of the United States to support efforts to remove the regime headed by Saddam Hussein from power in Iraq and to promote the emergence of a democratic government to replace that regime"—Section 3, at http://www.news.findlaw.com/hdocs/docs/iraq/libact103198.pdf.
3. http://www.whitehouse.gov/news/releases/2003/02/20030205-1.html.
4. http://www.yale.edu/lawweb/avalon/diplomacy/britain/br-1842d.htm.
5. Michael J. Glennon, "The New Interventionism," *Foreign Affairs* 78 no. 3 (1999): 2–7.
6. Tarcisio Gazzini, *The Changing Rules on the Use of Force in International Law* (Manchester: Juris, 2005), 149–153, and Donald R. Rothwell, "Anticipatory Self-Defence in the Age of International Terrorism," *University of Queensland Law Journal* 24, no. 2: (2005): 337–354. For a more skeptical view, see Chris-

tine Gray. *International Law and the Use of Force,* 2nd ed. (Oxford: Oxford University Press, 2004), 129–133.

7. John Negroponte, Speech to UN Security Council, November 8, 2002, http://usinfo.org/wf-archive/2002/021108/epf503.htm.
8. Explanation of Vote by Ireland, UN Security Council, November 8, 2002, at http://www.un.org/webcast/ireland110802.htm.
9. See "United Kingdom Explanation of its Vote on UN Security Council Resolution 1441: Statement by Ambassador Greenstock to the Security Council (2002)," reproduced in Shirley V. Scott, ed. *International Law and Politics. Key Documents* (Boulder, CO: Lynne Rienner: 2004), 112–113.
10. Military and Paramilitary Activities in and against Nicaragua *(Nicaragua v. United States of America)*, Merits, Judgment, ICJ Reports 1986, para. 241. http://www.icj-cij.org/docket/files/70/6503.pdf.
11. Brendan O'Neill, "Blair's Dodgy Dossier: Britain's Evidence of an Iraqi Threat is as Weak as the Opposition to War," *Spiked* (September 24, 2002), http://www.spiked-online.com/Articles/00000006DA63.htm.
12. Glennon, "The New Interventionism," 2.

FURTHER READING

"Congress and the United Nations Must Act to Stop an Illegal War Against Iraq." *Western States Legal Foundation*, 17 March 2003. www.wslfweb.org/docs/statement317.pdf.

Enemark, Christian, and Christopher Michaelsen. "Just War Doctrine and the Invasion of Iraq." *Australian Journal of Politics and History* 51, no.4 (2005): 545–563.

Gazzini, Tarcisio. *The Changing Rules on the Use of Force in International Law*. Manchester: Juris, 2005: 149–153.

Glennon, Michael J. "The New Interventionism." *Foreign Affairs* 78, no. 3 (1999): 2–7.

Gray, Christine. *International Law and the Use of Force*. Oxford: Oxford University Press, 2004.

Halliday, Dennis J. "Iraq and the UN's Weapon of Mass Destruction." *Current History* 98 (1999): 65–68.

Polk, William R. *Understanding Iraq*. London: I. B. Tauris, 2005.

Roberts, Adam. "Law and the Use of Force after Iraq." *Survival* 45, no. 2 (2003): 31–56.

Sands, Philippe. *Lawless World. America and the Making and Breaking of Global Rules from FDR's Atlantic Charter to George W. Bush's Illegal War*. Camberwell, Australia: Allen Lane, 2005.

"The United Nations Charter and the Use of Force Against Iraq." *Lawyers' Committee on Nuclear Policy*, October 2, 2002. www.lcnp.org/global/Iraqstatmt.3.pdf.

10

CONCLUSIONS: HAS THE INTERNATIONAL LAW RELATING TO THE USE OF FORCE CREATED A MORE PEACEFUL WORLD?

The World Peace Monument in Swayambhunath temple site, Kathmandhu, Nepal. Courtesy of Markus Koljonen.

The Adequacy of the Charter Regime to Address Contemporary Issues

- ***Document:*** "In Larger Freedom: Towards Development, Security and Human Rights for All," paragraphs 122–126, p. 33
- ***Date:*** March 21, 2005
- ***Where:*** United Nations, New York
- ***Significance:*** "In Larger Freedom" was the UN Secretary-General's follow-up report to the Millennium Summit of September 2000. In the report the Secretary-General addressed a range of issues affecting the security and prosperity of the world's people, including the degree of consensus and respect accorded the international law on the use of force.

DOCUMENT A

E. Use of Force

122. Finally, an essential part of the consensus we seek must be agreement on when and how force can be used to defend international peace and security. In recent years, this issue has deeply divided Member States. They have disagreed about whether States have the right to use military force pre-emptively, to defend themselves against imminent threats; whether they have the right to use it preventively to defend themselves against latent or non-imminent threats; and whether they have the right—or perhaps the obligation—to use it protectively to rescue the citizens of other States from genocide or comparable crimes.

123. Agreement must be reached on these questions if the United Nations is to be—as it was intended to be—a forum for resolving differences rather than a mere stage for acting them out. And yet I believe the Charter of our Organization, as it stands, offers a good basis for the understanding that we need.

124. Imminent threats are fully covered by Article 51, which safeguards the inherent right of sovereign States to defend themselves against armed attack. Lawyers

have long recognized that this covers an imminent attack as well as one that has already happened.

125. Where threats are not imminent but latent, the Charter gives full authority to the Security Council to use military force, including preventively, to preserve international peace and security. As to genocide, ethnic cleansing and other such crimes against humanity, are they not also threats to international peace and security, against which humanity should be able to look to the Security Council for protection?

126. The task is not to find alternatives to the Security Council as a source of authority but to make it work better. When considering whether to authorize or endorse the use of military force, the Council should come to a common view on how to weigh the seriousness of the threat; the proper purpose of the proposed military action; whether means short of the use of force might plausibly succeed in stopping the threat; whether the military option is proportional to the threat at hand; and whether there is a reasonable chance of success. By undertaking to make the case for military action in this way, the Council would add transparency to its deliberations and make its decisions more likely to be respected, by both Governments and world public opinion. **I therefore recommend that the Security Council adopt a resolution setting out these principles and expressing its intention to be guided by them when deciding whether to authorize or mandate the use of force.**

SOURCE: *In Larger Freedom: Towards Development, Security and Human Rights for All,* Report of the Secretary-General for decision by Heads of State and Government in September 2005. http://www.un.org/largerfreedom/chap3.htm.

- ***Document B:*** Extract from World Summit Outcome (General Assembly resolution 60/1)
- ***Date:*** September 15, 2005
- ***Where:*** United Nations, New York
- ***Significance:*** A reaffirmation by world leaders of their ongoing support for the Charter framework on the use of force

---

DOCUMENT B

Use of Force under the Charter of the United Nations

77. We reiterate the obligation of all Member States to refrain in their international relations from the threat or use of force in any manner inconsistent with the Charter. We reaffirm that the purposes and principles guiding the United Nations are, inter alia, to maintain international peace and security, to develop friendly relations among nations based on respect for the principles of equal rights and self determination of peoples and to take other appropriate measures to strengthen universal peace, and to that end we are determined to take effective collective measures for the prevention

and removal of threats to the peace and for the suppression of acts of aggression or other breaches of the peace, and to bring about by peaceful means, in conformity with the principles of justice and international law, the adjustment or settlement of international disputes or situations that might lead to a breach of the peace.

78. We reiterate the importance of promoting and strengthening the multilateral process and of addressing international challenges and problems by strictly abiding by the Charter and the principles of international law, and further stress our commitment to multilateralism.

79. We reaffirm that the relevant provisions of the Charter are sufficient to address the full range of threats to international peace and security. We further reaffirm the authority of the Security Council to mandate coercive action to maintain and restore international peace and security. We stress the importance of acting in accordance with the purposes and principles of the Charter.

80. We also reaffirm that the Security Council has primary responsibility in the maintenance of international peace and security. We also note the role of the General Assembly relating to the maintenance of international peace and security in accordance with the relevant provisions of the Charter.

SOURCE: 2005 World Summit Outcome, General Assembly Resolution A/Res/60/1, October 24, 2005, paras 77–80, pp 21–22. http://www.un.org/summit2005/documents.html.

ANALYSIS

This book began by tracing the historical process by which efforts have been made to develop a body of international law prohibiting States from engaging in armed hostilities as a policy option. We have seen how the Covenant of the League of Nations attempted to reduce the frequency of occasions on which States might resort to the use of force and how the Kellogg-Briand Pact outlawed war. Although both treaties failed to prevent the outbreak of World War II, they constituted important steps towards a system of international law in which sovereign States have no legal right to initiate war.

These developments culminated in the adoption of the Charter of the United Nations in 1945. The Charter has since then been the centerpiece of the international regime regulating the use of force. It contains a general prohibition of the use of force in Article 2(4), to which there are two exceptions. First, States may resort to the use of force in self-defense (Article 51 of the Charter). Second, the use of force is permissible in the context of collective security, i.e., when authorized by the UN Security Council. The general prohibition of the use of force is not only embodied in the Charter but also forms part of customary international law and binds all States.

Document A is part of a set of major reform proposals by Secretary-General Kofi Annan. This section addresses the international law of the use of force and its relevance to the contemporary world. The document lists several of the current issues of contention within the international law on the use of force that we have considered in this book: anticipatory and pre-emptive self-defense and the idea of humanitarian intervention. The Secretary-General claimed that Article 51 is sufficiently flexible to allow anticipatory self-defense. Non-imminent threats can, Annan argued, be dealt with by the Security Council, which has the full authority to draw on a range of options, including force, to deal with potential threats to international peace and security. Annan argued that the Council's responsibility for the maintenance of international peace and security extends to major domestic crises such as the genocide in Rwanda and the crimes against humanity being perpetrated in the Darfur region of Sudan. Annan concluded that the UN Charter as it stands provides an adequate basis for establishing a broad consensus on the legal response to some of the key contemporary issues of international security.

In September 2005, heads of state and government attended a major United Nations summit designed to review progress toward meeting the goals of the 2000 Millennium Declaration. World leaders considered the report excerpted in Document A and in turn agreed on a range of policy guidance for the Secretariat and United Nations agencies, funds and programs. Document B is an extract from the product of the 2005 Summit. In the Outcomes document, members of the international community reaffirmed their commitment to the Charter regime on the use of force. Despite the UN Charter being more than sixty years old, there would seem to be no doubt of its ongoing central role in world affairs.

This brings us to our final questions for consideration in this book. Is the world a more peaceful place because of the international legal prohibition on the use of force? Have the creation and gradual refinement of this body of law made any real-world difference? Amazingly, even those who do quantitative analysis of the historical incidence of warfare are divided as to whether, viewed in the context of the last two hundred years, the period since 1945 has been a more peaceful era.[1] In the 1990s, for example, the world appeared to be witnessing a decline in inter-State conflicts, but because of the terrible bloodshed of internal wars, the decade will go down as one of the worst of the last two centuries. The data on wars since 1945 looks very different according to whether, for example, one calculates wars per State in the international system or the sheer number of conflicts, and whether one compares the numbers of wars or the numbers of battle deaths.

It is far from the case that armed conflict ended in 1945. But the authors of this volume would nevertheless argue that the world *is* a more peaceful place with the Charter regime in place than it would have been had the San Francisco negotiations broken down without agreement on the final Charter text. While violent conflicts around the world continue to pose a challenge to international peace and security, the adoption of the UN Charter with its general prohibition of the use of force in international relations has meant that the use of force by States for political gain has become unacceptable, and any State considering breaking that rule can expect censure. As Louis Henkin explained in 1971:

> The sense that war is not done has taken hold, and nations more readily find that their interests do not in fact require the use of force after all. Expectations of international violence no longer underlie every political calculation of every nation, and war plans lie buried deep in national files. Even where force is used, the fact that it is unlawful cannot be left out of account and limits the scope,

the weapons, the duration, the purposes for which force is used.[2]

It is difficult to identify and measure deterrence, but this does not mean that it does not exist. According to Thomas Franck:

> Even a cursory examination of the post-Charter historic record makes clear that, in actual practice, almost all states, almost all the time, do abide by the strictures of Articles 2(4) and 51, refraining from resolving problems they may have with other states by recourse to force.[3]

The introduction into international law of a general prohibition of the use of force has provided impetus for the development of a range of related bodies of law, which have reinforced the purposes and objectives of the UN Charter. These bodies of law include the law of armed conflict, the law of arms control and disarmament, and international human rights law. In addition, there is an emergent body of international criminal law whose advocates are seeking to end impunity for those who commit war crimes or crimes against humanity. One could go further and point to international economic law as helping create and maintain peaceful relations among States. The availability of mechanisms for the peaceful resolution of international disputes, such as international arbitration or judicial proceedings, reinforces the impact of the substantive law. The International Court of Justice has, for example, issued judgments in a considerable number of cases concerning disputed boundaries that might otherwise have been settled through physical confrontation.[4]

Nonetheless, assessing whether the international law on the use of force has made the world a more peaceful place is a tricky exercise, not least because of the methodological difficulty of measuring the impact of international law on foreign policy.[5] Research indicates that the record is very mixed: some major foreign policy decisions, such as the French decision to sink the Greenpeace flagship *Rainbow Warrior* moored in Auckland, New Zealand, were taken without the decision-makers having sought or received any advice as to the legality of the proposed course of action.[6] In other decision-making situations in which use of force has been contemplated, such as that in the United States during the Cuban Missile Crisis, the advice of international lawyers has been integral to the decision-making process. The involvement of international law considerations in that situation would seem to have contributed to the peaceful resolution of that crisis.[7]

Idealists, including many international lawyers, would like international law to determine foreign policy. Theirs is an image of a world governed by law. This image has motivated many of the protagonists of the development of an international law prohibiting the use of force by States for political purposes. Thomas Schoenbaum has provided a contemporary outline of this image in his book *International Relations. The*

DID YOU KNOW?

In History: International Law and the Cuban Missile Crisis

The Cuban Missile Crisis is generally regarded as one of the most serious incidents of the Cold War. On October 16, 1962, U.S. reconnaissance photography provided evidence of the Soviet deployment of medium-range ballistic missiles in Cuba. A specially created Executive Committee of the U.S. National Security Council first considered responding with use of force, such as an air strike or invasion. Having received legal advice, they rejected both options, settling for what was a strategically less decisive action for which some relatively plausible legal justification could be found. After eight days of Committee deliberations, the United States imposed what it referred to as a "quarantine" on all Soviet cargo ships bound for Cuba. Soviet ships turned back, and the Soviet Union and the United States went on to negotiate the removal of those missiles already installed in Cuba. The international law on the use of force had therefore contributed to the peaceful resolution of the dispute.[8]

The *Rainbow Warrior* at the port of Genoa in June 2006. Courtesy of Creative Commons Attribution Share Alike.

Path Not Taken.[9] He regards as controversial his thesis that international law and international institutions must be the focal points of foreign policy and international relations. Schoenbaum argues that this is now more possible than in the past because there has been a paradigm shift in how States view their interests. Individual State interests are now supplemented with State interests rooted in cooperation with closely associated and allied States and State interests held in common with all of international society.

From the perspective of most nonlawyers, and even of the less idealistic of the lawyers, even to ask whether we can get world peace through international law may be to pose the wrong question. While it may be true that we will not have world peace without law, this does not mean that law is in itself capable of bringing about that peace. International law must either reflect what States would do anyway or prescribe norms and try to create acceptance of them.[10] Neither of these options is on its own likely to bring about a fundamental shift to ensure world peace.

From the pragmatic perspective of the realist, it would seem that idealists are fond of telling us what States *should* do, but that is of little help if States are not likely to heed those exhortations. The hope that sovereign States will, of their own volition, eventually submit all their disputes to binding adjudication would, from this perspective, seem an illusion.[11] As David Ziegler has argued:

> Advocates of world law seek not to create accepted laws but to win acceptance for laws already created. One way to win acceptance would be enlightened self-interest. The same motivation would lead all students to be honest on examinations. But

> this incentive has not been effective over past centuries, and it is hard to imagine what kind of radical change would suddenly make it effective now.[12]

Within the current international legal order, this is a particular challenge in respect of the major powers. Whereas less powerful States not aligned with the United States can expect the Security Council to enforce Article 2(4) of the UN Charter against them, it is much less likely that the United Nations could enforce the prohibition on the use of force against the United States. One of the reasons for this is that the global order, of which Article 2(4) is integral, prioritizes order over justice. This means that there is a politics to Articles 2(4) and 51 of the UN Charter and to their interpretation, for they generally serve the interests of status quo powers and, at times, place at a disadvantage any State with a genuine grievance.[13] Despite apparent disparities in application of the norm, States generally regard Article 2(4) of the UN Charter as not just any rule of international law but a cornerstone principle of the international order, where order is understood as implying a measure of predictability in political relations, a basis on which participants can plan for their future.[14]

Map of the Western Hemisphere showing the full range of the nuclear missiles under construction in Cuba. The CIA created this map and used it during the secret meetings on the Cuban crisis. Courtesy of the John F. Kennedy Presidential Library and Museum, Boston.

Operation Enduring Freedom, Djibouti, Africa. Members of the 3rd U.S. infantry and French naval commandos during a recent joint-combined exercise in Djibouti. Courtesy of U.S. Marine Corporal Adam C. Schnell, U.S. Army.

The importance attached to Article 2(4) as a fundamental rule of our contemporary international order has been reinforced by a study by Mark Weisburd.[15] Weisburd grouped the approximately 110 uses of force from 1945 to 1991 according to the reaction of the international community. He found that the use of force most likely to evoke third-State sanctions was the classic invasion: one involving a border crossing by regular troops of the States initiating the use of force with the purpose of either subjugating the State invaded, seizing a portion of its territory, or replacing an unfriendly government.[16] In this category he included, for example, the attack on Egypt by the United Kingdom and France in 1956; the Indian invasion of Goa in 1961; and the 1979 Soviet invasion of, and subsequent war in, Afghanistan. The second category of uses of force included postcolonial wars, wars continuing unresolved national liberation or postcolonial wars, outside intervention in civil strife, maintenance of preeminence by dominant States within a region, neocolonial wars, and uses of limited force. Although not approved, uses of force in this second group have not generally evoked general sanctions from third States. A third category of uses of force—those aimed at dislodging a European power from a colonial territory or involving multilateral intervention in civil strife—were those most likely to receive affirmative approval. The study by Weisburd demonstrated that the uses of force most likely to evoke sanctions were those in the first category, which were most clearly illegal, and which posed a significant threat to the international status quo.

It is easy to be cynical about the achievements of Article 2(4), and those contemplating deprecating its success to date would do well to bear in mind that we could easily face worse global prospects than we do today. As early as 1970, Thomas

Franck, a leading U.S. international lawyer, claimed that the prohibition against the use of force had been "eroded beyond recognition."[17] Michael Glennon has more recently argued that the Charter regime is defunct.[18] Thirty-six years after his article, Franck clarified that the purpose of his comments had not been to claim that the prohibition on first use of military force was no longer binding on States "but, to the contrary, to warn that, though an essential cornerstone of the postwar order, it was being progressively undermined by the conduct both of the Soviet Union and of the United States."[19] Even if the objective of an author is to issue a "wake-up call" to the U.S. government, any reduction in worldwide confidence in Article 2(4) does little to help the cause of international law.

On its own, international law may not be able to bring about world peace in the current international structure, but this is not to say that it can make no useful contribution toward that objective. Lawyers have a role to play to assist with incremental steps toward that end by continuing to contribute to refining the law. While the broad outline of the use of force regime during the era of the UN Charter is very clear, there are, as we have seen, several finer points that are far from settled. These include the content and scope of the right of self-defense, intervention for humanitarian protection purposes as a controversial exception to the general prohibition on the use of force, and the international criminal liability of individual political leaders responsible for launching a war of aggression.

The technical term for the degree of clarity of law is its "determinacy." Determinacy is usually achieved "by a rule text's explicit statement of a boundary between the permissible and the impermissible, or by the designation of a process for clarifying, in a contested instance, the meaning of a rule."[20] Increasing the determinacy of law is important, because this will make it easier to know when the law is being flouted. This is useful because it means that international law can function to discredit a course of action that is obviously illegal. As Ian Brownlie put it, "in attempting to provide effective legal controls the jurist must concentrate on the immediate source of danger—the use of force—and characterize the conditions in which it is prohibited in such a way that States can only give justifications for their illegal acts in terms of considerable implausibility."[21] Although the task of increasing the determinacy of the law of the use of force is in process, assisted by pronouncements of the Security Council and the International Court of Justice, it will never be completed, because the nature of the security threats facing States is constantly evolving. Terrorism is one issue that has, as we have seen, raised questions for this legal regime.

DID YOU KNOW?

When Have States Invoked Self-Defense in the Charter Era?

During the era of the UN Charter, States using force without Security Council authorization can justify their actions only on the basis of individual or collective self-defense. Not surprisingly, Article 51 has been invoked a number of times. Examples include:

- By the USSR in relation to Hungary in 1956 and to Afghanistan in 1979
- By Portugal in relation to Guinea in 1969, Senegal in 1969 and 1971, and Zambia in 1969
- By the United States in relation to the Dominican Republic in 1965, Libya in 1986, Panama in 1989, and Afghanistan in 2001
- By the United Kingdom when using force in response to the Argentine invasion of the Falkland Islands in 1982
- By Israel in relation to Egypt in 1967, the bombing of the Osirak nuclear reactor in Iraq in 1981; and its wall in the occupied Palestinian territory, construction of which began in 2002
- By South Africa in relation to Angola and Zambia, 1976–1979
- By India in relation to its invasion of East Pakistan in 1971
- By Vietnam in relation to Kampuchea in 1978
- By Tanzania in relation to Uganda in 1979

Apart from the difficulties arising from the lack of determinacy of some international rules, the regime governing the use of force faces other challenges. For instance, national leaders virtually never admit that a use of force is illegal but instead provide a rationale for their actions. The rationale is not always based in any obvious way on international law. An example of a justification not based on international law was that of the United States in regard to the 1983 invasion of Grenada by the United States and the Organization of Eastern Caribbean States. The United States justified this invasion on the need to protect U.S. nationals, to forestall further chaos, and to assist in the restoration of law and order.[22] President Reagan did not refer expressly to international law in any of his official explanations for the invasion.[23]

More usual, however, is to provide a legal rationale based on one of the two exceptions to the Charter prohibition on the use of force: Security Council authorization or self-defense. States generally insist that they are acting in full compliance with the international law of the use of force even at the risk of failing the "laugh test." They may do so through distorting the meaning of the law or distorting the facts to fit the law, but it is extremely rare to challenge the legitimacy of the law in question. "Vietnam averred that it had been invaded by Cambodia. Moscow alleged that the Soviet occupation of Afghanistan was launched at the invitation of the legitimate Afghan government. The UK government insisted that weapons of mass destruction were deployed in Iraq, poised to attack at forty-five minutes' notice."[24]

The fact that there have been wars since 1945 and that States have justified their actions in terms of the UN Charter, even when to do so has often been far-fetched,

Secretary-General Kofi Annan addresses the sixty-first session of the General Assembly at UN Headquarters in New York, September 19, 2006. Courtesy of Marco Castro, UN Photo.

has not weakened the legal standing of this body of law. As the International Court of Justice observed in its 1986 *Nicaragua* judgment:

> If a State acts in a way prima facie incompatible with a recognized rule, but defends its conduct by appealing to exceptions or justifications contained within the rule itself, then whether or not the State's conduct is in fact justifiable on that basis, the significance of that attitude is to confirm rather than to weaken the rule.[25]

It has generally been difficult to "fudge" authorization by the Security Council, because the requisite resolution has either been passed or not been passed, and during the Cold War the Security Council was stymied by the veto. In recent years, however, some attempts have been to do so, most notably in the case of Iraq. The fact that the legal justification based on purported Council authorization was so far-fetched added to the perceived illegitimacy of the invasion and scarred the reputation of U.S. foreign policy. This highlights the fact that international law fulfils roles in international society other than that of incorporating binding obligations. International law serves an important role in providing the language and medium through which States, NGOs, and other international actors communicate with each other, and it thereby functions to justify and legitimize—or delegitimize as the case may be—the actions of States.[26]

International law as "legitimator" is often overlooked in favor of a focus on international law as rules that are difficult to enforce. When focus is placed on instances of illegal or dubious uses of force in defiance of the Charter, international law is often denigrated as ineffective. Supporters of international law acknowledge its failures but point out that illegal actions take place in domestic legal systems without comparable questioning of whether that legal system really exists in any meaningful way. Indeed, as Ian Brownlie has pointed out, a fair degree of common sense prevails within States in assessing the performance of law. According to Brownlie,

> It does not seem sensible to say, for example, that because the rule of law is weak in a particular region and murders common, we can conclude that the law of the United Kingdom is not a reality. That kind of logic involves saying that if an ideal score of one hundred is not achieved any other lesser score is not to be counted.[27]

A possible future alternative could involve a radical political restructuring that would somehow render the current State-based system obsolescent and usher in an era of world government. If this were to come

DID YOU KNOW?

Extract from Barack Obama's Responses to a Survey of Presidential Candidates on International Law and U.S. Foreign Policy

Question: What are your views of the doctrine of pre-emptive use of force?

President-Elect Obama: I will not hesitate to use force, unilaterally if necessary, to protect the American people or our vital interests whenever we are attacked or imminently threatened. There is no greater responsibility than that of acting as the commander in chief of our armed forces. And I can tell you that whenever I might send our men and women into harm's way, I will clearly define the mission, seek out the advice of our military commanders, objectively evaluate intelligence, and ensure that our troops have the resources and the support they need. There are some circumstances beyond self-defense in which I would be prepared to consider using force, for example to participate in stability and reconstruction operations, or to confront mass atrocities. But when we do use force in situations other than self-defense, we should make every effort to garner the clear support and participation of others—as President George H. W. Bush did when we led the effort to oust Saddam Hussein from Kuwait in 1991. The consequences of forgetting that lesson in the context of the current conflict in Iraq have been grave.

Source: "International Law 2008—Barack Obama." Responses of Barack Obama to questions on the role of international law in U.S. foreign policy as part of a candidate survey conducted by the American Society of International Law, http://www.asil.org/obama.cfm.

about, the whole question of the effectiveness of international law would by then have become moot. The fact that States both make international law and are the subjects of that law is inextricable from the international system as it has evolved to date. The system of international law can thus be usefully judged only on its own terms.[28]

Notes

1. Meredith Reid Sarkees, Frank Whelon Wayman, and J. David Singer, "Inter-State, Intra-State, and Extra-State Wars: A Comprehensive Look at Their Distribution over Time, 1816–1997," *International Studies Quarterly* 47 (2003): 49–70.
2. Louis Henkin, "The Reports of the Death of Article 2(4) are Greatly Exaggerated," *American Journal of International Law* 65, no. 3 (1971): 544.
3. Thomas M. Franck, "The Power of Legitimacy and the Legitimacy of Power: International Law in an Age of Power Disequilibrium," *American Journal of International Law* 100, no. 1 (2006): 97.
4. For a list, see Franck, "The Power of Legitimacy and the Legitimacy of Power," 98 fn. 40.
5. See Markus Burgstaller, *Theories of Compliance with International Law* (Leiden: Martinus Nijhoff, 2005).
6. Antonio Cassese, "The Role of Legal Advisers in Ensuring That Foreign Policy Conforms to International Legal Standards," *Michigan Journal of International Law* 14 (1992–3): 145.
7. Radhika Withana, *Power, Politics, Law: International Law and State Behaviour During International Crises* (Leiden: Martinus Nijhoff, 2008), 167–198.
8. This sidebar draws on Shirley V. Scott and Radhika Withana, "The Relevance of International Law for Foreign Policy When National Security Is at Stake: Lessons from the Cuban Missile Crisis," *Chinese Journal of International Law* 3 (2004): 163–187.
9. Thomas J. Schoenbaum, *International Relations—The Path Not Taken. Using International Law to Promote World Peace and Security* (Cambridge, UK: Cambridge University Press, 2006).
10. David W. Ziegler, *War, Peace, and International Politics*, 5th ed. (Glenview, IL: Scott, Foresman, 1989), 186.
11. Cornelius F. Murphy, Jr. *The Search for World Order. A Study of Thought and Action* (Dordrecht: Martinus Nijhoff, 1985), 183.
12. Ziegler, *War, Peace, and International Politics*, 187.
13. Alberto R. Coll, "The Limits of Global Consciousness and Legal Absolutism: Protecting International Law from Some of Its Best Friends," *Harvard International Law Journal* 27, no. 2 (1986): 612.
14. This draws on the definition of Quincy Wright, *The Role of International Law in the Elimination of War* (Manchester, UK: Manchester University Press, 1961), 7.
15. A. Mark Weisburd, *Use of Force. The Practice of States since World War II* (University Park: Pennsylvania State University Press, 1997).
16. Weisburd provides a fuller list of criteria in his *Use of Force*, 28.

17. Thomas J. Franck, "Who Killed Article 2(4)? Or: Changing Norms Governing the Use of Force by States," *American Journal of International Law* 64, no. 4 (1970): 835.
18. Michael J. Glennon, *Limits of Law. Prerogatives of Power: Interventionism after Kosovo* (New York: Palgrave, 2001).
19. Franck, "The Power of Legitimacy," 94.
20. Franck, "The Power of Legitimacy," 94.
21. Ian Brownlie, *International Law and the Use of Force by States* (Oxford: Clarendon, 1963), 436.
22. Anthony Clark Arend, "International Law and the Recourse to Force: A Shift in Paradigms," *Stanford Journal of International Law* 27, no. 1 (1990–91): 12.
23. Robert J. Beck, *The Grenada Invasion: Politics, Law and Foreign Policy Decision-Making* (Boulder, CO: Westview Press, 1993), 76.
24. Franck, "The Power of Legitimacy," 97.
25. *Case Concerning Military and Paramilitary Activities in and Against Nicaragua* (Merits), [1986] *ICJ Reports*: 98.
26. For a clear exposition of these roles, see Onuma Yasuaki, "International Law in and with International Politics: The Functions of International Law in International Society," *European Journal of International Law* 14, no. 1 (2003): 105–139.
27. Ian Brownlie, *The Rule of Law in International Affairs. International Law at the Fiftieth Anniversary of the United Nations* (The Hague: Martinus Nijhoff, 1998), 14.
28. Brownlie, *The Rule of Law*, 15.

FURTHER READING

Art, Robert J., and Kenneth N. Waltz, eds. *The Use of Force: Military Power and International Politics*. 7th ed. Lanham, MD: Rowman & Littlefield, 2009.

Bowring, Bill. *The Denigration of the International Legal Order?* Oxford: Routledge-Cavendish, 2008.

Falk, Richard A. *The Costs of War. International Law, the UN, and World Order after Iraq*. New York: Routledge, 2008.

Gazzini, Tarcisio. *The Changing Rules on the Use of Force in International Law*. Manchester: Juris Publishing, 2005.

Hovell, Devika. "Chinks in the Armour: International Law, Terrorism and the Use of Force." *UNSW Law Journal* 27, no. 2 (2004): 398–427.

Lowe, Vaughan, et al., eds. *The United Nations Security Council and War: The Evolution of Thought and Practice Since 1945*. Oxford: Oxford University Press, 2008.

Schoenbaum, Thomas J. *International Relations—The Path Not Taken. Using International Law to Promote World Peace and Security*. Cambridge, UK: Cambridge University Press, 2006.

Weisburd, A. Mark. *Use of Force. The Practice of States since World War II*. University Park, PA: Pennsylvania State University Press, 1997.

Withana, Radhika. *Power, Politics, Law: International Law and State Behaviour During International Crises*. Leiden: Martinus Nijhoff, 2008.

SELECT BIBLIOGRAPHY

Akehurst, Michael. "The Use of Force to Protect Nationals Abroad." *International Relations* 5 (1977): 3–29.

Aldrich, George H. "Taliban, Al Qaeda, and the Determination of Illegal Combatants." *American Journal of International Law* 96, no. 4 (2002): 891–898.

Alexandrov, Stanimir A. *Self-Defence against the Use of Force in International Law*. The Hague: Kluwer, 1996.

Allain, Jean. *A Century of International Adjudication: The Rule of Law and its Limits*. The Hague: T. M. C. Asser Press, 2000.

Ambrosius, Lloyd E. *Woodrow Wilson and the American Diplomatic Tradition: The Treaty Fight in Perspective*. Cambridge: Cambridge University Press, 1987.

Amnesty International. "Draft Comprehensive Convention on International Terrorism: A Threat to Human Rights Standards." Statement to the UN General Assembly 56th Session (2002), October 22, 2002.

Andreu-Guzman. Frederic, ed. *Terrorism and Human Rights No. 2—New Challenges and Old Dangers*, International Commission of Jurists Occasional Papers No. 3. Geneva: International Commission of Jurists 2003.

Annan, Kofi. *In Larger Freedom: Towards Security Development and Human Rights for All*. Report of the United Nations Secretary-General for decision by Heads of State and Government in September 2005. http://www.un.org/largerfreedom/.

———. *Supplement to an Agenda for Peace*. Report by the United Nations Secretary-General, January 25, 1995. UNSC S/1995/1.

Arbour, Louise. "The Responsibility to Protect as a Duty of Care in International Law and Practice." *Review of International Studies* 34 (2008): 445–458.

Arend, Anthony C. "International Law and the Pre-emptive Use of Military Force." *The Washington Quarterly* 26, no. 2 (2003): 89–103.

———, and Robert J. Beck. *International Law and the Use of Force: Beyond the UN Charter Paradigm*. London: Routledge, 1993.

Art, Robert J., and Kenneth N. Waltz, eds. *The Use of Force: Military Power and International Politics*. 7th ed. Lanham, MD: Rowman & Littlefield, 2009.

Barros, James. *Betrayal from Within. Joseph Avenol, Secretary-General of the League of Nations, 1933–1940*. New Haven, CT: Yale University Press, 1969.

Baxter. R. R. "Passage of Ships Through International Waterways in Time of War." *British Year Book of International Law* 31 (1954): 187–216.

Beck, Robert J. *The Grenada Invasion: Politics, Law and Foreign Policy Decision-Making*. Boulder, CO: Westview, 1993.

Bederman, David J. *International Law in Antiquity*. Cambridge, UK: Cambridge University Press, 2001.

Bellamy, Alex J. "Whither the Responsibility to Protect? Humanitarian Intervention and the 2005 World Summit." *Ethics & International Affairs* 20, no. 2 (2006): 143–169.

Beres, Louis R. "Israel and Anticipatory Self Defense." *Arizona Journal of International and Comparative Law* 8, no. 1 (1991): 89–99.

Berger, Stefan, ed. *A Companion to Nineteenth-Century Europe*. Malden, MA: Blackwell Publishing, 2006.

Berkowitz, Peter, ed. *Terrorism, the Laws of War and the Constitution: Debating the Enemy Combatant Cases*. Stanford: Hoover Institution Press, 2005.

Berman, Nathaniel. "Legitimacy through Defiance: From Goa to Iraq [Symposium: Speaking Law to Power: International Law and Foreign Policy]." *Wisconsin International Law Journal* 23 (2005): 93–126.

Bhuta, Nehal. "'Paved with Good Intentions'—Humanitarian War, the New Interventionism and Legal Regulation of the Use of Force." *Melbourne University Law Review* 28 (2001): 843–858.

Bingham, Tony. "The *Alabama* Claims Arbitration." *International and Comparative Law Quarterly* 54 (2005): 1–25.

Blix, Hans. "Oral Introduction of the 12th Quarterly Report of UNMOVIC." UN Security Council, March 7, 2003. http://www.un.org/Depts/unmovic/SC7asdelivered.htm.

———. *Why Nuclear Disarmament Matters*. Cambridge, MA: MIT Press, 2008.

Blumenthal, David A., and Timothy L. H. McCormack, eds. *The Legacy of Nuremberg: Civilising Influence or Institutionalised Vengeance?* Leiden: Martinus Nijhoff, 2008.

Borrie, John, and Vanessa Martin Randin, eds. *Thinking Outside the Box in Multilateral Disarmament and Arms Control Negotiations*. United Nations Institute for Disarmament Research, 2006.

Bothe, Michael. "Terrorism and the Legality of Pre-emptive Force." *European Journal of International Law* 14, no. 2 (2003): 227–240.

———, Mary Ellen O'Connell, and Natalino Ronzitti, eds. *International Law and the Use of Force after the Cold War*. Ardsley, NY: Transnational, 2005.

Bourantonis, Dimitris, Ifantis Kostas, and Tsakanos Panayotis, eds. *Multilateralism and Security Institutions in an Era of Globalization*. London: Routledge, 2008.

Bowett, Derek W. "Collective Self-Defence under the Charter of the United Nations." *British Yearbook of International Law* 32 (1955–56): 130–161.

———. *Self Defence in International Law*. Manchester: Manchester University Press, 1958.

Bowring, Bill. *The Denigration of the International Legal Order?* Oxford: Routledge-Cavendish, 2008.

Boyle, Francis A. "The Relevance of International Law to the 'Paradox' of Nuclear Deterrence," *Northwestern University Law Review* 80, no. 6 (1986): 1407–1448.

Brackman, Arnold C. *The Other Nuremberg: The Untold Story of the Tokyo War Crimes Trials*. New York: Morrow, 1987.

Brierly, James L. *The Covenant and the Charter* (Cambridge, UK: Cambridge University Press, 1947): 23.

Brown, Chris, Nardin Terry, and Nicholas Rengger, eds. *International Relations in Political Thought. Texts from the Ancient Greeks to the First World War.* Cambridge: Cambridge University Press, 2002.

Brown-John, Lloyd. "The 1974 Definition of Aggression: A Query." *Canadian Yearbook of International Law* 15 (1977): 301–317.

Brownlie, Ian. *International Law and the Use of Force by States.* Oxford: Clarendon Press, 1963.

Bugnion, Francois. "The International Committee of the Red Cross and Nuclear Weapons: from Hiroshima to the Dawn of the 21st Century." *International Review of the Red Cross* 87, no. 859 (2005): 511–524.

Bulloch, John, and Harvey Morris. *Saddam's War: Origins of the Kuwait Conflict and the International Response.* London: Faber and Faber, 1991.

Buscher, Frank M. *The US War Crimes Trial Program in Germany, 1946–1955.* New York: Greenwood Press, 1989.

Byers, Michael. "Preemptive Self-defense: Hegemony, Equality and Strategies of Legal Change." *Journal of Political Philosophy* 11, no. 2 (2003): 171–190.

———. "Terrorism, the Use of Force and International Law after 11 September." *International and Comparative Law Quarterly* 51, no. 2 (2002): 401–414.

———. *War Law: Understanding International Law and Armed Conflicts.* New York: Grove, 2005.

Byrn-Jones, David. *Frank B. Kellogg: A Biography.* New York: Putnam, 1937.

Caron, David D. "War and International Adjudication: Reflections on the 1899 Peace Conference." *American Journal of International Law* 94 (2000): 4–30.

Carr, Edward Hallet. *The Twenty Years' Crisis 1919–1939.* London: Macmillan, 1940.

Cassese, Antonio. *International Criminal Law.* 2nd ed. Oxford: Oxford University Press, 2008.

———. "Terrorism is Also Disrupting Some Crucial Legal Categories of International Law." *European Journal of International Law* 12, no. 5 (2001): 993–1001.

———. *Terrorism, Politics and Law: The Achille Lauro Affair.* London: Polity, 1989.

Ceadel, Martin. *The Origins of War Prevention: the British Peace Movement and International Relations, 1730–1854.* Oxford: Clarendon, 1996.

Chadwick, Elizabeth. *Traditional Neutrality Revisited: Law, Theory and Case Studies.* The Hague: Kluwer, 2002.

Charter of the Organisation of African Unity, 1963. http://www.africa-union.org/root/au/Documents/Treaties/text/OAU_Charter_1963.pdf.

Chatfield, Charles. *The American Peace Movement. Ideals and Activism.* New York: Twayne, 1992.

Chatterjee, S. K. "Some Legal Problems of Support Role in International Law: Tanzania and Uganda." *International and Comparative Law Quarterly* 30, no. 4 (1981): 755–768.

Chesterman, Simon. "Humanitarian Intervention and Afghanistan." In Jennifer M. Welsh, ed. *Humanitarian Intervention and International Relations.* Oxford: Oxford University Press, 2006, 163–175.

Claude, Inis L. *Swords into Plowshares.* New York: Random House, 1964.

Clements, Kendrick A. *Woodrow Wilson, World Statesman.* rev. ed. Chicago: IR Dee, 1999.

"Coalition of the Willing? Make That War Criminals." *Sydney Morning Herald*, 26 February 2003. http://www.smh.com.au/articles/2003/02/25/1046064028608.html.

"Congress and the United Nations Must Act to Stop an Illegal War Against Iraq." *Western States Legal Foundation*, March 17, 2003. www.wslfweb.org/docs/statement317.pdf.

Constitutive Act of the African Union, 2000. http://www.au2002.gov.za/docs/key_oau/au_act.htm.

Coogan, John W. *The End of Neutrality: The United States, Britain, and Maritime Rights, 1899–1915.* Ithaca, NY: Cornell University Press, 1981.

Cooper, John Milton. *Breaking the Heart of the World: Woodrow Wilson and the Fight for the League of Nations*. Cambridge, UK: Cambridge University Press, 2001.

Cumings, Bruce. *The Origins of the Korean War: II, the Roaring of the Cataract, 1947–1950*. Princeton, NJ: Princeton University Press, 1990.

D'Amato, Anthony. "Israel's Air Strike upon the Iraqi Nuclear Reactor." *American Journal of International Law* 77, no. 3 (1983): 584–588.

D'Angelo, John R. "Resort to Force by States to Protect Nationals: The US Rescue Mission to Iran and Its Legality under International Law." *Virginia Journal of International Law* 21 (1981): 485–519.

Darnton, John. "A Victory for Tanzania: a Worry for Africa," *New York Times* (April 16, 1979): A8.

Davies, R. W. "Edward Hallett Carr 1892–1982." *Proceedings of the British Academy* 69 (1983): 473–511.

Davis, Calvin DeArmond. *The United States and the First Hague Peace Conference*. Ithaca, NY: Cornell University Press, 1962.

DiFilippo, Anthony. *Japan's Nuclear Disarmament Policy and the US Security Umbrella*. New York: Palgrave Macmillan, 2006.

Dinstein, Yoram. "Comments on War." *Harvard Journal of Law and Public Policy*. 27 (2003–2004): 877–892.

———. *War, Aggression and Self-defence*. 4th ed. Cambridge, UK: Cambridge University Press, 2005.

Dixon, Martin, and Robert McCorquodale, *Cases and Materials on International Law*. 3rd ed. London: Blackstone Press, 2000.

Drumbl, Mark A. "Self-Defense and the Use of Force: Breaking the Rules, Making the Rules, or Both?" *International Studies Perspectives* 4, no. 4 (2003): 409–431.

Egan, Patrick T. "The Kosovo Intervention and Collective Self-Defence." *International Peacekeeping* 8, no. 3 (2001): 39–58.

Elagab, Omer, and Jeehan Elagab, eds. *International Law Documents Relating to Terrorism*. 3rd ed. London: Routledge-Cavendish, 2007.

Enemark, Christian, and Christopher Michaelsen. "Just War Doctrine and the Invasion of Iraq," *Australian Journal of Politics and History* 51, no.4 (2005): 545–563.

Epstein, Leon D. "Partisan Foreign Policy: Britain in the Suez Crisis," *World Politics* 12, no. 3 (1960): 201–224.

Evans, Gareth. "The Responsibility to Protect: an Idea Whose Time has Come . . . and Gone?" *International Relations* 22, no. 3 (2008): 283–298.

Evans, Graham, and Jeffrey Newnham. *The Penguin Dictionary of International Relations*. London: Penguin, 1998.

Evans, Mark. Ed. *Just War Theory: A Reappraisal*. Edinburgh: Edinburgh University Press, 2005.

Eyffinger, Arthur. *The 1899 Hague Peace Conference: "The Parliament of Man, the Federation of the World."* The Hague: Kluwer Law International, 1999.

Falk, Richard A. "Kosovo, World Order and the Future of International Law." *American Journal of International Law* 93, no. 4 (1999): 847–857.

———. "Nuclear Weapons, International Law and the World Court: A Historic Encounter." *American Journal of International Law* 91, no. 1 (1997): 64–74.

———. *The Costs of War. International Law, the UN, and World Order after Iraq*. New York: Routledge, 2008.

Fassbender, Bardo, *Targeted Sanctions and Due Process*. Berlin: Humboldt-Universität zu Berlin, 2006. http://www.un.org/law/counsel/Fassbender_study.pdf.

Ferencz, Benjamin B. "The United Nations Consensus Definition of Aggression: Sieve or Substance?" *Journal of International Law and Economics* 10, no. 2 (1975): 701–724.

Ferrell, Robert H. *Peace in Their Time: The Origins of the Kellogg-Briand Pact.* Hamden, CT: Archon Books, 1968.

———. "The Peace Movement." In Alexander DeConde, ed. *Isolation and Security*. Durham, NC: Duke University Press, 1957.

Fisher, Eugene M., and M. Cherif Bassiouni. *Storm over the Arab World*. Chicago: Follett, 1972.

Fisk, Robert. *The Great War for Civilisation: the Conquest of the Middle East.* London: Fourth Estate, 2005.

Fleming, Denna Frank. *The United States and the League of Nations, 1918–1920*. New York: G. P. Putnam's Sons, 1932.

Franck, Thomas M. "The Power of Legitimacy and the Legitimacy of Power: International Law in an Age of Power Disequilibrium." *American Journal of International Law* 100, no. 1 (2006): 88–106.

———. "Who Killed Article 2(4)? Or: Changing Norms Governing the Use of Force by States." *American Journal of International Law* 64, no. 4, (1970): 809–836.

Freedman, Lawrence, and Efraim Karsh. *The Gulf Conflict: 1990–1991*. Princeton, NJ: Princeton University Press, 1993.

Friedrichs, Jörg. "Defining the International Public Enemy: The Political Struggle Behind the Legal Debate on International Terrorism." *Leiden Journal of International Law* 19, no. 1 (2006): 69–91.

Gageby, Douglas. *The Last Secretary-General: Sean Lester and the League of Nations*. Dublin: Town House, 1999.

Garvey, Jack I. "The UN Definition of 'Aggression': Law and Illusion in the Context of Collective Security." *Virginia Journal of International Law* 17, no. 2 (1977): 177–199.

Gazzini, Tarcisio. *The Changing Rules on the Use of Force in International Law*. Manchester: Juris, 2005.

Gill, Terry D. "The Second Gulf Crisis and the Relation between Collective Security and Collective Self-Defense." *Grotiana* 10, no. 1 (1989): 47–76.

Glennon, Michael J. *Limits of Law. Prerogatives of Power: Interventionism after Kosovo*. New York: Palgrave, 2001.

———. "The Fog of Law: Self-Defense, Inherence and Incoherence in Article 51 of the United Nations Charter." *Harvard Journal of Law and Public Policy* 25, no. 2 (2002): 539–558.

———. "The New Interventionism." *Foreign Affairs* 78, no. 3 (1999): 2–7.

———, and Serge Sur, eds. *Terrorism and International Law*. Leiden: Martinus Nijhoff, 2008.

Golan, Galia. *Reform Rule in Czechoslovakia: the Dubcek Era, 1968–1969*. Cambridge, UK: Cambridge University Press, 1973.

———. *The Czechoslovak Reform Movement: Communism in Crisis, 1962–1968*. Cambridge, UK: Cambridge University Press, 1971.

Goldsmith, Peter. "Advice to British Government on the legality of military action against Iraq," March 7, 2003. http://www.ico.gov.uk/upload/documents/library/freedom_of_information/notices/annex_a_-_attorney_general's_advice_070303.pdf.

Goodman, Ryan. "Humanitarian Intervention and Pretexts for War." *American Journal of International Law* 100, no. 1 (2006): 107–141.

Goodrich, Leland M. "From League of Nations to United Nations." *International Organization* 1 (1947): 3–21.

Goulden, Joseph C. *Korea: The Untold Story of the Korean War*. New York: Times Books, 1982.

Granoff, Jonathan. "Nuclear Weapons, Ethics, Morals and Law." *Brigham Young University Law Review* (2000): 1413–1442.

Gray, Christine. *International Law and the Use of Force*. 2nd ed. Oxford: Oxford University Press, 2004.

———. "The US National Security Strategy and the New 'Bush Doctrine' on Preemptive Self-Defense." *Chinese Journal of International Law* 1, no. 2 (2002): 437–448.

Greenwood, Christopher-. "International Law and the 'War against Terrorism'." *International Affairs* 78, no. 2 (2002): 301–317.

———. "The Concept of War in Modern International Law." *International and Comparative Law Quarterly* 36 (1987): 283–306.

Greig, Don W. "Self-Defence and the Security Council: What Does Article 51 Require?" *International Comparative Law Quarterly* 40 (1991): 366–402.

Grosek, Edward. *The Secret Treaties of History*. Buffalo, New York: William S. Hein & Co., 2007.

Gross, Leo. "The Charter of the United Nations and the Lodge Reservations." *American Journal of International Law* 41 (1947): 531–554.

Guicherd, Catherine. "International Law and the War in Kosovo." *Survival* 41, no. 2 (1999): 19–33.

Guillaume, Gilbert. "Terrorism and International Law." *International and Comparative Law Quarterly* 53, no. 3 (2004): 537–48.

Gupta, Sanjay. "The Doctrine of Pre-emptive Strike: Application and Implications during the Administration of President George W. Bush." *International Political Science Review* 29, no. 2 (2008): 181–196.

Hahn, Peter L. "The Suez Crisis: A Crisis That Changed the Balance of Power in the Middle East," May 8, 2008. http://www.america.gov/st/peacesec-english/2008/May/20080522120851WRybakcuH0.4956781.html.

Halberstam, David. *The Coldest Winter: America and the Korean War*. New York: Hyperion, 2007.

Hall, William Edward. *The Rights and Duties of Neutrals*. London: Longmans, 1874.

Halliday, Dennis J. "Iraq and the UN's weapon of mass destruction." *Current History* 98 (1999): 65–68.

Hargrove, John L. "The *Nicaragua* Judgment and the Future of the Law of Force and Self-defense." *American Journal of International Law* 81, no. 2 (1987): 135–152.

Harris, George C. "Terrorism, War and Justice: The Concept of the Unlawful Enemy Combatant." *Loyola of Los Angeles International & Comparative Law Review* 26, no. 1 (2003): 31–46.

Hemleben, Sylvester John. *Plans for World Peace Through Six Centuries*. Chicago: University of Chicago Press, 1943.

Henkin, Louis. "The Invasion of Panama under International Law: A Gross Violation." *Columbia Journal of Transnational Law* 29 (1991): 293–317.

———. "The Reports of the Death of Article 2(4) Are Greatly Exaggerated." *American Journal of International Law* 65, no. 3 (1971): 544–548.

Herz, John H. "Idealist Internationalism and the Security Dilemma." *World Politics* 2 (1950): 157–180.

Heykal, Mohammed H. *Cutting the Lion's Tail: Suez Through Egyptian Eyes*. London: Andre Deutsch, 1986.

Higgins, Rosalyn. *Problems and Process: International Law and How We Use It*. Oxford: Clarendon Press, 1994.

———, and Maurice Flory, eds. *Terrorism and International Law*. London: Routledge, 1997.

Hilpold, Peter. "Humanitarian Intervention: Is There a Need for a Legal Reappraisal?" *European Journal of International Law* 12, no. 3 (2001): 437–467.

Hoopes, Townsend, and Douglas Brinkley, *FDR and the Creation of the UN*. New Haven, CT: Yale University Press, 1997.

Hovell, Devika. "Chinks in the Armour: International Law, Terrorism and the Use of Force." *UNSW Law Journal* 27, no. 2 (2004): 398–427.

Hurst, Michael, ed. *Key Treaties for the Great Powers 1814–1914*. 2 vols. Newton Abbot: David & Charles, 1972.

International Commission on Intervention and State Sovereignty. *The Responsibility to Protect*. 2001. http://www.iciss.ca/report2-en.asp.

International Court of Justice. "Legality of the Threat or Use of Nuclear Weapons." Advisory Opinion of 8 July 1996. *ICJ Reports* 1996.

———. "Submission by Belgium to the International Court of Justice." 10 May 1999. http://www.icj-cij.org/docket/files/105/4515.pdf.

———. "The Corfu Channel Case," *Summaries of Judgements*, Judgement of 9 April 1949, p. 7. http://www.icj-cij.org/docket/files/1/1647.pdf.

Janis, Mark Weston. *The American Tradition of International Law: Great Expectations, 1789–1914*. Oxford: Clarendon, 2004.

Jennings, Robert Y. "The *Caroline* and McLeod Cases." *American Journal of International Law* 32, no. 1 (1938): 82–99.

Jervis, Robert. "Was the Cold War a Security Dilemma?" *Journal of Cold War Studies* 3, no. 1 (2001): 36–60.

Johnson, D. H. N. "Some Legal Problems of International Waterways, with Particular Reference to the Straits of Tiran and the Suez Canal." *Modern Law Review* 31, no. 2 (1968): 153–164.

Josephson, Harold. *James T. Shotwell and the Rise of Internationalism in America*. London: Associated University Presses, 1975.

———. "Outlawing War: Internationalism and the Pact of Paris." *Diplomatic History* 3, no. 4 (1979): 377–390.

Joyner, Christopher C. "United States Action in Grenada: Reflections on the Lawfulness of Invasion." *American Journal of International Law* 78, no. 1 (1984): 121–144.

Kaplan, Neil J. "The Attack on Osirak: Delimitation of Self-Defense under International Law." *New York Law School Journal of International and Comparative Law* 4 (1982–83): 131–156.

Karoubi, Mohammad Taghi. *Just or Unjust War? International Law and Unilateral Use of Armed Force by States at the Turn of the 20th Century*. Aldershot: Hants, 2004.

Kaysen, Carl, Robert S. McNamara, and George W. Rathjens. "Nuclear Weapons after the Cold War." *Foreign Affairs* 70, no. 4 (1991): 95–110.

Keeton, Edward David. *Briand's Locarno Policy. French Economics, Politics, and Diplomacy, 1925–1929*. New York: Garland, 1987.

Kelsen, Hans. "Collective Security and Collective Self-Defense under the Charter of the United Nations." *American Journal of International Law* 42, no. 2 (1948): 783–796.

Kusin, Vladimir. *The Intellectual Origins of The Prague Spring; The Development of Reformist Ideas in Czechoslovakia, 1956–1967*. Cambridge, UK: Cambridge University Press, 1971.

LaFeber, Walter. *The American Age. US Foreign Policy at Home and Abroad, 1750 to the Present*. 2nd ed. New York: W.W. Norton, 1989.

Lambert, Joseph J. *Terrorism and Hostages in International Law: A Commentary on the Hostages Convention 1979*. Cambridge, UK: Grotius Publications, 1990.

Larsen, Jeffrey Arthur, and James M. Smith. *Historical Dictionary of Arms Control and Disarmament*. Lanham, MD: Scarecrow Press, 2005.

Lauterpacht, Eli. "The Contemporary Practice of the United Kingdom in the Field of International Law. Survey and Comment III. August 16–December 31, 1956." *International and Comparative Law Quarterly* 6, no. 2 (1957): 301–336.

Legum, Colin, ed. *Africa Contemporary Record*, London: Africana Publishing Co., Vol. XI, 1980.

Lifton, Robert J., and Richard Falk. *Indefensible Weapons*. Toronto: Canadian Broadcasting Commission, 1982.

Lloyd, Lorna. *Peace Through Law. Britain and the International Court in the 1920s*. Woodbridge, UK: Boydell, 1997.

Lobe, Jim. "Law Groups Say US Invasion Illegal," *Common Dreams News Centre* 21 March 2003, http://www.commondreams.org/headlines03/0321-10.htm.

Lodge, Henry Cabot. *The Senate and the League of Nations*. New York: Scribner, 1925.

Lowe, Vaughan, et al., Adam Roberts, Jennifer Walsh, and Dominik Zaum, eds. The United Nations Security Council and War: The Evolution of Thought and Practice since 1945. Oxford: Oxford University Press, 2008.

Luck, Edward C., *UN Security Council: Practice and Promise*. London: Routledge, 2006.

Maier, Harold. G. ed. "Appraisals of the ICJ's Decision: *Nicaragua v. United States* (Merits)." *American Journal of International Law* 81 (1987): 77–183.

Malanczuk, Peter, ed. *Akehurst's Modern Introduction to International Law*. 7th ed. New York: Routledge, 1997.

Malkasian, Carter. *The Korean War: Essential Histories*. London: Osprey, 2008.

Marston, Geoffrey. "Armed Intervention in the 1956 Suez Canal Crisis: the Legal Advice Tendered to the British Government," *International and Comparative Law Quarterly*, 37, no. 4 (1988): 773–817.

Martel, Joll, and James Gordon. *The Origins of the First World War*, 3rd ed. New York: Pearson Longman, 2007.

Matheson, Michael J. "Opinions of the International Court of Justice on the Threat or Use of Nuclear Weapons." *American Journal of International Law* 91, no. 3 (1997): 417–435.

McCormack, Timothy L. H. "Anticipatory Self-Defence in the Legislative History of the United Nations Charter." *Israel Law Review* 25, no. 1 (1991): 1–42.

McWhinney, Edward. *The September 11 Terrorist Attacks and the Invasion of Iraq in Contemporary International Law*. Leiden: Martinus Nijhoff, 2004.

McWilliams, Wayne C., and Harry Piotrowski. *The World Since 1945*. Boulder, CO: Lynne Rienner, 2005.

Mearsheimer, John J. "Nuclear Weapons and Deterrence in Europe." *International Security* 9, no. 3 (1984–1985): 19–46.

Mee, Charles L., Jr. *The End of Order. Versailles 1919*. London: Secker & Warburg, 1981.

Meisler, Stanley. *United Nations: The First Fifty Years*. New York: The Atlantic Monthly Press, 1995.

Meltzer, Bernard D. "A Note on Some Aspects of the Nuremberg Debate." *University of Chicago Law Review* 14, no.3 (1947): 455–469.

Merrills, J. G. *International Dispute Settlement*. 4th ed. Cambridge, UK: Cambridge University Press, 2005.

Mettraux, Guénaël, ed. *Perspectives on the Nuremberg Trial*. Oxford: Oxford University Press, 2008.

Miller, Arthur S., and Martin Feinrider. *Nuclear Weapons and Law*. Westport, CT, and London: Greenwood Press, 1984.

Miller, David H. *The Drafting of the Covenant*, 2 vols. New York: G. P. Putnam's Sons, 1928.

———. *The Peace Pact of Paris. A Study of the Briand-Kellogg Treaty*. New York: G. P. Putnam's Sons, 1928.

Miller, Lynn H. "The Contemporary Significance of the Doctrine of Just War." *World Politics* 16, no. 2 (1964): 254–286.

Moorehouse, Frank. *Dark Palace: The Companion Novel to Grand Days*. Milsons Point, Australia: Random House, 2000.

———. *Grand Days*. Chippendale, Australia: Pan Macmillan, 1993.

Munro, Hector A. "The Case of the Corfu Minefield." *Modern Law Review* 10, no. 4 (1947): 363–376.

Murphy, Cornelius F., Jr. *The Search for World Order. A Study of Thought and Action*. Dordrecht: Martinus Nijhoff, 1985.

Murphy, Sean D. *Humanitarian Intervention: the United Nations in an Evolving World Order*. Philadelphia: University of Pennsylvania Press, 1996.

———. "Terrorism and the Concept of Armed Attack in Article 51 of the UN Charter." *Harvard International Law Journal* 43, no. 1 (2002): 41–63.

Murray, Gilbert. *From the League to UN*. London: Oxford University Press, 1948.

Myers, Denys P. *Handbook of the League of Nations. A Comprehensive Account of its Structure, Operation and Activities*. Boston: World Peace Foundation, 1935.

———, and Paul J. G. D'Arcy, eds. *The Secret Treaties of Austria-Hungary Vol. I. Texts of the Treaties and Agreements*. Cambridge, MA: Harvard University Press, 1920.

Nanda, Ved P. *Nuclear Weapons and the World Court*. Ardlsey, NY: Transnational, 1998.

Nasaw, David. *Andrew Carnegie*. New York: Penguin, 2006.

Neff, Stephen C. *War and the Law of Nations. A General History*. Cambridge, UK: Cambridge University Press, 2005.

Negroponte, John. "Speech to UN Security Council," 8 November 2002. http://usinfo.org/wf-archive/2002/021108/epf503.htm.

Nutting, Anthony. *Nasser*. London: Constable, 1972.

O'Connell, Mary Ellen. *International Law and the Use of Force: Cases and Materials*. 2nd ed. New York: Foundation, 2009.

———. *The Power and Purpose of International Law: Insights from the Theory and Practice of Enforcement*. Oxford: Oxford University Press, 2008.

O'Neill, Brendan. "Blair's Dodgy Dossier: Britain's Evidence of an Iraqi Threat Is as Weak as the Opposition to War." *Spiked* (September 24, 2002). http://www.spiked-online.com/Articles/00000006DA63.htm.

Patel, Bimal N. *The World Court Reference Guide. Judgments, Advisory Opinions and Orders of the Permanent Court of International Justice and the International Court of Justice (1922–2000)*. The Hague: Kluwer, 2002.

Paul, David W. "Soviet Foreign Policy and the Invasion of Czechoslovakia." *International Studies Quarterly* 15, no. 2 (1971): 159–202.

Paust, Jordan J. *Beyond the Law: The Bush Administration's Unlawful Responses in the "War" on Terror*. Cambridge, UK: Cambridge University Press, 2007.

———. "There Is No Need to Revise the Laws of War in Light of September 11th." *The American Society of International Law Task Force Papers on Terrorism*. November 2002. http://www.asil.org/taskforce/paust.pdf.

———. "War and Enemy Status after 9/11." *Yale Journal of International Law* 28, no. 2 (2003): 325–335.

Pedersen, Susan. "Review Essay: Back to the League of Nations." *The American Historical Review* 112 (2007). http://www.historycooperative.org/journals/ahr/112.4/pedersen.html.

Politi, Mauro, and Guiseppe Nesi, eds. *The International Criminal Court and the Crime of Aggression*. Aldershot, UK: Ashgate, 2004.

———, eds. *The Rome Statute of the International Criminal Court: A Challenge to Impunity.* Aldershot, UK: Ashgate, 2001.

Polk, William R. *Understanding Iraq.* London: I. B. Tauris, 2005.

Ralston, Jackson H. *International Arbitration, from Athens to Locarno.* Stanford, CA: Stanford University Press, 1929.

Ramraj, Victor V., Michael Hor, and Kent Roach, eds. *Global Anti-Terrorism Law and Policy.* Cambridge, UK: Cambridge University Press, 2005.

Randelzhoffer, Albrecht. "Article 2(4)." In Bruno Simma, ed. *The Charter of the United Nations. A Commentary.* Oxford: Oxford University Press, 1994, 111.

———. "Article 51." In Bruno Simma, ed. *The Charter of the United Nations. A Commentary,* 2nd ed. Oxford: Oxford University Press, 2002, 788–806.

Reisman, W. Michael. "Nuclear Weapons in International Law." *New York Law School Journal of International and Comparative Law* 4 (1982–1983): 339–343.

Rengger, Nicholas. "On the Just War Tradition in the Twenty-First Century." *International Affairs* 78 no. 2 (2002): 353–363.

Richardson, Louise. "The Concert of Europe and Security Management in the Nineteenth Century." In Helga Haftendorn, Robert O. Keohane, and Celeste A. Wallander. *Imperfect Unions: Security Institutions over Time and Space.* Oxford: Oxford University Press, 1999, 48–79.

Roberts, Adam. "Law and the Use of Force after Iraq." *Survival* 45, no. 2 (2003): 31–56.

Röling, B. V. A. "The 1974 UN Definition of Aggression." In Antonio Cassese, ed. *The Current Legal Regulation of the Use of Force.* Dordrecht: Martinus Nijhoff, 1986, 413–422.

Ronzitti, Natalino. "Lessons of International Law from NATO's Armed Intervention against the Federal Republic of Yugoslavia." *The International Spectator,* XXXIV, no. 3 (1999): 45–54.

———. ed. *Maritime Terrorism and International Law.* Dordrecht: Martinus Nijhoff, 1990.

———. *Rescuing Nationals Abroad Through Military Coercion and Intervention on Grounds of Humanity.* Dordrecht: Martinus Nijhoff, 1985.

Rosand, Eric. "Security Council Resolution 1373, the Counter-Terrorism Committee, and the Fight against Terrorism." *American Journal of International Law* 97, no. 2 (2003): 333–341.

Rosenne, Shabtai. "International Court of Justice." In Rüdiger Wolfrum, ed. *Max Planck Encyclopedia of Public International Law.* Oxford: Oxford University Press, 2008. online edition, http://www.mpepil.com/.

———, with the assistance of Yaël Ronen. *The Law and Practice of the International Court, 1920–2005.* 4th ed. Leiden: Martinus Nijhoff, 2006.

Ruggie, John. "The UN and the Collective Use of Force: Whither or Whether?" *International Peacekeeping* 3, no. 4 (1996): 1–20.

Sands, Philippe. *Lawless World. America and the Making and Breaking of Global Rules from FDR's Atlantic Charter to George W. Bush's Illegal War.* Camberwell, Australia: Allen Lane, 2005.

Sapiro, Miriam. "Iraq: The Shifting Sands of Preemptive Self-Defense." *American Journal of International Law* 97, no. 3 (2003): 599–607.

Sarkees, Meredith Reid, Frank Whelon Wayman, and J. David Singer. "Inter-State, Intra-State, and Extra-State Wars: A Comprehensive Look at Their Distribution over Time, 1816–1997." *International Studies Quarterly* 47 (2003): 49–70.

Saul, Ben. *Defining Terrorism in International Law.* Oxford: Oxford University Press, 2006.

Schachter, Oscar. "Self-Defense and the Rule of Law." *American Journal of International Law* 83, no. 2 (1989): 259–77.

———. "The Right of States to Use Armed Force," *Michigan Law Review* 82, no. 5/6 (1984): 1620–1646.

Scharf, Michael P. "Results of the Rome Conference for an International Criminal Court." *American Society of International Law—Insights*, August 1998, http://www.asil.org/insigh23.cfm.

Schild, Georg. "The Roosevelt Administration and the United Nations: Re-creation or Rejection of the League Experience?" *World Affairs* 158 (1995): 26–34.

Schlesinger, Stephen C. *Act of Creation. The Founding of the United Nations. A Story of Superpowers, Secret Agents, Wartime Allies and Enemies, and Their Quest for a Peaceful World*. Boulder, CO: Westview Press, 2003.

Schlochauer, Hans-Jürgen. "Arbitration." In Rudolf Bernhardt, ed. *Encyclopedia of Public International Law* Instalment 1 (1981): 16.

Schmitt, Michael N. "US Security Strategies: A Legal Assessment." *Harvard Journal of Law & Public Policy* 27, no. 3 (2004): 737–764.

Schoenbaum, Thomas J. *International Relations—The Path Not Taken. Using International Law to Promote World Peace and Security*. Cambridge, UK: Cambridge University Press, 2006.

Scott, Shirley V., ed. *International Law and Politics. Key Documents*. Boulder, CO: 2006.

———, and Radhika Withana. "The Relevance of International Law for Foreign Policy When National Security is at Stake: Lessons from the Cuban Missile Crisis." *Chinese Journal of International Law* 3 (2004): 163–187.

Shotwell, James T. *War as an Instrument of National Policy and Its Renunciation in the Pact of Paris*. New York: Harcourt, Brace and Company, 1929.

Simma, Bruno, ed. *The Charter of the United Nations. A Commentary*. 2nd ed. New York: Oxford University Press, 2002.

Singh, Nagendra. "The Right to Self-Defense in Relation to the Use of Nuclear Weapons." *Indian Yearbook of International Affairs* 5 (1956): 3–37.

———, and Edward McWhinney. *Nuclear Weapons and Contemporary International Law*. The Hague: Martinus Nijhoff, 1989.

Smith, Bradley F., ed. *The American Road to Nuremberg: The Documentary Record, 1944–1945*. Stanford: Hoover Institution Press, 1982.

Smith, Michael. "Blair Planned Iraq War from Start." *Sunday Times* (May 1, 2005). http://www.timesonline.co.uk/article/0,,2087-1592724,00.html.

Sobel, Russell S. "The League of Nations Covenant and the United Nations Charter: An Analysis of Two International Constitutions." *Constitutional Political Economy* 5, no. 2 (1994): 173–192.

Spiermann, Ole. "'Who Attempts Too Much Does Nothing Well': The 1920 Advisory Committee of Jurists and the Statute of the Permanent Court of International Justice." *British Yearbook of International Law* 73 (2002): 187–260.

Stahn, Carsten. "Terrorist Acts as 'Armed Attack': The Right to Self-Defense, Article 51 (1/2) of the UN Charter, and International Terrorism." *Fletcher Forum of World Affairs* 27, no. 2 (2003): 35–53.

Starr, Harvey. "A Collective Goods Analysis of the Warsaw Pact after Czechoslovakia." *International Organization* 28, no. 3 (1974): 521–523.

Stone, Julius. *Aggression and World Order: A Critique of United Nations Theories of Aggression*. London: Stevens, 1958.

———. "Hopes and Loopholes in the 1974 Definition of Aggression." *American Journal of International Law* 71, no. 2 (1977): 224–246.

Taft, William H., and Todd F. Buchwald. "Pre-emption, Iraq and International Law." *American Journal of International Law* 97, no. 3 (2003): 557–563.

Terry, James P. "The Panama Intervention: Law in Support of Policy." *Naval Law Review* 39, no. 4 (1990): 110–118.

Ticehurst, Rupert. "The Martens Clause and the Laws of Armed Conflict." *International Review of the Red Cross* 317 (April 30, 1997): 125–134.

Ulfstein, Geir. "Terrorism and the Use of Force." *Security Dialogue* 34, no. 2 (2003): 153–167.

United Nations. "Declaration of Principles of International Law Concerning Friendly Relations and Co-operation among States in Accordance with the Charter of the United Nations," United Nations General Assembly Resolution 2625 (XXV). October 24, 1970.

Van Krieken, Peter J., and David McKay, eds. *The Hague—Legal Capital of the World.* Cambridge, UK: Cambridge University Press, 2005.

Verzijl, J. H. W. *International Law in Historical Perspective. Part IX-B The Law of Neutrality.* Akogeb aab den Rijn: Sijthoff & Noordhoff, 1979.

Walter, Christian, Silja Vöneky, Volker Röben, and Frank Schorkopf, eds. *Terrorism as a Challenge for National and International Law: Security versus Liberty?* Berlin: Springer, 2004.

Waltz, Kenneth. "The Spread of Nuclear Weapons: More May Be Better." *Adelphi Papers* No. 171. London: International Institute for Strategic Studies, 1981.

Walzer, Michael. *Just and Unjust Wars: A Moral Argument with Historical Illustrations.* New York: Basic Books, 1977.

Wanhong, Zhang. "From Nuremberg to Tokyo: Some Reflections on the Tokyo Trial (On the Sixtieth Anniversary of the Nuremberg Trials)." *Cardozo Law Review* 27, no. 4 (2005–2006): 1673–82.

Weisburd, A. Mark. *Use of Force. The Practice of States Since World War II.* University Park: Pennsylvania State University Press, 1997.

Werke, Gerhard. *Principles of International Criminal Law.* The Hague: T. M. C. Asser Press, 2005.

Weston, Burns H. "Nuclear Weapons versus International Law: A Contextual Reassessment." *McGill Law Journal* 28 (1982–1983): 542–590.

Wheeler, Nicholas J. *Saving Strangers: Humanitarian Intervention in International Society.* Oxford: Oxford University Press, 2002.

Wiltz, John E. *From Isolation to War, 1931–1941.* London: Routledge and Kegan Paul, 1968.

Withana, Radhika. *Power, Politics, Law: International Law and State Behaviour During International Crises.* Leiden: Martinus Nijhoff, 2008.

Witten, Samuel M. "The International Convention for the Suppression of Terrorist Bombings." *American Journal of International Law* 92, no. 4 (1998): 774–781.

Wright, Quincy. "The Corfu Channel Case." *American Journal of International Law* 43, no. 3 (1949): 491–494.

———. "The Goa Incident." *American Journal of International Law* 56 (1962): 617–632.

———. *The Role of International Law in the Elimination of War.* Manchester, UK: Manchester University Press, 1961.

Ziegler, David W. *War, Peace, and International Politics.* 5th ed. Glenview, IL: Scott Foresman, 1989.

Zimmern, Alfred. *The League of Nations and the Rule of Law, 1918–1935.* Holmes Beach, FL.: Gaunt, 1998.

Young, John W., and John Kent. *International Relations since 1945.* Oxford: Oxford University Press, 2004.

Ziring, L., Robert E. Riggs, and Jack C. Plano, *The United Nations. International Organization and World Politics.* 4th ed. Belmont, CA: Thomson Wadsworth, 2005.

ELECTRONIC RESOURCES

Basic Documents

Second Peace Conference: The Hague, 18 October 1907
http://www.icrc.org/ihl.nsf/FULL/185?OpenDocument

The second Hague Convention was the first formal agreement about law of war, the use of weapons, war crimes. and neutrality.

The Charter of the United Nations
http://www.un.org/aboutun/charter/

The Covenant of the League of Nations
http://avalon.law.yale.edu/20th_century/leagcov.asp

Treaty on the Non-Proliferation of Nuclear Weapons (NPT)
http://www.un.org/events/npt2005/npttreaty.html

The Kellogg-Briand Pact 1928
http://www.yale.edu/lawweb/avalon/imt/kbpact.htm

The 1949 Geneva Conventions and their 1977 and 2005 Additional Protocols
http://www.icrc.org/Web/Eng/siteeng0.nsf/html/genevaconventions

"The Responsibility to Protect": Report of the International Commission on Intervention and State Sovereignty
http://www.iciss.ca/report-en.asp

This report is about the so-called "right of humanitarian intervention": the question of when, if ever, it is appropriate for states for take coercive—and, in particular, military—action, against another state for the purpose of protecting people at risk in that other state. The report's central theme is "The Responsibility to Protect," the idea that sovereign states have a responsibility to protect their own citizens from avoidable catastrophe, but that when they are unwilling or unable to do so, that responsibility must be borne by the broader community of states.

United States Federal Agencies and Departments

White House
http://www.whitehouse.gov/

National Security Council
http://www.whitehouse.gov/administration/cop/nsc/

The National Security Council (NSC) is the President's principal forum for considering national security and foreign policy matters with his senior national security advisors and cabinet officials. Since its inception under President Truman, the Council's function has been to advise and assist the President on national security and foreign policies. The Council also serves as the President's principal arm for coordinating these policies among various government agencies.

Department of State, Office of the Legal Adviser
http://www.state.gov/s/l/index.htm

The Office of the Legal Adviser furnishes advice on all legal issues, domestic and international, arising in the course of the Department's work. This includes assisting Department principals and policy officers in formulating and implementing the foreign

policies of the United States, and promoting the development of international law and its institutions as a fundamental element of those policies.
http://www.state.gov/s/l/c8183.htm

The Office of the Legal Adviser publishes the annual *Digest of United States Practice in International Law* to provide the public with a ready source of current information on the views and practice of the Government of the United States in public and private international law.

Department of Defense
http://www.defenselink.mil/

Department of Justice
http://www.usdoj.gov/

National Archives and Records Administration
http://www.archives.gov/index.html

The National Archives and Records Administration is a public trust that provides continuing access to essential documents.

Foreign Governments

The following (English) Web sites of several foreign ministries contain wealth of information and documentation on issues related to international law and the use of force.

Australian Department of Foreign Affairs and Trade
http://www.dfat.gov.au

Canadian Department of Foreign Affairs and International Trade
http://www.dfait-maeci.gc.ca/

UK Foreign and Commonwealth Office
http://www.fco.gov.uk/en/

German Federal Foreign Office
http://www.auswaertiges-amt.de/diplo/en

French Ministry for Foreign and European Affairs
http://www.diplomatie.gouv.fr/en/

Ministry of Foreign Affairs of Russia
http://www.ln.mid.ru/bul_ns_en.nsf/kartaflat/en01

Ministry of Foreign Affairs of Japan
http://www.mofa.go.jp/

Ministry of Foreign Affairs of the People's Republic of China
http://www.fmprc.gov.cn/eng/

Swiss Federal Department of Foreign Affairs
http://www.eda.admin.ch/eda/en/home.html

Dutch Ministry of Foreign Affairs
http://www.minbuza.nl/en/home

Indian Ministry of External Affairs
http://meaindia.nic.in/

Intergovernmental Organizations

United Nations
http://www.un.org/Docs/sc/

Documents and information on the UN Security Council
http://www.un.org/ga/

Documents and information on the UN General Assembly
http://www.un.org/Depts/dhl/scbib.htm

This site contains only English-language monographs published between 1945 and 2002.
http://documents.un.org/welcome.asp?language=E

This site makes a database of "all types of official United Nations Documentation beginning in 1993 available and provides access to the resolutions of the General Assembly, Security Council, Economic and Social Council and the Trusteeship Council from 1946 onwards."
http://www.un.org/apps/pressreleases/

Press releases and meeting coverage of the UN
http://untreaty.un.org/English/treaty.asp

United Nations Treaty Collection
http://www.un.org/disarmament/

United Nations Office for Disarmament Affairs
http://www.icj-cij.org/

The website of the International Court of Justice provides a wealth of valuable and accessible information.
http://www.un.org/law/ilc/

Established in 1948, the International Law Commission's mandate is the progressive development and codification of international law, in accordance with Article 13(1)(a) of the Charter of the United Nations
Organization of American States (OAS)
http://www.oas.org/

The OAS is a multilateral forum for strengthening democracy, promoting human rights, and confronting shared problems such as poverty, terrorism, illegal drugs, and corruption. With four official languages—English, Spanish, Portuguese, and French—the OAS reflects the rich diversity of the Western hemisphere's peoples and cultures. It is made up of 35 member states: the independent nations of North, Central, and South America and the Caribbean. The government of Cuba, a member state, has been suspended from participation since 1962; thus only 34 countries participate actively. Nations from other parts of the world participate as permanent observers. This allows them to closely follow the issues that are critical to the Americas.
Organization for Security and Cooperation in Europe (OSCE)
http://www.osce.org/

With 56 participating States from Europe, Central Asia, and North America, the OSCE forms the largest regional security organization in the world. The OSCE is a primary instrument for early warning, conflict prevention, crisis management, and post-conflict rehabilitation in its area. The Organization deals with three dimensions of security—the politico-military, the economic and environmental, and the human dimension—and addresses a wide range of security-related concerns, including arms control, confidence- and security-building measures, human rights, national minorities, democratization, policing strategies, counterterrorism, and economic and environmental activities.
European Union (EU)
http://europa.eu/

The EU is an economic and political union of 27 member states, located primarily in Europe. It was established by the Treaty of Maastricht on November 1, 1993, upon the foundations of the preexisting European Economic Community.
North Atlantic Treaty Organization (NATO)
http://www.nato.int

NATO is an international military alliance of 26 States in Europe and North America. NATO members have agreed that an attack on one party would be considered an attack against them all (Article 5 of the North Atlantic Treaty).
Organization of the Islamic Conference (OIC)
http://www.oic-oci.org/

The Organization of the Islamic Conference (OIC) is the second-largest intergovernmental organization after the United Nations, with a membership of 57 States spread over four continents. The Organization is the collective voice of the Muslim world and was founded to safeguard and protect the interests of the Muslim world in the spirit of promoting international peace and harmony among various people of the world.
League of Arab States
http://www.arableagueonline.org

The League of Arab States is a regional organization of Arab states in Southwest Asia and North and Northeast Africa. It currently has 22 members. The main goal of the League is to "draw closer the relations between member States and co-ordinate collaboration between them, to safeguard their independence and sovereignty, and to consider in a general way the affairs and interests of the Arab countries."
African Union
http://www.africa-union.org/

The African Union is an intergovernmental organization consisting of 53 African states. Established on July 9, 2002, the AU was formed as a successor to the Organisation of African Unity (OAU). The most important decisions of the AU are made by the Assembly of the African Union, a twice-yearly meeting of the heads of state and government of its member states. The AU's secretariat, the African Union Commission, is based in Addis Ababa, Ethiopia.

Nongovernmental Organizations

Conflict Database International Crisis Group
http://www.crisisgroup.org

This site provides a database of news regarding practiced use of force. Furthermore, it provids reports, speeches, interviews, and articles of private authors and NGOs about conflicts as well as a conflict histories database according to country.
International Committee of the Red Cross: International Humanitarian Law
http://www.icrc.org/Eng/ihl

This site provides the view of the Red Cross regarding law and the use of force.
Security Council Report
http://www.securitycouncilreport.org

Security Council Report is an independent not-for-profit organization in affiliation with Columbia University's Center on International Organization. It publishes regular reports on the UN Security Council's existing and prospective agenda, supplemented by ad hoc

Update Reports on breaking news. The development of a longer-term research program focused on key thematic and structural issues confronting the Council will further support these efforts. Security Council Report provides valuable information to a range of audiences including member states, particularly the 10 elected members of the Council, but also the wider UN membership, the UN Secretariat itself, and the public.

International Commission of Jurists
http://www.icj.org/

The International Commission of Jurists is dedicated to the primacy, coherence and implementation of international law and principles that advance human rights. The ICJ provides legal expertise at both the international and national levels to ensure that developments in international law adhere to human rights principles and that international standards are implemented at the national level. The Commission was founded in Berlin in 1952, and its membership is composed of 60 eminent jurists who are representatives of the different legal systems of the world. Based in Geneva, the International Secretariat is responsible for the realization of the aims and objectives of the Commission.

International Law Association
http://www.ila-hq.org/

The International Law Association has branches around the world and a growing membership of academics and practicing professionals with an interest in international law. The main objectives of the Association are the study, clarification and development of both public and private international law. It is in the work of the various International Committees that these aims are pursued and biennial conferences provide a forum for comprehensive discussion and endorsement for the work of these committees.

Amnesty International
http://www.amnesty.org/

Amnesty International is a worldwide movement of people who campaign for internationally recognized human rights for all.

Human Rights Watch
http://www.hrw.org/

Human Rights Watch is one of the world's leading independent organizations dedicated to defending and protecting human rights.

International Action Network on Small Arms
http://www.iansa.org/

The International Action Network on Small Arms (IANSA) is the global movement against gun violence—a network of 800 civil society organizations working in 120 countries to stop the proliferation and misuse of small arms and light weapons.

Federation of American Scientists
http://www.fas.org/

The Federation of American Scientists (FAS) was founded in 1945 by scientists who had worked on the Manhattan Project to develop the first atomic bomb. With 70 Nobel Laureates on its Board of Sponsors, FAS provides timely, nonpartisan, technical analysis on complex global issues that hinge on science and technology.

Libraries, Databases and Research Institutes/Initiatives

American Library Association
http://www.ala.org/

Library of Congress
http://www.loc.gov/
Facts on International Relations and Security Trends (FIRST) Database
http://first.sipri.org/index.php

The integrated database system of the Stockholm International Peace Research Institute "contains clearly documented information from research institutes around the world."
International Institute for Strategic Studies (IISS)
http://webcat.iiss.org/uhtbin/cgisirsi.exe/x/0/0/49

An online catalogue covering a broad range of topics in international relations, security, and defense.
http://www.iiss.org/programmes/

A database that lists all papers, survivals, and strategic comments of the IISS.
The American Society of International Law
http://www.dcdata.com/asil/asil.htm

This site contains a "bibliographic index of articles and other content from ASIL publications."
http://www.asil.org/insights.htm

ASIL Insights makes various scholars' comments on current issues since 1996 available.
International Law Database: Use of Force
http://www.eisil.org/index.php?sid=116177061&cat=23&t=sub_pages

This site of the American Society of International Law, in English, offers "highest quality primary materials, authoritative web sites and helpful research guides to international law."
The Avalon Project
http://www.yale.edu/lawweb/avalon/avalon.htm

The Avalon Project at Yale Law School offers a wealth of digital documents relevant to the fields of law, history, economics, politics, diplomacy, and government.
http://www.yale.edu/lawweb/avalon/diplomacy/britain/br-1842d.htm

"The *Caroline* Case," Avalon Project.
National Implementation Database of ICRC
http://www.icrc.org/ihl-nat.nsf/WebALL!OpenView

This site provides documents of nations regarding the international humanitarian law.
Peace Palace Library
http://catalogue.ppl.nl:80/IMPLAND=Y/SRT=YOP/LNG=EN/
http://www.ppl.nl/index.php?option=com_wrapper&view=wrapper&Itemid=83

A bibliography on International Criminal Law, updated regularly.
Arms Control Association
http://www.armscontrol.org/

The Arms Control Association is a U.S. nonpartisan organization dedicated to promoting public understanding of, and support for, effective arms control policies. It produces a magazine on current issues in arms control, entitled *Arms Control Today*.
Project on International Courts and Tribunals
http://www.pict-pcti.org/.

The Project on International Courts and Tribunals has a synoptic chart of the International Judiciary in Context and much other useful information.

Legal Research on International Law Issues
http://www2.lib.uchicago.edu/~llou/forintlaw.html
Public International Law collection at the University of Utrecht
http://www.jb.law.uu.nl/jb-vol/volkenrecht-eng.html
Lauterpacht Research Centre for International Law, University of Cambridge.
http://www.law.cam.ac.uk/rcil/home.htm
Australian and New Zealand Society for International Law
http://law.anu.edu.au/anzsil/
Canadian Council on International Law
http://www.ccil-ccdi.ca/
British Institute for International and Comparative Law
http://www.biicl.org/
Council on Foreign Relations
http://www.cfr.org/

The Council on Foreign Relations is an independent, national (U.S.) membership organization and a nonpartisan center for scholars, that seeks to improve the understanding of U.S. foreign policy and international affairs.

INDEX

ABOUT THE AUTHORS

SHIRLEY V. SCOTT is an associate professor in the School of Social Sciences and International Studies at the University of New South Wales (UNSW) in Sydney, Australia. She is the author of *International Law in World Politics. An Introduction* (Lynne Rienner, 2004) and *The Political Interpretation of Multilateral Treaties* (Martinus Nijhoff, 2004), and editor of *International Law and Politics. Key Documents* (Lynne Rienner, 2004). She has also published many articles on the political functioning of international law in key journals including the *European Journal of International Law*, the *European Journal of International Relations*, *International Relations*, *The Leiden Journal of International Law*, and the *Chinese Journal of International Law*.

ANTHONY JOHN BILLINGSLEY is a lecturer in the School of Social Sciences and International Studies at the University of New South Wales in Sydney, Australia. He specializes in international law, Middle East politics, international security and United States politics. Before joining UNSW, Anthony served in the Australian Department of Foreign Affairs and Trade, Westpac Banking Corp., the Higher Colleges of Technology, UAE, and the Australian Office of National Assessments. He is a graduate in Politics from UNSW and has master's degrees in politics (Strathclyde University) and international law (Australian National University) and a Ph.D. in Middle East politics and constitutional law (Macquarie University).

CHRISTOPHER MICHAELSEN is a research fellow at the Law Faculty of the University of New South Wales in Sydney, Australia, and specializes in public international law, human rights, and international security. Before joining UNSW, he served at the Office for Democratic Institutions and Human Rights of the Organization for Security and Co-operation in Europe, at the United Nations Department for Disarmament Affairs, and at the Australian National University's Strategic & Defence Studies Centre. Chris graduated in law from the University of Hamburg and holds a Master of Laws (LLM) degree from the University of Queensland.